A
I
C
H
G

FROM A WATER-COLOR PAINTING BY KAY SMITH

Independence Hall, Philadelphia, Pennsylvania, where the Declaration of Independence was adopted and signed. Prior to the adoption of the Declaration, the building, which was completed in 1734, was known as the State House.

FROM A WATER-COLOR SKETCH BY KAY SMITH

Carpenter's Hall, Independence Square, Philadelphia, Pennsylvania, the meeting place of the First Continental Congress in September 1774, and one of the most historic buildings in the United States.

THE PICTORIAL HISTORY OF THE AMERICAN REVOLUTION

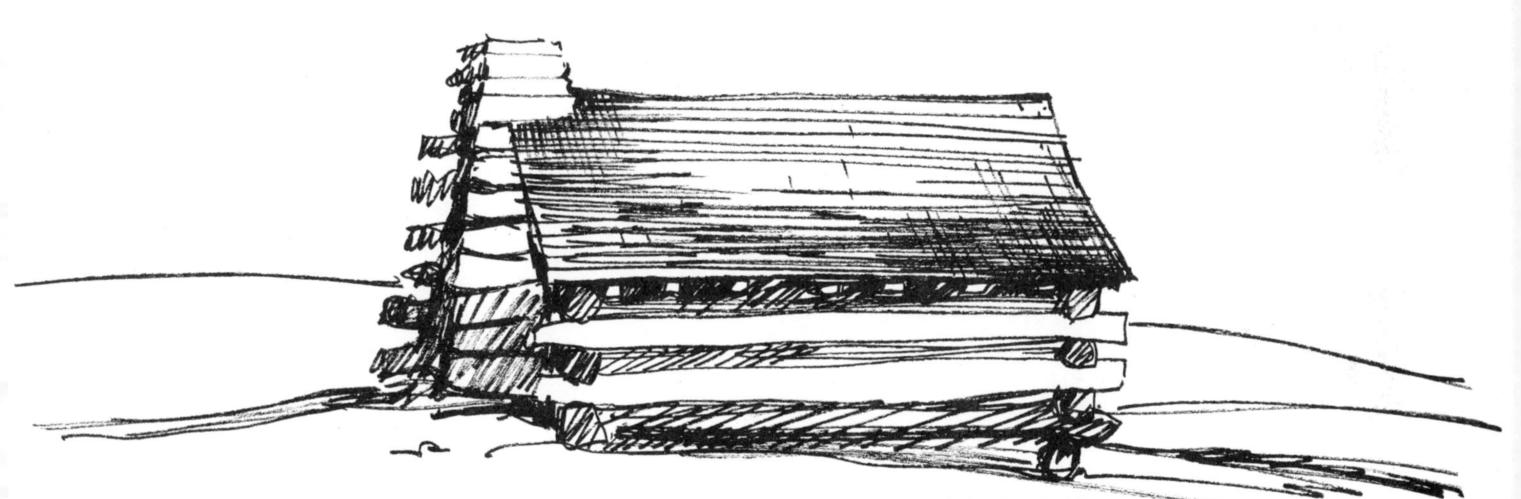

—Sketch by Kay Smith

Explanation of the eighteenth century print on the end papers

A French artist's painting of the surrender at Yorktown. The surrender of the English army commanded by General Cornwallis to the combined armies of the United States of America and France under the command of Generals Washington and Rochambeau at Yorktown and Gloucester, Virginia, October 19, 1781. This obviously distorted view of the surrender shows Yorktown in the background as a medieval European city and places the French fleet and troops in a dominant position in the foreground.

KEY TO THE PAINTING

- A Yorktown
- C English armies in formation
- D Stacks of British weapons
- E The French Army
- F The American Army
- G The French Navy under the command of Commodore Count de Grasse
- H Chesapeake Bay

THE PICTORIAL HISTORY
OF THE
AMERICAN REVOLUTION

AS TOLD BY

Eyewitnesses and Participants

by

RUPERT FURNEAUX

Featuring water-color paintings and sketches by

KAY SMITH

EDITED BY THOMAS C. JONES

Assistant to the editor

HARRIET B. HELMER

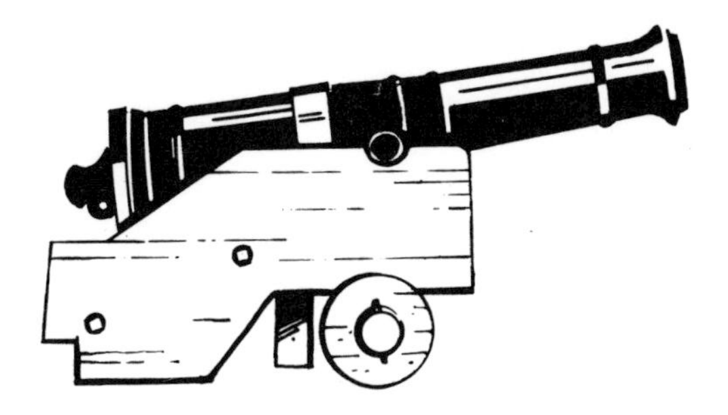

J. G. Ferguson Publishing Company / Chicago

BOUND IN HANDCRAFTED MISSION LEATHER BY BROWN & BIGELOW, ST. PAUL, MINNESOTA

ISBN: 0-385-02636-6

Library of Congress Catalogue Card No. 72-89979

Designed by Al Josephson

Lithographed in the United States of America
by Photopress, Inc., Broadview, Illinois

INTRODUCTION & ACKNOWLEDGMENTS

Some people feel that public apathy and political cynicism threaten the deepest foundations of the American republic as established by the Constitution of 1787. Whether or not this is true, the period of Bicentennial observances will serve to focus attention upon the years preceding the American Revolution, as well as the seven Revolutionary War years, to a degree that exceeds any previous national attention given to this era of American history. Events, places, and names such as the Boston Tea Party, Lexington, Concord, Valley Forge, Yorktown, Independence Hall, Paul Revere, John Paul Jones, George Washington, Lord Cornwallis, Benedict Arnold – and causes such as "taxation without representation," the Sugar and Stamp Acts, the Townshend Acts, the Coercive Acts – are to most Americans, at best, vaguely familiar reminders of grade-school history or high-school civics and history.

But compared with other more recent events and places of American history, the true glory of the war of American independence is little known and rarely appreciated for the heroic, miraculous victory for the underdog fighting against seemingly overwhelming odds.

Problems

Recognition of the true greatness of George Washington, as a man and a general, has somehow been lost to most American citizens with the passing of generations. Not only was he an inspired leader of men in the field, but, along with Robert Morris, he was largely instrumental in raising money to finance the army. He spent six years in the field with his troops without once returning to his beloved Mount Vernon. Since the rebel army consisted largely of militia who signed up voluntarily for limited periods, Washington and his generals were constantly plagued by the problems of recruiting, training, and inducing the men to stay in the service beyond their agreed commitments. That was long before the days of the draft, although certain navies were known to use strong-arm methods to fill out their crews.

Battle action covering thousands of miles

Few Americans today are aware of the great geographical range of the war. From the spectacular Citadel in Quebec City, in the frozen Canadian wilderness, to the semitropical fortress at Saint Augustine, Florida, and from the eastern seacoast to Kaskaskia, in the middle western plains country, the battle action covered one-fourth of the continent. From 1775 to 1782, there were major and minor battles and skirmishes in dozens of locations scattered widely throughout the colonies and the territories.

The truly international flavor of the conflict is not commonly known. Of course, the colonists were fighting for their freedom against King George III and the British regulars. Assisting the Crown were the Hessian mercenaries and some paid Indian tribes. The Americans were assisted by the French, some Indians, and volunteers from other European countries, such as Germany and Poland. The French were most instrumental in shaping the eventual victory through timely support at critical times. Particularly at Yorktown the presence of the French navy and ground troops in force proved to be decisive, not to mention their loan of hard cash to pay the American troops for the first time in months.

Exceptional work by the author

As publisher, we feel that the author, Rupert Furneaux, has prepared one of the most exciting stories of the American Revolution ever offered. By amassing a variety of accounts by eyewitnesses and participants, whose vivid descriptions convey to the reader all the drama, excitement, and pathos of the events, he has achieved a balance in reporting that makes the experience come alive. Through a skillful blending of his own explanatory comments with quotations from those who were at the scene, he has created a dramatic atmosphere seldom accomplished in historical narrative.

Such a remarkable performance demanded special effort in illustration. There is a very limited number of authentic contemporary illustrations of the Revolutionary period. For the most part, those that exist were drawn from memory or interpreted by artists from descriptions given to them by witnesses or participants. Since the author has used eyewitness action accounts as the device to tell the written story, we decided to adopt the same method to tell the visual story. We have reproduced sketches and maps from numerous books, as well as from libraries and historical societies.

Watercolors to capture the mood and setting

Kay Smith, a most accomplished illustrator and gifted watercolor painter, accepted our suggestion that she do on-the-scene sketches and paintings of the major battle areas and other historic landmarks. She traveled to the widespread locations to sketch and paint what she felt were scenes that told the story of each historic site. In both glowing color and dramatic black and white, her superb work is a convincing demonstration of the superiority of illustration over photography in creating an illusion and interpreting an event. Each painting and sketch has a versatility of treatment appropriate to the subject, varying from delicate pastels and washes to vivid strokes in all the colors of the spectrum. We feel that she has brilliantly accomplished our goal of achieving a suitable complement to the author's work.

There are many people who have contributed to the preparation of this volume. My editorial assistant, Harriet B. Helmer, has been unstinting in her devotion to this work. Al Josephson, the designer, has worked many hours to make the most effective use of the variety of illustrations and has created a format that is informative and dramatic. Photopress Incorporated – particularly Don Vendl and John Lauer – has extended every possible service to make this book a worthy addition to other material pertaining to the Revolutionary War. G. R. Grubb & Company faithfully reproduced many of the color sketches. The excellent service and careful typesetting of the Poole-Clarinda Company have been extremely helpful. We are indebted to Brown & Bigelow, Saint Paul, Minnesota, for their help and encouragement during the long period of production. The final link in the process is the binding, and we are grateful to Jim Stewart and the Engdahl Company for their consistent cooperation on this project.

A story worth telling

The Bicentennial deserves to be observed in many areas and in many ways, to commemorate the 200th birthday of American independence. It is our hope that this volume will convey the spirit, suffering, devotion, dedication, and inspiration that went into the founding of the nation. The story has been told here in a style designed to make the reader feel that he was *there.* The American Revolution was a series of episodes that drastically changed the history of mankind – a story worth telling that will never grow old.

Thomas C. Jones, Editor

A VIEW OF PART OF THE TOWN OF BOSTON IN NEW-ENGLAND

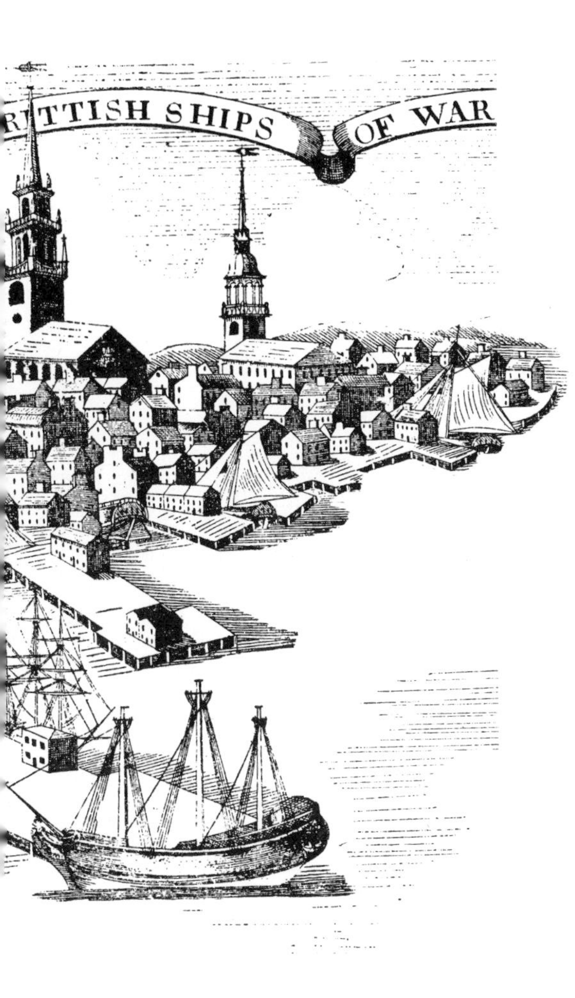

CONTENTS

(continued)

PAINTINGS AND SKETCHES IN COLOR

The Green Dragon tavern, a meeting place of the patriots

CHRONOLOGY OF THE PRINCIPAL EVENTS OF THE WAR

From *Harper's Encyclopaedia of United States History, Vol. VII*

Affair at Lexington

1775

April 19 . . . Battle of Lexington, Mass., at dawn.

April 27 . . . Col. Samuel H. Parsons and Benedict Arnold plan, at Hartford, Conn., the capture of Fort Ticonderoga, N. Y.

April 29 . . . Arnold leads his company from New Haven to Boston.

May 10 . . . Fort Ticonderoga captured by Ethan Allen.

May 12 . . . Crown Point, N. Y., captured by Americans.

May 16 . . . Americans under Benedict Arnold capture St. John, Canada.

May 25 . . . British Generals Howe, Clinton, and Burgoyne arrive at Boston from England with troops.

June 14 . . . Congress votes to raise 20,000 men.

June 15 . . . George Washington is unanimously elected by Congress commander-in-chief of the American forces.

June 17 . . . Battle of Bunker Hill, June 16-17; and burning of Charlestown.

June 22 . . . Resolved by Congress, "That a sum not exceeding two million of Spanish milled dollars be emitted by Congress in bills of credit for the defense of America."

July 3 . . . Washington takes command of the army at Cambridge.

July 6 . . . Declaration by Congress, the causes and necessity for taking up arms.

July 10 . . . First provincial vessel commissioned for naval warfare in the Revolution, sent out by Georgia.

July 15 . . . Importation of gunpowder, saltpeter, sulphur, and fire-arms permitted by act of Congress.

July 20 . . . Georgia joins the United Colonies.

July 21 . . . Franklin's plan of confederation and perpetual union. "The United Colonies of North America," considered by Congress.

July 27 . . . Congress resolves to establish an army hospital.

Aug. . . . British vessel, the *Betsy*, surprised by a Carolina privateer off St. Augustine bar, and 111 barrels of powder captured.

Aug. 23 . . . King issues a proclamation for suppressing rebellion and sedition in the colonies.

Sept. . . . American troops under Gen. Richard Montgomery sent into Canada to cut off British supplies.

Sept. . . . Col. Benedict Arnold, with a force of about 1,100 men, marches against Quebec *via* Kennebec River.

Sept. 17 . . . English ship seized off Tybee Island, Ga., by the Liberty people, with 250 barrels of powder.

Sept. 25 . . . British capture Col. Ethan Allen and thirty-eight men near Montreal.

Oct. 7 . . . Bristol, R. I., bombarded.

Marquis de Lafayette

Oct. 10 . . . Gen. William Howe supersedes General Gage as commander of the British army in America, who embarks for England.

Oct. 18 . . . Falmouth, Me., burned by British.

Nov. 2 . . . St. John, Canada, surrenders to Americans under Montgomery.

Nov. 4 . . . Congress orders a battalion to protect Georgia.

Nov. 7 . . . British fleet repulsed at Hampton, Va., Oct. 25, 1775, and Lord Dunmore declares open war.

Nov. 12 . . . Night attack of the British vessels *Tamar* and *Cherokee* on the schooner *Defence*, in Hog Island Channel, S. C.

Nov. 13 . . . Americans under Montgomery capture Montreal.

Nov. 29 . . . Benjamin Harrison, Benjamin Franklin, Thomas Johnson, John Dickinson, and John Jay, appointed by Congress a committee for secret correspondence with friends of America in Great Britain, Ireland, and other foreign nations.

Dec. 9 . . . Battle of Great Bridge, Va.

Dec. 13 . . . Congress appoints Silas Deane, John Langdon, and Christopher Gadsden, a committee to fit out two vessels of war, Nov. 25, orders thirteen vessels of war built and appoints Esek Hopkins commander.

Dec. . . . British vessels driven from Charleston Harbor, S. C., by artillery company under Colonel Moultrie, stationed on Haddrell's Point.

Dec. 31 . . . American forces united under Montgomery and Arnold repulsed at Quebec; General Montgomery killed.

1776

Jan. 1 . . . Washington unfurls the first Union flag of thirteen stripes at Cambridge, Mass.

Jan. 1 . . . Norfolk, Va., partly burned by Governor Dunmore.

Feb. 27 . . . Battle of Moore's Creek, N. C.; McDonald's loyalists routed by militia; seventy killed and wounded.

March 2 . . . Silas Deane appointed political agent to the French Court.

March 17 . . . Howe evacuates Boston.

March 23 . . . Congress authorizes privateering.

April 6 . . . Congress orders the ports open to all nations.

April 22 . . . North Carolina declares for independence.

May 4 . . . Rhode Island; May 10, Massachusetts; and May 14, Virginia, declare for independence.

May 6 . . . American forces under Gen. John Thomas retire from the siege of Quebec.

May 15 . . . Congress advises each colony to form a government independent of Great Britain.

June 7 . . . Resolution introduced in Congress by Richard Henry Lee, that "the United Colonies are and ought to be free and independent States; that they are absolved from all allegiance to the British crown, and that their political connection with Great Britain is and ought to be totally dissolved."

June 11 . . . Committee appointed by Congress to prepare a form of confederation.

June 11 . . . Committee appointed by Congress to draw up a Declaration of Independence.

June 12 . . . Board of war and ordnance appointed by Congress, consisting of five members, viz.: John Adams, Roger Sherman, Benjamin Harrison, James Wilson, and Edward Rutledge; Richard Peters elected secretary.

June 18 . . . American forces under General Sullivan retire from Canada to Crown Point, N. Y.

June 28 . . . Unsuccessful attack on Fort Moultrie by British fleet under Sir Peter Parker.

July 4. . . Declaration of Independence adopted by Congress.

July 9 . . . Declaration of Independence read to the army in New York by order of General Washington.

Aug. 22 . . . British General Lord Howe lands 10,000 men and forty guns near Gravesend, L. I.

Aug. 27 . . . Battle of Long Island.

Aug. 29-30 . . . Washington withdraws his forces from Long Island to the city of New York.

Sept. 9 . . . Congress resolves "that all Continental commissions in which heretofore the words 'United Colonies' have been used, bear hereafter the words 'United States.' "

Sept. 14 . . . Americans evacuate New York City.

Sept. 16 . . . British repulsed at Harlem Heights.

Sept. 22 . . . Benjamin Franklin, Silas Deane, and Arthur Lee appointed ambassadors to the Court of France.

Sept. 22 . . . Nathan Hale executed as a spy at New York.

Oct. 11-13 . . . Battle on Lake Champlain; British victory.

Oct. 18 . . . Thaddeus Kosciusko, a Pole, arrives; recommended to Washington by Dr. Franklin; appointed colonel of engineers by Congress.

Oct. 28 . . . Battle of White Plains, N. Y., British victory.

Oct. . . . Franklin sails for France in the *Reprisal*, of sixteen guns, one of the new Continental frigates, the first national vessel to appear in the Eastern Hemisphere.

Nov. 1 . . . Congress authorizes the raising of $5,000,000 by lottery for expenses of the next campaign.

Nov. 16 . . . Fort Washington on the Hudson captured by the British.

Nov. 18 . . . Americans evacuate Fort Lee, and retreat across New Jersey to Pennsylvania.

Nov. 28 . . . Eight thousand British troops land and take possession of Rhode Island.

Dec. 8 . . . Washington with his forces crosses the Delaware into Pennsylvania.

Dec. 8 . . . Sir Peter Parker takes possession of Rhode Island, and blockades the American fleet at Providence.

Dec. 12 . . . Maj.-Gen. Charles Lee captured by British at Baskingridge, N. J.

Dec. 26 . . . Battle of Trenton, N. J.

Dec. 30 . . . Congress resolves to send commissioners to the courts of Vienna, Spain, Prussia, and Tuscany.

Battle of Germantown

1777

Jan. 3 . . . Battle of Princeton.

Jan. . . . Washington's army encamps for the winter at Morristown.

Jan. 23 . . . Americans under General Maxwell capture Elizabethtown, N. J.

Feb. 6 . . . Letters of marque and reprisal granted by England against American ships.

Feb. 26 . . . Five vessels belonging to a British supply fleet are sunk near Amboy, N. J.

April 8 . . . Vermont declares itself an Independent State, Jan., 1777, and presents a petition to Congress for admission into the confederacy, which was denied.

April 26 . . . Danbury, Conn., destroyed by troops under ex-Governor Tryon.

May 23 . . . Colonel Meigs, with whale-boats from Guilford, attacks the British forces at Sag Harbor, destroying vessels and stores and taking ninety prisoners.

June 14 . . . Stars and Stripes adopted by Congress.

June 30 . . . British under General Howe evacuate New Jersey, crossing to Staten Island.

July 1 . . . British under Burgoyne appear before Ticonderoga.

July 6 . . . American garrison withdraw from New York.

July 7 . . . Battle of Hubbardton, Vt.

July 10 . . . British Gen. Richard Prescott surprised and captured near Newport by Lieutenant-Colonel Barton.

July 27 . . . Miss Jane McCrea captured by Indians in British employ at Fort Edward, N. Y., and shot and scalped.

July 29 . . . On the approach of Burgoyne, General Schuyler evacuates Fort Edward, and retreats down the Hudson Valley.

July 31 . . . General Lafayette, who volunteers his services to Congress, is commissioned major-general.

Aug. 3 . . . Lafayette introduced to Washington in Philadelphia, and attached to his personal staff.

Aug. 6 . . . Battle of Oriskany, N. Y.

Aug. 16 . . . Battle of Bennington, Vt.

Aug. 19 . . . Gen. Philip Schuyler succeeded by Gen. Horatio Gates in command of the Northern army.

Aug. 22 . . . General Arnold sent to relieve Fort Schuyler, invested by British under St. Leger, who retreats and returns to Montreal.

Sept. 11 . . . Battle of Brandywine, Washington defeated.

Sept. 15 . . . Count Pulaski commissioned brigadier-general by Congress.

Sept. 19 . . . Battle of Stillwater, N. Y.; indecisive.

Sept. 20-21 . . . Three hundred of Wayne's troops slaughtered at Paoli.

Sept. 27 . . . British army occupies Philadelphia.

Oct. 4 . . . Battle of Germantown; Americans repulsed.

Oct. 6 . . . Forts Clinton and Montgomery captured by the British.

Oct. 7 . . . Battle of Saratoga, N. Y.

General Burgoyne's retreat up the Hudson River

Oct. 17 . . . General Burgoyne's army surrenders.

Oct. 22-23 . . . Successful defense of Fort Mifflin and Fort Mercer.

Oct. . . . Congress creates a new board of war, General Gates presiding.

Nov. 15 . . . Articles of Confederation adopted.

Nov. 16-20 . . . Forts Mifflin and Mercer besieged by the British and captured.

Nov. . . . Congress recommends to the several States to raise by taxes $5,000,000 for the succeeding year.

Dec. 4 . . . Howe leaves Philadelphia with 14,000 men to drive Washington from his position at Whitemarsh, but does not attack.

Dec. 8 . . . Howe hurriedly returns to Philadelphia.

Dec. 18 . . . American army goes into winter quarters at Valley Forge, on the Schuylkill.

Dec. . . . Gen. Charles Lee released in exchange for General Prescott.

1778

Jan. 5 . . . Battle of the Kegs.

Feb. 6 . . . Louis XVI, acknowledges the Independence of the colonies, and signs a treaty of alliance and commerce.

Feb. . . . Baron von Steuben joins camp at Valley Forge.

April 22 . . . Bill introduced by Lord North in Parliament concerning peace negotiations with America reaches Congress April 15, and is rejected.

May 2 . . . French treaty reaches Congress by messenger.

May 4 . . . Deane's treaty with France ratified.

May 18. . . Mischianza, a festival, is given at Philadelphia by the British officers in honor of Sir William Howe (who had been succeeded by Sir Henry Clinton), six days before his return to England.

May 20 . . . Affair at Barren Hill.

May 25 . . . British raid in Warren and Bristol, R. I.

May 31 . . . Col. Ethan Allen, released from imprisonment, returns to Bennington, Vt.

June 10 . . . Earl of Carlisle, George Johnstone, and William Eden, appointed peace commissioners to America, with Prof. Adam Ferguson as secretary.

June 18 . . . British evacuate Philadelphia and retire across the Delaware into New Jersey.

June 18 . . . Americans break camp at Valley Forge and follow.

June 28 . . . Battle of Monmouth Court House, N. J., British retreat.

June 29. . . "Molly Pitcher" commissioned sergeant by Washington for bravery at Monmouth.

July 4 . . . Massacre of inhabitants in Wyoming Valley, Pa., by Indians and Tories.

July 4 . . . Expedition from Virginia under Maj. George Rogers Clark captures the British fort at Kaskaskia.

July 9 . . . Articles of Confederation signed by delegates from eight states–New Hampshire, Massachusetts, Rhode Island, Connecticut, Pennsylvania, New York, Virginia, and South Carolina.

July 21 . . . Delegates from North Carolina sign them.

July 24 . . . Delegates from Georgia sign them.

July 29. . . French fleet, under Count D'Estaing, enters Narraganset Bay.

Aug. 6 . . . M. Gerard, minister from France to America, received in Congress.

Aug. 11 . . . Congress rejects the bills of Parliament, and refuses to negotiate with Great Britain until her fleets and armies are withdrawn and she acknowledges the Independence of the colonies.

Aug. 12 . . . Gen. Charles Lee by court-martial for disobedience, misbehavior, and disrespect to Washington, suspended from command for one year.

Aug. 29 . . . Battle of Rhode Island.

Aug. 31 . . . Americans evacuate Rhode Island, Aug. 30, and British occupy Newport.

Sept. 5 . . . British under General Grey burn Bedford village, in Dartmouth, Mass., and seventy American vessels lying at the wharfs.

Sept. 14 . . . Benjamin Franklin appointed minister to the Court of France.

Nov. 10 . . . Massacre by Indians and Tories at Cherry Valley, N. Y.

Dec. 29 . . . British troops under Howe capture Savannah; the Americans retreat across the Savannah River.

Northern American army hutted in cantonments from Danbury, Conn., to Elizabethtown, N. J., for the winter.

1779

Maj.-Gen. Benjamin Lincoln, commanding the Southern forces, establishes his first post at Purysburg, on the Savannah River.

Jan. 2 . . . Congress calls upon the States for their quotas of $15,000,000 for the year, and $6,000,000 annually for eighteen years to follow as a sinking-fund.

Jan. . . . Vincennes, Ind., captured by the British.

Jan. 12 . . . British under General McLane take possession of Castine, Me.

Feb. 3 . . . British under Major Gardiner driven from Port Royal Island by General Moultrie.

Feb. . . . Franklin commissioned sole minister plenipotentiary to France, and Adams recalled.

Feb. 14 . . . Battle of Kettle Creek, Ga., American victory.

Feb. 20 . . . Americans under Major Clark capture Vincennes.

March 3 . . . Battle of Brier Creek, Ga., British victory.

March 26 . . . Salt works at Horseneck, Conn., destroyed by General Tryon.

April . . . American ministers recalled, except at Versailles and Madrid.

June 20 . . . Americans repulsed at Stono Ferry, S. C.

June . . . Spain declares war against Great Britain.

July 5 . . . British under Tryon plunder New Haven; July 8, burn Fairfield; July 12, burn Norwalk.

July 16 . . . Americans under Wayne take by storm Fort Stony Point, N. Y.

July 25 . . . Expedition against the British at Fort Castine, Me., repulsed.

Aug. 13 . . . American fleet arrive at Penobscot, July 25, and are dispersed by British fleet.

Aug. 14 . . . Congress agrees to a basis of terms for a peace with Great Britain.

July-Sept. . . . General Sullivan's campaign against the Six Nations; the Indian villages of the Genesee Valley destroyed.

Sept. 3 . . . British fleet at Tybee captured by Count D'Estaing.

Sept. . . . Congress votes thanks and a gold medal to Major Lee, for surprising and capturing (Aug. 19) the British garrison at Paulus's Hook.

Sept. 17 . . . Congress guarantees the Floridas to Spain if she takes them from Great Britain, provided the United States should enjoy the free navigation of the Mississippi River.

Sept. 23 . . . Naval engagement off Flamborough Head, England; the *Bonhomme Richard* (American), John Paul Jones commander, captures the British gunship *Serapis*.

Sept. 27 . . . John Jay appointed minister to Spain, and John Adams to negotiate a peace with Great Britain.

Sept. 23-Oct. 9 . . . Siege of Savannah, Ga., by Americans and French, fails; Pulaski killed.

Oct. 1 . . . A company of British regulars and four armed vessels in the Ogeechee River, Ga., surrenders to Colonel White.

Oct. 11-25 . . . British evacuate Rhode Island.

Nov. 17 . . . M. Gerard succeeded by the Chevalier de la Luzerne as minister from France to the United States.

Dec. . . . American army winters at Morristown.

Dec. 26 . . . General Clinton sails from New York against Charleston.

1780

Jan. . . . Washington reprimands General Arnold, by order of Congress, for misconduct charged by the council of Philadelphia.

Jan. 10 . . . Gen. Charles Lee dismissed from the army.

March . . . Congress sends General Gates to succeed Baron de Kalb, who, by the surrender of General Lincoln, had been commander-in-chief in the South.

April 10 . . . General Clinton lays siege to Charleston.

April 14 . . . Battle at Monck's Corner, S. C.

May 6 . . . Fort Moultrie, S.C., surrendered to Captain Hudson of the British navy.

May 11 . . . Lafayette rejoins the army, after a visit to France, bringing a commission from the French government to Washington as lieutenant-general and vice-admiral of France, so that he may be commander-in-chief of the united forces of France and the United States.

May 12 . . . Charleston, S. C., capitulates.

May 29 . . . Massacre of Americans under Colonel Buford at Waxhaw, on the North Carolina border, by British under Tarleton.

June 3 . . . General Clinton proclaims South Carolina subject to England.

June 20 . . . Battle of Ramsour's Mills, N. C.

June 23 . . . Battle at Springfield, N. J.; General Clinton burns the town.

July 10 . . . French army of 6,000 men, under Rochambeau, reaches Newport Harbor, R. I.

July 30 . . . Battle of Rocky Mount, S. C.

Aug. 3 . . . Command in the highlands of the Hudson with West Point given to Gen. Benedict Arnold.

Aug. 6 . . . Battle of Hanging Rock, S. C.

Aug. 16 . . . Battle of Camden, S. C.; Gates defeated.

Aug. 18 . . . Battles of Musgrove Mills and Fishing Creek, S. C.

Sept. 21 . . . Maj. John André, British adjutant-general, meets Benedict Arnold near Stony Point, N. Y.

Sept. 23 . . . Major André captured near Tarrytown.

Sept. 24 . . . Arnold escapes to the British vessel *Vulture*.

Sept. 26 . . . Battle of Charlotte, N. C.

Sept. 29 . . . André convicted as a spy by military board, Gen. Nathanael Greene, president, and hung at Tappan, New York Oct. 2.

Oct. . . . Congress votes John Paulding, David Williams, and Isaac Van Wart, captors of André, its thanks, a silver medal, and a pension of $200 each yearly, for life.

Oct. 6 . . . Henry Laurens, minister from United States, seized on his way to Holland by a British frigate, Sept. 3, imprisoned in the Tower of London.

Battle of King's Mountain

Oct. 7 . . . Battle of King's Mountain, S. C.

Oct. 10 . . . Congress resolves that western lands to be ceded shall be formed into republican States, and become equal members of the Union.

Oct. 14 . . . Gen. Nathanael Greene appointed to command of the armies in the South, superseding General Gates.

Dec. . . . Col. John Laurens appointed a special minister to France to secure a loan.

1781

Jan. 1 . . . Pennsylvania troops break camp at Morristown, Jan. 1, demanding back pay. Congress appoints a commission, which accedes to their demand.

Jan. 5-6 . . . Benedict Arnold plunders Richmond, Va.

Jan. . . . Robert R. Livingston appointed secretary of foreign affairs by Congress.

Jan. 17 . . . Battle of Cowpens, S. C.; American victory.

Jan. 23-27 . . . Mutiny of New Jersey troops quelled by Gen. Robert Howe.

Feb. 2 . . . Young's house, near White Plains, surprised by British.

Jan. 28-Feb. 13 . . . Skillful retreat of Americans under General Greene from Cowpens to the River Dan, pursued by Cornwallis.

March 1 . . . Final ratification of Articles of Confederation announced by order of Congress.

March 15 . . . Battle of Guilford Court House, N. C.

April 24 . . . British under Generals Phillips and Benedict Arnold occupy Petersburg.

April 25 . . . Battle of Hobkirk's Hill, S. C.

May . . . Union of Vermont with the British proposed to Col. Ira Allen at Isles aux Noix, Canada.

May 20 . . . Cornwallis joins Arnold at Petersburg, Va.

June 5 . . . Augusta, Ga., taken by Colonel Clark, Sept. 14, 1780; retaken by British, Sept. 17, 1780; capitulates to Americans.

June 18 . . . General Wadsworth captured, and imprisoned at Castine, Me.

June 21 . . . British abandon Fort Ninety-six.

June 22 . . . Jonas Fay, Ira Allen, and Bazaleel Woodward appointed to represent the cause of Vermont in the Continental Congress.

July 6 . . . General Lafayette attacks Cornwallis near Green Springs, Va., and is repulsed.

Aug. 4 . . . Cornwallis retires with his army to Yorktown.

Aug. . . . R. R. Livingston appointed secretary of foreign affairs by Congress.

Aug. 20 . . . Congress requires Vermont to relinquish territory east of the Connecticut and west of the present New York line before admission as a State.

Aug. 25 . . . Combined armies of Americans and French start for Yorktown, Va., from the Hudson River.

Aug. 30 . . . Count de Grasse, with the French fleet, arrives in the Chesapeake.

Sept. 3 . . . Lafayette joins French troops under Count de St. Simon at Green Springs, and they occupy Williamsburg, about 15 miles from Yorktown, Sept. 5.

Sept. 6 . . . Benedict Arnold plunders and burns New London, Conn., and captures Fort Griswold.

Sept. 7 . . . British fleet under Admiral Graves appears in the Chesapeake.

Sept. 8 . . . Indecisive battle of Eutaw Springs, S. C.

Sept. 14 . . . Washington and Count Rochambeau reach Williamsburg.

Yorktown

Oct. 5-19 . . . Siege of Yorktown.

Oct. 19 . . . Cornwallis surrenders at Yorktown.

Oct. 24 . . . Sir Henry Clinton, with fleet of thirty-five vessels and 7,000 troops, arrives at the Chesapeake, and returns to New York Oct. 29.

Oct. 30 . . . Benjamin Lincoln appointed Secretary of War by Congress.

Dec. 13 . . . Day of public thanksgiving and prayer observed throughout the United States.

Dec. 31 . . . Henry Laurens released from imprisonment in the Tower of London.

1782

April 19 . . . Holland recognizes the independence of United States.

May 5 . . . Sir Guy Carleton, appointed to succeed Clinton, lands in New York.

June 14 . . . Orders received by Sir James Wright at Savannah for the evacuation of the province.

July 11 . . . Savannah, Ga., evacuated by the British.

Oct. 8 . . . Treaty of amity and commerce concluded by Mr. Adams, on part of the United States, with Holland.

Nov. 30 . . . Preliminary articles of peace signed at Paris by Richard Oswald for Great Britain, and by John Adams, Benjamin Franklin, John Jay, and Henry Laurens for the United States.

Dec. 14 . . . British evacuate Charleston, S. C.

Dec. 24 . . . French army embarks from Boston for San Domingo, having been in the United States two years five months and fourteen days.

1783

Feb. 5 . . . Sweden recognizes independence of United States.

Feb. 25 . . . Denmark recognizes independence of United States.

March 15 . . . Congress being unable to pay either officers or men of the army, an anonymous address is circulated, March 11, 1783, advising the army at Newburg, N. Y., to enforce its claims. The situation is critical, but Washington, by an admirable address, obtains from the officers a declaration of confidence in Congress and the country.

March 22 . . . Congress grants five years' full pay to officers in lieu of half-pay for life, promised Oct. 21, 1780.

March 24 . . . Spain recognizes independence of United States.

April 11 . . . Congress proclaims a cessation of hostilities, which is read to the army April 19.

April 15 . . . Congress ratifies the preliminary treaty with Great Britain.

July . . . Independence of the United States recognized by Russia.

Sept. 3 . . . Definitive treaty signed by David Hartley on the part of Great Britain, and by Benjamin Franklin, John Adams, and John Jay on the part of the United States.

Nov. 2 . . . Washington issues his "Farewell Address to the Army" from Rocky Hill, near Princeton, N. J.

Nov. 3 . . . By general order of Congress, proclaimed Oct. 18, the army is disbanded, a small force remaining at West Point.

Nov. 25 . . . British evacuate New York City.

Dec. 4 . . . General Washington bids farewell to his officers at Fraunces Tavern, corner Pearl and Broad Streets, New York City.

Dec. 4 . . . British evacuate Long Island and Staten Island (withdrawing their last armed man sent for the purpose of reducing the colonies to subjection).

Dec. 23 . . . Washington resigns his commission as commander-in-chief at the Statehouse, Annapolis, Md., and retires to Mount Vernon.

1784

Jan. 14 . . . Congress ratifies the definitive treaty of peace.

NC
NJ
NY
C
V
NE
G
M
P
UNITE OR DIE
Water-town 33
Chensford
Concord
34
Cambridg
39
Woburn:
Roxbury
35
36
Dorchester
Brantry
Lyn
Salē
Hingam
Hull
CAnn=

Statue of Nathan Hale, Capitol Building, Hartford, Connecticut

GRIFFIN'S WHARF
The Boston Tea Party

The Old South Church in Boston where many of the colonial leaders worshiped

John Adams believed that the Revolution was in the hearts and minds of the people from the founding of the first colonies. The original settlers crossed the Atlantic to escape intolerance and injustice. Their descendants enjoyed a semblance of freedom until 1763 when, at the end of the French and Indian War in which many colonists had fought, the British government attempted to force the colonists to pay part of the cost of the war, which had benefited England more than the colonies. Most of the colonists were loyal to the King and acknowledged certain obligations to England, but they objected to being taxed without representation. British blunders goaded them from passive resistance into open revolt. The cataclysm came on December 16, 1773.

The government in London imposed a tax on tea imported into the colonies. The amount was trivial, a mere three pence, which failed to raise the price above that of the smuggled

John Hancock, first to sign the Declaration of Independence, in a bold hand so that no one would mistake his signature

Samuel Adams, less known than his brother, John Adams, but one of the moving spirits of the American Revolution

Dr. Joseph Warren, President of the provincial congress and major general who was killed during the retreat from Breed's Hill

commodity. Therein lay the catch. If the colonists bought the imported tea, they accepted the constitutionality of external taxation. At Philadelphia and New York, the East India Company's ships were turned back. On November 14, 1773, the *Dartmouth*, laden with 114 chests of tea, reached Boston.

The church bells summoned the patriots to assemble. Harangued by Samuel Adams, John Hancock, William Molineaux, and Joseph Warren, they demanded that the royal governor, Thomas Hutchinson, return the tea to England or remove the tax. He refused. Two more vessels entered the harbor, joining the *Dartmouth* at Griffin's Wharf in Boston Harbor.

The patriots assembled again on December 16. "Who knows," asked John Rowe, "how tea will mingle with salt water?" Samuel Adams proclaimed that the citizens could do no more to save their country. His words constituted a prearranged signal. A war whoop sounded from the gallery of the Old South Meeting House. It was answered in kind from the doorway by a group of men disguised as Indians. Shouts filled the hall: "Boston Harbor a teapot tonight! Hurrah for Griffin's Wharf! The Mohawks are coming! Every man to his tent!" They were heard by John Andrews, who sat in his house nearby drinking tea. He hurried to the Meeting House but was unable to enter the door, the crush was so great. As the throng rushed out, the din reached deafening proportions. "You'd have thought that the inhabitants of the infernal regions had broken out," he recalled.

The mob swept down Milk Street, into Hutchinson Street and onto Griffin's Wharf. Alongside the wharf lay the *Dartmouth*, and the *Eleanor* and the *Beaver*, with 226 chests containing 90,000 pounds of dutied tea, valued at £25,000.

Who were "the Mohawks?"

Who "the Mohawks" were remains one of the mysteries of American history. Half a century later, John Adams said he did not know the identity of a single participant. Their names were enshrouded in secrecy, which encouraged speculation and, possibly, falsification. One list of names was supplied by an alleged participant at the age of 93. Another recorded his reminiscences at the age of 113, seventy-five years after the event.

The presence at Griffin's Wharf of Thomas Melvill, a Princeton graduate with an M.A. degree from Harvard, was attested by the tea found in his boots the next morning. The merchant, Lendall Pitts, was reported as being active. Most of the alleged participants were artisans. James Brewer, a blockmaker, offered his house on Summer Street as a meeting place for some of his friends. Mrs. Brewer helped blacken their faces with burnt cork and sent them on their way. John Crane, Thomas Bolter, and Samuel Fenno, all housewrights, are said to have met at Crane's house on the corner of Hollis and Tremont Streets. After joining their neighbors, the Bradlee brothers, they hastened to the waterfront. Some of the participants were young apprentices, like Peter Slater and Robert Sessions, who appeared at the wharf when they learned what was going on. Most were Bostonians, but the party probably included men from many of the neighboring towns and from as far away as Worcester. Best known among the alleged participants were William Molineaux, Thomas Young, and Paul Revere, the silversmith, whose name became famous in 1775.

An eyewitness account

What may be an authentic account of the Boston Tea Party was supplied in 1834 by George Hewes.

It was now evening, and I immediately dressed myself in the costume of an Indian, equipped with a small hatchet, which I and my associates called a "tomahawk," with which, and a club, after having painted my face and hands with coal dust in the shop of a blacksmith, I repaired to Griffin's Wharf, where the ships lay that contained the tea. When I first appeared in the street after being thus disguised, I fell in with many who were dressed, equipped and painted as I was, and who fell in with me and marched in order to the place of our destination.

When we arrived at the wharf, there were three of our members who assumed an authority to direct our operations, to which we readily submitted. They divided us into three parties, for the purpose of boarding the three ships which contained the tea at the same time. The name of him who commanded the division to which I was assigned was Leonard Pitt. The names of the other commanders I never knew. We were immediately ordered by the respective commanders to board all the ships at

The home of General Joseph Warren

the same time, which we promptly obeyed. The commander of the division to which I belonged, as soon as we were on board the ship, appointed me boatswain, and ordered me to go to the captain and demand of him the keys to the hatches and a dozen candles. I made the demand accordingly, and the captain promptly replied, and delivered the articles, but requested me at the same time to do no damage to the ship or rigging. We then were ordered by our commander to open the hatches and take out all the chests of tea and throw them overboard, and we immediately proceeded to execute his orders, first cutting and splitting the chests with our tomahawks, so as thoroughly to expose them to the effects of the water.

In about three hours from the time we went on board, we had thus broken and thrown overboard every tea chest to be found in the ship, while those in the other ships were disposing of the tea in the same way, at the same time. We were surrounded by British armed ships, but no attempt was made to resist us. We then quietly retired to our several places of residence, without having any conversation with each other, or taking any measures to discover who were our associates, nor do I recollect our having had the knowledge of the name of a single individual concerned in that affair, except that of Leonard Pitt, the commander of my division, whom I have mentioned. There appeared to be an understanding that each individual should volunteer his services, keeping his own secret, and risk the consequence for himself. No disorder took place during that transaction, and it was observed at that time that the stillest night ensued that Boston had enjoyed for many months.

Facsimile of the first money coined by the United States

Looters were apprehended

During the time we were throwing the tea overboard, there were several attempts made by some of the citizens of Boston and its vicinity to carry off small quantities of it for their family use. To effect that object, they would watch their opportunity to snatch up a handful from the deck, where it became plentifully scattered, and put it into their pockets. One Captain O'Connor, whom I well knew, came on board for that purpose, and when he supposed he was not noticed, filled his pockets, and also the lining of his coat. But I had detected him and gave information to the captain of what he was doing. We were ordered to take him into custody, and just as he was stepping from the vessel, I seized him by the skirt of his coat, and in attempting to pull him back, I tore it off; but, springing forward, by a rapid effort he made his escape. He had, however, to run a gauntlet through the crowd upon the wharf, each one, as he passed, giving him a kick or a stroke.

Another attempt was made to save a little tea from the ruins of the cargo by a tall, aged man who wore a large cocked hat and a white wig, which were fashionable at that time. He had skillfully slipped a little tea into his pockets, but was detected. They seized him and, taking his hat and wig from his head, threw them, together with the tea, of which they had emptied his pockets, into the water. In consideration of his advanced age, he was permitted to escape, with now and then a slight kick.

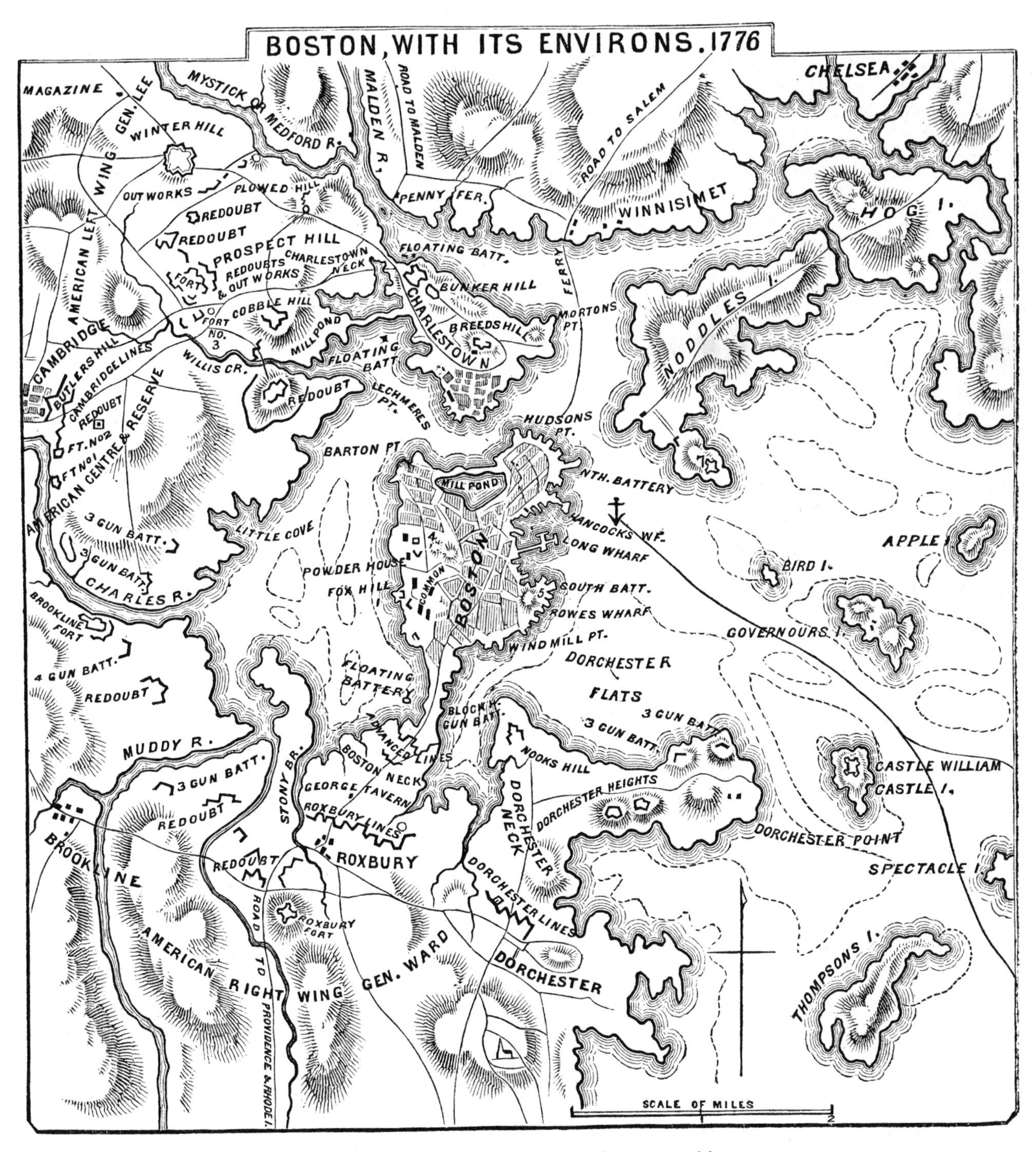

A simple map of Boston and nearby communities

The next morning, after we had cleared the ships of the tea, it was discovered that very considerable quantities of it were floating upon the surface of the water, and to prevent the possibility of any of its being saved for use, a number of small boats were manned by sailors and citizens, who rowed them into those parts of the harbor wherever the tea was visible, and by beating it with oars and paddles, so thoroughly drenched it as to render its entire destruction inevitable.

As the work progressed, a large crowd gathered at the wharf to watch the proceedings in silent approval. It was so quiet

Patrick Henry, whose fiery speeches helped enflame the colonists

that a witness standing at some distance could hear the steady whack-whack of the hatchets. By nine o'clock, less than three hours from the time they had begun, the gangs had finished their task. The next day, John Adams wrote in his diary:

> This is the most magnificent Movement of all. There is a Dignity, a Majesty, a Sublimity in this last Effort of the Patriots that I greatly admire. This Destruction of the Tea is so bold, so daring, so firm, intrepid, and inflexible, and it must have so important Consequences and so lasting that I cannot but consider it as an Epoch in History.

London responded by closing the port

The government in London punished the Bostonians by closing the port, and by other Intolerable Acts, as the colonists named them. This repression united the colonists, who sent delegates to form the First Continental Congress. They refused to submit to oppression and tyranny. On the other hand, the King and his ministers were determined to bring them to heel by armed might. "Blows must decide," declared King George, whether the colonists would be free or remain subservient to Britain. He sent more and more troops to Boston, the hotbed of sedition. The colonists secreted arms and ammunition and drilled their militia. Ancient muskets were taken from the walls where they had hung for fifteen years, since the farmers and fishermen, merchants and planters had fired them in the French and Indian War.

"The next gale that sweeps from the north will bring the clash of arms," declared Patrick Henry.

A panorama of Boston in 1775

LEXINGTON

"Do something," Lord Dartmouth, the secretary of state for the colonies, urged General Thomas Gage, the British commander-in-chief and governor of the Massachusetts Bay Colony. "It would be better that the conflict be brought on quickly than in a riper state of rebellion." He meant that the general should strike first and scotch the dangerous snake of liberty.

The British government's order reached General Gage on April 14, 1775. Five days later, in Benjamin Franklin's words, Gage "drew the sword and began the war."

Gage planned to destroy the arms cache which the colonists had collected at Concord, sixteen miles north of Boston. He also intended to arrest the two ringleaders of rebellion, Samuel Adams and John Hancock, who had taken refuge at the Reverend Clark's parsonage at Lexington, six miles short of Concord.

Gage began his preparations on April 15. To cover up his actions he announced that the unusual activity was due to the need for his soldiers to learn new military tactics. The break in routine and the surreptitious collection of landing boats beneath the sterns of the warships anchored in the harbor fooled no one. Some great evil was being planned, concluded Dr. Joseph Warren, the leader of the citizens' Committee of Safety. He told his friends throughout the countryside that if the British left Boston by water, which would indicate a raid on Concord, two lanterns would be hung in the steeple of the Old North Church.

Paul Revere at Lexington
–From a sketch by Howard Pyle

"What a glorious morning this is"

On the night of April 18, eight hundred British Grenadiers and Light Infantrymen stole stealthily through the streets of Boston and embarked in the waiting boats. Their precautions were in vain. Long before they had landed on the opposite shore, Paul Revere had been dispatched by Warren. From across the bay the church steeple flashed the warning message. Twice intercepted by British patriots, his horse taken from him, Revere reached Clark's parsonage before dawn. From Lexington came the crackle of musketry. "What a glorious morning this is – I mean for America," announced Adams.

The British soldiers, who were led by Colonel Francis Smith, a gallant old officer, and Major Pitcairn of the marines,

Skirmish at Lexington, as sketched by Paul Revere

soon learned that their plan had been detected. Lieutenant William Sutherland spotted "vast numbers" of militiamen skulking on the skyline. Another young officer, Lieutenant John Barker, realized, "All our precautions were in vain for the inhabitants rose out of their beds."

By four thirty that morning, fifty or sixty militiamen had assembled at Lexington, including twenty-three-year-old Sylvanus Wood, who at nearby Woburn had been aroused by the peal of church bells:

> By this time many of the company had gathered around the captain at the hearing of the drum, where we stood, which was about halfway between the meeting house and Buckman's tavern. Parker says to his men, "Every man of you who is equipped, follow me, and those of you who are not equipped, go into the meeting house and furnish yourselves from the magazine, and immediately join the company." Parker led those of us who were equipped to the north end of Lexington Common, near the Bedford Road, and formed us in single file. I was stationed about in the center of the company. While we were standing, I left my place and went from one end of the company to the other and counted every man who was paraded, and the whole number was thirty-eight and no more.

According to the deposition of Jonas Parker, one of many collected to prove the innocence of the colonists and the guilt of the British, he ordered his men not to fire unless they were fired upon.

Sylvanus Wood had just finished counting the militiamen and had regained his place in the line, when he perceived the British troops marching into Lexington, between the meeting house and Buckman's tavern. Thomas Willard, peering from the window of a house, had an even better view:

"Lay down your arms, damn you"

I saw, as I suppose, about four hundred regulars in one body coming up the road, who marched toward the north part of the Common, back of the meeting house of the said Lexington, and as soon as said regulars were against the east end of the meeting house, the commanding officers said something, which I know not; but upon that, the regulars ran till they came within about eight or nine rods of about a hundred of the militia of Lexington who were collected on the Common, at which time the militia of Lexington dispersed; then the officers made a huzza and the private soldiers succeeded them. Directly after this, an officer rode before the regulars to the other side of the body, and hallooed after the militia of Lexington and said, "Lay down your arms, damn you. Why don't you lay down your arms?" and there was not a gun fired till the militia of Lexington were dispersed.

Sylvanus Wood was in the thick of the fight:

The British troops approached us rapidly in platoons, with a general officer on horseback at their head. The officer came up to within about two rods of the center of the company, where I stood, the first platoon being about three rods distant. They there halted. The officer then swung his sword, and said, "Lay down your arms, you damned rebels, or else you are all dead men. Fire!" Some guns were fired at us by the British from the first platoon, but no person was killed or hurt, being probably charged only with powder.

Just at this time, Captain Parker ordered every man to take care of himself. The company immediately dispersed; and while the company was dispersing and leaping over the wall, the second platoon of the British fired and killed some of our men. There was not a gun fired by any of Captain Parker's company, within my knowledge. I was so situated that I must have known it, had anything of the kind taken place before a total dispersion of our company.

Lieutenant Barker declared afterwards that two to three hundred men were assembled on the common. As the regulars approached, the militia fired one or two shots,

"Upon which our men, without any orders, rushed in upon them, fired and put 'em to flight; several of them were killed—we could not tell how many, because they were got behind Walls and into the Woods. We had a Man of the 10th Light Infantry wounded, nobody else hurt. We then formed on the Common, but with some difficulty, the Men were so wild they could hear no orders."

Ensign Lister also said that the militia fired first. Each side blamed the other for what may have been an accidental discharge, as Major Pitcairn thought, according to Ezra Stiles, who later became President of Yale College:

> Riding up to them, he [Major Pitcairn] ordered them to disperse; which they not doing instantly, he turned about to order his troops to draw out so as to surround and disarm them. As he turned, he saw a gun in a peasant's hand, from behind a wall, flash in the pan without going off; and instantly, or very soon, two or three guns went off by which he found his horse wounded, and also a man near him wounded. These guns he did not see; but believing they could not come from his own people, doubted not, and so asserted that they came from our people, and that thus they began the attack. The impetuosity of the king's troops was such that a promiscuous, uncommanded, but general fire took place which Pitcairn could not prevent, though he struck his staff or sword downwards with all earnestness, as the signal to forbear or cease firing.

Ordered to withhold fire, according to Pitcairn

In the report he made to General Gage, Pitcairn stated that he told his troops on no account to fire without orders. He observed nearly two hundred rebels on the village green:

> When I came up within about one hundred yards of them, they began to file off towards some stone walls on our right flank. The Light Infantry, observing this, ran after them. I instantly called to the soldiers not to fire, but to surround and disarm them, and after several repetitions of these positive orders, some of the rebels who had jumped over the wall fired four or five shots at the soldiers, and at the same time several shots were fired from a meeting house on our left. Upon this, without any order or regularity, the Light Infantry began a scattered fire, and continued contrary to repeated orders.

Lieutenant Sutherland also thought the militia fired first:

> I heard Major Pitcairn's voice call out, "Soldiers, don't fire, keep your ranks, form and surround them." Instantly some of the villains who got over the hedge fired at us, which our men for the first time returned, which set my horse a-going, who galloped me down a road above six hundred yards among the middle of them before I turned him. In returning, a vast number who were in a wood at the right of the Grenadiers, fired at me, but the distance was so great that I only heard the whistling of the balls, but saw a great number of people in the wood. In consequence of their discovering [revealing] themselves, our Grenadiers gave them a smart fire.

The colonial view

The pastor of Lexington, the Reverend John Clark, on the other hand, blamed the British:

> The foremost officer, who was within a few yards of our men, brandishing his sword and then pointing toward them, with a loud voice said to the troops, "Fire! By God, fire!" which was instantly followed by a discharge of arms from the said troops, succeeded by a very heavy and close fire upon our part, dispersing, so long as any of them were within reach. Eight were

BOSTON
AND
VICINITY
1776
by Henry Pelham.
MEDFORD
Causeway
CAMBRIDGE
to Concord
Lane
Winter Hill Fort
Charleston
Mt. Prospect
PART
OF
MALDEN
To Waterlown
To Newton
Cambridge Neck
CHARLES'S RIVER
BROOKLINE
MALDEN RIVER
Lechmere's Farm
Charlestown Common
To Malden
To Dedham
Stoney Brook
Lynes Pt.
Bunker's Hill
Upper Road to Milton
CHARLESTOWN
MISTICK or MEDFORD RIVER
Mill Pond
Ferry
Morton's Pt.
ROXBURY
Brown's House
Common
BOSTON
To Salem
Old Works
Long Wharf
Noddles Island
Foster's Hill
Dorchester Neck
PART
OF
DORCHESTER
New Works
1776
Bird Island
BOSTON
Dorchester Point
Governours Island
Chelsea
MILTON RIVER
Castle Island
Ship Channel
Apple Island
HARBOUR
Snake Island
Thompson Island
Shirley Point
PART
OF
NAHANT BAY
MILTON
Squantum
Spectacle Island
Pulling Pt.
G. Hayward Lith 171 Pearl Str N.Y.

Jonathan Harrington, who was mortally wounded in front of his house

left dead upon the ground! Ten were wounded. The rest of the company, through divine goodness, were (to a miracle) preserved unhurt in this murderous action!

Twelve of the militiamen present testified on April 25 that the regulars fired on the company before a gun was fired upon them. Jonas Parker, who repeatedly said he would never run from the British and continued to fire his gun, was killed by a bayonet. Jonathan Harrington fell mortally wounded in front of his own house on the north of the Common. His wife, who was watching from the window, saw him fall and start up again, the blood gushing from his breast. He stretched out his hands toward her and fell again. Rising once more to his knees, he crawled toward his house, to expire at her feet. Isaac Murray and Robert Munroe died where they stood in line. Caleb Harrington was shot down as he ran to replenish his powder, and Samuel Headley, John Brown, and Asehel Porter were killed after they had left the Common.

A volley by the redcoats at Lexington

FROM A WATER-COLOR SKETCH BY KAY SMITH

Connecticut Hall at Yale College, New Haven, the residence of Nathan Hale during his college days from 1769 to 1773 just prior to the war.

FROM A WATER-COLOR SKETCH BY KAY SMITH

The Old North Church, the oldest public building in Boston, Massachusetts—important in American history as it was from the spire of this church that the lanterns signaled the approach of the British.

CONCORD

Realizing that he had entered a hornet's nest, Colonel Smith sent a messenger galloping to Boston to request reinforcements. Then, following a final volley, the British marched off to Concord. On the deserted Lexington common, Sylvanus Wood helped to carry the wounded to the meeting house, and then he, too, set out for Concord "with my gun."

From the neighboring towns and villages the minutemen, who were from sixteen to sixty years of age, converged on Concord. The inhabitants of Concord had sent Reuben Brown to Lexington to learn what was happening. He returned with the startling news that the people of Lexington had been fired upon by the King's troops, who were treble in number to the militiamen at Concord. Brown had hardly returned to the town before the British came in sight at the distance of a quarter of a mile, their arms glittering in the early morning sunshine, their pipes and drums playing a lively tune.

Minuteman statue at the North Bridge—Concord

"We had grand music"

From Concord, a party of militia went out to meet the British, among them Corporal Amos Barrett:

> We at Concord heard they was a-coming. The bell rung at three o'clock for an alarm. As I was then a Minuteman, I was soon in town and found my captain and the rest of my company at the post. It wasn't long before there was other minute companies. One company, I believe, of minutemen was raised in almost every town to stand at a minute's warning. Before sunrise, there was, I believe, 150 of us and more.
>
> We thought we would go and meet the British. We marched down towards Lexington about a mile and a half, and we see them a-coming. We halted and stayed there until we got within about a hundred rods, then we was ordered to about-face and marched before them with our drums and fifes a-going—and also the British. We had grand music.

Pastor William Emerson watched Captain Minot assemble his men on a hill overlooking the meeting house:

> Scarcely had we formed before we saw the British troops at the distance of a quarter of a mile, glittering in arms, advancing towards us with the greatest celerity. Some were for making a stand, notwithstanding the superiority of their number; but others, more prudent, thought best to retreat till our strength

Colonel Barrett's house

should be equal to the enemy's by recruits from neighboring towns that were continually coming to our assistance.

A British private's view of the scene at Concord:

> On a hill near Concord, there was assembled a number of people – about seven hundred – at exercise; they were ready prepared for us, being all loaded with powder and ball. We then halted and looked at them, as cocks might do on a pit before they fight. But it was not our business to wait long looking at them, so we fixed our bayonets and immediately charged them up the hill, in order to disperse them; but we were greatly mistaken, for they were not to be dispersed so easily, the whole of them giving us a smart fire; but we returned the compliment and pursued them with charged bayonets, till we entered the town of Concord, where we cut down what they call their Liberty Pole.

As the British entered Concord, the colonists withdrew across the river, assembling on another hill, from where they watched the King's troops ransacking the houses for the military provisions which they had come to destroy. Learning that there were two bridges across the river, Colonel Smith sent out detachments; one commanded by Captain Pole to secure the South Bridge, and the other by Captain Parsons to hold the North Bridge. Accompanying Parsons was Captain Walter Slone Laurie, who remained with two companies at the North Bridge while Parsons advanced with four companies in the direction of Colonel James Barrett's farm house two miles distant, to destroy the military supplies which were reported to have been cached there.

In the town, Colonel Smith ordered his men to search for and destroy the military stores, which they succeeded in doing only partially, for the early warning had enabled the people to hide and disperse most of their supplies. The troops broke open sixty barrels of flour and scattered their contents, half of which was subsequently saved, knocked off the trunnions of three twenty-four-pound cannons, and burned sixteen new carriage wheels – a poor haul for so much effort.

According to one British officer, the inhabitants were told that they need be under no apprehensions of injury to their persons and properties, and the troops behaved with the utmost levity, though the people were very sulky, and many of them very surly without provocation. One fellow had the impudence to strike Major Pitcairn of the marines, while he was searching for the military stores according to orders.

Quick witted rebels

A quantity of precious flour was saved, due to the astuteness of Timothy Wheeler, who had charge of some of it in his barn, together with several casks of his own.

A British officer demanding entrance, he readily took his key and gave him admission. The officer expressed his pleasure at the discovery, but Captain Wheeler, with much affected simplicity, said to him, putting his hand on a barrel:

This is my flour. I am a miller, sir; yonder stands my mill; I get my living by it. In the winter, I grind a great deal of grain and get it ready for market in the spring. This (pointing to one barrel) is the flour of wheat; this (pointing to another) is the flour of corn; this is the flour of rye; this (putting his hand on his own casks) is *my* flour; this is *my* wheat; this is *my* rye; this is *mine*.

"Well," said the officer, "we do not injure private property," and withdrew, leaving this important discovery untouched.

Even more remarkable was the exploit of the widow Martha Moulton, which she described nearly a year later in her petition for recompense. The heroine of Concord was accorded the sum of three pounds for her good services in boldly and successfully preventing the burning of the Court House. Taking her life in her hands, she persuaded the soldiers to extinguish the fire, setting the example of bringing a pail of water to the scene.

"Fire, fellow soldiers. For God's sake, fire!"

The search of Concord was interrupted by the sound of heavy firing from the North Bridge. Amos Barrett described the onset of the fight to recapture the bridge:

When we was on the hill by the bridge, there was about eighty or ninety British came to the bridge and there made a halt. After a while, they begun to tear up the plank of the bridge. Major Buttrick said if we were all of his mind, he would drive them away from the bridge; they should not tear that up. We all said

The battlefield at Concord

we would go. We then wasn't loaded; we were all ordered to load—and had strict orders not to fire till they fired first, then to fire as fast as we could.

Colonel Bartlett, who had taken command of the 450 militiamen, ordered Major Buttrick to dislodge the British. Observing the militia approaching, British Captain Laurie withdrew his 100 men across the bridge, ordering them to tear up its planks, an action which caused American Major Buttrick to hasten his march. As the militiamen neared the bridge, the British opened fire, killing Captain Davis and another man, upon which Buttrick called out, "Fire, fellow soldiers. For God's sake, fire."

The action at North Bridge was described by four eyewitnesses, two British, John Barker and J. Lister, and two colonists, Amos Barrett and the Reverend William Emerson. Lieutenant Barker wrote:

> The Rebels marched into the Road and were coming down upon us, when Cap'n. Laurie made his Men retire to this side of the Bridge (which by the bye he ought to have done at first, and then he would have had time to make a good disposition, but at this time he had not, for the Rebels were got so near him that his people were obliged to form the best way they could); as soon as they were over the Bridge, the three companies got one behind the other so that only the front one could fire; the Rebels when they got near the Bridge halted and fronted, filling the road from the top to the bottom. The fire soon began from a dropping shot on our side, when they and the front company fired almost at the same instant, there being nobody to support the front company. The others not firing, the whole were forced to quit the Bridge and return toward Concord; some of the Grenadiers met 'em in the road and then advanced to intercept the Rebels, who had got this side the Bridge and on a good height, but seeing the manoeuvre they thought proper tó retire again over the Bridge.

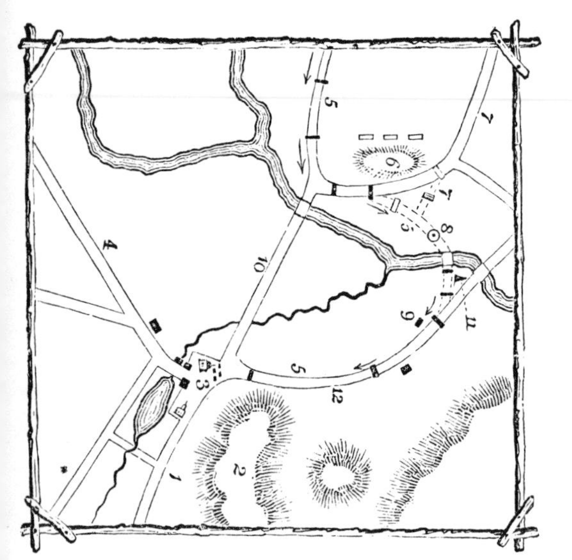

Plan of the action at Concord.

1. Lexington Road.
2. Hills and high land where the liberty pole stood.
3. Center of the town, and main body of the British.
4. Road to the South Bridge.
5,5,5. Road to the North Bridge and to Colonel Barrett's, two miles from the center of the town.
6. High ground a mile north of the meeting-house, where the militia assembled.
7. Road along which they marched to dislodge the British at North Bridge.
8. Spot where Davis and Hosmer fell.
9. Reverend Mr. Emerson's house.
10. Bridges and roads made in 1793, when the old roads with dotted lines were discontinued.
11. The monument. The arrows show the return of Captain Parsons, after the firing at the North Bridge.
12. The place where reinforcements met him.

From Frothingham's History of the Siege of Boston

Atrocity claims

Lister added to Lieutenant Barker's narrative the important fact that "the weight of their fire was such that we was obliged to give way, then run with the greatest precipitance." The four British men who had been killed, he claimed, were afterwards "scalped, their eyes gouched out, their noses and ears cut off," and he remarked, "Such barbarity exercised upon this corps could scarcely be paralleled by the most uncivilized savages." Lister, who had fled before the Americans came up, could hardly have been an eyewitness to such atrocities. His story may have been derived and enlarged from the unfortunate incident when a wounded British soldier was killed by a young militiaman who struck the fallen man with a hatchet as he tried to rise.

In their counter-accusation, the Americans claimed that, at Lexington, "the savage barbarity exercised upon the bodies of our unfortunate brethren who fell is almost incredible. Not

The Battle of Concord Bridge, as viewed by a contemporary artist

contented with shooting down the unarmed, aged, and infirm, they (the British troops) disregarded the cries of the wounded, killing them without mercy, and mangling their bodies in the most shocking manner."

On the colonial side, Amos Barrett was in the thick of the fight:

> Captain Davis's minute company marched first, then Captain Allen's minute company, the one I was in next; we marched two deep. It was a long causeway, being round by the river. Captain Davis had got, I believe, within fifteen rods of the British, when they fired three guns one after the other. I see the balls strike the river on the right of me. As soon as they fired them, they fired on us—their balls whistled well. We then was all ordered to fire that could fire and not kill our own men. It is strange that there warn't no more killed, but they fired too high. Captain Davis was killed, and Mr. Hosmer and a number wounded. We soon drove them from the bridge. When I got over, there was two lay dead and another almost dead. We did not follow them. There was eight or ten that was wounded, and a-running and hobbling about, looking back to see if we was after them.
>
> We then saw the whole body a-coming out of town. We then was ordered to lay behind a wall that run over a hill, and then when they got nigh enough, Major Buttrick said he would give the word "fire," but they did not come quite so near as he expected before they halted. The Commanding Officer ordered the whole battalion to halt and officers to the front march. The officers then marched to the front. There was laying behind the wall about two hundred of us with our guns cocked, expecting every minute to hear the word "fire." Our orders was, if we fired, to fire two or three times and then retreat. If we had fired, I believe that we could have killed almost every officer there was in the front, but we had no orders to fire and there wasn't a gun fired.
>
> They stayed about ten minutes and then marched back, and we after them.

The Old Manse, Concord, built in 1769 by Ralph Waldo Emerson's grandfather from which he observed the fight on the bridge

They seemed to "drop from the clouds"

Pastor Emerson watched the British retreat in disorder. They were allowed to return unmolested to Concord, where Colonel Smith spent two hours re-forming his troops—a near fatal delay, for by then thousands of militiamen, roused by the firing, were massing along the roads to Lexington. They seemed to "drop from the clouds," thought one British soldier.

Tramping sullenly along the road, the regulars were sniped by unseen marksmen sheltered behind trees and walls, as Lieutenant Barker experienced:

> They were all lined with people who kept an incessant fire upon us, as we did too upon them, but not with the same advantage, for they were so concealed there was hardly any seeing them: in this way we marched between nine and ten miles, their number increasing from all parts while ours was reducing by deaths, wounds, and fatigue; and we were totally surrounded with such an incessant fire as it is impossible to conceive; our ammunition was likewise near expended.

Philada July 5. 1775

Mr Strahan,

You are a Member of Parliament, and one of that Majority which has doomed my Country to Destruction.— —You have begun to burn our Towns, and murder our People. — Look upon your Hands! — They are stained with the Blood of your Relations! — You and I were long Friends: — You are now my Enemy, — and

I am, Yours,

B Franklin

Benjamin Franklin announces the end of a long friendship.

The enemy marched very fast and left many dead and wounded, and a few "tired," states Colonel Loammi Baldwin, who, earlier in the day, had left his farm to take up arms.

Colonel Smith's contingent was saved from annihilation by the arrival at Lexington of three regiments of British infantry and two of marines, commanded by Lord Percy, with whom marched Lieutenant Frederick Mackenzie of the Welsh Fusiliers:

> We could observe a considerable number of the Rebels but they were much scattered, and not above fifty of them to be seen in a body in any place. Many lay concealed behind the stone walls and fences. They appeared most numerous in the road near the church, and in a wood in the front, and on the left flank of the line where our regiment was posted. A few cannon shots were fired at those on and near the road, which dispersed them. The flank companies now retired and formed behind the brigade, which was soon fired upon by the Rebels most advanced. A brisk fire was returned, but without much effect. As there was a piece of open morassy ground in front of the left of our regiment, it would have been difficult to have passed it under the fire of the Rebels from behind the trees and walls on the other side. Indeed no part of the brigade was ordered to advance; we therefore drew up near the morass, in expectation of orders how to act, sending an officer for one of the six-pounders. During this time the Rebels endeavored to gain our flanks and crept into the covered ground on either side, and as close as they could in front, firing now and then in perfect security. We also advanced a few of our best marksmen who fired at those who showed themselves.

"All that were found in the houses were put to death."

"We were obliged to force almost every house on the road, for the rebels had taken possession of them and galled us exceedingly," stated Lieutenant Barker. They suffered for their temerity for "all that were found in the houses were put to death." Others rode up, "crept down" near enough to fire a shot, mounted and rode off, getting ahead of the column where they repeated their maneuver.

As the regulars neared Cambridge, the number of their enemies and their fire increased. "Even women had firelocks," claimed one eyewitness.

Concluding his story of that disastrous day, Mackenzie wrote:

> During the whole of the march from Lexington the Rebels kept an incessant irregular fire from all points at the column, which was the more galling as our flanking parties, which at first were placed at sufficient distances to cover the march of it, were at last, from the different obstructions they occasionally met with, obliged to keep almost close to it. Our men had very few opportunities of getting good shots at the Rebels, as they hardly ever fired but under cover of a stone wall, from behind a tree, or out of a house, and the moment they had fired they lay down out of

The Barrett Farm, where the British ended their march on the 19th of April, 1775

The monument at Concord commemorating the battle of April 19, 1775 with the following inscription:

HERE,
On the 19th of April, 1775,
was made the first forcible resistance to
BRITISH AGGRESSION.
On the opposite bank stood the American militia, and on this spot the first of the enemy fell
in the WAR OF THE REVOLUTION,
which gave Independence to these United States.
In gratitude to God, and in the love of Freedom,
This Monument was erected,
A.D. 1836.

sight until they had loaded again, or the column had passed. In the road indeed in our rear, they were most numerous and came on pretty close, frequently calling out "*King Hancock forever.*"

An ill-planned and ill-executed expedition

The exhausted troops passed through Charlestown and stumbled across the Neck into Boston as dusk was falling, Lieutenant Barker remarking, "Thus ended this expedition, which from beginning to end was ill-planned and ill-executed."

The Americans had lost 49 men killed, 39 wounded, and 5 missing. The British had lost 73 men killed, and 200 wounded or missing.

When he heard the news of the engagement, John Adams called the event, "the most shocking New England ever beheld," and he reflected that "the fight was between those whose parents but a few generations ago were brothers; I shudder at the thought, and there is no knowing where our calamities will end."

Benjamin Franklin on his return to Philadelphia from Europe remarked in his dry way, "His (General Gage's) troops made a most vigorous retreat–twenty miles in three hours–scarce to be paralleled in history. The feeble Americans, who pelted them all the way, could scarcely keep up with them."

"The most artful villains in the world"

The British troops, Lord Percy reported to General Gage, had behaved with "their usual intrepidity and spirit," and he called the Americans "the most artful villains in the world," an accusation which did nothing to explain away the unpalatable fact that 1,800 disciplined soldiers had been routed by bands of rustic farmers, by men who had shown a determination and perseverance that boded ill for the future.

Whoever had fired first, the first blow of the Revolution had been struck, and the Americans set out to exploit it to the full. The Massachusetts Provincial Congress deputized a committee to collect depositions from participants and eyewitnesses, and draw up a *Narrative of the Massacre*, and their version of the affair was dispatched so expeditiously that Captain Richard Derby of Salem reached London with the report on May 29, eleven days ahead of General Gage's messenger. In England, the news that British veterans had been forced to retreat by a "rude rabble" was received with astonishment, though few Englishmen understood the significance of these skirmishes.

As night fell on April 19, thousands of determined minutemen and militia, clad in their homespun garments and carrying an assorted medley of weapons, converged on Boston, flocking round the town, which they cut off from the surrounding countryside.

TICONDEROGA

At Lexington and Concord, the colonists had defended themselves against aggression. Now, they seized the initiative, though who first conceived the idea of taking the King's fort at Ticonderoga is uncertain. The credit seems to belong to lawyer John Brown, who had been sent to Canada to test the feelings of the French residents. From Montreal he wrote on March 29, 1775, to the Massachusetts Committee of Safety:

> One thing I must mention to be kept as a profound secret; the fort at Ticonderoga must be seized as soon as possible should hostilities be commenced by the King's troops.

The desirability of capturing the famous fort was obvious. Located at the confluence of lakes Champlain and George, it dominated the water route from Canada, from where the British could launch a counter offensive against the rebellious colonists. But, the seizure of the King's fort, however justified now that his troops had struck "the first blow," would constitute an offensive act which the colonists were loath to commit. While the Committee of Safety considered its advisability, chance intervened.

On the day following the actions at Lexington and Concord, Colonel Samuel Parsons left the American camp at Cambridge to return to Connecticut to recruit men for the siege of Boston, and for the long struggle which he believed lay ahead. The colonists' lack of cannons worried him, and he was wondering how to obtain such weapons when he met Colonel Benedict Arnold, who was on his way to Cambridge with his company of militiamen from New Haven.

Arnold told him that there were plenty of cannons at Ticonderoga, and further, that the fort appeared weakly garrisoned and run down. Parsons continued his journey and Arnold hurried to Cambridge where he urged the Committee to give him authority to seize the fort. The Committee agreed that Arnold could enlist "not more than 400 men" from Massachusetts.

Fort Ticonderoga

Explanation of the ground plan: a, entrance and wicket gate; *b,* counterscarp twenty feet wide; *cc,* bastions; *d,* underground room and ovens; *e e e e,* barracks and officers' quarters; *f,* court or parade-ground; *g g,* trench or covert-way, sixteen feet wide and ten feet deep; *h,* the place where Ethan Allen and his men entered by a covert-way from the outside.

Ethan Allen and his Green Mountain Boys

Meanwhile, Parsons had encountered John Brown and Colonel James Easton who, understanding the need for cannon, had set out with forty men for Castleton, in the Hampshire Grants, the district which later became the state of Vermont. They ran into Ethan Allen, who had already decided with his Green Mountain Boys, the hardy frontiersmen of that district, to capture the fort at the "Meeting Place of Waters," or, as the Indians had named this tongue of land with their word, *Ticonderoga*.

The old stone fort, or Fort Ti, as it is still affectionately known to Americans, had been built by the French in 1750 to replace the earthworks constructed in 1690. During the years of peace, since 1763, it had been allowed to decay, and its eighty heavy and twenty smaller cannons, and twelve mortars,

Map showing the strategic location of Fort Ticonderoga on the waterway linking the interior of New England and New York with Lake Champlain and the Saint Lawrence River.

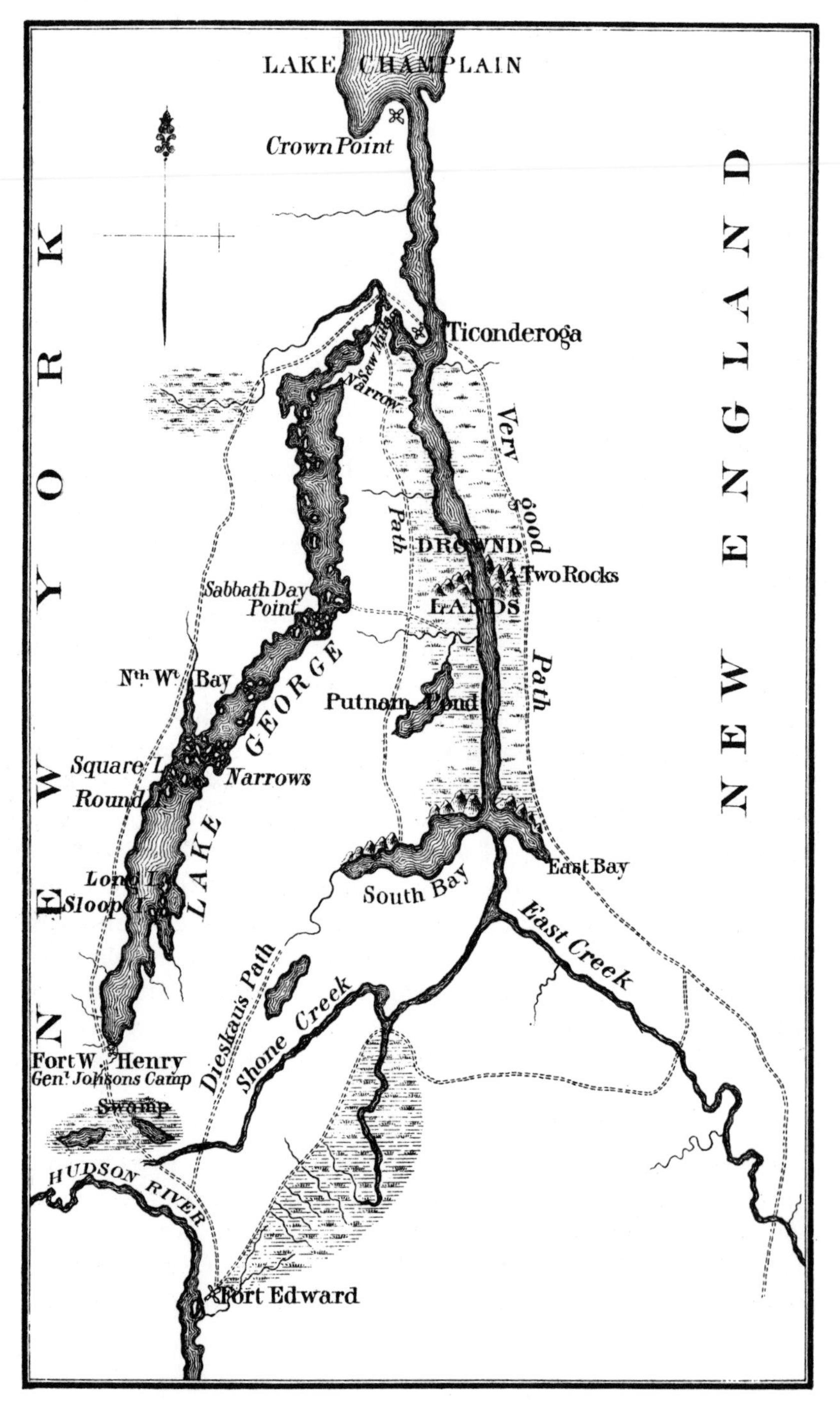

After years of neglect, this is how Fort Ticonderoga appeared before reconstruction.

represented a rich prize. Two independent expeditions were now converging, both led by fiery, impetuous, and ambitious men—the energetic and bold Ethan Allen, the local hero, and the hot-headed and rash Benedict Arnold, the one-time apothecary, shipmaster, and horse trader.

When they met at Castleton, where Arnold had dashed ahead of his troops, the two officers clashed. Waving his commission from the Massachusetts Committee of Safety, Arnold told Allen that he had no authority from anyone. Allen pointed to his 175 men, and Arnold's lack of troops. Allen refused to hand over command, but he grudgingly agreed that Arnold should march at his side.

The expedition reached Ticonderoga in the early hours of May 10, 1775. Walking side by side, Allen and Arnold approached the wicket gate which stood open. As the sleepy sentry snapped his fusee, he was cut on the head and disarmed, and the Green Mountain Boys—among them Seth Warner—poured into the courtyard, "giving three huzzas" as they approached the barracks where the eighty-three-man garrison and two officers, Captain William Delaplace and Lieutenant Jocelyn Feltham, were still asleep.

In his account of the action in his *Narrative of Captivity*, Allen said that a sentry made a pass at one of his officers. "My first thought was to kill him with my sword but, in an instant, I altered the design and fury of the blow to a slight cut on the side of the head, upon which he dropped his gun and asked quarter, which I readily granted, demanding the place where the commanding officer slept." The soldier pointed to a pair of stairs which led to the second story of the barracks.

Deliver the fort "in the name of the Great Jehovah and the Continental Congress"

Allen called to the commanding officer to come forth instantly, and the captain, he says, came to the door with his

Major General Benedict Arnold

breeches in his hand. It was not, however, Captain Delaplace who appeared, but Lieutenant Feltham. Allen ordered him to deliver the fort instantly, and upon being asked his authority, he announced it, "in the name of the Great Jehovah, and the Continental Congress," holding his sword over Feltham's head.

"This surprise," says Allen, "was carried into execution in the gray of the morning. The sun seemed to rise with a superior luster, and Ticonderoga and its dependencies smiled on its conquerors, who tossed about the flowing bowl, and wished success to Congress and the freedom of America."

The prisoners—two officers, some forty privates and subalterns, and various women and children—were rounded up, and Seth Warner, of the Green Mountain Boys, was dispatched to capture the fort at Crown Point, further up the lake. This expedition succeeded and yielded a prize of more than a hundred cannons.

To their chagrin and fury, Arnold and Allen were ordered to abandon both forts and return to Boston bringing the captured cannons. Later, Congress relented and sent a thousand soldiers to garrison these valuable posts. The captured cannons could not be moved without transport, and they did not reach Boston until January, 1776.

Looking across Lake Champlain to the west, old Fort Ticonderoga with Mount Defiance in the background in the nineteenth century before reconstruction

Faneuil Hall, Boston, where many of the meetings of the enraged colonists served to solidify their resistance to the Crown

THE SIEGE OF BOSTON

The British had challenged and the colonists had responded, to the astonishment of the British. On the night of April 19, 1775, they withdrew to Boston, and from there they watched the campfires of the rebellious colonists flickering in a wide half-circle. The jubilant Americans had not gone home. They meant to continue the war which the British had begun. The crash of the volley fired at Lexington spread in waves, reverberating from village to village and from farm to farm, evoking horror, anger, and resolution. Twenty thousand armed men converged on Boston, a miracle of spontaneous determination.

That night the Massachusetts Committee of Safety dispatched post riders to spread the conflagration. Israel Bisset reached Philadelphia on April 23, riding the distance in just over five days, three days quicker than stagecoach time. "We conjure you by all that is sacred to send help," appealed the Committee. "Our all is at stake," it entreated. The call to arms rang from north to south. In Kentucky, the pioneer farmers named their new village Lexington. When the royal governor of Georgia heard the news, he forecast, "A general rebellion throughout America is coming suddenly and swiftly." The prophetic vision of "A Gentleman of Rank" residing in New

England was even more acute for he wrote, "thus, Sir, a civil war is commenced; but how or where it will end, He only knows whose hands are all the corners of the earth."

"To arms, to arms"

Throughout the Thirteen Colonies the people understood that the die had been cast. "To arms, to arms," came the cry.

B I C K E R S T A F F'S

BOSTON ALMANACK,

For the Year of our LORD 1770. Being the fecond Year after Leap Year.

The HON. JAMES OTIS, jun. ESQ;

B O S T O N:

Printed by MEIN and FLEEMING, and to be SOLD by JOHN MEIN, at the *LONDON BOOK-STORE*, North-fide of *KING-STREET.*

[Price feven Coppers fingle, and 25 s. Old Tenor, or 3 s. 4. Lawful the Dozen.]

The cover of Bickerstaff's Boston Almanack of 1770 featured a print of James Otis, one of the real firebrands of the revolutionary spirit.

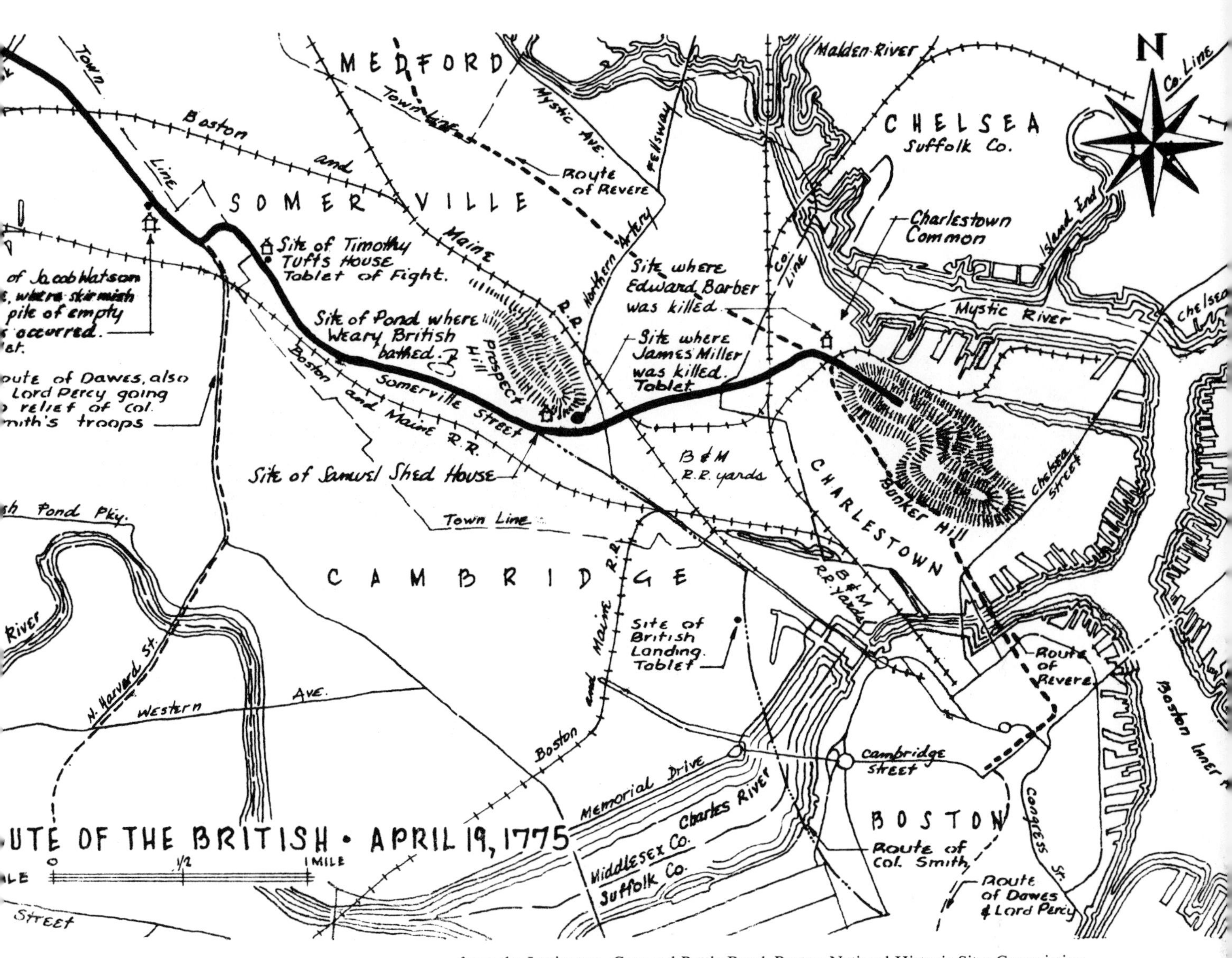

—from the Lexington—Concord Battle Road, Boston National Historic Sites Commission

The streets of Philadelphia reverberated to the sound of pipe and drum.

From the Quaker City, Silas Deane, the Connecticut delegate to the forthcoming Second Continental Congress, wrote to his wife:

> The militia are constantly out, morning and evening at exercise; and there are already thirty companies in this city in uniform, well armed, and have made a most surprising progress.

In Virginia, the colony which, with Massachusetts, had given the impetus to the revolution, the royal governor, Lord Dunmore, on the night of April 20, sent a body of marines to seize a store of powder. His action sparked such beligerent protest that he was forced to pay for the powder. His empty threat to turn the whole country into a "solitude," and to free

Boston from Dorchester Heights in 1774

and arm the slaves, ranged the colony solidly behind Massachusetts.

"The late unhappy affair at Boston," a letter writer from New York told his friend, "has the most amazing effects throughout every part of America." In his own city he was astonished to find, "the most violent proposals meeting with universal approbation."

All was in commotion.

In Boston, all was in commotion. The war had come suddenly and unexpectedly. From within the city and its suburbs streamed the refugees, those who were as anxious to get out as were the militiamen to get in. Hannah Winthrop was determined to avoid being trapped in Charlestown, as she explained to her friend Mercy Warren:

> To stay in this place was impracticable. Thus with precipitancy were we driven to the town of Andover, following some of our acquaintance, five of us to be conveyed with one poor tired horse and chaise. Thus we began our pilgrimage, alternatively walking and riding, the roads filled with frightened women and children, some in carts with their tattered furniture, others on foot, fleeing into the woods.

To her terror was added the horror of "passing through the bloody field at Menotomy which was strewn with mangled bodies. We met one affectionate father with a cart, looking for his murdered son and picking up his neighbor's who had fallen in the battle, in order for their burial."

The British failed to understand the determination and resolution of the colonists. Even after their courageous stand on April 19, the regulars continued to pour scorn upon the mili-

FROM A WATER-COLOR SKETCH BY KAY SMITH

The residence of Paul Revere in Boston, Massachusetts, as it appears among the buildings of the historic city.

FROM A WATER-COLOR SKETCH BY KAY SMITH

The Longfellow House, Cambridge, Massachusetts, built in 1759 by Major John Vassall, a wealthy young Royalist. After the battles of Lexington and Concord and Bunker Hill this house was used for a time as a hospital for the wounded American soldiers. On July 2, 1775, General Washington came to Cambridge to take command of the Continental forces. Two weeks later he moved into this house and for the next ten months he made it his headquarters. Years later it was the home of Henry Wadsworth Longfellow, the poet.

tary capabilities of the farmers and tradesmen who made up the militia. The loyalist lady, Ann Hulton, sister of the Commissioner of Customs, who wrote home a long description of the affairs at Lexington and Concord, lamented, "We are now cut off from all communication with the country, and many people must soon perish with famine in this place," and she entreated for "the Lord to preserve us all."

The Old State House, Boston

"A scene too black for human sight"

A naval officer, who is quoted by Willard, grieved to relate the details of the "fatal 19th of April," calling it a "scene too black for human sight," and he lamented "the woes of this devoted and unhappy country." Another British officer, a naval surgeon, expressed the sentiments of many of his fellow officers, naval and military:

> There is a large body of them [rebels] in arms near the town of Boston. Their camp and quarters are plentifully supplied with all sorts of provisions, and the roads are crowded with carts and carriages, bringing them rum, cider, etc. from the neighboring towns, for without New England rum, a New England army could not be kept together; they could neither fight nor say their prayers, one with another; they drink at least a bottle of it a man a day. This army, which you will hear so much said, and see so much wrote about, is truly nothing but a drunken, canting, lying, praying, hypocritical rabble, without order, subjection, discipline, or cleanliness; and must fall to pieces of itself in the course of three months, notwithstanding every endeavor of their leaders, teachers, and preachers, though the last are the most canting, hypocritical, lying scoundrels that this, or any other country ever afforded.

The young Lord Percy, who had experienced the fighting qualities of the militiamen, took a more realistic view, expressing his opinions in a letter written the day after his return to Boston, to his friend, Edward Harvey, the adjutant general of the British army:

> Whoever looks upon them as an irregular mob will find himself much mistaken. They have men amongst them those who know very well what they are about, having been employed as Rangers against the Indians and Canadians, and this country being much covered with woods, and hilly, is very advantageous for their method of fighting.
>
> You may depend upon it, that as the rebels have now had time to prepare, they are determined to go through with it, nor will the insurrection here turn out so despicable as it is perhaps imagined at home. For my part, I never believed, I confess, that they would have attacked the King's troops or have the perseverance I found in them yesterday.

Were the colonists determined "to go through with it," as Percy believed? In the makeshift camps around Boston, it did not look so, for almost as soon as the militiamen had assembled, they began to melt away, to return home to plant or work, or to collect clothes and supplies. Timothy Pickering, the

12d 1776 MASSACHUSETTS STATE 12d
No 2763 Octot 18
TWELVE PENCE
This Bill entitles the Bearer to receive One shilling oute of the Treasury of this State by the 18 of Octo 1784 and shall be received for that sum in all payments Agreeable to an Act of said State
D Cheever Comittee
12d 12d

Massachusetts twelve pence bill

General John Thomas,
a colonial officer

commissioner of deeds at Salem, did not think that the affair of the 19th had made hostilities inevitable. He told the hastily convened council of militia officers that "negotiation might still effect a compromise." Fortunately for the colonists, his was almost a lone voice. At this first council of war, the soldiers expressed their determination to fight. But how? Within four days of the skirmishes at Lexington and Concord, Artemas Ward, the Massachusetts general appointed to command the siege of Boston, found it necessary to inform Congress:

> Gentlemen: my situation is such that if I have not enlisting officers immediately I shall be left all alone. It is impossible to keep the men here, excepting something be done. I, therefore, pray that the plan may be completed and handed to me this morning, and that you, Gentlemen of Congress, issue orders for enlisting men.

When General Thomas, who commanded at Roxbury, lamented that his force had shrunk from 6,000 to 2,500 men, Ward replied that his own camp was too thin for him to send help.

No arsenal and no funds

The problems faced by the Massachusetts Provincial Assembly, and its Committee of Safety, were fearful. Their militiamen were unorganized and ill-disciplined, and there was no obligation for them to stay. The Colony possessed no arsenal and no funds, and, as well as needing to raise an army, it must form a government to replace the one that had been overthrown. On the departure of John Hancock, and Samuel and John Adams to attend the meeting of the Second Continental Congress at Philadelphia, James Warren, the president of the assembly, took charge of the situation, which was graphically described by John Trumbull, the gifted son of the governor of Connecticut, who would later achieve fame as an artist:

> The entire army, if it deserved the name, was but an assemblage of brave, enthusiastic, undisciplined country lads; the officers in general quite as ignorant of military life as the troops, excepting a few elderly men, who had seen some irregular service among the provincials under Lord Amherst (in the previous war against the French).

John Hancock's residence
on Beacon Hill, Boston

Fortunately, this state of affairs did not last long. The New England colonies rallied quickly from the first shock of war and the hurried departure and quick return of their militiamen, whom they now organized into regiments–enlisting troops, paying and supplying them, and commissioning officers, a procedure which engendered much jealousy. Corporal Amos Farnsworth noted in his diary: "April 26, 27, 28, 29. Was a struggling with the officers which should be the highest in office."

In answer to the call for an army of 30,000 men, Massachusetts quickly raised 11,500, Connecticut 2,300, New Hampshire 1,200, and Rhode Island 1,000. With them came officers, several already famous, others still to win renown, such as Colonel John Stark and Colonel Enoch Poor of New Hampshire. Artemas Ward himself had served under Abercrombie at Ticonderoga in 1758, General Pomeroy had fought at the siege of Louisburg, and General Richard Prescott had served throughout the French and Indian War. The militiamen were mostly farmers and mechanics, born and bred to fire a musket.

"What! Ten thousand peasants keep five thousand King's troops shut up!"

When, on May 25, the *Cerebus*, carrying reinforcements from England and the three major generals, Howe, Clinton and Burgoyne, neared Boston, Burgoyne called to the skipper of a packet boat just outside the harbor asking for news. On being told that the city was surrounded by 10,000 country people, he asked, "How many regulars are there?" When the answer "5,000" came, he cried in astonishment, "What! Ten thousand peasants keep five thousand King's troops shut up. Well, let *us* get in and we'll soon find some elbow room."

By that date, a little over a month from the first assembly of militiamen, the siege of the city had become better organized. General Ward's plea to Congress had been answered, and the recently recruited regiments had been supplied with food, weapons, and powder. By early June, 7,500 militiamen from New England had formed a ring around Boston.

Within the city, General Gage retained a precarious foothold, cut off from the countryside and supplied from England by a 3,000-mile sea link. He was hemmed in, and his position was untenable should the Americans occupy either Dorchester Heights to the south, or the low hills on the Charlestown peninsula.

Major General John Stark, a colonial officer

A brief autobiography of John Adams in his own handwriting

Sir Quincy December 30 1815

I was born Octr 19. 1735 in Quincy then the North Parish in Braintree, my Father was John Adams born in the Same Parish, My Grandfather was Joseph Adams Junior born in the Same Parish, My Great Grandfather was Joseph Adams Senior, and my Great Great Grandfather was Henry Adams who came from England. These all lived died and were buried in this Parish as their Gravestones in the Congregational Church yard distinctly show to this day My Mother was Suzanna Boylston a Daughter of Peter Boylston of Brookline, I was educated partly at the public Grammar School and partly at a private Accademy under Mr Joseph Marsh, both in this Parish. In 1751 I entered Harvard College in Cambridge In 1755 took my degree of Batchelor of Arts, and immediately undertook the Care of the Publick Grammar School in Worcester where I lived in the Family and Studied Law in the Office of James Putman, till 1758 when I took my Second Degree at Colledge and the Oath of an Attorney in Boston In 1761 I was admitted a Barrister at Law in Boston in the Superiour Court of Judicature of the Province of Massachusetts Bay. In 1764 I married a daughter of the Reverend William Smith Abigail Smith, of Weymouth. In 1767 my Son John Quincy Adams was born in this Parish. * * * * *

In 1755 I took a decided part against France and Great Britain too; thorougly disgusted with their Folly. The Ignorance, the Cowardice or Treachery of her Conduct of the War against Canada, This Indignation was much increased by her degrading Treatment of our Troops through the whole War.

In 1760 and 1761, upon the first Appearance of the Design of Great Britain to deprive Us of our Liberties by Assorting the Souvereign Athority of Parliament Over Us. I took a decided Part against her, and have persevered for Fifty five Years in opposing and resisting to the Utmost of my power every Intance of her Injustice, and arbitrary Power, towards Us. I am, Sir with much respect

your humble Servant
John Adams

BUNKER HILL

The cannon shot warned General Gage that the colonists had stolen a march on him. For several days he had been planning to seize the three low hills, Morten's, Breed's, and Bunker, which rose on the Charlestown peninsula, and from where Boston could be bombarded. Foreseeing the British strategy, the colonists forestalled him, as Peter Brown, a young Massachusetts militiaman, told his mother in the letter he wrote a week later. On the night of Friday, June 16, he and his company had been ordered to march across the Neck and entrench on the hill overlooking Boston. But, instead of fortifying Bunker Hill as had been intended, Colonel William Prescott took his men to the lower height of Breed's, where the 1,800 militiamen set to work to construct a redoubt under the direction of the chief engineer, Colonel Richard Gridley, as Brown explained:

> We intrenched and made a fort of about ten rods long and eight wide, with a breastwork of about eight more. We worked there undiscovered until about five in the morning, before we saw our danger, being against eight ships of the line, and all Boston fortified against us.

Battle of Bunker's Hill, from a painting by Alonzo Chappel engraved by John Godfrey

Fortifying Breed's Hill on the night of June 16, 1775

Plan of the redoubt on Breed's Hill

Explanation of the plan—A A represents the situation of two strong fences, composed of stones and rails; *a* and *b*, two well-contrived flanks, so arranged that their fires crossed within twenty yards of the face of the redoubt; *c*, another well-arranged flank; *d*, a bastion, with its flanks *e* and *b*; *m*, a small portion of a trench, that extended from the eastern side of the redoubt to a slough at the foot of the hill toward the Mystic River. On the southeast side of the redoubt was a deep hollow. Two cannons were placed in embrasures at the front of the redoubt, in the two salient angles of which were large apple-trees.

This redoubt was eight rods square. The Bunker Hill Monument now occupies its center.

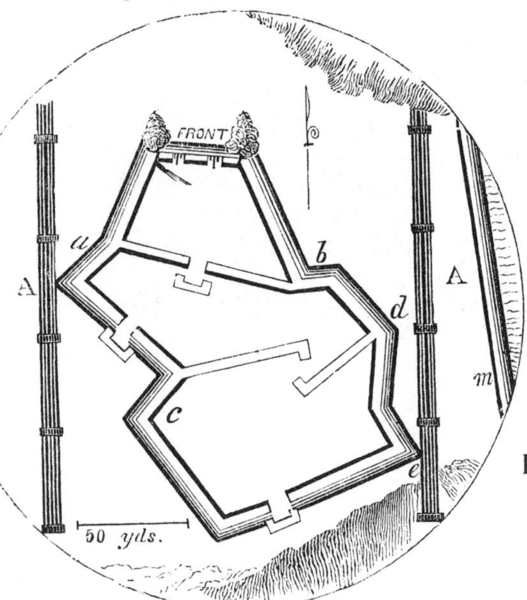

Cannon fire by the British caused some of our young country people to desert, apprehending danger in a clearer manner than the rest, who were more diligent in digging and fortifying ourselves against them.

In his account of the action, Prescott declared that, when the British bombardment began, "the engineer foresook me." Colonel Gridley became indisposed and could render little service, and most of the men under his command deserted. Nevertheless, the redoubt was constructed, as the Reverend Peter Thacher, an eyewitness from across the water, observed:

> The work was carried on in every animation and success so that by the dawn of the day they had nearly completed a small redoubt about eight rods square. At this time a heavy fire began from three men-of-war and a number of floating batteries, and from a fortification of the enemy's on Copp's Hill in Boston directly opposite to our little redoubt. These kept up an incessant shower of shot and bombs, by which one man pretty soon fell. Not discouraged by the melancholy fate of their companion, the soldiers labored indefatigably till they had thrown up a small breastwork extending from the north side of the redoubt to the bottom of the hill but were prevented, by the intolerable fire of the enemy, from completing them in such a manner as to make them defensible.

This breastwork was built about 100 yards to the east of Breed's Hill, on the shore of the Mystic River, and was manned by 200 Connecticut militiamen commanded by Captain Thomas Knowlton, and by Colonel John Stark's New Hampshire militiamen.

In the redoubt on the hill, Prescott was joined by Dr. Joseph Warren, the president of the provincial congress and newly appointed a major general, who, forsaking his rank, fought all day dressed in his fine clothes. Warren was killed during the retreat.

Howe was ordered to dislodge the colonists.

Sir William Howe, the senior British major general, was ordered to dislodge the colonists from the peninsula, a task he chose to accomplish by direct frontal attack, rejecting the advice of Henry Clinton, who suggested landing troops on the Neck in order to cut off the colonists' retreat. It was 2:00 P.M.

Attack on Bunker's Hill, June 17, 1775

before the British were ready, and an hour later before they landed at Morten's Point, on the southeastern tip of the peninsula. From his vantage point, Peter Brown watched their disembarkation:

> We espied forty boats or barges coming over full of regulars – it is supposed there were about three thousand of them – and about seven hundred of us left, not deserted, besides five hundred reinforcements, that could not get nigh to do us any good, till they saw that we must all be cut off, or some of them, so they advanced. When our officers saw that the regulars intended to land, they ordered the artillery to go out of the fort and prevent their landing, if possible; from whence the artillery captain took his field pieces, and went right home to Cambridge as fast as he could – for which he is now confined, and we expect he will be shot for it. The enemy landed and fronted before us, and formed themselves into an oblong square, so as to surround us, which they did in part.

The bombardment of Charlestown

"And now ensued one of the greatest scenes of war that can be conceived," wrote General John Burgoyne, who stood at Clinton's side in Boston, watching Howe's attack on the breastwork and General Robert Pigot's assault on the hill. As a preliminary, the British artillery was ordered to soften up the

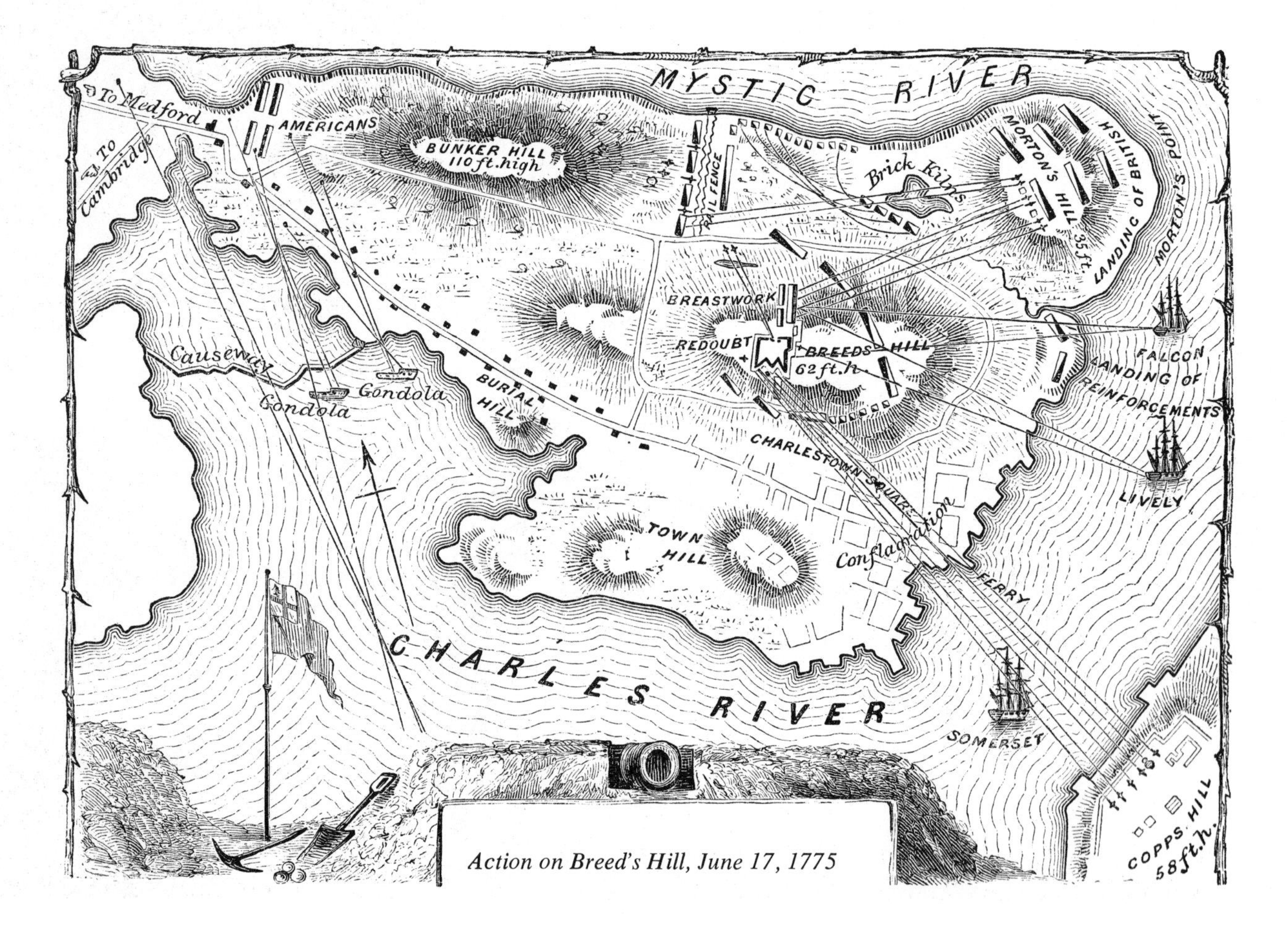

Action on Breed's Hill, June 17, 1775

defenses, a task it was unable to accomplish due to the blunder of the elderly officer who had sent 12-pound balls for the 6-pound caliber guns. A fellow officer described him as an "officer of rank who spends his whole time in dallying with the schoolmaster's daughters." His dereliction of duty was partly compensated for by the guns of the warships and floating batteries which cannonaded Charlestown, setting it in one great blaze. The church steeples, built of timber, became "great pyramids of fire." The hills surrounding the peninsula, Burgoyne remarked, were "covered with spectators, the enemy all in anxious suspense."

Although he considered Howe's disposition "exceedingly soldierlike," Burgoyne still had some doubts, as he expressed in these words:

> The roar of cannon, mortars and musketry, the crash of churches, ships upon the stocks, and whole streets falling in ruins to fill the eye; the storm of the redoubts, and the reflection that perhaps a defeat was a final loss to the British Empire in America to fill the mind, made the whole a picture and a complication of horror and importance beyond anything that ever came to my lot to be witness to.

Leading his troops in person, their bayonets gleaming in the brilliant sunshine, at the quick-step, Howe threw his men against the rail fence by the river, with the object of turning the colonists' left flank. They were surprised by the colonial militia which met them with fire "such as they never before faced." They had never seen a "sharper action," remarked several experienced officers. An officer, whose name was not recorded, described it thus:

> As we approached, an incessant stream of fire poured from the rebel lines; it seemed a continuous sheet of fire for near thirty minutes. Our light infantry was served up in companies against the grass fence, without being able to penetrate; indeed how could we penetrate; most of our grenadiers and light infantry, the moment of presenting themselves, lost three-fourths, and many nine-tenths of their men. Some had only eight and nine men a company left—some only three, four and five.

General William Howe, Commander in Chief of the British forces in America

Amos Farnsworth, a corporal in the Massachusetts militia, stood behind the rail fence:

> As the enemy approached, our men were not only exposed to the attack of a very numerous musketry, but to the heavy fire of the battery on Copp's Hill, four or five men-of-war, several armed boats or floating batteries in Mystic-river, and a number of field-pieces. Notwithstanding, we within the intrenchment, and at a breastwork without, sustained the enemy's attacks with great bravery and resolution, killed and wounded great numbers, and repulsed them several times; and after bearing, for about two hours, as severe and heavy a fire as perhaps ever was known, many having fired away all their ammunition, and having no reinforcement, although there was a great body of men nearby, we were overpowered by numbers and obliged to leave the intrenchment, retreating about sunset to a small distance

over Charlestown Neck. N.B. [note well] I did not leave the intrenchment until the enemy got in.

It was not as easy for the British as Farnsworth made it sound. Twice their soldiers broke and fled, an experience Howe had "never felt before." "The dead lay as thick as sheep in a fold," remarked John Stark, the farmer turned soldier. Peter Thacher from across the Mystic River watched the regulars rallied by their officers "with the most passionate gestures."

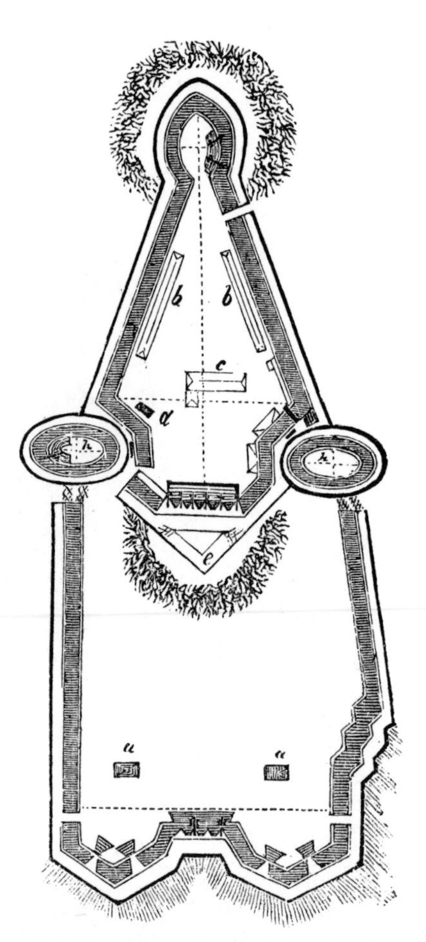

British fort on Bunker's Hill. This was a well-built redoubt. The parapet was from six to fifteen feet broad, the ditch from fourteen to eighteen feet wide, and the banquet about four feet broad. The galleries and parapet before them were raised about twenty feet high, and the merlons at the six-gun battery in the center were about twelve feet high.

a a, two temporary magazines; *b b*, barracks; *c*, guard-houses; *d*, magazine; *e*, advanced ditch; *h h*, bastions.

"Wait until you see the whites of their eyes"

While Howe attacked the rail fence, finally putting its defenders to flight, Pigot led his troops up the slopes of Breed's Hill, where the colonists, armed with ancient muskets, were dangerously short of ammunition, many possessing no more than a cup of powder, fifteen balls, and one flint. But they had learned from frontier wars the need for economical, slow, careful shooting, which was deadly accurate at close range, within fifty yards. "Fire low," their officers ordered, "aim at the white waistbands and pick off the officers." Colonel Prescott told them to "wait until you see the whites of their eyes." Robert Steele, a drummer boy, watched the British:

> They marched with a rather slow step nearly up to our entrenchment, and the battle began. The conflict was sharp, but the British soon retreated with a quicker step than they came up, leaving some of their killed and wounded in sight of us. They retreated towards where they landed and formed again and came up again, and a second battle ensued which was harder and longer than the first, but being a lad, and this the first engagement I was ever in, I cannot remember much more than great noise and confusion.

"Our people in confusion and talking about retreating"

During a lull in the fighting, young Steele was sent to the rear to bring up a pitcher of rum, and on his return to the hill he found "our people in confusion and talking about retreating," as the British advanced for the third time. "Our rum and water went very quick. It was very hot, but I saved my pitcher and kept it for sometime afterwards." I was in the fort when the enemy came in, and jumped over the walls, and ran half a mile, while balls flew like hail stones, and cannons roared like thunder."

One of the better accounts of the action was written by British Lieutenant Lord Rawdon, who described it in a letter to his uncle, the Earl of Huntingdon:

> Our cannon fired upon the entrenchment for some time, but it was so strong that our balls had no effect upon it, and their men kept so close behind it that they were in no danger. Our men at last grew impatient, and all crying out, "Push on, push on," advanced with infinite spirit to attack the work with their small arms. As soon as the rebels perceived this, they rose up and poured in so heavy a fire upon us that the oldest officers say they never saw a sharper action. They kept up this fire till we

were within ten yards of them; nay, they even knocked down my captain, close beside me, after we had got into the ditch of the entrenchment. Nothing, however, could long resist the courage of our men. The rebels were obliged to abandon the post, but continued a running fight from one fence, or wall, to another, till we entirely drove them off the peninsula of Charlestown.

Marine Adjutant Waller marched on the extreme left of Pigot's line:

When we came immediately under the work, we were checked by the severe fire of the enemy, but did not retreat an inch. We were now in confusion, after being broke several times in getting over the rails, etc. I did all I could to form the two companies on our right, which at last I effected, losing many of them. Major Pitcairn was killed close by me, with a captain and a subaltern; also a sergeant, and many of the privates; and had we stopped there much longer, the enemy would have picked us all off. I saw this, and begged Colonel Nesbitt of the 47th, to form on our left, in order that we might advance with our bayonets to the parapet. I ran from right to left, and stopped our men from firing; and when we had got in tolerable order, we rushed on, leaped the ditch, and climbed the parapet, under a most sore and heavy fire.

The Reverend Martin, who had come to the hill to encourage the wounded, described to Ezra Stiles how a soldier had rushed upon him with his bayonet: "Mr. Martin drew his Irish long-sword and defended himself, thrust and killed his adversary by letting out his bowels. Another fired and attacked him with the broad sword. Mr. Martin handled the sword – defended himself and killed his adversary by a stroke on the neck. He brought off his wounded."

Colonel Prescott found himself:

Left with perhaps 150 men in the fort. The enemy advanced and fired very hotly and meeting with a warm reception, there was a very smart firing on both sides. After a considerable time,

Colonel William Prescott's headquarters

finding our ammunition was almost spent, I commanded a cessation till the enemy advanced within 30 yards, when we gave them such a hot fire till they were obliged to retire nearly 150 yards before they could rally and come up again to the attack.

Our ammunition being nearly exhausted, could keep up only a scattering fire. The enemy, being numerous, surrounded our little fort, began to mount our lines and enter the fort with their bayonets. We was obliged to retreat through them, while they kept up as hot a fire as it was possible for them to make. We, having very few bayonets, could make no resistance. We kept the fort about one hour and twenty minutes after the attack with small arms.

"Our retreat was shameful and scandalous"

"Our retreat," claimed Captain John Chester, who came from Connecticut,

. . . was shameful and scandalous and owing to the cowardice, misconduct, and want of regularity of the provincial troops, though to do them justice there was a number of their officers and men that were in the fort and a very few others that did honor to themselves by a most noble, manly, and spirited effort in the heat of the engagement, and 'tis said many of them, the flower of the province, have sacrificed their lives in the cause. Some say they have lost more officers than men. Good Dr. Warren, God rest his soul, I hope is safe in Heaven! Had many of their officers the spirit and courage in their whole constitution that he had in his little finger, we had never retreated.

Many considerable companies of their men I saw that said there was not so much as a corporal with them. One in particular fell in the rear of my company and marched with us. The captain had mustered and ordered them to march and told them he would overtake them directly, but they never saw him till the next day. If a man was wounded, twenty more were glad of an opportunity to carry him away when not more than three could take hold of him to advantage. One cluster would be sneaking down on their bellies behind a rock, and others behind haycocks and apple trees.

"The success is too dearly bought"

The British had won the day, but at fearful cost, which Sir William Howe called "the fatal consequences of this action." The loss of so many brave officers filled him with horror, and he said in his report that "the success is too dearly bought."

The British had won, said Clinton, a "dear-bought victory," and he thought, "another such would have ruined us." The threat of American invincibility behind fortifications was to haunt the British generals throughout the war.

Of his 2,500 men engaged, Howe had lost 1,054–226 killed and 828 wounded, including 19 officers killed and 70 wounded. The Americans lost 140 killed, and 271 wounded.

Following the battle, General Gage remained inactive, other than to fortify the captured hills, and the Americans strengthened their lines from Cambridge to Roxbury.

Bunker Hill memorial as it appeared about a century ago.

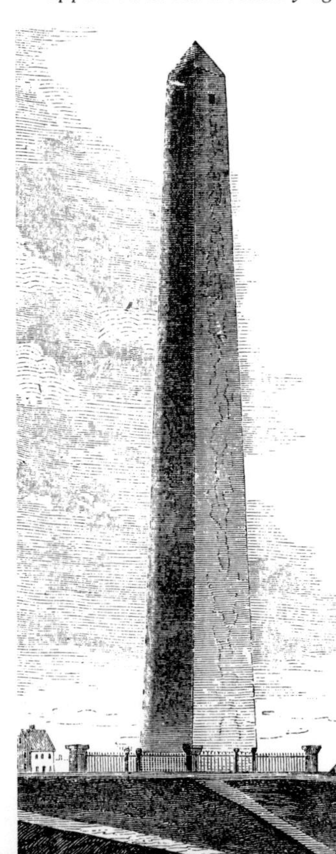

SELECTING THE COMMANDER-IN-CHIEF

Congress, urged by John Adams, reached two momentous decisions. It created a Continental Army, and it appointed George Washington its Commander-in-Chief. It also named four major-generals, Artemas Ward, Charles Lee, who had had experience with the British and Polish armies, Horatio Gates, a one-time major in the British army, and Philip Schuyler, the New York landowner and patrician, and eight brigadiers.

His appointment filled him with "inexpressible concern," Washington told his wife. Far from seeking it, he had used every endeavor in his power to avoid it, not only because it meant being parted from her and his family, but "from a consciousness of its being a trust too great for my capacity." He accepted it as "a kind of destiny." He set out for Boston, unaware, probably, of two tiny incidents which provide some insight into the state of public opinion at home and abroad. On June 11, 1775, a letter writer from New Jersey (whose correspondence was published in the London *Morning Post and Daily Advertiser*) related that a party of Danes and Germans had crossed the Atlantic "to support liberty in America, and to acquire settlements which they would defend with the peril of their lives and spend their best blood in the cause of America."

General George Washington, from a painting by John Trumbull, who served as an aide to the General, engraved by A. B. Durand from an original owned by Yale University

The other small incident was noted by Frank More, a diligent collector of revolutionary trivia and poetry, in his diary:

> The following droll affair happened at Kinderhook, New York. A young fellow, an enemy to the liberties of America, going to a quilting frolic, where a number of young women were collected, and he the only man in company, began his aspersions on Congress, as usual, and held forth some time on the subject. The girls, exasperated at his impudence, laid hold of him, stripped him naked to the waist, and instead of tar, covered him with molasses, and for feathers took the downy tops of flags, which grow in the meadows, and coated him well and then let him go. He has prosecuted every one of them, and the matter has been tried before Justice S—. We have not as yet heard his worship's judgment. It is said Parson Buel's daughter is concerned in the affair.

Throughout the colonies, several diarists relate that soldiers were parading in their homespun, wearing on their chests the motto, LIBERTY OR DEATH.

Janet Shaw, the loyalist "Lady of Quality," as she described herself, witnessed one such parade in Wilmington, North Carolina:

> They at last, however, assembled on the plain field, and I must really laugh when I recollect their figures: 2,000 men in their shirts and trousers, preceded by a very ill-beat drum and a fiddler, who was also in his shirt with a long sword and a pigtail, who played with all his might. They made indeed a most unmartial appearance. But the worst figure there can shoot from behind a bush and kill even a General Wolfe.

Her prediction proved true. The southern riflemen, armed with the Kentucky rifle, were able to pick off officers at 200 yards, twice the range of the old-fashioned musket.

Washington at Cambridge

Washington reached the American camp at Cambridge on July 2, 1775. The problems he faced were practically impossible to solve. He needed to create an army from a conglomeration of forces raised haphazardly by the four New England states – Massachusetts, Connecticut, New Hampshire, and Rhode Island – and the southern regiments yet to come. These Yankee soldiers were volunteers, rugged individualists, resentful of discipline, ignorant of military procedure, and lacking clothing, weapons, ammunition, and other supplies with which to wage a prolonged war. They stoutly resisted any at-

tempt to weld them into a unified force, and they possessed the defects of their virtues. To them all men were equal. They chose their own officers whom each unit controlled like a town meeting, in which everyone had a voice. Their loyalties were confined to their own states.

The difficulties of introducing military discipline and simple tactics to the volunteers were "truly daunting," Washington told the president of Congress. He had no staff. Confusion and disorder reigned in every department. Many of the men had gone home. When he called for "return" of the powder possessed by the deserters, he was pleased with the results, until he learned that the inexperienced officers had recorded, not the powder in stock, but all that had been supplied since April, irrespective of the amount that had been used. He was shocked to discover that there was only enough powder for about nine shots by each soldier.

The officers were "the most indifferent kind of people I ever saw."

General Washington wrote to his brother that the officers, in general, were "the most indifferent kind of people I ever saw." He had already broken one colonel and five captains for cowardice and fraud. Nevertheless, he felt that they had nothing to fear from the enemy "provided we can keep our men watchful and vigilant." He complained that the promises of Congress had not been fulfilled:

General George Washington
–This portrait by John Trumbull was painted in 1790
during President Washington's residence in New York City
and now hangs in New York City Hall

My situation is inexpressibly distressing, to see the winter fast approaching upon a naked army, the time of their service within a few weeks of expiring, and no provision yet made for such important events. Added to these, the military chest is totally exhausted; the paymaster has not a single dollar in hand; the commissary-general assures me he has strained his credit, for the subsistence of the army, to the utmost. The quarter-master-general is precisely in the same situation; and the greater part of the troops are in a state not far from mutiny, upon the deduction from their stated allowance. I know not to whom I am to impute this failure; but I am of opinion, if the evil is not immediately remedied, and more punctually observed in future, the army must absolutely break up.

Joseph Reed, a delegate to Congress, understood Washington's difficulties, as he told his wife on October 11:

To attempt to introduce discipline and subordination into a new army must always be a work of much difficulty, but where the principles of democracy so universally prevail, where so great an equality, and so thoroughly a levelling spirit predominates, either no discipline can be established, or he who attempts it must become odious and detestable.

To give her some notion of this state of affairs, he described how he had seen a captain from Connecticut shaving one of his men.

A sketch of George Washington made on the battlefield

"Death stalked among us."

The situation within beleaguered Boston was little better. "Death stalked among us," stated Attorney-General Jonathan Sewell, who took ship to England. "There were as many dead folks in the street as live ones," remarked one resident, who declared, "We pass them with less emotion and attention than we used to pass dead sheep and oxen in the days of yore."

Suspected of being a spy, John Leach, a teacher, was thrown into the Stone Jail:

From the 2d July to the 19th, a complicated scene of oaths, curses, debauchery and the most horrid blasphemy, committed by the Provost Marshal (the brutal William Cunningham) his deputy and his soldiers who were our guards, soldier prisoners, and the sundry women for our neighbors; some placed over our heads, and some in rooms each side of us. They acted such scenes as was shocking to nature and language, horrible to hear, as if it came from the very suburbs of hell. When our wives, children and friends came to see us (which was seldom they were permitted), we seemed to want them gone, notwithstanding we were so desirous of their company, as they were exposed to hear the most abandoned language, as was grating to the ears of all sober persons.

The official coach used by General Washington

Leach's small son, bringing his father's dinner and overhearing the Provost drink "damnation to the rebels," seized the empty mug and called for "success to the Yankees," upon which he was forbidden further access to his father.

Timothy Newell, a selectman and the deacon of the Brattle Street church, who kept a journal, noted on August 1, that he had invited two gentlemen to dinner, "to dine upon rats." Lord Percy was more fortunate, he killed a foal and had it roasted; Major Musgrave less so, for his fat mare was stolen, killed and sold in the market for beef.

The officers of the garrison attempted to keep up their spirits by theatrical performances, as British Lieutenant Hunter described in his journal:

> Plays were acted twice every week by the officers and some of the Boston ladies. Miss Sally Fletcher acted the part of Zara. She was a very pretty girl and did it very well. A farce called *The Blockade of Boston*, written, I believe, by General Burgoyne, was acted. The enemy knew the night it was to be performed and made an attack on the mill at Charlestown at the very hour the farce began. I happened to be on duty in the redoubt at Charlestown that night. The enemy came along the mill dam and surprised a sergeant's guard that was posted at the mill. Some shots were fired, and we all immediately turned out and manned the works. A shot was fired by one of our advanced sentries, and instantly the firing commenced in the redoubt, and it was a considerable time before it could be stopped. Not a man of the enemy was within three miles of us, and the party that came along the mill dam had effected their object and carried off the sergeant's guard. However, our firing caused a general alarm at Boston, and all the troops got under arms.
>
> An orderly sergeant that was standing outside the playhouse door heard the firing and immediately ran into the playhouse, got upon the stage and cried, "Turn out! Turn out! They are hard at it hammer and tongs." The whole audience thought that the sergeant was acting a part in the farce, and that he did it so well that there was a general clap, and such a noise that he could not be heard for a considerable time. When the clapping was over, he again cried, "What the deuce are you all about? If you won't believe me, by Jesus, you need only go to the door, and there you will see and hear both!" If it was the intention of the enemy to put a stop to the farce for that night, they certainly succeeded, as all the officers immediately left the playhouse and joined their regiments.

Colonists "at least a hundred years" behind the times

Another British officer found the inhabitants of Massachusetts "at least a hundred years behind hand with the people of England in every refinement," and "with the most austere show of devotion, destitute of every principle or religion of common honesty," and he described them as "the most arrant cheats and hypocrites on the whole continent of America." But, "the women are very handsome, but, like old mother Eve, very frail. Our camp has been well supplied in that way since we have been on Boston Common, as if our tents were pitched on Blackheath [the London Common]."

In September, General Gage was recalled to England and Sir William Howe took his place as Commander-in-Chief in North America.

This sketch depicts General Washington stopping a brawl in camp—one of the many examples of the lack of discipline with which he was plagued

CAMBRIDGE CAMP

The regiments from Pennsylvania, Maryland, and Virginia added to Washington's troubles when they reached the camp. They persisted in firing their rifles, wasting valuable powder, and they became so insubordinate that, as one of their number, Aaron Wright, recorded, thirty-four had to be put in irons, and one was whipped for stealing. Another shot the man who had stabbed him with his bayonet. One of the riflemen, Jesse Lukens, "blushed with shame" at what he had witnessed:

> We were excused from all working parties, camp guards, and camp duty. This indulgence, together with the remissness of discipline and care in our young officers, had rendered the men rather insolent for good soldiers. They had twice before broke open our guardhouse and released their companions who were confined there for small crimes, and once when an offender was brought to the post to be whipped, it was with the utmost difficulty that they were kept from rescuing him in the presence of

The buildings of Harvard College in Cambridge

all their officers—they openly damned them and behaved with great insolence. However, the colonel was pleased to pardon the man and all remained quiet.

But on Sunday last, the adjutant having confined a sergeant for neglect of duty and murmuring, the men began again and threatened to take him out. The adjutant, being a man of spirit, seized the principal mutineer and put him in also, and came to report the matter to the colonel, where we, all sitting down after dinner, were alarmed with a huzzaing, and, upon going out, found they had broke open the guardhouse and taken the man out. The colonel and lieutenant colonel, with several of the officers and friends, seized the fellow from amongst them and ordered a guard to take him to Cambridge at the Main Guard, which was done without any violent opposition, but in about 20 minutes, 32 of Captain Ross' company with their loaded rifles swore before God they would go to the Main Guard and release the man or lose their lives, and set off as hard as they could run—it was in vain to attempt stopping them.

The guard was reinforced to five hundred men who were ordered to load their rifles and fix boyonets, and another regiment was ordered under arms, as "the generals were determined to subdue by force the mutineers." George Washington himself came to the scene.

Our 32 mutineers who had gone about half a mile towards Cambridge and taken possession of a hill and woods, beginning to be frightened at their proceedings, were not so hardened but upon the General's ordering them to ground their arms they did

> it immediately. The General then ordered another of our companies (Captain Nagle's) to surround them with their loaded guns, which was immediately done and did the company great honor. However, to convince our people that it did not altogether depend upon themselves, he ordered two of the ringleaders to be bound. I was glad to find our men all true and ready to do their duty except these 32 rascals—26 were conveyed to the Quarter Guard on Prospect Hill and 6 of the principals to the Main Guard.
>
> You cannot conceive what disgrace we are all in and how much the General is chagrined that only one regiment should come from colonies south of Massachusetts and that it should set so infamous an example.

The mutineers, Lukens recorded, had since been tried by court-martial and fined twenty shillings, and were now sorry for their behavior.

Facing a crisis

Washington also faced a more serious problem. The enlistments of many of the militiamen, who had contracted to serve for specific terms, expired in December. Would they reenlist or go home? It was one of the great crises of the Revolution, and Washington was fearful of the outcome. By November 19, only 2,540 men had reenlisted, and, as he informed Congress, "our situaton is truly alarming."

The Connecticut militia, whose term of duty expired on December 10, began to pack up on the first. Sworn at by General Lee, they marched off, Simeon Lyman remarking on his return home, "I got a good supper and lay in a good bed."

Diarist Amos Farnsworth ignored the crisis. He had a more important matter on his mind, the salvation of his soul:

> *Friday, Decr. 15th.* Alas what a backward Hart have I and how Slothfull that before I am aware, my Hart is Sat on the things of this world and Deceives me.
>
> *Saturday, Decr. 16th.* Oh my dulness to Duty! Oh that I did take more delite in the ways of Godliness. Quicken me, oh God, of thy own mear good pleasure because I am dull of understanding.
>
> *Friday, Decr. 29th.* I thought on a life of Religion, but with too much Coldness.
>
> *Saturday and Lords-day, Decr. 30, 31.* Alas what gloomy time is this to my Sole; oh that God would Cause light to arise out of the midst of darkness and Shew to me his Salvation.

Lacking money and supplies

The new recruits and the fresh enlistments failed to meet Washington's hopes, as he told Joseph Reed, to whom he wrote on January 14: "We are now without any money in our treasury, powder in our magazines, or arms in our stores." But those evils were small in comparison with that which disturbed his repose. His worst fears had been realized:

Washington's headquarters in Cambridge—later the residence of Henry Wadsworth Longfellow (also shown in color in a sketch by Kay Smith)

> The discontented officers (for I do not know how else to account for it) have thrown such difficulties or stumbling blocks in the way of recruiting, that I no longer entertain a hope of completing the army by voluntary enlistments, and I see no move or likelihood of one, to do it by other means. In the last two weeks we have enlisted but about a thousand men, whereas I was confidently bid to believe, by all the officers I conversed with, that we should by this time have had the regiments nearly completed.

The total number of soldiers amounted on paper to about 10,500, but many had not joined the army, and others had carried away their firelocks without leave. A month later, the situation had not improved. The regiments were at little more than half strength, and the siege of Boston stagnated.

QUEBEC

Once again the colonists seized the initiative, though only after considerable hesitation by Congress. Loath as yet to commit the nation to a war for outright independence, the delegates took from May 19 to June 27 to debate and approve the plan for an expedition against Canada, the base from where the British could launch a counter-attack on their rebel subjects. As long as they held Quebec and Montreal, the British troops could advance southward following the waterway, the classic invasion route, which ran, with one twenty-mile portage, from Montreal to New York, via lakes Champlain and George and the Hudson River. In 1759, the fate of the North American continent had been decided at Quebec.

In 1775, the opportunity to add Canada to the Thirteen Colonies seemed very inviting. General Guy Carleton, the gover-

The walled city of Montreal from the south bank of the Saint Lawrence River, as it appeared in an old French print in 1760

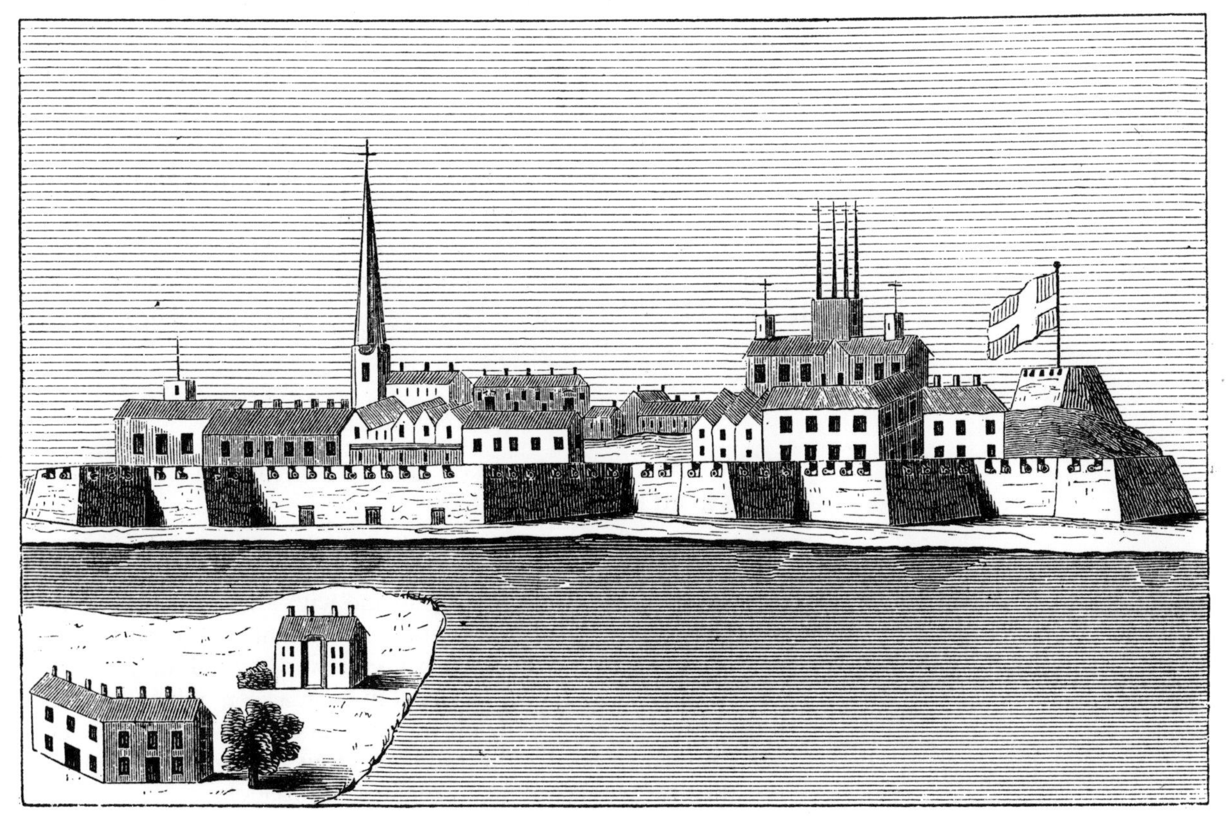

The old French city of Montreal

nor-general of Canada, had only 450 regular soldiers. However, he was an energetic and resourceful soldier who had gained the cooperation of the settlers, whom the Americans hoped to win to their cause. Time was the essential factor, for the terrible Canadian winter lay only four months ahead. Indecision, hesitation, disunion, jealousy, and unpreparedness delayed the start of the expedition to annex Canada.

However, the expedition to capture key points in Canada was approved, and three thousand men under General Philip Schuyler and General Richard Montgomery were sent to Lake Champlain. When General Schuyler, who had been appointed to lead the expedition, fell ill, General Montgomery took his place. He had risen to the rank of captain in the British army while fighting under Wolfe in Quebec during the French and Indian War and had retired to marry and settle in New York.

Montgomery suffered an early disappointment when the Green Mountain Boys refused to join the expedition, rejecting the entreaties of their Colonel, Ethan Allen, whom they set aside, appointing Seth Warner in his place. Allen joined the expedition as a volunteer, collecting en route a number of Canadian sympathizers, and later Warner brought a small contingent to assist Montgomery.

They crossed the lake in flat bottom boats and marched to St. Johns where they arrived September 6, 1775. Fort St. Johns was fourteen miles from Montreal. They were immediately attacked by a party of Indians who forced them to retreat to their boats and take refuge on Isle aux Noix, which commands the entrance to Lake Champlain. Another group of Indians, who had been rejected by General Carleton, joined General Montgomery and his troops. Thus reinforced, he decided to return to St. Johns and lay siege to it.

While this was occurring, Colonel Ethan Allen, with a party of about 150 men composed of Americans and Indians marched to the banks of the St. Lawrence River which they crossed at night about three miles below Montreal. However, the small force of British and Canadian troops defending Montreal had been alerted and they attacked and beat back Allen's men and took Allen prisoner.

Ethan Allen becomes a prisoner

As Allen described in his *Narrative*, no sooner had he handed his sword to an officer than:

> A savage, part of whose head was shaved, being almost naked and painted, with feathers intermixed with the hair on the other side of his head, came running to me with an incredible swiftness; he seemed to advance with more than mortal speed (as he approached near me, his hellish visage was beyond all description; snakes' eyes appear innocent in comparison of his; his features extorted, malice, death, murder, and the wrath of devils and damned spirits are the emblems of his countenance) and in less then twelve feet of me, presented his firelock.

At the instant of his present, I twitched the officer to whom I gave my sword, between me and the savage, but he flew round with great fury, trying to single me out to shoot me without killing the officer. But by this time I was nearly as nimble as he, keeping the officer in such a position that his danger was my defense. But in less than half a minute I was attacked by just such another imp of hell. Then I made the officer fly around with incredible velocity for a few seconds, when I perceived a Canadian taking my part against the savages; and in an instant an Irishman came to my assistance with a fixed bayonet and drove away the fiends, swearing by Jesus, he would kill them. The escaping from so awful a death made even imprisonment happy.

Allen spent two years in captivity in England before he was exchanged.

Montgomery was still in the vicinity of Fort St. Johns and had captured Fort Chambly, a small fortress five miles above St. Johns. His whole detachment did not exceed twenty-five hundred men at this time, and he was very short of supplies and ammunition. The capture of Fort Chambly with its ammunition and provisions on November 3, 1775, enabled him to press the siege against St. Johns, which fell on November 13. With the surrender of St. Johns, General Carleton left Montreal by water for Quebec shortly before it fell to General Montgomery.

After taking Montreal, Montgomery put his troops to work constructing flatboats with which to attack the British armaments, which consisted of eleven armed vessels with a large quantity of military stores. The Americans managed to overwhelm the British forces, and Montgomery proceeded directly to Quebec. He arrived December 5, 1775, and immediately

Fort Chambly, an important link in the chain of forts on the Canadian-American waterway via Lake Champlain (also shown in color in a sketch by Kay Smith)

demanded that the city surrender. General Carleton refused to recognize the demand. Montgomery opened fire, which did little damage to the Quebec fortress.

Winter weather in Canada is scarcely conducive to the conduct of any kind of campaign. Nevertheless, with a deteriorating morale, it became apparent that Montgomery would have to take some action to hold the troops. Four attacks were to be made at the same time—two diversionary or false attacks and two real ones. The false attacks were by Cape Diamond and St. Johns Gate, and the real ones were under Cape Diamond and by Drummond's Wharf and the Potash. The attacks were to begin at daybreak on December 31. Unfortunately, word leaked out concerning the American plans, and the result was disastrous. General Montgomery led nine hundred men through a crossfire and he was wounded in the first wave.

Six grueling weeks of swampy wilderness

During the same weeks that Fort St. Johns was under siege, Colonel Benedict Arnold, with fifteen hundred men, was navi-

A sketch of the tortuous march of the colonial troops under General Arnold through a trackless wilderness to Quebec in the autumn of 1775
Courtesy Archives Nationales du Quebec

Point Levi from Durham Terrace in Quebec City

gating the rocks and shoals of the Kennebec River, 130 miles north of Boston, with the capture of Quebec as the objective. Much of this rugged trip involved long portages over rocky and sometimes swampy wilderness. Provisions began to run low and approximately one third of the detachment deserted on some slight pretense. Nevertheless, six weeks after his departure from Boston, November 14, 1775, Arnold arrived on the plains of Canada. They made camp at Point Levy across the St. Lawrence River from Quebec. That very evening he crossed the river and launched an attack at the gate of St. Louis. Unknown to Arnold, Quebec had the day before been reinforced with a detachment of troops under Colonel MacLean. There had also been some pieces of cannon added to the defenses from a navy frigate. As a result, the Americans sustained a costly defeat, with many casualties, and withdrew to Point au Tremble, twenty miles from Quebec City.

Arnold lacked artillery and he now realized that there was little or no chance to take Quebec without it. He returned to Point Levy where he could intercept supplies and communications. There he awaited the arrival of General Montgomery from Montreal.

Several of the men kept journals describing the hazards of their famous march – sixteen-year-old John Joseph Henry, who recorded his reminiscences late in life after he had become a judge in Pennsylvania, twenty-two-year-old Abner Stocking, George Morrison, Captain Simeon Thayer, Henry Dearborn, and the young doctor, Isaac Senter.

Having raised a volunteer force of a thousand frontiersmen and woodsmen, which included the remarkable Daniel Morgan and the young Aaron Burr, who served as the Commander's aide, Arnold divided his force into three divisions. The van was led by the southern riflemen, commanded by Captains Morgan, Smith, and Hendricks; the second division was commanded by Lieutenant Colonel Christopher Greene and Major Bigelow, with Captains Thayer, Topham, and Hubbard; and the third division was headed by Majors Meigs and Febiger (a Danish volunteer), whose companies were officered by Dearborn, Ward, Godrich, and Hanchet. The rear was brought up by Colonel Roger Enos.

The uniform of the British Marine
Courtesy Archives Nationales du Quebec

"The soldiers were of as rude and hardy a race as ourselves."

The soldiers from Massachusetts, Rhode Island, and Connecticut, John Joseph Henry recalled, "were of as rude and hardy a race as ourselves," whereby he meant the riflemen from Pennsylvania to whom he belonged, "and as unused to the discipline of a camp and as fearless as we were."

From Cambridge, where rifleman Jesse Lukens took leave of his comrades "with a wet eye" – and whom he envied, for they would "spend the winter at Quebec in joy and festivities amongst the sweet nuns" – Arnold's troops were ferried to the mouth of the Kennebec River, where they transferred to the batteaux which had been hastily constructed from green wood.

The terrible hardships of the march – the misery of struggling through the trackless wilderness, the soldiers nearly starving and exhausted by the portages, with their clothes torn to shreds – began on September 24, 1775, when the expedition encountered the first rapids on the Kennebec, Abner Stocking wrote in his diary on September 29:

> This day we arrived to the second carrying place, called Skowhegan Falls. Though this was only 60 rods over, it occasioned much delay and great fatigue. We had to ascend a ragged rock, near on 100 feet in height and almost perpendicular. Though it seemed as though we could hardly ascend it without any burden, we succeeded in dragging our batteaux and baggage up it.

Another diarist, James Melvin, did not allow the torture and fatigue to influence his matter-of-fact language:

> Rained all last night and this day . . . marched through hideous woods and mountains. The company were ten miles wading knee-deep. One man fainted in the water. Here a boat was stove, with four men, and one man drowned. They agreed to part and the heartiest to push forward as fast as they could. I was not well, having the flux. We went twenty-one miles.

A waterfront scene in old Quebec

A street in the lower part of old Quebec City

The street where General Arnold was wounded

Buildings in old Quebec, with the Citadel in the background

A nineteenth century view of Quebec showing the Citadel and the city from the south shore of the Saint Lawrence River

By the time the Norridgewock Falls were reached, most of the batteaux were nothing but wrecks. The men were suffering from diarrhea and were greatly fatigued. Ahead lay the trackless wilderness and the Great Carrying Place where the boats would have to be carried from the Kennebec to the Dead River. Dr. Isaac Senter wrote in his journal on October 24:

> As the number of falls increased, the water became consequently more rapid. The heights of land upon each side of the river, which had hitherto been inconsiderable, now became prodigiously mountainous, closing, as it were, up the river with an aspect of an immense height. The river was now become very narrow, and such a horrid current as rendered it impossible to proceed in any other method than by hauling the batteaux up by the bushes, painters, etc.
>
> Here we met several boats returning loaded with invalids, and lamentable stories of the inaccessibleness of the river, and the impracticability of any further progress into the country; among which was Mr. Jackson, complaining of the gout most severely, joined to all the terrors of approaching famine. I was now exhorted in the most pathetic terms to return, on pain of famishing upon contrary conduct, and the army were all returning except a few who were many miles forward with Col. Arnold. However, his elocution did not prevail; I therefore bid him adieu and proceeded.
>
> Not far had I proceeded before I discovered several wrecks of batteaux belonging to the front division of riflemen, etc. with an increased velocity of the water. A direful howling wilderness, not describable. With much labour and difficulty I arrived with the principal part of my baggage (leaving the batteaux made fast) to the encampment. Two miles from thence I met the informants last mentioned, where were Col. Greene's division, etc. waiting for the remainder of the army to come up, that they might get some provisions, ere they advanced any further. Upon enquiry, I found them almost destitute of any eatable whatever, except for a few *candles*, which were used for supper, and breakfast the next morning, by boiling them in water, gruel, etc.
>
> *Wednesday 25*. Every prospect of distress now came thundering on with a twofold rapidity. A storm of snow had covered the ground of nigh six inches deep, attended with very severe weather. We now waited in anxious expectation for Col. Enos' division to come up, in order that we might have a recruit of provisions ere we could start off the ground.

Ordered to send back those men indisposed either in body or mind.

Arnold, in order to employ the provisions to the best advantage, had left orders for the two rear divisions, those commanded by Greene and Enos, to send back those men who were indisposed either in body or mind. At the council of war, or the "council of grimacers" as Dr. Senter called it, Enos and his men decided to return home, taking their provisions with them. About Enos' desertion, Captain Dearborn had this to say:

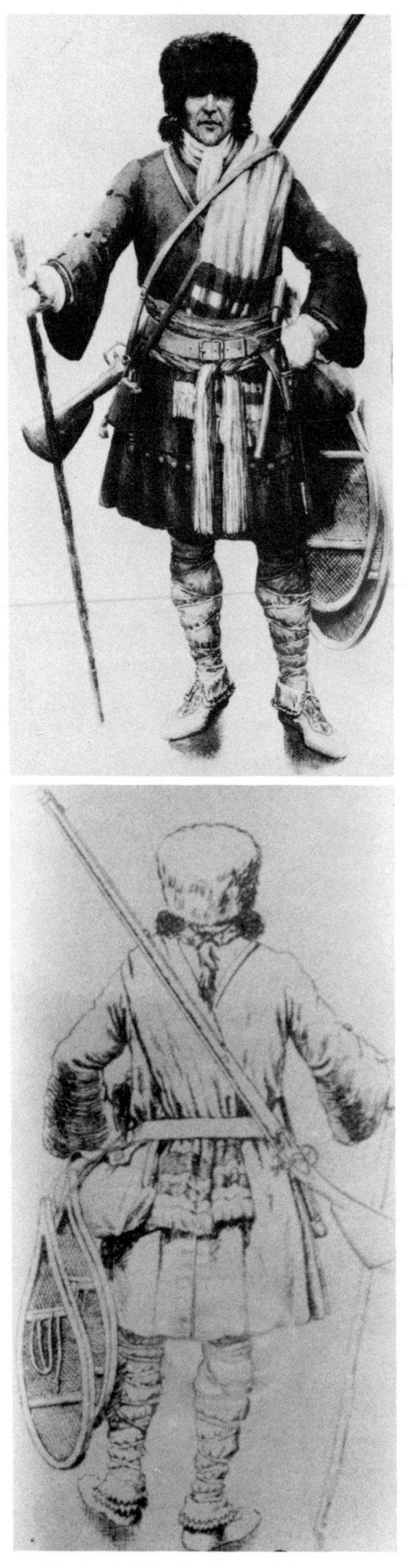

Front and back views of the winter uniforms used by the French in Canada.
Courtesy Archives Nationales du Quebec

Here a Very unhappy Circumstance happen'd to us, in our March, Which proved very fatal and Mortifying to us all.

When we were at the great Carrying Place we had the unhappy news of Col. Enos, and the three Company's in his Division, being so Imprudent as to return back two or three days before, which disheartened and discouraged our men very much, as they Carri'd Back more than their part, or quota of Provision, and Ammunition, and our Detachment, before being but Small, and now loosing these three Companies, We were Small, indeed, to think of entering such a place as Quebec. But being now almost out of Provisions, we were Sure to die if we attempted to Return Back, and We Could be in no Worse Situation if we proceeded on our rout. Our men made a General Prayer, that Col. Enos and all his men might die by the way, or meet with some disaster, Equal to the Cowardly dastardly and unfriendly Spirit they discover'd in returning Back without orders, in such a manner as they had done. And then we proceeded forward.

A court martial and acquittal

Colonel Enos' decision to abandon the march was severely criticized. On his return to Cambridge, he requested and was granted, in the absence of his comrades, a court martial, which acquitted him of blame. In his defense, he claimed that because his officers were determined to turn back, he felt it was his duty to go with them, a decision for which he had some technical justification, for Arnold had told him to send back the men he could not provision. Enos later resigned his commission and left the army.

The loss of these companies reduced the strength of Arnold's force to 675 gaunt scarecrows. Before the "deserters" left, John Joseph Henry acquired from one a much prized rifle, and he lamented, "Our provisions are exhausted; we have no meat of any kind." Captain Simeon Thayer found the traveling very bad:

> We sunk half leg deep every step, but our Pilot says it is better ahead. We lost one man belonging to Capt. Topham's company who must inevitably have perish'd, to wit; Samuel Nichols. We find now that the Pilot knows no more the way than the most ignorant of ourselves; we traveled about five miles and encamped. This night we had the good fortune to kill a partridge, of which we made good soup and some supper.

Several of the men, wrote Dr. Senter, devoured the whole of their flour, "determined (as they expressed it) to have a full meal, letting the morrow look out for itself." Unaware in which direction lay the Chaudière River, he recorded:

> In this state of uncertainty we wandered through hideous swamps and mountainous precipices, with the conjoint addition of cold, wet and hunger, not to mention our fatigue—with the terrible apprehension of famishing in this desert. The pretended pilot was not less frightened than many of the rest; added to

TRENTON
SARATOGA
YORKTOWN
EUTAW
MILITARY
COSTUME
of the
REVOLUTION.

citadel
Quebec City Kay Smith

FROM A WATER-COLOR SKETCH BY KAY SMITH

Saint Louis Gate in Quebec City, Canada, the western entrance to the old walled city.

(left) The Citadel, the imposing fort overlooking the Saint Lawrence River in Quebec City, Canada, was originally constructed by the French about 1665 and has figured prominently in the defense of Quebec on several occasions including the French and Indian War in 1759 and the American Revolutionary War in 1775 and 1776.

FROM A WATER-COLOR PAINTING BY KAY SMITH

FROM A WATER-COLOR SKETCH BY KAY SMITH

This delightful scene in Savannah, Georgia, shows a former powder storehouse dating back to the eighteenth century, on the far right, and on the left, an adjoining tavern formerly known to have been a pirate lair in the eighteenth and nineteenth centuries, both of which are next to the plot that was James Oglethorpe's first experimental garden.

that the severe execrations he received from the front of the army to the rear, made his office not a little disagreeable. Several of the men towards evening were ready to give up any thoughts of ever arriving at the desired haven. Hunger and fatigue had so much the ascendancy over many of the poor fellows, added to their despair of arrival, that some of them were left in the river, nor were heard of afterwards.

They eventually reached the Chaudière, proceeding with renewed vigor, knowing that it would conduct them to an inhabited area, the town of Sartigan:

Thursday, November 2nd. Not more than eight miles had we marched when a vision of horned cattle, four-footed beasts, etc. rode and drove by animals resembling Plato's two footed featherless ones. Upon a nigher approach our vision proved real! Exclamations of joy, echoes of gladness resounded from front to rear with a *Te Deum.* Three horned cattle, two horses, eighteen Canadians and one American. A heifer was chosen as victim to our wants, slain and divided accordingly. Each man was restricted to one pound of beef. Soon arrived two more Canadians in birch canoes, laden with a coarse kind of meal, mutton, tobacco, etc. Each man drew likewise a pint of this provender. The mutton was destined for the sick. They proceeded up the river in order to the rear's partaking of the same benediction. We sat down, eat our rations, blessed our stars, and thought it luxury. Upon a general computation, we marched from 20 to 30 miles per day. Twenty miles only from this to the settlements. Lodged at the great falls this night.

Marching with his division, some miles behind Senter, John Joseph Henry recorded this anecdote:

There were two women attached to those companies, who arrived before we commenced the march. One was the wife of Sergeant Grier, a large, virtuous and respectable woman. The other was the wife of a private of our company, a man who lagged upon every occasion. These women being arrived, it was presumed that all our party were up. We were on the point of entering the marsh, when some one cried out "Warner is not here." Another said he had "sat down sick under a tree, a few miles back." His wife begging us to wait a short time, with tears of affection in her eyes, ran back to her husband. We tarried an hour. They came not. Entering the pond (Simpson foremost), and breaking the ice here and there with the buts of our guns and feet, as occasion required, we were soon waist deep in the mud and water. As is generally the case with youths, it came to my mind, that a better path might be found than that of the more elderly guide. Attempting this, in a trice the water cooling my armpits, made me gladly return into the file. Now Mrs. Grier had got before me. My mind was humbled, yet astonished, at the exertions of this good woman. Her clothes more than waist high, she waded before me to the firm ground. No one, so long as she was known to us, dared intimate a disrespectful idea of her. Her husband, who was an excellent soldier, was on duty in Hendrick's boat, which had proceeded to the discharge of the lake with Lieutenant M'Cleland.

Two scenes from old Quebec

She appeared "fresh and as rosy as ever."

Henry recalled, in a footnote to his narrative, the arrival in December at Quebec of the "wife or widow" of James Warner, who had fallen behind on the march. She appeared "fresh and as rosy as ever:"

> The story Mrs. Jemima Warner told was extremely affecting and may be worth remembering, as it is something like a sample of the whole of our distresses and intolerable disasters.
>
> The husband was a great eater. His stores of provisions after the partition, at the head of the Chaudière, were in a little time consumed. The consummate wife ran back from the marsh and found her beloved husband sitting at the foot of a tree, where he said he was determined to die.
>
> The tender-hearted woman attended her ill-fated husband several days, urging his march forward; he again sat down. Finding all her solicitations could not induce him to rise, she left him, having placed all the bread in her possession between his legs with a canteen of water. She bore his arms and ammunition to Quebec, where she recounted the story.

"Difficulties beyond description"

An early harbor scene in Quebec

The tribulations of the long march were summed up by an officer, who wrote on December 5:

> The difficulties that our detachment underwent in the woods are beyond description. For forty days I waded more or less, my feet continually wet, except nights; the most of the time freezing weather; we were at an allowance of half a pint of flour a man for a fortnight, and half that time no meat; climbing hills, passing through morasses, cedar swamps, and drowned lands, wading creeks and rivers at the same time; the number that we we lost was small, not exceeding three or four, and these with hunger.

The Commander of the long march, Benedict Arnold, described it thus:

"The officers and men, inspired and fired with the love of liberty and their country, pushed on with a fortitude superior to every obstacle."

> In about eight weeks we completed a march of near six hundred miles, not to be paralleled in history; the men having with the greatest fortitude and perseverance hauled their batteaux up rapid streams, being obliged to wade almost the whole way, near 180 miles, carried them on their shoulders near forty miles, over hills, swamps and bogs almost impenetrable, and to their knees in mire; being often obliged to cross three or four times with their baggage. Short of provisions, part of the detachment disheartened and gone back; famine staring us in the face; an enemy's country and uncertainty ahead. Notwithstanding all these obstacles, the officers and men, inspired and fired with the love of liberty and their country, pushed on with a fortitude superior to every obstacle, and most of them had not one day's provisions for a week.

Arnold lay within one mile of Quebec, awaiting Montgomery, who arrived on December 2, short of half his men because 300 Connecticut soldiers had abandoned the expedition following the capture of Montreal and had returned to Ticonderoga. General Schuyler interpreted their claim to "sickness" as "homesickness," noting that, having been discharged, "they slung their packs, crossed the lake and undertook a march of two hundred miles with the greatest alacrity."

Arnold's hope of capturing the city by surprise was gone. Before Carleton had arrived, his second-in-command, Colonel MacLean had raised a force of 1,700 men, sufficient to defend the city's long but very strong walls against the equal number of men with whom Arnold and Montgomery planned to capture the city.

Montgomery decided to storm Quebec on the night of December 31, by a surprise night attack, and to this end he and

General Richard Montgomery

Plaque commemorating the spot where
General Montgomery fell on December 31, 1775

Sailing ships in the harbor of the Quebec waterfront in the eighteenth century

Arnold divided their forces, Arnold to attack from the north, and Montgomery from the river side. Favored by a heavy fall of snow, which obscured their movements from the enemy, the attackers reached the walls about midnight and succeeded in penetrating within the city where they became lost within the maze of narrow streets. Arnold was wounded in the leg, and was carried away. Montgomery was killed when the Lower Town was almost within his grasp, and in fact the rumor had reached Carleton that it had fallen. He hurried reinforcements to the threatened walls, as the Americans wavered. Unable to find their way in the narrow streets, shot upon from the houses, their powder too wet to fire, denied the leadership of their fallen heroes, they hesitated fatally. Too late, Morgan ordered his men to clear the houses of their foes. By dawn many had been killed, including Captain Hendricks. A British sortie proved decisive; overwhelmed, the survivors surrendered. Sixty men had been killed or wounded, and four hundred were taken prisoners. About half the force escaped across the ice. The British and Canadians lost only eighteen men.

"Led on by the intrepid Daniel Morgan"

The glorious failure had several chroniclers. George Morrison accompanied Morgan:

> All eyes are now directed to the place from whence the rockets are to ascend; they are let off precisely at five o'clock—instantly the enemy beat to arms, for when they saw the signals they conjectured that ill was intended them. Our advance party, consisting of thirty men, impetuously rush on and attack a battery on a wharf. Captain Morgan, being in front, advances to their aid, followed by Captain Hendricks. We fire into the portholes

with our rifles with such effect that the enemy cannot discharge a single cannon—save one on our approach that did no damage. Perhaps there is no similar instance in modern warfare of a battery being silenced by a few riflemen. Several discharges of musketry are now made upon us from the houses and other unexpected places. Colonel Arnold receives a bad wound in his leg, and is carried to the hospital. We now scale the battery with our ladders, led on by the intrepid Daniel Morgan, our brave captain. This bold act so confounds the guard that thirty of them instantly surrender and are immediately secured. This affair occupies us but about twenty minutes—one killed and six or seven wounded.

Believing that the city was nearly won, the riflemen laid their ladders against the wall:

Our gallant officers are mounting followed by several men, when a furious discharge of musketry is let loose upon us from behind houses. In an instant we are assailed from different quarters with a deadly fire. We now find it impossible to force the battery or guard the portholes any longer. We rush on to every part, rouse the enemy from their coverts, and force a body of them to an open fight; some of our riflemen take to the houses and do considerable execution. We are now attacked by thrice our number. The battle becomes hot, and is much scattered; but we distinguish each other by hemlock sprigs previously placed in our hats. All our officers act most gallantly. Betwixt every peal the awe-inspiring voice of Morgan is heard, whose gigantic stature and terrible appearance carry dismay among the foe wherever he comes.

Abner Stocking climbed the precipice leading to a blockhouse:

Montgomery, who was himself in front, assisted with his own hands to cut down or pull up the pickets, and open a passage for his troops; but the excessive roughness and difficulty of the way had so lengthened his line of march that he found it absolutely necessary to halt a few minutes in order to collect a force with which he might venture to proceed. Having reassembled about two hundred men, whom he encouraged alike by his voice and his example, he advanced boldly and rapidly at their head to force the barrier. One or two persons had now ventured to return to the battery, and, seizing a slow-match standing by one of the guns, discharged the piece, when the American front was within forty paces of it. This single accidental fire was a fatal one. The general (Montgomery) with Captains McPherson and Cheeseman, two valuable young officers near his person, the first of whom was his aid, together with his orderly sergeant and a private, were killed on the spot.

The advantages of the ground in front, a vast superiority of numbers, and dry and better arms gave the enemy an irresistible power.

Rifleman Henry supplied a detailed description of the fight:

This second barrier was erected across and near the mouth of a narrow street, adjacent to the foot of the hill, which opened into a larger one, leading soon into the main body of the lower town.

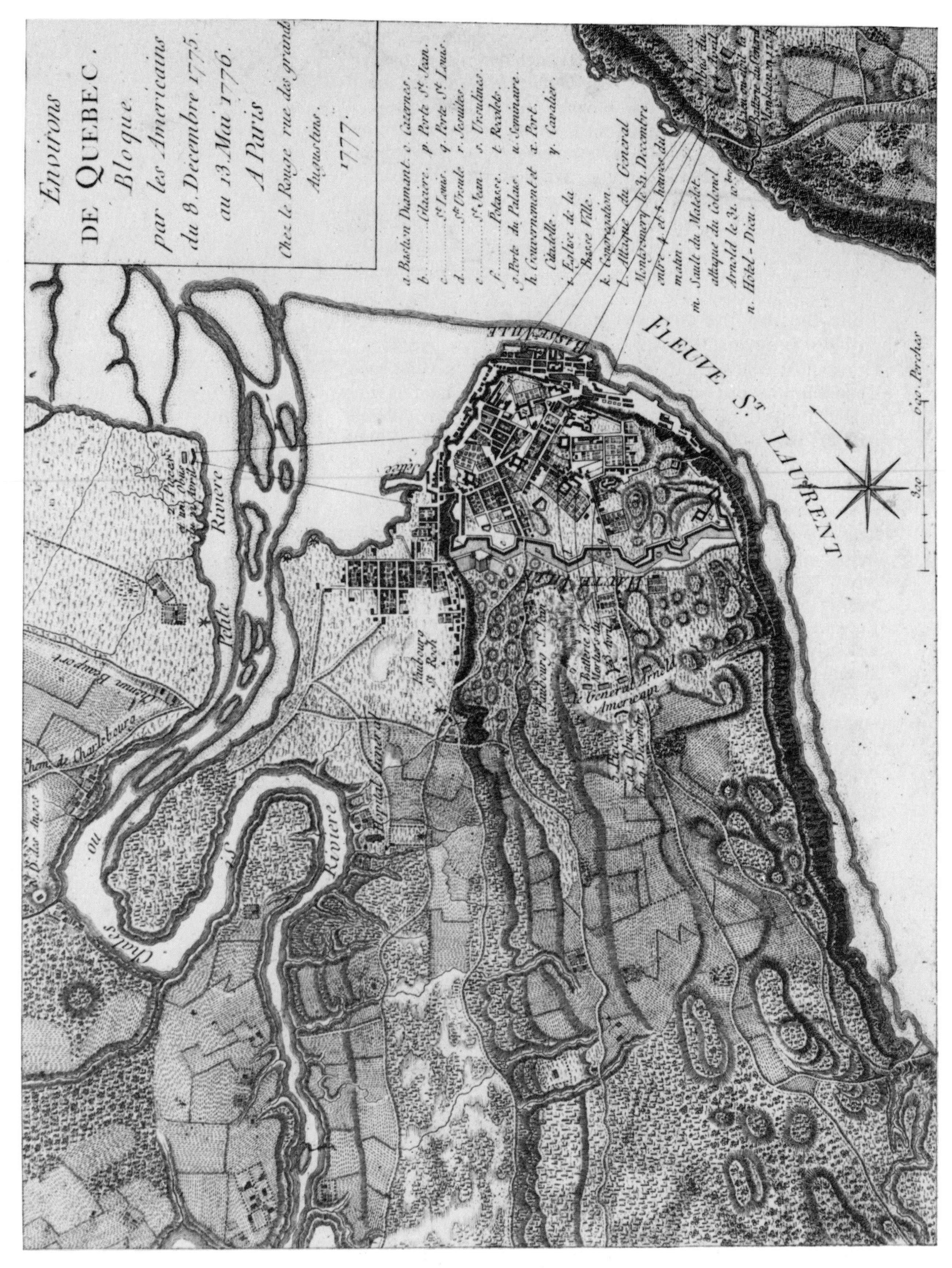

A map of Quebec as it appeared in 1775

Here it was that the most serious contention took place: this became the bone of strife. The admirable Montgomery, by this time (though it was unknown to us), was no more; yet, we expected momentarily to join him. The firing on that side of the fortress ceased, his division fell under the command of a Colonel Campbell, of the New York line, a worthless chief, who retreated without making an effort, in pursuance of the general's original plan. The inevitable consequence was, that the whole of the forces on that side of the city, and those who were opposed to the dastardly persons employed to make the false attacks, embodied and came down to oppose our division. Here was sharp shooting. We were on the disadvantageous side of the barrier, for such a purpose. Confined in a narrow street hardly more than twenty feet wide, and on the lower ground, scarcely a ball, well aimed or otherwise, must take effect upon us. Morgan, Hendricks, Steele, Humphreys, and a crowd of every class of the army, had gathered into the narrow pass, attempting to surmount the barrier, which was about twelve or more feet high, and so strongly constructed, that nothing but artillery could effectuate its destruction. There was a construction fifteen or twenty yards within the barrier, upon a rising ground, the cannon of which much overtopped the height of the barrier; hence, we were assailed by grape-shot in abundance. This erection we call the platform. Again, within the barrier, and close in to it, were two ranges of musketeers, armed with musket and bayonet, ready to receive those who might venture the dangerous leap. Add to all this, that the enemy occupied the upper chambers of the houses, in the interior of the barrier, on both sides of the street, from the windows of which we became fair marks. The enemy, having the advantage of the ground in front, a vast superiority of numbers, dry and better arms, gave them an irresistible power, in so narrow a space. Humphreys upon a mound, which was speedily erected, attended by many brave men, attempted to scale the barrier, but was compelled to retreat, by the formidable phalanx of bayonets within, and the weight of fire from the platform and the buildings. Morgan, brave to temerity, stormed and raged, Hendricks, Steele, Nichols, Humphreys, equally brave, were sedate, though under a tremendous fire. The platform, which was within our view, was evacuated by the accuracy of our fire, and few persons dare venture there again. Now it was, that the necessity of the occupancy of the houses, on our side of the barrier, became apparent. Orders were given by Morgan to that effect. We entered—this was near daylight. The houses were a shelter, from which we could fire with much accuracy. Yet, even here, some valuable lives were lost. Hendricks, when aiming his rifle at some prominent person, died by a straggling ball through his heart. He staggered a few feet backwards and fell upon a bed, where he instantly expired. He was an ornament of our little society. The amiable Humphreys died by a like kind of wound, but it was in the street, before we entered the buildings. Many other brave men fell at this place; among these were Lieutenant Cooper of Connecticut, and perhaps fifty or sixty noncommissioned officers, and privates. The wounded were numerous, and many of them dangerously so. Captain Lamb of the York artil-

Captain Hendricks

lerists, had nearly one half of his face carried away by a grape or canister shot. My friend Steele lost three of his fingers, as he was presenting his gun to fire; Captain Hubbard and Lieutenant Fisdle, were also among the wounded. When we reflect upon the whole of the dangers at this barricade, and the formidable force that came to annoy us, it is a matter of surprise, that so many should escape death and wounding, as did.

General Guy Carleton

"Every man threw down his gun."

Daniel Morgan (who following his capture was exchanged), in a letter written after his return home, described how, following Arnold's retirement:

I took his place, for, although there were three field officers present, they would not take the command, alleging that I had seen service and they had not. I ordered the ladder, which was on two men's shoulders, to be placed (every two men carried a ladder). This order was immediately obeyed and for fear the business might not be executed with spirit, I mounted myself and was the first man who leaped into the town among McLeod's guard, who were panic struck and after a faint resistance ran into a house that joined the battery and platform.

I lighted on the end of a heavy piece of artillery which hurt me exceedingly and perhaps saved my life, as I fell from the gun upon the platform where the bayonets were not directed.

Colonel Charles Porterfield, who was then a cadet in my company, was the first man who followed me. The rest lost not a moment, but sprang in as fast as they could find room. All this was in a few seconds. I ordered the men to fire into the house and follow up their fire with their pikes (for besides our rifles we were furnished with long espontoons). This was done and the guard was driven into the street.

I went through a sally port at the end of the platform, met them in the street, and ordered them to lay down their arms, if they expected quarter. They took me at my word, and every man threw down his gun. We then made a charge upon the battery and took it and everything that opposed us, until we arrived at the barrier-gate where I was ordered to wait for General Montgomery. And a fatal order it was, as it prevented me from taking the garrison, having already made half the town prisoners. The sally port through the barrier was standing open. The guard left it, and the people came running in seeming platoons and gave themselves up in order to get out of the way of the confusion. I went up to the edge of the Upper Town with an interpreter to observe what was going on, as the firing had ceased. I found no person in arms at all. I returned and called a council of war of what officers I had, for the greater part had missed their way and had not got into the town.

Morgan was overruled; he sacrificed his own opinion to the arguments of the officers and "lost the town."

The British Major, Henry Caldwell, believed that had the Americans "acted with more spirit, they might have pushed in at first and possessed themselves of the whole of the Lower Town, and let their friends in at the other side, before our people had time to have recovered from a certain degree of panic, which seized them on the first news of the post being surprised."

"We were now all soldiers, even the wounded in their beds."

Dr. Senter had remained at the base camp to care for the wounded, and one of the first to be brought in was Arnold. Learning that the victorious enemy was in pursuit of the retreating Americans, Dr. Senter urged Colonel Arnold for his own safety to be carried back into the country where they would not readily find him:

> He would neither be removed, nor suffer a man from the hospital to retreat. He ordered his pistols loaded, with a sword on his bed, adding that he was determined to kill as many as possible if they came into the room. We were now all soldiers; even the wounded in their beds were ordered to have a gun by their side, and if they did attack the Hospital, to make the most vigorous defense possible.

Carleton did not pursue. He treated his prisoners kindly, hoping thereby to win them back to loyalty. Of these prisoners, Major Caldwell scornfully remarked, "You can have no conception what kind of men composed their officers. Of those we took, one major was a blacksmith, another a hatter. Of their captains, there was a butcher, a tanner, a shoemaker, and a tavern-keeper. Yet they all pretended to be gentlemen."

When Carleton was reinforced by the arrival of nine hundred soldiers from England, the colonists retreated, evacuating Montreal and returning to Ticonderoga, where we shall hear again of Arnold.

DORCHESTER HEIGHTS

In January, 1776, Henry Knox arrived at the camp outside Boston, bringing fifty-three pieces of artillery, the loot of Ticonderoga. From the fort the cannon had been floated down Lake George on scows, carried over the mountains on sleds, and drawn to Boston by eighty yoke of oxen. And this prodigious feat had been accomplished in the depths of winter. The possession of heavy cannon made it possible for the colonists to batter the British in Boston and force their evacuation of the city. To achieve that, they needed to occupy Dorchester Heights, to the south, which the British had neglected to fortify.

The journals which were composed by eyewitnesses, outside and inside Boston, tell the story of events from March 4 to March 17.

General Heath described the operations in which he played a conspicuous part:

General Henry Knox arriving with artillery

Major John Trumbull

March 4th. There was an almost incessant roar of cannon and mortars during the night, on both sides. The Americans took possession of Dorchester Heights and nearly completed their works on both the hills by morning. Perhaps there never was so much work done in so short a space of time. The adjoining orchards were cut down to make the abatis; and a very curious and novel mode of defense was added to these works. The hills on which they were erected were steep, and clear of trees and bushes. Rows of barrels, filled with earth, were placed round the works. They presented only the appearance of strengthening the works; but the real design was, in case the enemy made an attack, to have rolled them down the hill. They would have descended with such increasing velocity as must have thrown the assailants into the utmost confusion, and have killed and wounded great numbers.

"We were in high spirits"

Major John Trumbull was a member of the force which occupied the Heights:

Our movement was not discovered by the enemy until the following morning, and we had an uninterrupted day to strengthen the works which had been commenced the night preceding. During this day we saw distinctly the preparations which the enemy was making to dislodge us. The entire waterfront of Boston lay open to our observation, and we saw the embarkation of troops from the various wharves, on board of ships, which hauled off in succession, and anchored in a line in our front, a little before sunset, prepared to land the troops in the morning.

We were in high spirits, well prepared to receive the threatened attack. Our positions, on the summits of two smooth, steep hills, were strong by nature, and well fortified. We had at least twenty pieces of artillery mounted on them, amply supplied with ammunition, and a very considerable force of well-armed infantry. We waited with impatience for the attack, when we meant to emulate, and hoped to eclipse, the glories of Bunker's Hill.

In the evening the Commander-in-Chief visited us and examined all our points of preparation for defense. Soon after his visit the rain, which had already commenced, increased to a violent storm, and heavy gale of wind, which deranged all the enemy's plan of debarkation, driving the ships foul of each other, and from their anchors in utter confusion, and thus put a stop to the intended operation.

John Rowe, a Boston merchant, a man of moderate views, too cautious to take sides, observed the operations from within the town:

March 5. This morning we perceived a battery erected on the hill on Dorchester Neck. This has alarmed us very much. About 12 the General sent off six regiments; perhaps this day or tomorrow determines the fate of this truly distressed place. All night both sides kept a continual fire. Six men of the 22nd are wounded in a house at the south end; one boy lost his leg. A very severe storm; it blew down my rail fences, both sides the front of the house.

March 6. This morning the country people have thrown a strong work on another place on the Neck at Dorchester Neck. Gen'l Howe has ordered the troops ashore again, and tis now out of doubt that Gen. Howe will leave this town with his troops, &c. which has put the inhabitants of this town into great disorder, confusion, and much distress.

On Dorchester Heights, Heath noted:

On the night of the 7th Capt. Erving made his escape out of Boston. He reported, that the British were preparing to leave the town; that they were putting their cannon, mortars, shot, shells, &c. on board the store ships; that some of the shot and shells, sent into the town by the Americans, had been well directed.

Rowe watched the British preparations:

March 7. The troops and inhabitants very busy in getting all the goods and effects on board the shipping in the harbor; 'tis impossible to describe the distresses of this unfortunate town.

March 8. My situation has almost distracted me. John Inman, Archy McNeil, and Duncan are determined to leave me. God give me comfort in my old age. I try to do what business I can, but I am dispirited, disappointed, and nothing but cruelty and ingratitude falls to my lot.

March 9. This day Gen. Robinson pressed the ship *Minerva* into the service; nothing but hurry and confusion—every person striving to get out of this place. A great deal of firing on both sides this night.

General Sir William Howe

On March 10, Heath saw that "the British were putting their cannon, military stores, and baggage on board the supply ships and transports. This evening the Yankees carried two pieces of cannon, and two small mortars, onto Noddles Island, to disturb the British shipping; but the enemy being quiet at their different works, they were not molested from that quarter."

The evacuation of Boston

The next day, Rowe found that his warehouse had been broken into and plundered by the British soldiers whom he saw "making havoc in every house." The loyal inhabitants were alarmed for their safety after the British had gone. Deacon Newell watched them leave. He thought this "unhappy, distressed town" relieved from a set of men of "unparalleled wickedness, profanity, debauchery and cruelty." When the Americans entered the town, Heath noticed that "the inhabitants discovered joy inexpressible." Taking with him eleven hundred Tories, Sir William Howe sailed to Halifax, Nova Scotia.

The colonists had won a great victory; the evacuation of Boston left no British soldier on American soil. Washington's problem was—where would the British strike next?

Believing that Howe would sail to New York, Washington rode there for, "it is the object worthy of their attention, and it is the place that we must use every endeavor to keep from them."

CHARLESTON

General Charles Cornwallis

Prompted by the enthusiastic optimism of the governors of the southern colonies, which were, they urged, strongholds of loyalism, the British government, early in 1776, dispatched a naval and military expedition to recapture Charleston, South Carolina, from where a waterway ran inland which could facilitate reconquest. Admiral Sir Peter Parker sailed from Cork in Ireland on February 13, 1776, with eleven warships, and thirty-one transports, carrying two thousand troops commanded by Lord Cornwallis, with orders to rendezvous off Cape Fear with a contingent from Boston led by General Clinton. The frigate *Syren*, 28 guns, preceded the fleet and reached Cape Fear on January 3, after a "very disagreeable passage of seven weeks and four days," reported her Captain, Tobias Furneaux, my ancestor, who thus, though the part he played was small, became a "participant" in the Revolutionary War.

"All was hurry and confusion."

The arrival of the fleet on the coast of South Carolina on May 31 did not catch the colonists wholly unprepared, for they had learned, from captured documents, of the projected raid, to counter which General Charles Lee had been ordered to the Southern Department. In his absence, the defense of Charleston had been entrusted to the old Indian-fighter, Colonel William Moultrie, who kept vigilant watch:

> The sight of these vessels alarmed us very much; all was hurry and confusion—the President with his council busy in sending dispatches to every part of the country, to hasten down the militia—men running about the town looking for horses, carriages, and boats to send their families into the country; and as they were going out through the town gates to go into the country, they met the militia from the country marching into town; traverses were made in the principal streets; fleches thrown up at every place where troops could land; military works going on everywhere, the lead taken from the windows of the churches and dwelling houses, to cast into musket balls, and every preparation to receive an attack, which was expected in a few days.

The threat to the colony was not as serious as it might have been, for the North Carolina loyalists, in expectation of prompt assistance from England, and impatient of delay, had risen and had been defeated in February at Moore's Bridge where 850 of them were either killed or taken prisoner.

Learning that the British fleet had been sighted, Lee hurried to Charleston with two thousand troops, reaching on June 4, the town, where, says Moultrie, "his presence gave us great spirits," largely because "he taught us to think lightly of the enemy."

Sullivan's Island, believed Moultrie, was "the key to the harbor," the mouth of which was protected by the two islands–James to the south and Sullivan's to the north–where the old fortifications had been partly repaired and named Fort Moultrie. Behind Sullivan's Island lay Long Island, from which it was separated by a narrow creek called The Breech, the depth of which was about seven feet.

In order to capture Charleston, the British needed to silence the guns of Fort Moultrie.

Fort Sullivan, which later became Fort Moultrie

In order to capture Charleston, the British needed to silence the guns of Fort Moultrie, which commanded the channel into the harbor. To guard against attack by the two thousand troops which the British were expected to land on Long Island, the colonists built earthworks on The Breech, placing there two cannon and eight hundred men, with another fifteen hundred held in reserve.

The British delay in launching their assault, due to gale-force winds, gave time for the colonists to strengthen Fort Moultrie, where, by the end of June, a double line of palmetto logs, seven feet high, had been laid, and twenty-six cannon had been installed. But the gunners possessed only sufficient powder for twenty-eight discharges by each gun, and the western

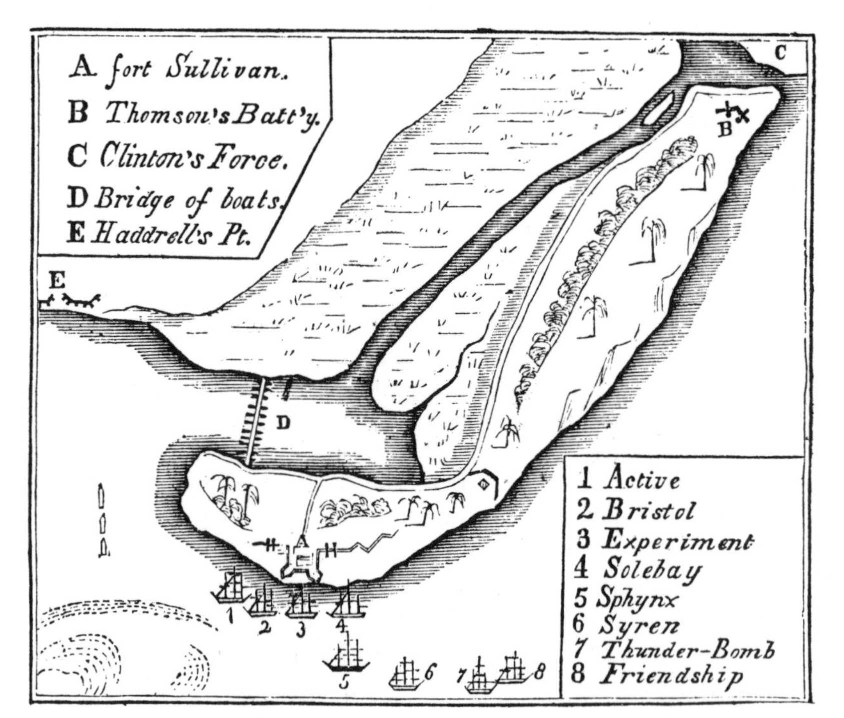

General layout of Sullivan's Island

end of the fort lay exposed to enfilading fire, should naval vessels succeed in passing the fort and anchoring above it. Moultrie knew that two frigates in this position could knock out the fort. "Our fort," he says, "at this time was not nearly finished; the mechanics and negro laborers were taken from all the works about the town, and sent down to the Island to complete our fort. We worked very hard, but could not get it nearly finished before the action." He could maintain the fort, Moultrie told Lee.

Sir Peter Parker, Admiral of the British fleet

"We had scarcely manned our guns, when the ships of war came sailing up."

On the morning of June 28, Moultrie, while on a visit to the advanced post at The Breech, three miles to the eastward of the fort, saw a number of the enemy's boats in motion, "as if they intended a descent on our advanced post," and, at the same time, saw the men-of-war "loose their top-sails." He galloped back to the fort, and by the time he reached it, the ships were already under sail:

> I immediately ordered the long roll to beat, and officers and men to their posts. We had scarcely manned our guns, when the ships of war came sailing up, as if in confidence of victory; as soon as they came within the reach of our guns, we began to fire; they were soon abreast of the fort, let go to their anchors, with springs upon their cables, and begun their attack most furiously.

At 9.00 A.M. Admiral Parker had signaled to the land forces that he intended to attack the forts at flood tide. By 11.30 A.M. the two 50-gun warships, the *Experiment* and his own flagship, the *Bristol*, and the *Active*, 28, and the *Thunder* bomb-vessel, with the *Solebay*, 28, slightly outside them, were firing their broadsides into Fort Moultrie at a range of 800 yards, too far to be effective. The battleships were passed by the three frigates, *Sphinx, Aetaeon* and *Syren* which failed to get above the fort and so enfilade it. Guided by a local pilot, the *Sphinx* and *Aetaeon* ran aground on shoals, the *Sphinx* losing her bowsprit, a fate which Tobias Furneaux in the *Syren* narrowly avoided. His was the only frigate which was able to fire its guns with any effect. Had all four vessels been able to get into position, Moultrie believed "they would have enfiladed us in such a manner, as to have driven us from our guns."

The bombardment continued for ten hours, the guns of the fort replying with great effect, killing 40 and wounding 71 men on the *Bristol*, 23 and 56 on the *Experiment*, 1 and 6 on the *Active*, with 8 wounded on the *Solebay*. Not one man who was stationed on the quarter-deck of the *Bristol* escaped being either killed or wounded. The Commodore himself escaped with bruises, and the loss of his breeches.

Early in the action Moultrie was joined by Captain Lamperer, whom he describes as a "brave and experienced seaman, who had been Master of a man-of-war, and Captain of a respectable privateer." Together they watched the approach of the British warships:

> He said to me: "Well, Colonel, what do you think of it now?" I replied that "we should beat them." "Sir," said he, "when those ships (pointing to the men-of-war) come to lay alongside of your fort, they will knock it down in half an hour," (and that was the opinion of all the sailors). Then I said, "We will lay behind the ruins and prevent their men from landing."

Only Moultrie wrote a coherent eyewitness account of the action:

> At one time the Commodore's ship (the *Bristol*) swung round with her stern to the fort, which drew the fire of all the guns that could bear upon her: we supposed he had had the springs of her cables cut away. The words that passed along the platform by officers and men, were, "mind the Commodore, mind the two fifty-gun ships:" most all the attention was paid to the two fifty-gun ships, especially the Commodore, who, I dare say, was not at all obliged to us for our particular attention to him; the killed and wounded on board those two fifty-gun ships confirms what I say.

When, during the action, General Lee visited the fort, the men of the garrison went to unbar the gate, which led the seamen in the tops of the battleships to believe that, in Moultrie's words, "we were quitting the fort," and that "we hung up a man in the fort:"

> That idea was taken from this circumstance; when the action begun, (it being a warm day) some of the men took off their coats and threw them upon the top of the merlons. I saw a shot take one of them and throw it into a small tree behind the platform, it was noticed by our men and they cried out "look at the coat."

"Several times," reported a surgeon on board one of the warships in a letter he wrote home on July 9, "the battery appeared to be silenced for more than an hour," when , "it was thought that the fort was abandoned." This mistaken idea was due, states Moultrie, to the need of the garrison to reserve their powder, in case the troops were able to attack the fort from the rear. He believed that:

> Had we as much powder as we could have expended in the time, the men-of-war must have struck their colors, or they

Fort Moultrie

FROM A WATER-COLOR SKETCH BY KAY SMITH

The residence of Thomas Heyward, Charleston, South Carolina, a signer of the Declaration of Independence.

FROM A WATER-COLOR SKETCH BY KAY SMITH

Fort Moultrie, Sullivan's Island, Charleston, South Carolina, the site of old Fort Sullivan where the first decisive southern battle of the American Revolution was fought.

would certainly have been sunk, because they could not retreat, as the wind and tide were against them; and if they had proceeded up to town, they would have been in a much worse situation. They could not make any impression on our fort; built of palmetto logs and filled in with earth, our merlons were 16 feet thick, and high enough to cover the men from the fire of the tops. The men that we had killed and wounded received their shots mostly through the embrasures.

Colonel William Moultrie

"Never did men fight more bravely, and never were men more cool."

"Never did men fight more bravely, and never were men more cool," Moultrie said—an opinion which was shared by the British surgeon who remarked, "The Provincials reserved their fire until the shipping were advanced within point blank shot; their artillery was surprisingly well served; it was slow but decisive indeed; they were very cool, and took great care not to fire except when their guns were exceedingly well directed," and he also remarked that "one would have imagined that no battery could have resisted their (ships') incessant fire."

The day was very hot, and the men on the fort's gun platforms were served with grog in buckets, of which "we partook heartedly" remarked Moultrie:

> I never had a more agreeable draught than that which I took out of one of those buckets at the time; it may be very easily conceived what heat and thirst a man must feel in this climate, to be upon a plat-form on the 28th June, admist 20 or 30 heavy pieces of cannon, in one continual blaze and roar; and clouds of smoke curling over his head for hours together; it was a very honorable situation, but a very unpleasant one.

The action was watched from a distance of six miles, by "thousands of our fellow citizens, looking on with anxious hopes and fears, some of whom had their fathers, brothers, and husbands in the battle; whose hearts must have been pierced at every broadside."

"Don't let liberty expire with me today"

Another of the fort's defenders, Major Barnard Elliott, who wrote to his wife the next day, described these incidents of the fight:

> As soon as I got to my battery after leaving you, we took up several places on the inside of the cabin, upon which were brass screws, all bespattered with blood, and other ornaments of the man-of-war. The firing continued till near ten o'clock, and I have the pleasure to inform you that we have lost but ten men and twenty-two wounded. Dr. Faysseaux came up this morning with the latter. He tells me that Richard Baker, our nephew, behaved gallantly, as did all the officers and men.
>
> The expression of a Sergeant McDaniel, after a cannon ball had taken off his shoulder and scooped out his stomach, is worth recording in the annals of America: "Fight on, my brave boys; don't let liberty expire with me today!"

Young, the barber, an old artillery man, who lately enlisted as sergeant, has lost a leg. Several arms are shot away. Not an officer is wounded.

My old grenadier, Sergeant Jasper, upon the shot carrying away the flag-staff, called out to Col. Moultrie: "Colonel, don't let us fight without our flag!"

"What can you do?" replied the Colonel. "The staff is broke."

"Then sir," said he, "I'll fix it to a halbert and place it on the merlon of the bastion next to the enemy," which he did, through the thickest fire.

"One of the most furious and incessant fires I ever saw and heard"

The bombardment was described by Lee, in a letter to Congress, as "one of the most furious and incessant fires I ever saw and heard," and Lord Rawdon, who stood on Long Island, called it "by far the grandest sight I ever beheld," and he thought "a severer action has seldom been seen."

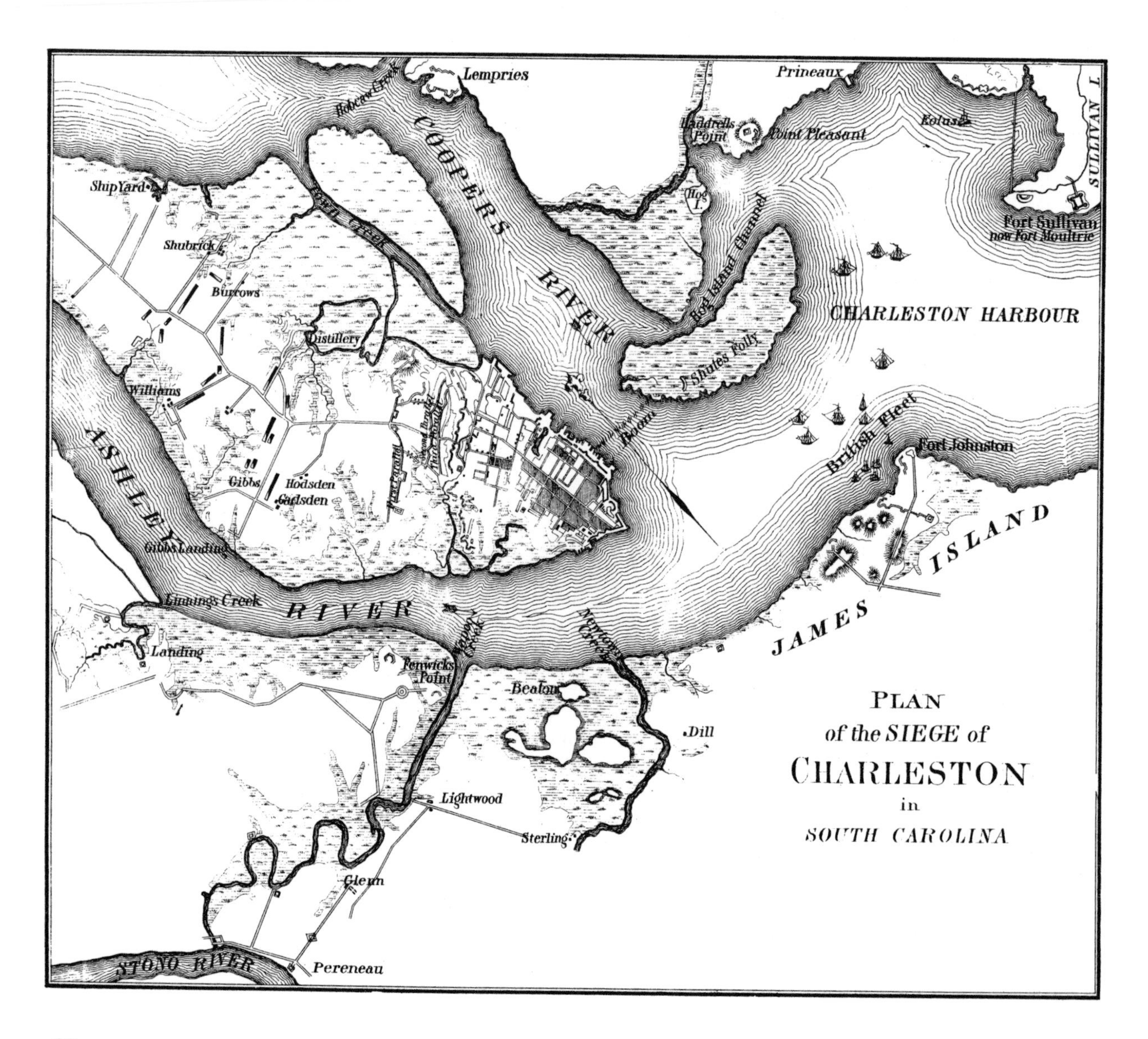

PLAN of the SIEGE of CHARLESTON in SOUTH CAROLINA

The harbor of Charleston in 1780, with the Provost—used as a British prison—appearing conspicuously in the background (also shown in color in a sketch by Kay Smith)

"At length," said Moultrie, "the British gave up the conflict; the ships slipped their cables, and dropped down with the tide, out of reach of the guns, all except the *Aetaeon;* she remained aground until the next morning when her Captain set her on fire. The American Captain Jacob Milligan, with a few seamen, boarded her and pointed and fired her guns at the retreating enemy, carrying away her bell as a prize. They had scarcely left her when she blew up, and from the explosion issued a grand pillar of smoke, which soon expanded itself at the top, and to appearance, formed the figure of a palmetto tree. The ship immediately burst into a great blaze that continued till she burnt down to the water's edge."

General Clinton to his "unspeakable mortification" had been unable to bring his troops into action. He was "cruelly deceived," stated Lord Rawdon, "by assurances from many people, who pretended to know the country, of there being a ford between Sullivan's Island and this place. At low water indeed there is a great extent of sand dry between the two islands, but intersected by channels of a hundred yards wide and seven or eight feet deep."

Concluding his account of the action, a civilian letter-writer told his correspondent:

> It is astonishing and almost incredible to think, that a palmetto log fort, with twelve guns (those were all they could bring to bear on the vessels), and three hundred men, should make such havoc with so formidable a fleet of British vessels. At the time of attacking the fort, their troops endeavored to land on the Island, and were twice repulsed by Thompson's Rangers, about three hundred men. Be assured the foregoing account is true in every particular. There are many other circumstances of the spirit and bravery of individuals, which would appear still more incredible for young soldiers, that I have not time to relate. I expect in about ten days we shall have another brush with them, and doubt not but through the Divine favor we shall be equally successful.

Abandoning the assault, the British warships sailed to New York, where we shall rejoin them.

THE DECLARATION

Thus far the colonists had fought to establish their rights and to resist tyranny, and the British had fought to teach them a lesson. There had been no formal declaration of war or of colonial independence; the patriots hoped for reconciliation. King George made that impossible. He hired German mercenaries to subdue his rebellious subjects and he rejected their petitions. Though many wavered, the patriots' determination hardened. An Englishman living in America, Thomas Paine, precipitated the issue. In his pamphlet *Common Sense*, which had an enormous circulation, he tore the veil from royalty and ridiculed the veneration in which it was held. He depicted King George as a harsh and savage brute. His words became the determining factor in the great debate, and the desire for independence became, in John Adams' words, a torrent.

On May 15, 1776, the Virginia Convention instructed its delegates to Congress to propose a resolution asserting independence, and three weeks later Richard Henry Lee formally proposed:

> RESOLVED, That these United Colonies are, and of right ought to be, free and independent States, that they are absolved from all allegiance to the British Crown, and that all political connection between them and the State of Great Britain is, and ought to be, totally dissolved.

It was agreed to set up a Committee of five to prepare a draft, and Thomas Jefferson was entrusted with the task.

Jefferson wrote several accounts describing his composition of the draft, and the debate in Congress. His own story has been published by Julian P. Boyd, the editor of his Papers:

Thomas Jefferson

> It appearing in the course of these debates that the colonies of New York, New Jersey, Pennsylvania, Delaware, Maryland & South Carolina were not yet matured for falling from the parent stem, but that they were fast advancing to that state, it was thought most prudent to wait a while for them, and to postpone the final decisions to July 1, but that this might occasion as little delay as possible a committee was appointed to prepare a declaration of independence. The Commee. were John Adams, Dr. Benjamin Franklin, Roger Sherman, Robert R. Livingston and myself. Committees were also appointed at the same time to prepare a plan of confederation for the colonies, and to state the terms proper to be proposed for foreign alliance.

The committee for drawing the Declaration of Independence desired me to do it. It was accordingly done and being approved by them, I reported it to the house on Friday the 28th of June when it was read and ordered to lie on the table.

On Monday the 1st of July the house resolved itself into a commee. of the whole & resumed the consideration of the original motion made by the delegates of Virginia, which being again debated through the day, was carried in the affirmative by the votes of N. Hampshire, Connecticut, Massachusetts, Rhode Island, N. Jersey, Maryland, Virginia, N. Carolina, & Georgia. S. Carolina and Pennsylvania voted against it. Delaware having but two members present, they were divided: the delegates for New York declared they were for it themselves, & were assured their constituents were for it, but that their instructions having been drawn near a twelvemonth before, when reconciliation was still the general object, they were enjoined by them to do nothing which should impede that object. They therefore thought themselves not justifiable in voting on either side, and asked leave to withdraw from the question, which was given them.

The Commee. rose and reported their reolution to the house. Mr. Rutledge of S. Carolina then requested the determination might be put off to the next day, as he believed his collegues, tho' they disapproved of the resolution, would then join in it for the sake of unanimity. The ultimate question whether the house would agree to the resolution of the committee was accordingly postponed to the next day (July 2), when it was again moved and S. Carolina concurred in voting for it. In the meantime a third member had come post from the Delaware counties and turned the vote of that colony in favor of the resolution. Members of a different sentiment attending that morning from Pennsylvania also, their vote was changed, so that the whole 12 colonies who were authorized to vote at all, gave their voices for it and thus supplied the void occasioned by the withdrawing of their delegates from the vote.

Congress proceeded the same day (July 2) to consider the Declaration of Independence, which had been reported and laid on the table the Friday preceding, and on Monday referred to a commee. of the whole, the pusillanimous idea that we had friends in England worth keeping terms with still haunted the minds of many. For this reason those passages that conveyed censures on the people of England were struck out, lest they should give them offence. The clause too, reprobating the enslaving the inhabitants of Africa, was struck out in compliance to South Carolina & Georgia, who had never attempted to restrain the importation of slaves and who on the contrary still wished to continue it. Our Northern brethren also I believe felt a little tender under those censures; for tho' their people have very few slaves themselves yet they had been pretty considerable carriers of them to others. The debates having taken up the greater parts of the 2d. 3d. & 4th days of July were, in the evening of the last closed. The declaration was reported by the commee. agreed to by the house, and signed by every member present except Mr. Dickinson.

Benjamin Franklin, from a sketch appearing in a history of the period

Jefferson wrote his draft Declaration in two weeks, and it was debated in Congress on July 2, 3 and 4. Many delegates feared at first to take the plunge, particularly those representing the middle colonies. Such action, they argued, was premature, and they urged delay. At the first count only nine colonies voted for approval; South Carolina, Pennsylvania, Delaware and New York held back. The arrival of the new delegate from Delaware, Caesar Rodney, and abstentions by others, changed the vote. On July 4, with New York abstaining but approving, twelve of the Thirteen Colonies voted:

> That these United Colonies are, and of right, ought to be, free and independent states; that they are absolved from all allegiance to the British Crown, and that all political connection between them, and the state of Great Britain is, and ought to be, totally dissolved.

Congressional Hall—in Independence Hall in Philadelphia—where the Declaration of Independence was signed on July 4, 1776.
—Sketched by Kay Smith

John Adams called it the greatest question "which ever was debated," and writing to his wife, Abigail, on July 2, said:

> The second day of July, 1776, will be the most memorable epoch in the history of America. I am apt to believe that it will be

celebrated by succeeding generations as the great anniversary festival. It ought to be commemorated as the day of deliverance, by solemn acts of devotion to God Almighty. It ought to be solemnized with pomp and parade, with shows, games, sports, guns, bells, bonfires, and illuminations, from one end of this continent to the other, from this time forward, forevermore.

You will think me transported with enthusiasm, but I am not. I am well aware of the toil, and blood, and treasure, that it will cost us to maintain this declaration, and support and defend these States. Yet, through all the gloom, I can see the rays of ravishing light and glory. I can see that the end is more than worth all the means, and that prosperity will triumph in that day's transaction, even although we should rue it, which I trust in God we shall not.

King George III at the time of his accession to the throne

The Declaration was joyously hailed in New York, where, as Isaac Bangs, a lieutenant in the Massachusetts militia, wrote:

Last night the statue in the Bowling Green representing George Rex [King George III] was pulled down by the populace. In it were 4,000 pounds of lead, and a man undertook to take 10 ozs. of gold from the superfices, as both man & horse were covered with gold leaf. The lead, we hear, is to be run up into musket balls for the use of the Yankies, when it is hoped that the emanations from the leaden George will make as deep impressions in the bodies of some of his redcoated and Tory subjects, and that they will do the same execution in poisoning and destroying them as the super-abundant emanations of the folly and pretended goodness of the real George have made upon their minds, which have effectually poisoned and destroyed their souls, so that they are not worthy to be ranked with any beings who have any pretensions to the principles of virtue and justice; but would to God that the unhappy contest might be ended, without putting us to the disagreeable necessity of sending them to dwell with those beings, for the company of whom alone their tempers and dispositions are now suitable.

The great Declaration came at a vital moment. Sir William Howe had sailed from Nova Scotia and was threatening New York. In the words of the modern historian, John Richard Alden (*The American Revolution*, 1954) it gave the patriot cause new nobility and dignity.

The Great Seal of King George III, the purse and Chancellor's mace

SIGNERS OF THE DECLARATION OF INDEPENDENCE.

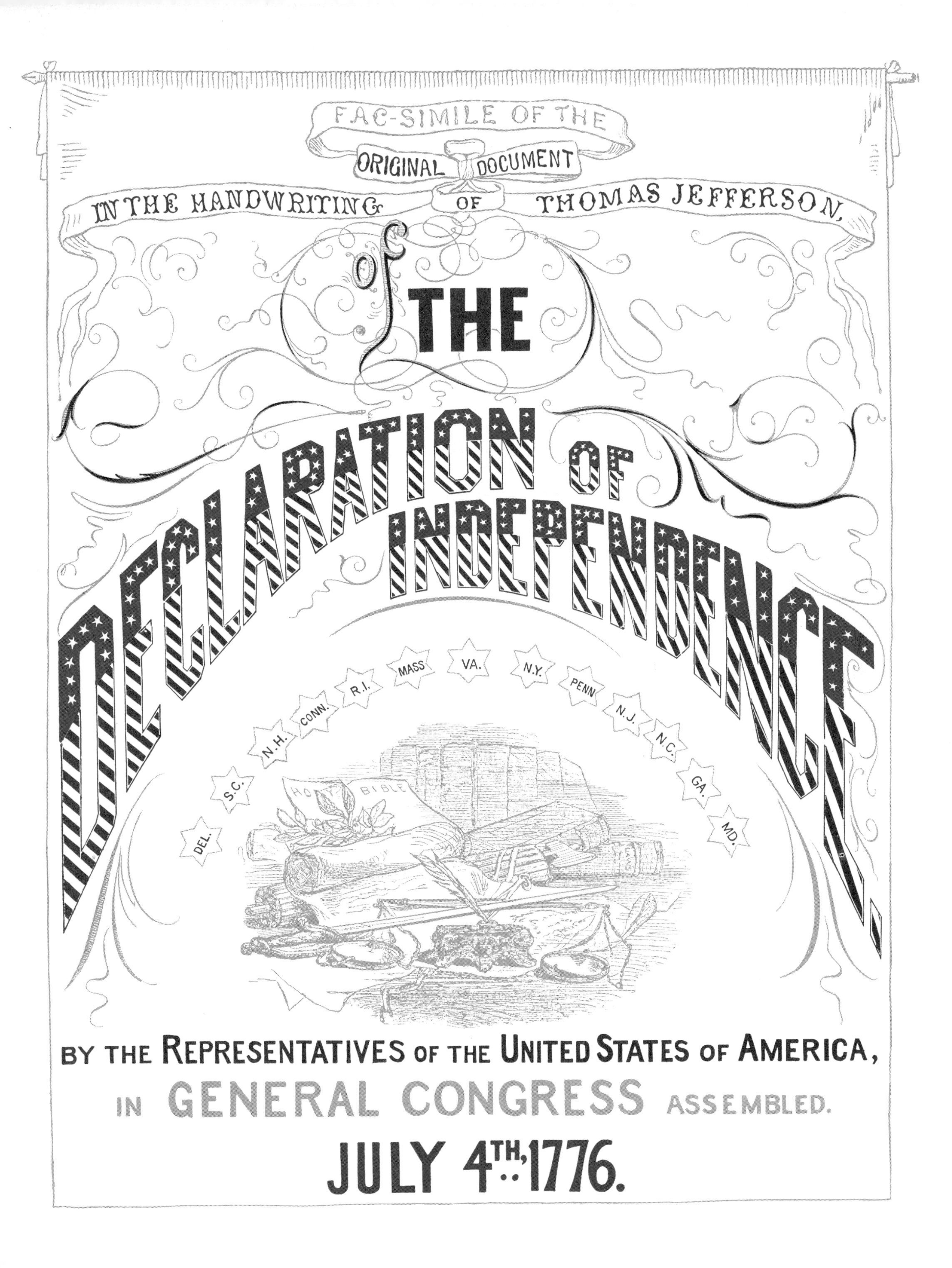
FAC-SIMILE OF THE
ORIGINAL DOCUMENT
IN THE HANDWRITING OF THOMAS JEFFERSON,
OF THE
DECLARATION OF INDEPENDENCE.
DEL.
S.C.
N.H.
CONN.
R.I.
MASS
VA.
N.Y.
PENN
N.J.
N.C.
GA.
MD.
HOLY BIBLE
BY THE REPRESENTATIVES OF THE UNITED STATES OF AMERICA,
IN GENERAL CONGRESS ASSEMBLED.
JULY 4TH, 1776.

A Declaration by the Representatives of the UNITED STATES OF AMERICA, in General Congress assembled

When in the course of human events it becomes necessary for one people to dissolve the political bands which have connected them with another, and to assume among the powers of the earth the separate and equal station to which the laws of nature & of nature's god entitle them, a decent respect to the opinions of mankind requires that they should declare the causes which impel them to the separation.

We hold these truths to be self-evident; that all men are created equal; that they are endowed by their creator with certain inalienable rights; that among these are life, liberty, & the pursuit of happiness; that to secure these rights, governments are instituted among men, deriving their just powers from the consent of the governed; that whenever any form of government ~~shall~~ becomes destructive of these ends, it is the right of the people to alter or to abolish it, & to institute new government, laying it's foundation on such principles & organising it's powers in such form, as to them shall seem most likely to effect their safety & happiness: prudence indeed will dictate that governments long established should not be changed for light & transient causes: and accordingly all experience hath shewn that mankind are more disposed to suffer while evils are sufferable, than to right themselves by abolishing the forms to which they are accustomed but when a long train of abuses & usurpations, [begun at a distinguished period &] pursuing invariably the same object, evinces a design to ~~subject~~ reduce them under absolute Despotism ~~to arbitrary power~~, it is their right, it is their duty, to throw off such government & to provide new guards for their future security. such has been the patient sufferance of these colonies; & such is now the necessity which constrains them to [expunge] alter their former systems of government. the history of ~~his~~ the present king of Great Britain ~~majesty~~, is a history of [unremitting] repeated injuries and usurpations, [among which, appears no solitary fact ~~there was not one single fact~~ to contradict the uniform tenor of the rest, ~~all of which~~] but all have [have] in direct object the establishment of an absolute tyranny over these states. to prove this, let facts be submitted to a candid world, [for the truth of which we pledge a faith yet unsullied by falsehood]

he has refused his assent to laws the most wholesome and necessary for the public good:

he has forbidden his governors to pass laws of immediate & pressing importance, unless suspended in their operation till his assent should be obtained, and when so suspended, he has utterly neglected ~~utterly~~ to attend to them.

he has refused to pass other laws for the accomodation of large districts of people unless those people would relinquish the right of representation in the legislature, a right inestimable to them & formidable to tyrants only:

he has called together legislative bodies at places unusual, uncomfortable, & distant from the depository of their public records, for the sole purpose of fatiguing them into compliance with his measures;

he has dissolved Representative houses repeatedly [& continually] for opposing with manly firmness his invasions on the rights of the people:

~~[illegible]~~, he has refused for a long ~~space of time~~ time after such dissolutions* to cause others to be elected whereby the legislative power, incapable of annihilation, have returned to the people at large for their exercise, the state remaining in the mean time exposed to all the dangers of invasion from without, & convulsions within:

he has endeavored to prevent the population of these states; for that purpose obstructing the laws for naturalization of foreigners; refusing to pass others to encourage their migrations hither, & raising the conditions of new ap-propriations of lands:

he has [suffered] obstructed the administration of justice [totally to cease in some of these ~~colonies~~ states] by refusing his assent to laws for establishing judiciary powers:

he has made [our] judges dependant on his will alone, for the tenure of their offices and the amount + & payment of their salaries:

he has erected a multitude of new offices [by a self-assumed power,] & sent hither swarms of officers to harrass our people & eat out their substance.

he has kept among us in times of peace ~~[illegible]~~ standing armies [& ships of war] without ~~our~~ the consent of our legislatures

he has affected to render the military, independent of & superior to the civil power:

he has combined with others to subject us to a jurisdiction foreign to our constitutions and unacknoleged by our laws; giving his assent to their acts of pretended ~~acts~~

of legislation, for quartering large bodies of armed troops among us;

for protecting them by a mock-trial from punishment for any murders

which they should commit on the inhabitants of these states;

for cutting off our trade with all parts of the world;

for imposing taxes on us without our consent;

in many cases

for depriving us of the benefits of trial by jury;

for transporting us beyond seas to be tried for pretended offences:

for abolishing the free system of English laws in a neighbouring province, establishing therein an arbitrary government and enlarging it's boundaries so as to render it at once an example & fit instrument for introducing the same absolute rule into these col~~onies~~; colonies [states]

† abolishing our most valuable ~~important~~ Laws

for taking away our charters, & altering fundamentally the forms of our governments;

for suspending our own legislatures & declaring themselves invested with power to

legislate for us in all cases whatsoever.

by declaring us out of his protection & waging war against us.

he has abdicated government here, [withdrawing his governors, & declaring us out

of his allegiance & protection:]

he has plundered our seas, ravaged our coasts, burnt our towns & destroyed the

lives of our people:

Scotch and other

he is at this time transporting large armies of foreign mercenaries to compleat

the works of death, desolation & tyranny, already begun with circumstances

scarcely paralleled in the most barbarous ages and totally

of cruelty & perfidy unworthy the head of a civilized nation.

he has constrained to

excited domestic insurrections amongst us and has

he has endeavored to bring on the inhabitants of our frontiers the merciless Indian

savages, whose known rule of warfare is an undistinguished destruction of

all ages, sexes, & conditions [of existence.]

he has incited treasonable insurrections of our fellow-citizens with the

allurements of forfeiture & confiscation of our property

he has constrained others ~~[illegible]~~ taken captive ~~[illegible]~~ the high seas to bear arms against their country ~~[illegible]~~ to become the executioners of their friends & brethren or to fall themselves by their hands.

he has waged cruel war against human nature itself, violating it's most sa-

-cred rights of life & liberty in the persons of a distant people who never of-

fended him, captivating & carrying them into slavery in another hemis-

-where, or to incur miserable death in their transportation thither. this piratical warfare the opprobrium of infidel powers, is the warfare of the Christian king of Great Britain [determined to keep open a market where MEN should be bought & sold he has prostituted his negative for suppressing every legislative attempt to prohibit or to restrain this ~~determining to keep open a market where MEN should be bought & sold~~: execrable commerce: and that this assemblage of horrors might want no fact of distinguished die, he is now exciting those very people to rise in arms among us, and to purchase that liberty of which he has deprived them by murdering the people upon whom he also obtruded them: thus paying off former crimes committed against the liberties of one people, with crimes which he urges them to commit against the lives of another.]

in every stage of these oppressions we have petitioned for redress in the most humble terms: our repeated petitions have been answered only by repeated injuries. a prince whose character is thus marked by every act which may define a tyrant, is unfit to be the ruler of a free people [who mean to be free. future ages will scarce believe that the hardiness of one man, adventured within the short compass of twelve years only, to build a foundation, so broad & undisguised for tyranny ~~[illegible]~~ over a people fostered & fixed in principles of ~~liberty~~ freedom.]

Nor have we been wanting in attentions to our British brethren: we have warned them from time to time of attempts by their legislature to extend an unwarrantable jurisdiction over [these our states]. we have reminded them of the circumstances of our emigration & settlement here, [no one of which could warrant so strange a pretension: that these were effected at the expence of our own blood & treasure, unassisted by the wealth or the strength of Great Britain: that in constituting indeed our several forms of government, we had adopted one common king, thereby laying a foundation for perpetual league & amity with them: but that submission to their parliament was no part of our constitution, nor ever in idea if history may be credited: and] we have appealed to their native justice & magnanimity [as well as to] & we have conjured them by the ties of our common kindred to disavow these usurpations which [were likely to] would inevitably interrupt our connection & correspondence ~~& connection~~. They too have been deaf to the voice of justice & of consanguinity, We must therefore [& when occasions have been given them, by the regular course of their laws, of removing from their councils the disturbers of our harmony, they have by their free election re-established them in power. at this very time too they are permitting their chief magistrate to send over not only soldiers of our common blood, but Scotch & foreign mercenaries to invade & destroy us ~~deluge us in blood~~. these facts have given the last stab to agonizing affection, and manly spirit bids us to re-nounce for ever these unfeeling brethren. we must endeavor to forget our former love for them, and to hold them as we hold the rest of mankind, enemies in war, in peace friends. we might have been a free & a great people together; but a communication of grandeur & of freedom it seems is below their dignity. be it so since they will have it: the road to ~~glory &~~ & to glory happiness is open to us too; we will ~~must~~ ~~climb~~ tread it ~~in~~ apart from them, ~~a separately state~~, and] we must therefore acquiesce in the necessity which ~~pro~~ denounces our ~~eternal~~ ~~separation~~ [~~eternal~~] separation! and hold them as we hold the rest of mankind enemies in war, in peace friends.

We therefore the representatives of the United States of America in General Congress assembled, appealing to the supreme judge of the world for the rectitude of our intentions do in the name & by authority of the good people of these [states,] colonies [reject and renounce all allegiance & subjection to the kings of Great Britain & all others who may hereafter claim by, through, or under them; we utterly dissolve ~~& break~~ off all political connection which may ~~have~~ heretofore have subsisted between us & the people or parliament of Great Britain; and finally we do assert and declare these colonies to be free and independant states, and that as free & independant states they ~~shall hereafter~~ have full power to levy war, conclude peace, contract alliances, establish commerce, & to do all other acts and things which independant states may of right do. And for the support of this declaration] we mutually pledge to each other our lives, our fortunes & our sacred honour.

John Penn John Hancock John Hart
Wm Floyd Wm. Paca
Geo. Read Wm Hooper Saml Adams
Step. Hopkins Thos Nelson jr. Geo. Clymer
Charles Carroll of Carrollton Elbridge Gerry
Thos M:Kean Saml Huntington
Roger Sherman
Wm Whipple Thomas Lynch Junr.
Geo Taylor Josiah Bartlett Benja. Franklin
Wm Williams Richd Stockton
John Morton
Oliver Wolcott Jno Witherspoon Geo. Ross
Thos. Stone Samuel Chase Robt Treat Paine
George Wythe Matthew Thornton
Frans Lewis Th Jefferson Benja Harrison
Lewis Morris Abra Clark Phil. Livingston
Cæsar Rodney
Arthur Middleton Fras Hopkinson
Geo Walton Carter Braxton James Wilson
Richard Henry Lee Thos Heyward Junr.
Benjamin Rush John Adams Robt Morris
Lyman Hall Joseph Hewes Button Gwinnett
Francis Lightfoot Lee
William Ellery Edward Rutledge Jas. Smith

Printed in U.S.A.

NEW YORK

In June, 1776, Sir William Howe struck at New York, as Washington expected. It was of far greater importance than Boston, which lay on the road to nowhere. New York was a rich prize, for from it ran the strategic waterway to Canada, the control of which could decide the war.

Washington reached the city on April 13, and, with the arrival of regiments from the south, his army soon amounted to 8,300 troops, among them a contingent from New Jersey led by their 58-year-old Colonel, William Alexander, a veteran of the French and Indian War, who claimed the title of Lord Stirling, which the British House of Lords had denied his father.

Recruiting and retaining soldiers, and the provision of equipment and stores, remained the serious problem.

In the matter of equipment Benjamin Franklin demonstrated his scientific genius. He advocated, on February 11, the employment of pikes, bows and arrows as ancient and good weapons "not wisely laid aside;"

1. Because a Man may shoot as truly with a Bow as with a common Musket.
2. He can discharge 4 arrows in the time of charging and discharging one Bullet.
3. His object is not taken from his view by the smoke of his own side.
4. A Flight of Arrows seen coming upon them terrifies and disturbs the Enemy's Attention to his Business.
5. An Arrow striking in any part of a Man, puts him *hors de combat* 'till 'tis extracted.
6. Bows and Arrows are more easily provided every where than Muskets & Ammunition.

His suggestion was not as archaic as it sounds; the mediaeval British long-bow had a range of 200 yards, twice that of the musket, and it had greater accuracy at 100 yards. Against serried ranks of soldiers, unprotected by body-armor, the bow could have been most effective.

Captain Alexander Graydon, of the Continental Line, described his experiences in recruiting in Pennsylvania at this time:

> The object now was to raise my company, and as the streets of the city had been pretty well swept by the preceding and contemporary levies, it was necessary to have recourse to the country. My recruiting party was therefore sent out in various directions; and each of my officers, as well as myself, exerted

himself in the business. Among the many unpleasant peculiarities of the American service, it was not the least that the drudgery, which in old military establishments belongs to sergeants and corporals, here devolved on the commissioned officers; and that the whole business of recruiting, drilling, &c. required their unremitted personal attention. This was more emphatically the case in recruiting; since the common opinion was that the men and the officers were never to be separated, and hence, to see the persons who were to command them, and above all, the captain was deemed of vast importance by those inclining to enlist; for this reason I found it necessary, in common with my brother officers, to put my feelings most cruelly to the rack; and in an excursion I once made to Frankford, they were tried to the utmost.

"I struck him with the utmost force between the eyes."

A number of fellows at the tavern, at which my party rendezvoused, indicated a desire to enlist, but although they drank freely of our liquor, they still held off. I soon perceived that the object was to amuse themselves at our expense, and that if there might be one or two among them really disposed to engage, the others would prevent them. One fellow in particular, who had made the greatest shew of taking the bounty, presuming on the weakness of our party, consisting only of a drummer, corporal, my second lieutenant and myself, began to grow insolent, and manifested an intention to begin a quarrel, in the issue of which he no doubt calculated on giving us a drubbing. The disgrace of such a circumstance presented itself to my mind in colors the most dismal, and I resolved, that if a scuffle should be unavoidable, it should, at least, be as serious as the hangers which my lieutenant and myself carried by our sides could make it. Our endeavor, however, was to guard against a contest; but the moderation we testified, was attributed to fear.

At length the arrogance of the principal ruffian rose to such a height, that he squared himself for battle and advanced toward me in an attitude of defiance. I put him by, with an admonition to be quiet, though with a secret determination that, if he repeated the insult, to begin the war, whatever might be the consequence. The occasion was soon presented; when taking excellent aim, I struck him with the utmost force between the eyes and sent him staggering to the other end of the room. Then instantly drawing our hangers, and receiving the manful cooperation of the corporal and drummer, we were fortunate enough to put a stop to any further hostilities. It was some time before the fellow I had struck recovered from the blow, but when he did, he was quite an altered man. He was as submissive as could be wished, begging my pardon for what he had done, and although he would not enlist, he hired himself to me for a few weeks as a fifer, in which capacity he had acted in the militia; and during the time he was in this employ, he bore about the effects of his insolence, in a pair of black eyes.

This incident would be little worthy of relating, did it not serve in some degree to correct the error of those who seem to conceive the year 1776 to have been a season of almost universal patriotic enthusiasm. It was far from prevalent in my opin-

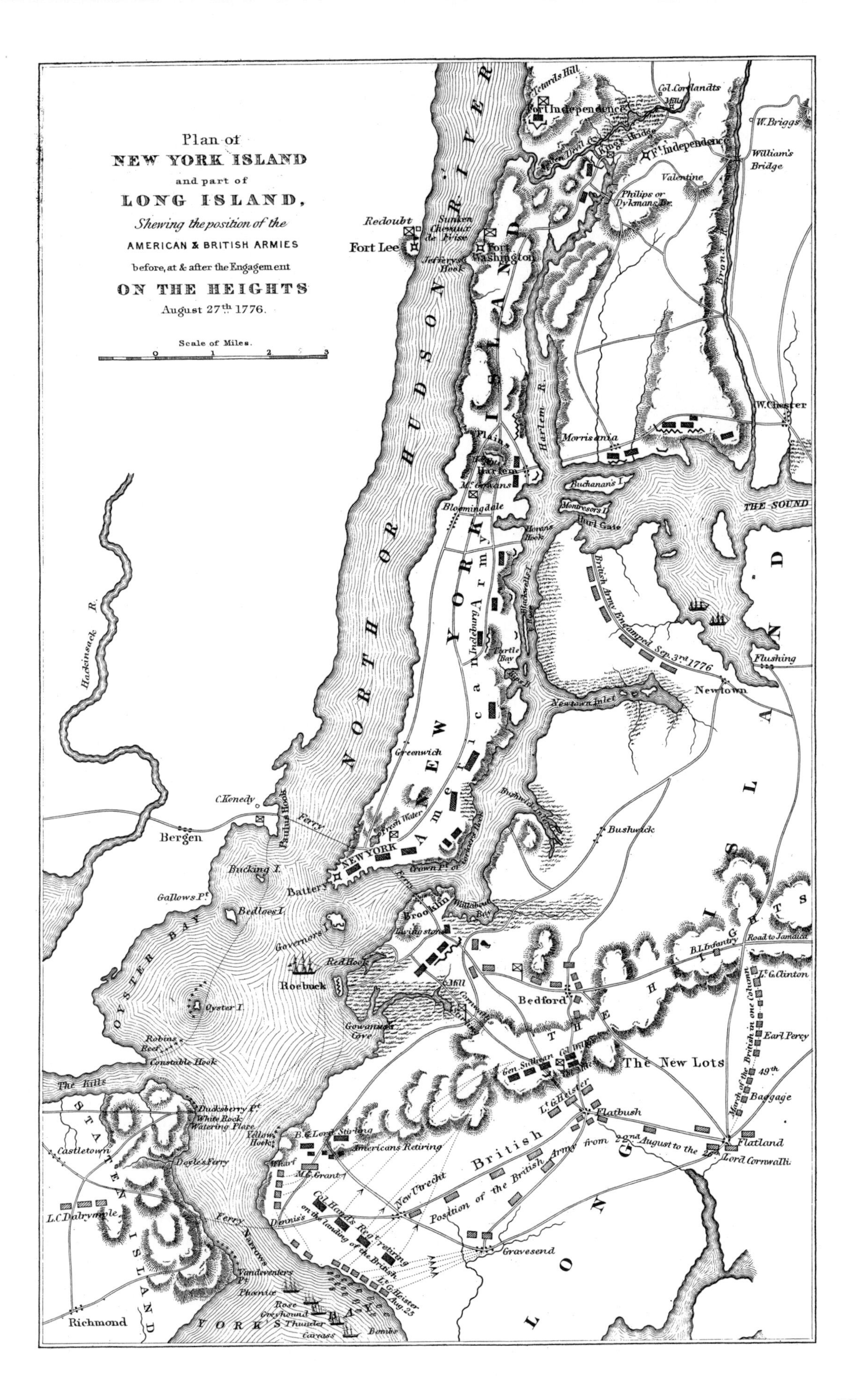
Plan of
NEW YORK ISLAND
and part of
LONG ISLAND,
Shewing the position of the
AMERICAN & BRITISH ARMIES
before, at & after the Engagement
ON THE HEIGHTS
August 27th 1776.
Scale of Miles.
NORTH OR HUDSON RIVER
NEW YORK ISLAND
Fort Lee
Fort Washington
Fort Independence
Kings Bridge
Harlem
Bloomingdale
Hurl Gate
THE SOUND
Flushing
Newtown
Greenwich
NEW YORK
Bergen
Battery
Governors I.
Bedloes I.
OYSTER BAY
Brooklin
Red Hook
Roebuck
Bedford
The New Lots
Flatbush
Flatland
Gravesend
New Utrecht
British Army from 22nd August to the 27th
Americans Retiring
Narrows
STATEN ISLAND
Richmond
Castletown
The Kills
LONG ISLAND
THE HEIGHTS
Lt. G. Clinton
Earl Percy
Lord Cornwallis
Gen. Sullivan
Morrisania
W. Chester
Harlem R.
Hackinsack R.
Bronx R.

Major General Nathanael Greene

> ion among the lower ranks of the people, at least in Pennsylvania. At all times, indeed, licentious, leveling principles are much to the general taste, and were of course popular with us; but the true merits of the contest were little understood or regarded. The opposition to the claims of Britain originated with the Better sort; it was truly aristocratic in its commencement; and as the oppression to be apprehended had not been felt, no grounds existed for general enthusiasm. The cause of liberty, it is true, was fashionable, and there were great preparations to fight for it; but a zeal proportioned to the magnitude of the question was only to be looked for in the minds of those sagacious politicians who inferred effects from causes, and who, as Mr. Edmund Burke expresses it, "snuffed the approach of tyranny in every tainted breeze."

Returning to base with few recruits, Graydon and another officer encountered a solitary recruit for whom they tossed a coin, Graydon winning. He was a small gainer for "he was never fit for anything better than the inglorious post of camp color man."

"The army continues healthy."

Sixteen-year-old Joseph Plumb Martin felt the urge to enlist. He was anxious to be called "a defender of my country," and to become a soldier. He left his grandfather's home in Massachusetts and was sent to New York where he began the extensive journal which has made him famous as perhaps the typical soldier of the Revolution. Another Massachusetts man, Colonel Loammi Baldwin reached New York about the same time. He complained to his wife of the difficulties of enforcing discipline:

> The army continues healthy. The inhabitants of the holy ground have brought some of the officers and a number of the soldiers into difficulty. The whores (by information) continue their employ which is become very lucrative. Their unparalleled conduct is a sufficient antidote against any desires that a person can have that has one spark of modesty or virtue left in him and the last atom must certainly be lost before he can associate himself with these bitchfoxly jades, jilts, haggs, scrums, prostitutes and all these multiplyed into one another and then their full character not displayed.

He never exchanged a word with these women, except in the execution of duty, he assured his wife.

General Nathanael Greene, who was stationed at Brooklyn, found other causes for comment:

> Complaint having been made by the inhabitants situated near the mill pond, that some of the soldiers come there to go into swimming in the open view of the women & that they come out of the water & run to the houses naked with a design to insult & wound the modesty of female decency. 'Tis with concern that the General finds himself under the disagreeable necessity of expressing his disapprobation of such a beastly conduct. Whoever has been so void of shame as to act an infamous part, let them veil their past disgrace by their future good behavior,

for they may depend upon it, any new instances of such scandalous conduct will be punished with the utmost severity.

A Massachusetts officer, Lieutenant Isaac Bangs, was not unmindful of the advantages of social discourse:

In the Afternoon I visited a very agreeable Young Ladie of this City, Miss – –, with whom I had before had a small acquaintance, as I had, while on Guard, shewn this young Ladie & the Company with her the Civility due to Persons of their appearance, Viz., of shewing them the Works, &c. She, in her Turn, was not so ungrateful as to take no Notice of me, but as I accidentally passed the House for several Times, I observed that she seemed to Compliment me with more respect than is usual, or than I deserved; but as I was bashful, I no more than returned the Compliment, & passed by till at length I made bold to enter the House with the Gentleman that was with me; but as he was in a great Hurry I could not tarry long, but was obliged to depart, bitterly against my will; however I gave her Intimation that I should again call in, & as I could not discover but that it would be agreeable, I took this opportunity to spend an Afternoon with her. I found her playing upon her Spinet, upon which she performed to admiration; her Musick, joined to an agreeable Person, gave me very favorable Ideas of my New Acquaintance. I spent the After Noon with her in her own Apartment, Reading & Chatting, &c., till about 5 o'clock, when her Mother came and asked us to Tea. The Father was absent, but her Mother was an agreable Woman, plainly dressed. They were Germans, who soon after they were married came into this Country. I know not whether they have an Estate or not. After Tea we spent About an Hour in the same Manner as before, when I was obliged to Attend Duty & took my leave, but Not till I had provided myself with some entertaining Books from her Library.

Pulling down the statue of George III in New York, July 9, 1776.

New York was a hotbed of loyalism.

Bangs, and all the rebel soldiers, needed to be careful with whom they associated in New York, a hotbed of loyalism. The Tories, as the loyalists were called, were given a rough time, as the contemporary historian of the city, Judge Thomas Jones, himself a loyal supporter of King George, complained:

A republican mob, raised and led by a number of staunch Presbyterians searched the whole town in pursuit of Tories and found and dragged several from their lurking holes, where they had taken refuge to avoid the undeserved vengeance of an ungovernable rabble. When they had taken several of these unhappy victims, destined to the will, sport, and the caprice of a banditti, and diversion of republicans and rebels, they placed them on sharp rails with one leg on each side; each rail was carried upon the shoulders of two tall men, with a man on each side to keep the poor wretch straight and fixed in his seat. In this manner were numbers of these poor people paraded through the most public and conspicuous streets in the town.

Another observer, Peter Elting, reported in a letter to a friend, "There is hardly a Tory face to be seen this morning."

The wretched Tories were accused of plotting to murder General Washington "the best man on earth," as Dr. William Eustis described him in an indignant letter. A member of that general's own guard, Thomas Hickey, was tried, found guilty and hanged in the presence of the whole army, as Washington's Order Book (June 28) records:

> The unhappy Fate of Thomas Hickey, executed this day for Mutiny, Sedition and Treachery, the General hopes will be a warning to every Soldier, in the Army, to avoid those crimes and all others, so disgraceful to the character of a Soldier, and pernicious to his country, whose pay he receives and Bread he eats. And in order to avoid those Crimes, the most certain method is to keep out of temptation of them, and particularly to avoid lewd Women, who, by the dying Confession of this poor Criminal, first led him into practices which end in an untimely and ignominous Death.

The news of the Declaration of Independence did not cause much stir within Washington's army.

The news received, a few days later, of the Declaration of Independence, did not cause much stir within Washington's army, according to Brigadier John Lacey:

> Lieut. Col. Johnston brought with him the Declaration of Congress of the Independence of America on the 4th inst. It made a little Buzz, but soon subsided & was forgotten. A few Officers left the Armey in consequence of it.

A few days earlier, Samuel Webb, Washington's aide, had spotted the sails of the long-awaited British fleet. The warships hove to under the lee of Long Island which indicated to Webb that the British intended to land there.

The Reverend Shewkirk, pastor of the Moravian Church, saw several warships sail up the Narrows where they fired their guns upon the city, knocking down houses and killing several people:

> This affair caused a great fright in the city. Women and children and some with their bundles came from the lower parts, and walked to the Bowery, which was lined with people. Mother Bosler had been brought down into their cellar. Phil Syphers, with their child, which was sick, came again to our house.

With the warships from Charleston, commanded by Sir Peter Parker, which anchored off Staten Island on August 1, came Lord Rawdon:

> The fair nymphs of this isle are in wonderful tribulation, as the fresh meat our men have got here has made them as riotous as satyrs. A girl cannot step into the bushes to pluck a rose without running the most imminent risk of being ravished, and they are so little accustomed to these vigorous methods that they don't bear them with the proper resignation, and of consequence we have most entertaining courts-martial every day. To the southward they behaved much better in these cases, if I may judge from a woman who having been forced by seven of our men made a complaint to me "not of their usage," she

said—No, thank God, she despised that—but of their having taken an old prayer book for which she had a particular affection. A girl of this island made a complaint the other day to Lord Percy of her being deflowered, as she said, by some grenadiers. Lord Percy asked her how she knew them to be grenadiers, as it happened in the dark. "Oh, good God," cried she, "they could be nothing else, and if your Lordship will examine I am sure you will find it so."

Lord Viscount Richard Howe, Rear Admiral of the British fleet.

Following the arrival of the British there occurred a ludicrous incident, which provided cause for comment by several diarists. Admiral Lord Howe and his brother, the military commander, had been authorized by the British government to offer peace terms to the rebels, but the negotiations failed to get off the ground, due to an unfortunate technicality. An officer from the *Eagle*, man-of-war, brought ashore a letter, as he informed Colonel Reed, "from Lord Howe to Mr. Washington:"

"Sir," says Colonel Reed, "we have no person in our army with that address."

"Sir," says the officer, "will you look at the address?" He took out of his pocket a letter which was thus addressed: George Washington, Esq., New York.

"No, sir," says Colonel Reed, "I cannot receive that letter."

"I am very sorry," says the officer, "and so will be Lord Howe, that any error in the superscription should prevent the letter being received by *General Washington*."

"So high is the Vanity and Insolence of these men."

The Americans refused to accept the letter, which drew from Ambrose Serle the comment, "So high is the Vanity and Insolence of these men." In rejecting the British overture, Washington was fully aware of the danger in which his small army stood. The need for discipline was greater than ever:

It is with great concern, the General understands, that Jealousies &c. are arisen among the troops from the different Provinces, of reflections frequently thrown out, which can only tend to irritate each other, and injure the noble cause in which we are engaged, and which we ought to support with one hand and one heart. The General most earnestly entreats the officers, and soldiers, to consider the consequences; that they can no way assist our cruel enemies more effectually, than making division among ourselves.

Ten days later he again cautioned his men:

The practice of Sentries sitting down while on their post is so unsoldierly, that the General is ashamed to see it prevail so much in the army. At night especially, it is of the most dangerous consequence, as it occasions a Sentinel's sleeping on his post, when otherwise he would be watchful.

Washington mustered less than 10,000 men to oppose the 25,000 British and German soldiers who had not as yet disembarked from the fleet.

Lord Stirling, General William Alexander

LONG ISLAND

"Crack! Crack! An alarm from Red-Hook. Crack! Crack! Crack! The alarm repeated from Cobble-Hill. Orders are given for the drums to beat *to arms*," noted the Reverend Philip Fithian, the chaplain of the New Jersey militia, on the morning of August 22. The terrible storm of wind, thunder, and lightning overnight had led him to think that the British warships would put to sea, yet "the enemy have been landing for some time down at the Narrows." Learning that the British had put ashore on Long Island several thousand men, he equipped himself for action, taking his gun, canteen, knapsack, and blanket.

The landing near Gravesend Bay was unopposed, other than by some skirmishing, as a Hessian officer noted:

> The rebels approached twice, fired howitzers and used grape and ball, so that all our artillery had to come up. At noon I slept a little while, and was waked by two cannon balls which covered me with earth. The rebels have some very good marksmen, but some of them have wretched guns, and most of them shoot crooked. But they are clever at hunter's wiles. They climb trees, they crawl forward on their bellies for one hundred and fifty paces, shoot, and go as quickly back again. They make themselves shelters of boughs, etc. But today they are much put out by our green coats (the uniform of the German Jagers), for we don't let our fellows fire unless they can get good aim at a man, so that they dare not undertake anything more against us.

From his vantage point on the deck of the *Eagle*, Ambrose Serle watched the troops land:

> The disembarkation was effected upon the flat shore, near Gravesend, without the least resistance, the inhuman Rebels contenting themselves with burning as much of the people's corn as they could (though the great rains which fell last night very happily prevented much of their design), with driving off their cattle as far as their time would permit, and doing as much injury to the inhabitants, who are generally well disposed, as they possibly could. The soldiers and sailors seemed as merry as on a holiday, and regaled themselves with the fine apples, which hung everywhere upon the trees in a great abundance. After the landing was pretty well effected, I went with two or three gentlemen on shore to Mr. De Nuys's house, opposite the Narrows, whose family were rejoiced at the deliverance from the tyranny they had so long undergone from the Rebels. It was really diverting to see sailors and apples tumbling from the trees together.

"All that is worth living for is at stake"

By August 26, Sir William Howe had landed 21,000 men, three times the number of the defenders who were arrayed in two lines on the Quan hills, which crossed Long Island from west to east, and on Brooklyn Heights where Washington came to supervise the defense of the island and to exhort his men, as a watching soldier related:

> I also heard Washington say, "If I see any man turn his back today, I will shoot him through. I have two pistols loaded, but I will not ask any man to go further than I do. I will fight so long as I have a leg or an arm." He said that the time had come when Americans must be freemen or slaves. "Quit yourselves like men, like soldiers, for all that is worth living for is at stake."

On the 27th, Howe launched a three-pronged attack on the Quan hills. General James Grant advanced to turn the rebels' right, which was commanded by Lord Stirling, and the Hessians thrust at their center, commanded by General Sullivan. They were ordered to delay until Howe, leading the British right, had outflanked the American left which was commanded by Colonel Samuel Miles.

In the greatest silence, says Lord Rawdon, Howe's force, consisting of ten thousand soldiers and guided by Tories, advanced to capture Jamaica Pass, which, being little known, was thought to be lightly held:

General William Howe

We got through the pass at daybreak without any opposition and then turned to the left towards Bedford. When we were within a mile of that town, we heard firing in that part of the mountain where General Grant was expected. We fired two pieces of cannon to let him know we were at hand, which immediately turned the attention of the rebels stationed against Flatbush to us, and we soon saw them come through the woods to attack us. We routed them the first onset, and pursued them so close through the thickest woods that they never could rally.

On hearing Howe's signal guns, the Hessians attacked the American center and Grant their left, in order to hem them in as Howe encircled their left flank. With his men exposed, Colonel Miles fell back. He had not proceeded more than half a mile, when, according to Colonel Miles of the colonial forces:

We fell in with a body of 700 or 800 light infantry, which we attacked without any hesitation, but their superiority of numbers encouraged them to march up with their bayonets, which we could not withstand, having none ourselves. I therefore ordered the troops to push on towards our lines. I remained in the ground myself until they had all passed me (the enemy were then within less than 20 yards of us), and by this means I came into the rear instead of the front of my command. We had proceeded but a short distance before we were again engaged with a superior body of the enemy, and here we lost a number of men, but took Major Moncrieffe, their commanding officer, prisoner, but he was a Scotch prize, for Ensign Brodhead, who took him and had him in possession for some hours, was obliged to surrender himself. Finding that the enemy had possession of the ground between us and our lines, and that it was impossible to cut our way through as a body, I directed the men to make the best of their way as well as they could; some few got in safe, but there were 159 taken prisoners. I was myself entirely cut off from our lines and therefore endeavored to conceal myself, with a few men who would not leave me. I hoped to remain until night, when I intended to try to get to Hell Gate and cross the Sound; but about 3 o'clock in the afternoon was discovered by a party of Hessians and obliged to surrender. Thus ended the career of that day.

General John Sullivan

Realizing the hopelessness of the situation, Lord Stirling ordered retreat.

The encirclement of their left, and the collapse of their center, where Sullivan had been forced to follow Miles' example, brought the brunt of the attack upon Lord Stirling, a Rebel commanding officer. Realizing the hopelessness of the situation, he ordered retreat, which was gallantly covered by a force of Marylanders, 259 of whom were killed. Six diarists or letter writers described this part cf the action. The most lively account was supplied by an unknown soldier (who is quoted by Henry Onderdonk):

The enemy then advanced to us, when Lord Stirling, who commanded, immediately drew up in a line and offered them battle in the true English taste. The British then advanced within out 300 yards of us and began a very heavy fire from their cannon and mortars: for both the balls and shells flew very fast, now and then taking off a head. Our men stood it amazingly well; not even one showed a disposition to shrink. Our orders were not to fire till the enemy came within 50 yards of us; but when they perceived we stood their fire so coolly and resolutely, they declined coming any nearer, though treble our number.

In this situation we stood from sunrise till 12 o'clock, the enemy firing on us the chief part of the time, when the main body of British, by a route we never dreamed of, had surrounded us and driven within the lines, or scattered in the woods, all our men except the Delaware and Maryland battalions, who were standing at bay with double their number. Thus situated, we were ordered to attempt a retreat by fighting our way through the enemy, who had posted themselves and nearly filled every road and field between us and our lines. We had not retreated a quarter of a mile before we were fired on by an advanced party of the enemy and those in the rear playing their artillery on us.

Our men fought with more than Roman valor. We forced the advanced party which first attacked us to give way, through which opening we got a passage down to the side of a marsh, seldom before waded over, which we passed, and then swam a narrow river, all the while exposed to the enemy's fire.

"Good God! What brave fellows I must this day lose."

The soldier observed, "Most of our generals, on a high hill, viewing us with glasses as we were retreating." General Washington, wrung his hands and cried out, "Good God! What brave fellows I must this day lose."

The Pennsylvanian officer, Lieutenant James McMichael, said that a number of his men were drowned when they attempted to escape through the morass which lay on the American right and between them and the sea.

Colonel Samuel Attle commanded the Pennsylvanians who had not before faced the enemy. Forced to retreat, they held a small hill for some time until they were surrounded. Then, preferring any risk rather than falling into the hands of the Hessians, Attle and his men burst through the ranks in order "to throw ourselves into the mercy of a battalion of Highlanders!"

Writing to General Washington two days later from the warship *Eagle*, where he had been taken as a prisoner of war, Stirling described the end of the action:

In this position we stood, cannonading one another, till near eleven o'clock, when I found that General Howe, with the main body of the army, was between me and our lines, and saw that the only chance of escaping being all made prisoners was to pass the creek near the Yellow Mills; and in order to render this the more practicable, I found it absolutely necessary to attack a body of troops commanded by Lord Cornwallis, posted at the house near the Upper Mills. This I instantly did, with about half of Smallwood's, first ordering all the other troops to make the best of their way through the creek. We continued the attack a considerable time, the men having been rallied and the attack renewed five or six several times, and were on the point of driving Lord Cornwallis from his station, but large succors arriving rendered it impossible to do more than provide for safety. I endeavored to get in between that house and Fort Box, but on attempting it, I found a considerable body of troops in my front, and several in pursuit of me on the right and left, and a constant firing on me. I immediately turned the point of a hill which covered me from their fire, and I was soon out of the reach of my pursuers. I soon found it would be in vain to attempt to make my escape, and therefore went to surrender myself to General de Heister, commander-in-chief of the Hessians.

The soldiers who succeeded in escaping, made their way to Brooklyn, where they were met by Joseph Plumb Martin, whose regiment had been brought across the East River to resist the assault on the Heights, which Washington expected. He saw the end of the action on the American left wing.

As he and his comrades advanced, they met wounded soldiers – men with broken arms and legs, and some with broken heads – and they saw the opposing armies hotly engaged:

What were the feelings of most or all the young soldiers at this time, I know not, but I know what mine were. But let mine or theirs be what they might, I saw a lieutenant who appeared to have feelings not very enviable; whether he was actuated by fear or the canteen I cannot determine now. I thought it fear at the time, for he ran round among the men of his company, sniveling and blubbering, praying each one if he had aught against him, or if *he* had injured anyone that they would forgive him,

Retreat from Long Island, August 29, 1776

declaring at the same time that he, from his heart, forgave them if they had offended him, and I gave him full credit for his assertion; for had he been at the gallows with a halter about his neck, he could not have shown more fear or penitence. A fine soldier you are, I thought, a fine officer, an exemplary man for young soldiers! I would have then suffered anything short of death rather than have made such an exhibition of myself.

Martin's regiment pressed forward reaching the fighting zone:

By the time we arrived, the enemy had driven our men into the creek, or rather millpond (the tide being up), where such as could swim got across; those that could not swim, or could not procure anything to buoy them up, sunk. The British, having several field-pieces stationed by a brick house, were pouring the canister and grape upon the Americans like a shower of hail.

It was at this creek that the Maryland Volunteers had stood and many had died. Martin saw the end of their action:

When they came out of the water and mud to us, looking like water rats, it was a truly pitiful sight. Many of them were killed in the pond, and more were drowned. Some of us went into the water after the fall of the tide, and took out a number of corpses and a great many arms that were sunk in the pond and creek.

In search of something to eat

That night, Martin and his comrades encamped on the ground they had occupied:

The next day, in the afternoon, we had a considerable scratch with about an equal number of the British, which began rather unexpectedly, and a little whimsically. A few of our men (I mean of our regiment) went over the creek upon business that usually employed us, that is, in search of something to eat. There was a field of Indian corn at a short distance from the creek, with several cocks of hay about halfway from the creek to the cornfield; the men proposed to get some of the corn, or anything else that was eatable. When they got up with the haycocks, they were fired upon by about an equal number of the British, from the cornfield; our people took to the hay, and the others to the fence, where they exchanged a number of shots at each other, neither side inclining to give back. A number, say forty or fifty more of our men, went over and drove the British from the fence; they were by this time reinforced in their turn, and drove us back. The two parties kept thus alternately reinforcing until we had the most of our regiment in the action. After the officers came to command, the English were soon routed from the place, but we dare not follow them for fear of falling into some snare, as the whole British army was in the vicinity of us. I do not recollect that we had anyone killed outright, but we had several severely wounded, and some, I believe, mortally.

Martin's regiment held their ground until they were forced to retreat, their powder having been wetted by a rain storm. His stomach was as empty as his musket, he complained.

Washington expected that Howe would follow up his victory by immediately storming Brooklyn Heights. Howe failed to press home his advantage, losing thereby the opportunity to destroy the American army. He had planned with his brother, the Admiral, for the warships to sail up the East River to prevent the enemy's retreat to Manhattan. A strong north-easterly wind prevented the ships from getting into position, and Washington escaped the trap prepared for him, but not without difficulty, as the journals kept by several of his officers show.

A successful retreat

The Connecticut Captain, Benjamin Talmadge, became engaged in the fighting, it being "the first time in my life that I had witnessed the awful scene of a battle." He felt solemn beyond all description, and "very hardly could I bring my mind to attempt the life of a fellow creature." The British failure to storm the entrenchments gave Washington the "most wonderful" opportunity to slip away.

> To move so large a body of troops, with all their necessary appendages, across a river full a mile wide, with a rapid current, in face of a victorious, well-disciplined army, nearly three times as numerous as his own, and a fleet capable of stopping the navigation, so that not one boat could have passed over, seemed to present most formidable obstacles. But, in the face of these difficulties, the Commander-in-Chief so arranged his business, that on the evening of the 29th by 10 o'clock, the troops began to retire from the lines in such a manner that no chasm was made in the lines, but as one regiment left their station on guard, the remaining troops moved to the right and left and filled up the vacancies, while General Washington took his station at the ferry, and superintended the embarkation of the troops.

It was one of the "most anxious, busy nights" that Talmadge ever recollected. As dawn approached, the men who had been left to hold the lines became anxious for their safety; providentially, a dense fog cloaked their retreat, which resulted from a confusion of orders:

> When the sun rose we had just received orders to leave the lines, but before we reached the ferry, the Commander-in-Chief sent one of his Aides to order the regiment to repair again to their former station on the lines. Colonel Chester immediately faced to the right about and returned, where we tarried until the sun had risen, but the fog remained as dense as ever. Finally, the second order arrived for the regiment to retire, and we very joyfully bid those trenches a long adieu. When we reached Brooklyn ferry, the boats had not returned from their last trip, but they very soon appeared and took the whole regiment over to New York; and I think I saw General Washington on the ferry stairs when I stepped into one of the last boats that received the troops. I left my horse tied to a post at the ferry.

The confusion of orders was explained by Colonel Edward Hand, an officer under the command of General Thomas Mifflin, who had been placed in charge of the covering party. During the night Colonel Alexander Scammell, who acted as aide to General Washington, came to Mifflin with an order to march his men to the ferry. Hand led his men in that direction, meeting General Washington who asked:

> "Is not that Colonel Hand?" I answered in the affirmative. His Excellency said he was surprised at me in particular; that he did not expect that I would have abandoned my post. I answered that I had not abandoned it; that I had marched by order of my immediate commanding officer. He said it was impossible. I told him I hoped, if I could satisfy him I had the orders of General Mifflin, he would not think me particularly to blame. He said he undoubtedly would not.
>
> General Mifflin just then coming up, and asking what the matter was, His Excellency said: "Good God! General Mifflin, I am afraid you have ruined us by so unseasonably withdrawing the troops from the lines."
>
> General Mifflin replied with some warmth: "I did it by your order." His Excellency declared it could not be.
>
> General Mifflin swore: "By God, I did," and asked, "Did Scammell act as an aide-de-camp for the day, or did he not?" His Excellency acknowledged he did.
>
> "Then", said Mifflin, "I had orders through him." The General replied it was a dreadful mistake, and informed him that matters were in much confusion at the ferry, and, unless we could resume our posts before the enemy discovered we had left them, in all probability the most disagreeable consequences would follow. We immediately returned, and had the good fortune to recover our former stations and keep them for some hours longer without the enemy perceiving what was going forward.

General Thomas Mifflin

Despite this muddle, Washington succeeded in extricating 9,500 soldiers, due less to his own military genius, than to the hesitation of his enemies. Brigadier General John Morin Scott, who had opposed the retreat "from an aversion to giving the enemy a single inch of ground," admitted the fearful alternative:

> Invested by an enemy of double our number from water to water, scant in almost every necessary of life and without covering and liable every moment to have the communication between us and the city cut off by the entrance of the frigates into the East River. In such a situation we should have been reduced to the alternative of desperately attempting to cut our way through a vastly superior enemy with the certain loss of a valuable stock of artillery and artillery stores, which the contingent has been collecting with great pains; or by famine and fatigue have been made an easy prey to the enemy. In either case the campaign would have ended in the total ruin of our army.

Dejected troops and populace

The Reverend Shewkirk watched the troops return from Long Island:

> In the morning, unexpectedly and to the surprise of the city, it was found that all that could come back was come back; and that they had abandoned Long Island; when many had thought to surround the King's troops, and make them prisoners with little

trouble. The language was now otherwise; it was a surprising change, the merry tones on drums and fifes had ceased, and they were hardly heard for a couple of days. It seemed a general damp had spread; and the sight of the scattered people up and down the streets was indeed moving. Many looked sickly, emaciated, cast down, &c., the wet clothes, tents—as many as they had brought away—and other things, were lying about before the houses and in the streets to-day; in general everything seemed to be in confusion.

Oblivious of the opportunity they had missed, the British exulted in their easy victory. One officer called it "a damned crush," and another "a glorious achievement." He thought it would end the war, and "we shall all return covered with American laurels and have the cream of American lands allotted to us for our services." Only Sir George Collier, the Captain of the warship *Rainbow*, sounded a sour note. In a letter to a friend in England, he described the result of the battle in sarcastic terms:

> The having to deal with a generous, merciful, forbearing enemy, who would take no unfair *advantages*, must surely have been highly satisfactory to General Washington, and he was certainly very deficient in not expressing his gratitude to General Howe for his *kind* behavior towards him. Far from taking the rash resolution of hastily passing over the East River after Gates (whom he mistakenly believed to have been in Canada), and *crushing at once* a frightening, trembling enemy, he generously gave them time to recover from the torpid state the rebellion appeared in from its late shock.
>
> For *many succeeding* days did our brave veterans, consisting of twenty-two thousand men, stand on the banks of the East River, like Moses on Mount Pisgah, looking at their promised land, little more than half a mile distant. The rebel's standards waved insolently in the air from many different quarters of New York. The British troops could scarcely contain their indignation at the sight and at their own *inactivity*; the officers were *displeased and amazed*, not being able to account for the strange delay.

Great chain and mortars

MANHATTAN ISLAND
The Amazing Story of the First Submarine

Federal Hall, Manhattan Island

What to do next? That was Washington's Dilemma. Should he defend Manhattan, or evacuate his army and escape to New Jersey? Surrounded by water on three sides, the island could become a trap. David Bushnell, a Yale graduate, had an answer to the General's predicament. Unable himself to navigate the submarine which he had invented and built, the *Turtle*, he entrusted it to Sergeant Ezra Lee, who told the story of the voyage of the world's first submarine craft:

> Its shape was most like a round clam, and set up on its square side. It was high enough to stand in or sit in as you had occasion, with a composition head hanging on hinges. It had six glasses inserted in the head and made water-tight, each the size of a half-dollar piece, to admit light. In a clear day a person might see to read in three fathoms of water. The machine was steered by a rudder having a crooked tiller, which led in by your side through a water joint; then sitting on the seat, the navigator rows with one hand and steers with the other. It had two oars of about twelve inches in length, and four or five in width, shaped like the arms of a handmill, which led also inside the water joints, in front of the person steering, and was worked by means of a winch, and with hand labor, the machine might be impelled at the rate of three knots an hour for a short time.
>
> Seven hundred pounds of lead were fixed on the bottom for ballast, and two hundred weight of it was so contrived as to let it go in case the pumps choked, so that you could rise at the surface of the water. It was sunk by letting in water by a spring near the bottom, by placing your foot against which the water would rush in, and when sinking, take off your foot and it would cease to come in and you would sink no further; but if you had sunk too far, pump out water until you got the necessary depth. These pumps forced the water out of the bottom, one being on each side of you as you rowed. A pocket compass was fixed on the side, with a piece of bright wood on the north side, thus—and another on the east side, thus—to steer by while under water. Three round doors were cut in the head to let in fresh air until you wished to sink, and then they were shut down and fastened. There was also a glass tube twelve inches long and one inch in diameter, with a cork in it, with a piece of light wood fixed to it, and another piece at the bottom of the tube to tell the

depth of descent; one inch rise in the cork in the tube gave about one fathom of water.

It had a screw that pierced through the top of the machine with a water joint which was so very sharp that it entered wood with very little force, and this was turned with a winch or crank, and when entered fast in the bottom of the ship, the screw is then left, and the machine is disengaged by unscrewing another one inside that held the other. From the screw now fixed on the bottom of the ship, a line led to and fastened to the magazine to prevent its escape either side of the ship. The magazine was directly behind you on the outside, and was freed from you by unscrewing a screw inside. Inside the magazine was a clock machinery, which immediately sets a-going after it is disengaged, and a gun lock is fixed to strike fire to the powder at the set time after the clock should run down. The clock might be set to go longer or shorter; twenty or thirty minutes was the usual time to let the navigator escape. This magazine was shaped like an egg and made of oak dug out in two pieces, bound together with bands of iron, corked and paid over with tar so as to be perfectly light, and the clock was formed so as not to run until the magazine was unscrewed.

I will now endeavor to give you a short account of my voyage in this machine. The first night that was favorable after we got down to New York with it—for the time for a trial must be when it is slack water and calm, as it is unmanageable in a swell or strong tide—the British fleet lay a little above Staten Island. We set off from the city; the whale boats towed me as nigh the ships as they dared to go and then cast me off. I soon found that it was too early in the tide, as it carried me down by the ships. I, however, hove about and rowed for five glasses by the ship's bells before the tide slacked, so that I could get alongside of the man-of-war which lay above the transports.

The moon was about two hours high, and the daylight about one. When I rowed under the stern of the ship I could see the men on deck and hear them talk. I then shut down all the doors, sunk down and came under the bottom of the ship. Up with the screw against the bottom, but found it would not enter the copper-sheathed hull. I pulled along to try another place, but deviated a little one side and immediately rose with great velocity and come above surface two or three feet between the ship and the daylight, then sunk again like a porpoise. I hove about to try again, but on further thought I gave out, knowing that as soon as it was light the ship's boats would be rowing in all directions, and I thought the best generalship was to retreat as fast as I could, as I had four miles to go before passing Governor's Island. So I jogg'd as fast as I could, and my compass being then of no use to me, I was obliged to rise up every few minutes to see that I sailed in the right direction, and for this purpose keeping the machine on the surface of the water and the doors open. I was much afraid of getting around on the island, as the tide of the flood set on the north point.

While on my passage up to the city, my course, owing to the above circumstances, was very crooked and zigzag, and the enemy's attention was drawn down towards me from Governor's Island. When I was abreast of the fort on the island, 300

New York and the Narrows looking up the Hudson in the early nineteenth century

or 400 men got upon the parapet to observe me; at length a number came down to the shore, shoved off a 12-oared barge with five or six sitters and pulled for me. I eyed them, and when they had got within fifty or sixty yards of me, I let loose the magazine in hopes that if they should take me they would likewise pick up the magazine, and then we should all be blown up together. But as kind Providence would have it, they took fright and returned to the island, to my infinite joy. I then weathered the island and our people, seeing me, came off with a whale boat and towed me in. The magazine, after getting a little past the island, went off with a tremendous explosion, throwing up large bodies of water to an immense height.

Before we had another opportunity to try an experiment, our army evacuated New York and we retreated up the North River as far as Fort Lee. A frigate came up and anchored off Bloomingdale. I now made another attempt upon a new plan. My intention was to have gone under the ship's stern and screw on the magazine close to the water's edge. But I was discovered by the watch and obliged to abandon this scheme; then shutting my doors I drove under her, but my cork in the tube (by which I ascertained my depth) got obstructed and deceived me, and I descended too deep and did not touch the ship. I then left her.

Bushnell's submarine was tried at Philadelphia a year later, with equal lack of success, other than the "consternation" it caused among several British naval officers.

General Nathanael Greene

Nathanael Greene urged the abandonment and burning of the city of New York. Washington agreed to the former but would not allow the latter without the authority of Congress. He delayed his evacuation nearly fatally, for Howe was planning to do exactly that which he feared—to land his army on Manhattan Island and cut off the Americans' retreat, as Captain Frederick Mackenzie noted in his journal on September 9:

> It is supposed we shall land somewhere about Harlem, and by taking a position across the island, which is narrow in that part, endeavor to cut off all that part of the rebel army between us and New York, for if some ships go up the North River at the same time it will be almost impossible for any of them to escape. The island in that part affords some very advantageous positions, which would enable us to prevent those near New York from escaping to Kingsbridge, or receiving any assistance from thence. The destruction or capture of a considerable part of the rebel army in this manner would be attended with numerous advantages, as it would impress the remainder with a dread of being surrounded and cut off in every place where they took post, would increase their discontent, and probably be the means of breaking up the whole of their army, and reducing the Colonies to submission.

Joseph Plumb Martin was one of the sentinels stationed on the East River to watch for the expected British landing, at Kips Bay, at the present 34th Street:

> As soon as it was fairly light, we saw their boats coming out of a creek or cove on the Long Island side of the water, filled with British soldiers. When they came to the edge of the tide, they formed their boats in line. They continued to augment their forces from the island until they appeared like a large clover field in full bloom. And now was coming on the famous Kips Bay affair, which has been criticized so much by the historians of the Revolution. I was there and will give a true statement of all that I saw during that day.

It was a Sabbath morning, he says, the day the British always employed for their "delivry," if possible:

> We lay very quiet in our ditch waiting their motions, till the sun was an hour or two high. We heard a cannonade at the city, but our attention was drawn toward our own guests. But they being a little dilatory in their operations, I stepped into an old warehouse which stood close by me with the door open inviting me in and sat down upon a stool. The floor was strewed with papers which had in some former period been used in the concerns of the house but were then lying in "woeful confusion." I was very demurely perusing these papers when all of a sudden there came such a peal of thunder from the British shipping that I thought my head would go with the sound. I made a frog's leap for the ditch and lay as still as I possibly could and began to consider which part of my carcass was to go first. The British played their parts well; indeed they had nothing to hinder them. We kept the lines till they were almost leveled upon us, when our officers, seeing we could make no resistance—and no orders coming from any superior officer—and that we must soon

be entirely exposed to the rake of their guns, gave the order to leave the lines.

The retreat became a rout, for the fault of which the Reverend Benjamin Trumbull blamed the general officers. Adjutant General Reed, on the other hand, thought "our men behaved well, stood and returned the fire until, overcome by numbers, they were obliged to retreat. The enemy advanced very fast." A more critical opinion was voiced by the American General, George Clinton, who said that the main body "almost instantly retreated, nay fled, without possibility of rallying them, though General Washington with some other officers exerted themselves to effect it."

An American retreat

With the British extending across the island, the Americans had no choice but to retreat and fly if they could. Martin was one of them:

> We had not gone far before we saw a party of men, apparently hurrying on in the same direction with ourselves. We endeavored hard to overtake them, but on approaching them we found that they were not of our way of thinking; they were Hessians. We immediately altered our course and took the main road leading to King's Bridge. We had not long been on this road before we saw another party, just ahead of us, whom we knew to be Americans. Just as we overtook these, they were fired upon by a party of British from a cornfield and all was immediately in confusion again. I believe the enemy's party was small, but our people were all militia, and the demons of fear and disorder seemed to take full possession of all and everything on that day. When I came to the spot where the militia were fired upon, the ground was literally covered with arms, knapsacks, staves, coats, hats, and old oil flasks, perhaps some of those from the Maderia wine cellar in New York. All I picked up of the plunder was a block-tin syringe, which afterwards helped to procure me a Thanksgiving dinner. Myself and the man whom I mentioned as belonging to our company were all who were in company at this time, the other man having gone on with those who were fired upon; they did not tarry to let the grass grow much under their feet.
>
> We had to advance slowly, for my comrade, having been some time unwell, was now so overcome by heat, hunger, and fatigue that he became suddenly and violently sick. I took his musket and endeavored to encourage him on. He was, as I before observed, a nigh neighbour of mine when at home and I was loath to leave him behind, although I was anxious to find the main part of the regiment, if possible, before that night, for I thought that the part of it which was not in the lines was in a body somewhere. We soon came in sight of a large party of Americans ahead of us who appeared to have come into this road by some other route. We were within sight of them when they were fired upon by another party of the enemy. They returned but a very few shots and then scampered off as fast as their legs would carry them. When we came to the ground they had occupied, the same display of lumber presented itself as at

Bloomingdale Road during the Colonial period

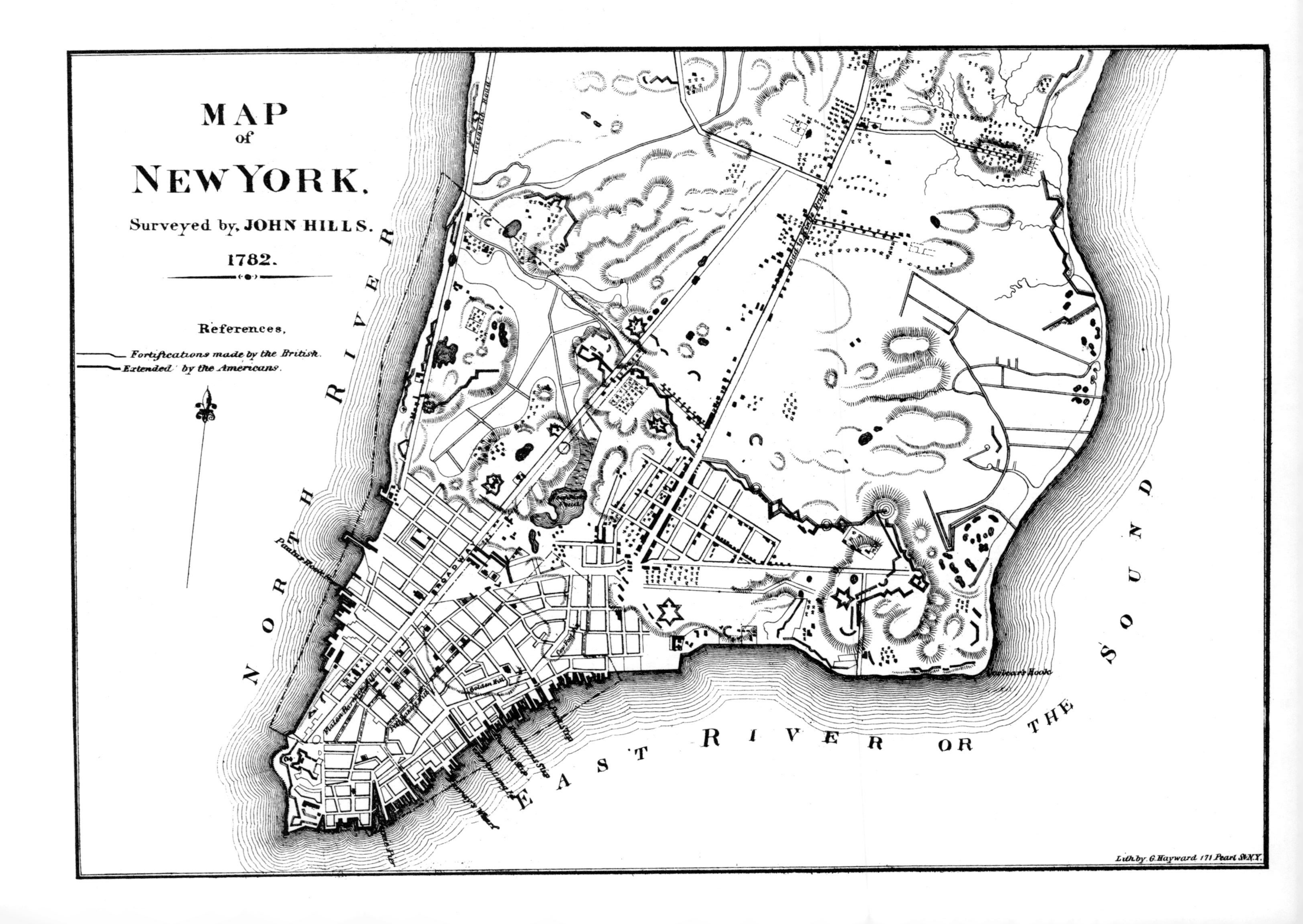
MAP
of
NEW YORK.
Surveyed by, JOHN HILLS.
1782.
References,
Fortifications made by the British.
Extended by the Americans.
NORTH RIVER
EAST RIVER OR THE SOUND
Greenwich Road
Road to Kings Bridge
BROADWAY
Paulus Hook
Golden Hill
Corlears Hook
Lith. by G. Hayward 171 Pearl St. N.Y.

the other place. We here found a wounded man and some of his comrades endeavoring to get him off. I stopped to assist them in constructing a sort of litter to lay him upon, when my sick companion, growing impatient, moved on, and as soon as we had placed the wounded man upon the litter I followed him.

Finding his retreat cut off, Martin and several others quitted the road and hid in the fields, in a small spot of boggy land covered with low bushes and weeds:

Into these I ran and squatting down concealed myself from their sight. Several of the British came so near to me that I could see the buttons on their clothes. They, however, soon withdrew and left the coast clear for me again. I then came out of my covert and went on, but what had become of my sick comrade or the rest of my companions I knew not. I still kept the sick man's musket. I was unwilling to leave it, for it was his own property and I knew he valued it highly and I had a great esteem for him. I had indeed enough to do to take care of my own concerns; it was exceeding hot weather, and I was faint, having slept but very little the preceding night, nor had I eaten a mouthful of victuals for more than twenty-four hours.

A scene in Central Park, Manhattan, at the time of the American Revolution

Saving a neighbor

He "waddled on," as fast as he could, crossing several fields and encountering again his sick friend:

I was exceeding glad to find him, for I had but little hope of ever seeing him again. He was sitting near the fence with his head between his knees. I tapped him upon the shoulder and asked him to get up and go on with me. "No," said he, at the same time regarding me with a most pitiful look, "I must die here." I endeavored to argue the case with him, but all to no purpose; he insisted upon dying there. I told him he should not die there nor anywhere else that day if I could help it, and at length with more persuasion and some force I succeeded in getting him upon his feet and to moving on.

Moving on, Martin and several men who had joined him were stopped by an officer who directed them to make a stand:

I told him I had a sick man with me who was wet and would die if exposed all night to the damp cold air, hoping by this to move his compassion, but it would not do. He was inexorable. I shall not soon forget the answer he gave me when I made the last-mentioned observation respecting the sick man. "Well," said he, "if he dies the country will be rid of one who can do it no good." Pretty fellow!

Seeing little chance of escaping from this "very humane gentleman" by fair means, Martin and his companion resolved to achieve their escape by other means. One soon offered:

There came to the sentinel I suppose an old acquaintance of his, with a canteen containing some sort of spirits. After drinking himself, he gave it to the sentinel who took a large pull upon it. They then fell into conversation together, but soon taking a hair from the same hound, it put them into quite "a talkative mood." I kept my eyes upon them and when I thought I saw a chance of getting [away] from them, I gave my companions a

The battle at Harlem Heights

> wink and we passed by the sentinel without his noticing us at all. A walk of a very few rods concealed us from his view by a turn in the road and some bushes, and thus we escaped from prison, for we thought we were hardly dealt by, to be confined by those whom we took to be our friends, after having labored so hard to escape being made prisoners by the common enemy.

Martin rejoined his own company which "rejoiced to see him."

A cocky but hesitant enemy

The British, "without loss of a man," states Ambrose Serle, ignoring the loss of two Hessians who were killed and fifteen wounded, spread across the island. Again Sir William Howe dallied, missing another opportunity to destroy the bulk of Washington's army. James Thacher described the incident which proverbially delayed pursuit:

> When retreating from New York, Major General Putnam, at the head of three thousand five hundred Continental troops, was in the rear and the last that left the city. In order to avoid any of the enemy that might be advancing in the direct road to the city, he made choice of a road parallel with and contiguous to the North River, till he could arrive at a certain angle, whence another road would conduct him in such a direction as

> that he might form a junction with our army. It so happened that a body of eight thousand British and Hessians were at the same moment advancing on the road, which would have brought them in immediate contact with General Putnam, before he could have reached the turn into the other road.
>
> Most fortunately, the British generals, seeing no prospect of engaging our troops, halted their own, and repaired to the house of Mr. Robert Murray, a Quaker and a friend of our cause; Mrs. Murray treated them with cake and wine, and they were induced to tarry two hours or more, Governor Tryon (the Royal Governor of New York) frequently joking her about her American friends. By this happy incident General Putnam, by continuing his march, escaped a recounter with a greatly superior force, which must have proved fatal to his whole party. One half-hour, it is said, would have been sufficient for the enemy to have secured the road at the turn, and entirely cut off General Putnam's retreat. It has since become almost a common saying among our officers that Mrs. Murray saved this part of the American army.

Whatever may be the truth behind this legend, Howe failed to follow up his advantage, allowing Washington to withdraw his troops to Harlem Heights. The British occupied New York which one British officer found "a melancholy spectacle" deserted by its 22,000 inhabitants, of whom only 500 remained. But "nothing," says Serle, "could equal the Expressions of Joy shouted by the Inhabitants, upon the arrival of the King's officers among them."

But not all the 500 were loyal, as the next event proves; Ambrose Serle and Lieutenant Mackenzie both described the fire which swept the city on September 20, which Serle declared had been started by some rebels who lurked about the town:

> Some of them were caught with matches and fire-balls about them. One man, detected in the act, was knocked down by a grenadier and thrown into the flames for his reward. Another, who was found cutting off the handles of the water buckets to prevent their use, was first hung up by the neck till he was dead and afterwards by the heels upon a signpost by the sailors. Many others were seized, on account of combustibles found upon them, and secured, and, but for the officers, most of them would have been killed by the enraged populace and soldiery.

Mackenzie stated that the brisk wind from the south spread the flames with such irresistible rapidity that:

> Notwithstanding every assistance was given which the present circumstances admitted, it was impossible to check its progress till about eleven this day, when by preventing it from crossing the Broad-way at the North part of the town, it was stopped from spreading any further that way, and about twelve, it was so far got under that there was no danger of its extending beyond those houses which were then on fire. It broke out first near the Exchange, and burnt all the houses on the West side of Broad Street, almost as far as the City Hall, & from thence all those in Beaver Street, and almost every house on the West

General Israel Putnam

side of the town between the Broad Way and the North River, as far as the College, amounting in the whole to about 600 houses, besides several churches, particularly Trinity Church, the principal one in town.

Mackenzie was in no doubt that the fire had been started willfully, for:

During the time the Rebels were in possession of the town, many of them were heard to say they would burn it, sooner than it should become a nest for the Tories—and several Inhabitants who were most violently attached to the Rebel cause have been heard to declare that they would set fire to their own houses sooner than they should be occupied by the King's troops.

The conflagration awakened Mackenzie's descriptive powers:

It is almost impossible to conceive a Scene of more horror and distress. The Sick, the Aged, Women and children, half-naked were seen going they knew not where, and taking refuge in houses which were at a distance from the fire, but from whence they were in several instances driven a second and even a third time by the devouring element, and at last in a state of despair, laying themselves down on the Common. The terror was increased by the horrid noise of the burning and falling houses, the pulling down of such wooden buildings as served to conduct the fire, (in which the Soldiers & Seamen were particularly active and useful) the rattling of above 100 wagons, sent in from the Army, and which were constantly employed in conveying to the Common such goods and effects as could be saved. The confused voices of so many men, the Shrieks and Cries of the Women and children, and seeing the fire break out unexpectedly in places at a distance, which manifested a design of totally destroying the City, with numberless other circumstances of private misery and distress, made this one of the most tremendous and affecting Scenes I ever beheld.

The bravery of Nathan Hale

Upon this scene of devastation, Lieutenant Nathan Hale, a native of Connecticut, came to spy, as he freely admitted when he was captured. His "martyrdom" had several chroniclers.

Stephen Hempstead, an officer of his company, who accompanied Hale part of the way, stated:

Hale had changed his uniform for a plain suit of citizen's brown clothes, with a round broad-brimmed hat, assuming the character of a Dutch schoolmaster, leaving all his other clothes, commission, public and private papers with me, and also his silver shoe buckles, saying they would not comport with his character of schoolmaster, and retaining nothing but his college diploma, as an introduction to his assumed calling. Thus equipped, we parted for the last time in life.

Having passed through the British lines, Hale stopped at a tavern:

Here there was no suspicion of his character being other than he pretended, until most unfortunately he was met in the crowd by a fellow countryman and an own relation (Samuel Hale, of Portsmouth, New Hampshire, but a Tory and a renegade), who had received the hospitality of his board and the attention of a brother from Captain Hale at his quarters at Winter Hill in Cambridge the winter before. He recognized him and most inhumanly and infamously betrayed him, divulging his true character, situation in the army &c. and having him searched, his diploma corroborated his relative's statement.

The melancholy particulars of Hale's end were learned later by Captain William Hull, from a British officer who came to Washington's camp under flag of truce:

> He said that Captain Hale had passed through their army, both of Long Island and York Island. That he had procured sketches of the fortifications, and made memoranda of their number and different positions. When apprehended he was taken before Sir William Howe, and these papers, found concealed about his person, betrayed his intentions. He at once declared his name, his rank in the American army, and his object in coming within the British lines.
>
> Sir William Howe, without the form of a trial, gave orders for his execution the following morning. He was placed in the custody of the Provost Marshal, who was a refugee, and hardened to human suffering and every softening sentiment of the heart. Captain Hale, alone, without sympathy or support, save that from above, on the near approach of death asked for a clergyman to attend him. It was refused. He then requested a Bible; that too was refused by his inhuman jailer.
>
> On the morning of his execution, my station was near the fatal spot, and I requested the Provost Marshal to permit the prisoner to sit in my marquee, while he was making the necessary preparations. Captain Hale entered; he was calm, and bore himself with gentle dignity, in the consciousness of rectitude and high intentions. He asked for writing materials, which I furnished him: he wrote two letters, one to his mother and one to a brother officer.

He was shortly after summoned to the gallows. Only a few persons were around him, yet his characteristic dying words were remembered. He said, "I only regret that I have but one life to lose for my country." Four years later, when a British officer suffered the same fate, the Americans mourned him as a brave man.

RETREAT TO NEW JERSEY

Following the flight of his army, which he described as "disgraceful and dastardly," Washington consolidated his position on Harlem Heights, where, almost immediately, there developed a small action in which Joseph Plumb Martin fought. Many men, he says, were killed on both sides, including Colonel Thomas Knowlton, who, we recall, had defended the rail-fence at Bunker Hill.

Though safe for the moment, Washington faced the same predicament as before. If Howe landed north of him, his position would become untenable. His army had become shrunken by desertions, which Major General Henry Knox attributed to the lack of good officers, "the radical evil of our army."

> We ought to have men of merit in the most extensive and unlimited sense of the word. Instead of which, the bulk of the officers of the army are a parcel of ignorant, stupid men, who might make tolerable soldiers, but are bad officers; and until Congress forms an establishment to induce men proper for the purpose to leave their usual employments and enter the service, it is ten to one they will be beat till they are heartily tired of it. We ought to have academies, in which the whole theory of the art of war shall be taught, and every other encouragement possible given to draw persons into the army that may give a luster to our arms. As the army now stands, it is only a receptacle for ragamuffins. You will observe, I am chagrined, not more so than at any other time since I've been in the army; but many late affairs, of which I've been an eyewitness, have so totally sickened me that unless some very different mode of conduct is observed in the formation of the new army, I shall not think myself obliged by either the laws of God or nature to risk my reputation on so cobweb a foundation.

"Unless some speedy and effectual measures are adopted by Congress, our cause is lost."

Washington was equally gloomy. "Unless some speedy and effectual measures are adopted by Congress, our cause is lost," he told its President. It was impossible to get good officers, and no reliance could be placed on the militia. He referred to their "lust for plunder."

> I enclose you the preceedings of a Court Martial held upon an Officer, who with a Party of Men had robbed a House a little beyond our lines of a number of valuable goods; among which (to show that nothing escapes) were four large Pier looking

Major General Henry Knox

Glasses, Women's Cloaths, and other Articles which one would think, could be of no earthly use to him. He was met by a Major of Brigade who ordered him to return the Goods, as taken contrary to Genl. Orders, which he not only peremptorily refused to do, but drew up his party and swore he would defend them at the hazard of his Life; on which I ordered him to be arrested, and tried for Plundering, Disobedience of Orders, and Mutiny; for the result I refer to the Proceedings of the Court; whose judgment appeared so exceedingly extraordinary, that I ordered a Reconsideration of the matter, upon which and with the Assistance of fresh evidence, they made Shift to Cashier him.

Retreat to White Plains

Howe resumed the offensive on October 12, landing his troops at Throgs Neck and Pells' Point, above Harlem Heights, and behind Washington, which forced him to abandon the Heights and retreat to White Plains, which he reached only just ahead of the British, whose advance was delayed by some spirited rear-guard action, as Colonel John Glover related. Early in the morning he saw the British landing:

I marched down to oppose their landing with about seven hundred and fifty men and three field-pieces, but had not gone

> more than half the distance before I met their advanced guard, about thirty men; upon which I detached a captain's guard of fifty men to meet them, while I could dispose of the main body to advantage.

Realizing that the enemy had the advantage, having possession of a small hill, Glover acted to the best of his judgment:

> This disposed of, I rode forward—(oh! the anxiety of mind I was then in for the fate of the day—the lives of seven hundred and fifty men immediately at hazard, and under God their preservation entirely depended on their being well disposed of; besides this, my country, my honor, my own life, and everything that was dear, appeared at that critical moment to be at stake. I would have given a thousand worlds to have had General Lee or some other experienced officer present, to direct or at least to approve of what I had done—looked around, but could see none, they all being three miles from me, and the action came on so sudden it was out of their power to be with me)—to the advance guard and ordered them to advance, who did, within fifty yards, and received their fire without the loss of a man; we returned it and fell four of them, and kept the ground till we exchanged five rounds.

The enemy pushing forward, Glover ordered a retreat, which was "masterly done" by the captain of the advance party:

> The enemy gave a shout and advanced; Colonel Reed's, laying under cover of a stone wall undiscovered till they came within thirty yards, then rose up and give them the whole charge; the enemy broke and retreated for the main body to come up.
>
> In this situation we remained about an hour and a half, when they appeared about four thousand, with seven pieces of artillery; they now advanced, keeping up a constant fire of artillery; we kept our post under cover of the stone wall before mentioned till they came within fifty yards of us, rose up and gave them the whole charge of the battalion; they halted and returned the fire with showers of musketry and cannon balls. We exchanged seven rounds at this post, retreated, and formed in the rear of Colonel Shepherd and on his left; they then shouted and pushed on till they came up on Shepherd, posted behind a fine double stone wall; he rose up and fired by grand divisions, by which he kept up a constant fire and maintained his part till he exchanged seventeen rounds with them, and caused them to retreat several times, once in particular so far that a soldier of Colonel Shepherd's leaped over the wall and took a hat and canteen off a captain that lay dead on the ground they retreated from.

Realizing that his men were outnumbered, Glover ordered a further retreat. They reached Dobbs Ferry after dark "after fighting all day without victuals or drink, laying as a picket all night, the heavens over us and the earth under us, which was all we had."

Martin was also concerned in the rear-guard action. He and a friend had been away from camp stealing turnips from a field, and on their return found the troops parading. He marched with his regiment, reaching an orchard where they were surprised by the Hessians:

> They would advance so far as just to show themselves above the rising ground, fire, and fall back and reload their muskets. Our chance upon them was, as soon as they showed themselves above the level ground, or when they fired, to aim at the flashes of their guns; their position was as advantageous to them as a breastwork. We were engaged in this manner for some time, when, finding ourselves flanked and in danger of being surrounded we were compelled to make a hasty retreat from the stone wall. We lost, comparatively speaking, very few at the fence, but when forced to retreat we lost, in killed and wounded, a considerable number. One man who belonged to our company, when we marched from the parade said, "Now I am going out to the field to be killed," and he said more than once afterwards that he should be killed, and he was. He was shot dead on the field. I never saw a man so prepossessed with the idea of any mishap as he was. We fell back a little distance and made a stand, detached parties engaging in almost every direction.

General Putnam had another lucky escape. Going out to reconnoiter, he chose to return alone. Not knowing the district

Nassau Hall, Princeton University

Philadelphia harbor during the days of the American Revolution

in which he found himself, and fearing that it may have been overrun by the enemy, he disguised his appearance by removing his cockade, his only emblem of rank, and secreted his sword and pistols under his coat, which he realized might result, if he was caught, in being hanged as a spy.

When Howe advanced on White Plains on October 28, Washington prudently withdrew, ferrying the bulk of his army across the Hudson into New Jersey. Unwisely, he left strong detachments to garrison the two forts, named Washington and Lee, which commanded the river. The internal plan of Fort Washington had already been disclosed to the British by a deserter, an officer who served under the fort's commander, Major Magaw. Howe sent the Hessians, commanded by Colonels Rall and Knyphausen, and two Highland regiments under Lord Cornwallis, to storm the fort, as an anonymous letter writer described to Robert Auchmuty, a loyalist refugee in London:

> The Hessians with great firmness marched through this way until they came to the north end of the steep mountain on Harlem River on the left side, which they began to clamber up notwithstanding the heavy fire from the rebels on the top of the hills, and after very great difficulties and labors gained the summit; which as soon as the rebels saw, they ran away towards the fort with great precipitation.

John Reuber, an officer in Colonel Rall's regiment, continued the story:

> At last, however, we got about on the top of the hill where there were trees and great stones. We had a hard time of it there together. Because they now had no idea of yielding, Col. Rall gave the word of command, thus: "All that are my grenadiers, march forwards!" All the drummers struck up the march the hautboy [oboe] players blew. At once all that were yet alive shouted, "Harrah!" Immediately all were mingled together, Americans and Hessians. There was no more firing, but all ran forward pell-mell upon the fortress.

The Highlanders scrambled up the hill, beginning (in the letter writer's account)—

> . . . a very spirited attack upon the rebels, who were in the bushes on top of the mountain, driving them from behind trees and rocks; and by this means greatly facilitating the operation of the Hessians, who had very hard work, some to scramble over the rocks and fight all the way, in order to make way for others to drag their cannon along a very steep road commanded on all sides.

Meanwhile, Lord Percy had attacked the rebel lines from the south; "with singular bravery, rushing into them with the greatest fury, and driving the rebels from line to line, and from work to work, till he got them crammed up in the fort, before the Hessians and Highlanders could get to it with their cannon."

Surrounded on all sides, the garrison surrendered, the prisoners numbering upwards of three thousand men. Lord Rawdon reported that the fort—

> . . . had been evacuated by the rebels so precipitately that the pots were left absolutely boiling on the fires, and the tables spread for dinner of some of their officers. In the fort they found but twelve men, who were all dead drunk. There were forty or fifty pieces of cannon found loaded, with two large iron sea mortars and one brass one, with a vast quantity of ammunition, provision and stores, with all their tents standing.

The fort's loss was the greatest disaster the Americans had so far suffered. With the Hudson crossings cleared of rebels, Rawdon expected Howe to march on triumphantly to Philadelphia:

> The fact is that their army is broken all to pieces, and the spirit of their leaders and abettors is also broken. However, I think one may venture to pronounce that it is well nigh over with them.

The defense of New York had cost Washington 329 officers, 4,000 soldiers taken prisoner, and 600 killed and wounded. With his "broken and dispirited army" reduced to 3,000 men, he retreated deeper into New Jersey, expecting Howe to follow hard on his heels.

—Sketch by Kay Smith

TRENTON

Lord Cornwallis

Successively, Washington withdrew across the Hackensack, Passaic and Delaware rivers, hotly pursued by Lord Cornwallis, to whom General Howe had entrusted twelve regiments. Howe retired to New York and Cornwallis halted at the Delaware unable to cross, for Washington had seized all the available boats. General Charles Lee, on his way to join Washington, stopped near Morristown, sending his 2,700 men towards the Delaware.

Resting at a house at Basking Ridge, Lee wrote to his friend, Horatio Gates. Referring to the loss of Fort Washington, he said, "There was never so damned a stroke," adding, "*entre nous*, a certain great man is most damnably deficient." Lee declared, "The Commander-in-Chief has thrown me into a situation where I have my choice of difficulties." If he stayed in New Jersey, he risked the loss of his army. He concluded his letter:

> I have neither guides, cavalry, medicines, money, shoes or stockings. I must act with the greatest circumspection. Tories are in my front, rear, and on my flanks. The mass of the people is strangely contaminated. In short, unless something which I do not expect turns up, we are lost. Our counsels have been weak to the last degree.

James Wilkinson, Gates's adjutant who sat waiting for Lee to finish his letter, told the sad story:

> I had risen from the table and was looking out an end window down a lane about one hundred yards in length, which led to the house from the main road, when I discovered a party of British dragoons turn a corner of the avenue at a full charge.
>
> Startled by this unexpected spectacle, I exclaimed, "Here, Sir, are the British cavalry!"
>
> "Where?" replied the General, who had signed his letter in the instant.
>
> "Around the house," for they had opened files and encompassed the building.

The Dragoons were led by young Banastre Tarleton, who described the incident in a letter to his mother. He had been given charge of the advance party, "a circumstance I shall esteem as one of the most fortunate in my life." Learning from a local resident that General Lee was not more than four or five miles ahead, Tarleton lit out in full pursuit and, after covering about three miles, seized two sentries who "in the dread of in-

Washington crossing the Delaware

stant death" informed him of Lee's whereabouts. Another prisoner pointed out the house where Lee was staying, guarded by only fifty men. Dashing on at full speed, Tarleton reached the house, making all the noise he could:

> The sentries were struck with a panic, dropped their arms, and fled. I ordered my men to fire into the house thro' every window and door, and cut up as many of the guards as they could. An old woman upon her knees begged for life and told me General Lee was in the house.

The Dragoons surrounded the house, from the windows of which Wilkinson peered:

> General Lee appeared alarmed, yet collected, and his second observation marked his self-possession: "Where is the guard? Damn the guard, why don't they fire?" and after a momentary pause, he turned to me and said, "Do, Sir, see what has become of the guard."
>
> The woman of the house at this moment entered the room and proposed to him to conceal himself in a bed, which he rejected with evident disgust. I caught up my pistols which lay on the table, thrust the letter he had been writing into my pocket, and passed into a room at the opposite end of the house, where I had seen the guard in the morning. Here I discovered their arms, but the men were absent. I stepped out of the door and perceived the dragoons chasing them in different directions, and receiving a very uncivil salutation, I returned into the house.

Wilkinson, who believed the enemy to be "a wanton murdering party," rather than a military reconnaissance, took up a defensive position and waited pistol in hand. He heard the British officer call, "If General Lee does not surrender in five

Major General Charles Lee of the American forces

minutes, I will set fire to the house." He threatened that if his order was not complied with immediately, he would put every person within to the sword, Tarleton stated. Two minutes later, Wilkinson heard a shout, "Here is the General. He has surrendered." He saw Lee hurried off, bareheaded, in his slippers, his collar open and his shirt very much soiled from several days' use. Except for one Colonel, the rest of Lee's staff was killed or wounded. Wilkinson escaped. To Tarleton, the capture of the famous rebel general was "a most miraculous event," and it appeared like a dream. Washington called Lee's capture a "severe blow," which he attributed to the prisoner's "own imprudence." A Hessian officer who acted as aide to Howe, when he heard of Lee's capture, was jubilant, calling him "the only rebel general we had to fear." Lee was later exchanged.

"The game is pretty near up"

Lee's soldiers joined Washington across the Delaware, raising the strength of his force to, on paper, 7,500, "many of them entirely naked and most so thinly clad as to be unfit for service." By one estimate, only 4,707 were fit for duty and the enlistment of the Continentals expired on December 31, 1776. Once again, following a series of retreats, the army was in danger of disintegration, a situation which Captain Ebenezer Huntington called "very gloomy." "The militia," he told his grandfather, "leave us the minute their times are out and would not stay tho' their eternal salvation was to be forfeited if they returned home."

Writing to his brother, Augustine, on December 18, Washington told him, "The game is pretty near up." He believed that when the Delaware froze, Howe would cross it and push on to Philadelphia.

"Something must be attempted to revive our expiring credit," Joseph Reed told him. "Is it not possible," he asked, "for the troops to make a diversion, or something more?" The greater the alarm, the more likely the success, and delay would be equal to a victory. Colonel John Fitzgerald, one of Washington's aides, believed that his chief intended to make some movement soon, but kept his own counsel.

By their Tory spies the British were kept informed of the low state of Washington's army. However, they failed to see that their posts, strung out on the eastern bank of the Delaware, were vulnerable to surprise attack. The Hessian detachment at Trenton, a village comprising 130 houses, and which lay across the Assanpink creek, was the most exposed. The 1,000 Germans commanded by Colonel Rall and Major von Dechow spent the evening of December 25 in seasonal festivities. Rall dined at the Trenton tavern. He drank a great deal of wine and sat up nearly all night playing cards. During the evening he was told that a loyalist freshly arrived from Pennsylvania was at the door and insisted on seeing him. Rall refused to interrupt his game. When the man scribbled a note and sent it in, Rall thrust it into his pocket unread, and retired to bed. An hour or so later, Lieutenant Wiederhold learned the truth. Towards daybreak he drank a cup of coffee and stepped from the guard house to get a breath of morning air. One hundred and fifty paces away a large force of rebels emerged from the woods. Lieutenant Piel rushed to rouse the inebriated Colonel Rall. Piel informed him that they were under attack. Thus brought to his senses, he groped for his uniform and weapons, rushed out and mounted his horse only to be mortally wounded later that morning.

For several days Washington, keeping his own counsel, had been planning a surprise raid on Trenton for Christmas night, when, as Colonel Fitzgerald forecast:

> They make a great deal of Christmas in Germany, and no doubt the Hessians will drink a great deal of beer and have a dance tonight. They will be sleepy tomorrow morning. Washington will set the tune for them about daybreak. The rations are cooked. New flints and ammunition have been distributed. Colonel Glover's fishermen from Marblehead, Massachusetts, are to manage the boats just as they did in the retreat from Long Island.

"A terrible night for the soldiers who have no shoes"

On Christmas night at six o'clock (as Fitzgerald later noted in his journal):

> The regiments have had their evening parade, but instead of returning to their quarters are marching towards the ferry. It is fearfully cold and raw and a snow storm setting in. The wind is northeast and beats in the faces of the men. It will be a terrible night for the soldiers who have no shoes. Some of them have tied old rags around their feet; others are barefoot, but I have not heard a man complain. They are ready to suffer any hardship and die rather than give up their liberty. I have just copied the order for marching. Both divisions are to go from the ferry to Bear Tavern, two miles. They will separate there; Washington will accompany Greene's division with a part of the artillery down the Pennington road; Sullivan and the rest of the artillery will take the river road.

The two sides of the Hessian flag

Nine fearful hours later, at three in the morning, Fitzgerald found a moment to keep up his record:

> I am writing this in the ferry house. The troops are all over and the boats have gone back for the artillery. We are three hours behind the set time. Glover's men have had a hard time to force the boats through the floating ice with the snow drifting in their faces. I have never seen Washington so determined as he is now. He stands on the bank of the river, wrapped in his cloak, superintending the landing of his troops. He is calm and collected, but very determined. The storm is changing to sleet, and cuts like a knife. The last cannon is being landed, and we are ready to mount our horses.

Colonel Knox (who, we recall, had carried the cannon from Ticonderoga to Boston) told his wife that a large part of the army—2,500 to 3,000 men—crossed the river with almost infinite difficulty. He brought across 18 fieldpieces.

> The floating ice in the river made the labor almost incredible. However, perseverance accomplished what at first seemed impossible. At two o'clock the troops were all on the Jersey side; we then were about nine miles from the object. The night was cold and stormy; it hailed with great violence; the troops marched with the most profound silence and good order.

Thomas Rodney was a member of the force commanded by Colonel John Cadwalader which had been ordered to cross the river further down. Rodney, who was second-in-command of a company of Philadelphia infantry which was sent ahead to cover the landing, told his father:

> We landed with great difficulty through the ice, and formed on the ferry shore, about 200 yards from the river. It was as severe a night as ever I saw, and after two battalions were landed, the storm increased so much, and the river was so full of ice, that it was impossible to get the artillery over; for we had to walk 100 yards on the ice to get on shore. Col. Cadwalader therefore ordered the whole to retreat again, and we had to stand at least six hours under arms—first to cover the landing and till all the rest had retreated again—and, by this time, the storm of wind, hail, rain and snow, with the ice, was so bad that some of the infantry could not get back till next day.

"Tell General Sullivan to use the bayonet."

Cadwalader eventually got his men across the river and occupied the Hessian post at Bordentown.

The two main divisions, those commanded by Generals Greene and Sullivan (who with Lord Stirling had been exchanged) parted at the Bear Tavern. Sullivan sent back a message that the snowstorm was wetting his men's muskets and making them unfit to fire. "Tell General Sullivan to use the bayonet," Washington ordered. He was resolved to take Trenton, he told Fitzgerald who rode at his side:

Colonel John Stark

> It was just 8 o'clock. Looking down the road I saw a Hessian running out from the house. He yelled in Dutch [meaning German] and swung his arms. Three or four others came out with their guns. Two of them fired at us, but the bullets whistled over our heads. Some of General Stephen's men rushed forward and captured two. The others took to their heels, running towards Mr. Calhoun's house, where the picket guard was stationed, about twenty men under Captain Altenbrockum. They came running out of the house. The Captain flourished his sword and tried to form his men. Some of them fired at us; others ran towards the village.
>
> The next moment we heard drums beat and a bugle sound, and then from the west came the boom of cannon. General Washington's face lighted up instantly, for he knew it was one of Sullivan's guns. We could hear a great commotion down towards the meeting-house, men running here and there, officers swinging their swords, artillerymen harnessing their horses. Captain Forrest unlimbered his guns. Washington gave the order to

The Battle of Trenton

advance, and we rushed on to the junction of King and Queen streets. Forrest wheeled six of his cannons into position to sweep both streets. The riflemen under Colonel Hand and Scott's and Lawson's battalions went upon the run through the fields to gain possession of the Princeton road. The Hessians were just ready to open fire with two of their cannons when Captain Washington and Lieutenant Monroe, with their men, rushed forward and captured them. We saw Colonel Rall riding up the street from his headquarters, which were at Stacy Pott's house. We could hear him shouting, "My brave soldiers, advance." His men were frightened and confused, for our men were firing upon them from fences and houses and they were falling fast. Instead of advancing, they ran into an apple orchard. The officers tried to rally them, but our men kept advancing and picking off the officers. It was not long before Rall tumbled from his horse and his soldiers threw down their guns and gave themselves up as prisoners.

While this was taking place, the New Hampshire Colonel John Stark drove the Hessians "pell mell" through the town, and Colonel St. Clair seized the bridge across the creek, cutting off their retreat to Bordentown to the south.

Colonel Knox, pleased to find that the force of the storm was at his back, and in the face of the enemy, entered the town:

And here succeeded a scene of war which I have often conceived, but never saw before. The hurry, fright and confusion of the enemy was not unlike that which will be when the last trump shall sound. They endeavored to form in streets, the heads of which we had previously the possession of with cannon and howitzers; these, in the twinkling of an eye, cleared the streets. The backs of the houses were resorted to for shelter. These proved ineffectual; the musketry soon dislodged them. Finally they were driven through the town into an open plain beyond. Here they formed in an instant. During the contest in the streets, measures were taken for putting an entire stop to their retreat by posting troops and cannon in such passes and roads as it was possible for them to get away by. The poor fellows after they were formed on the plain saw themselves completely surrounded. The only resource left was to force their way through numbers unknown to them. The Hessians lost part of their cannon in the town; they did not relish the project of forcing, and were obliged to surrender upon the spot, with all their artillery, six brass pieces, army colors &c.

"He has pounced on the Hessians like an eagle upon a hen."

Nine hundred Hessians were taken prisoner. Another 106 officers and men were killed. Only four hundred succeeded in escaping. Although American battle casualties were trivial—a mere two killed and three wounded—the soldiers had suffered severely from the hardships of the weather and the river crossing. The next day a thousand men reported as unfit for duty. Under the circumstances, this was a small price to pay for such a decisive victory. Summing up the night's work, Fitzgerald wrote:

It is a glorious victory. It will rejoice the hearts of our friends everywhere and give new life to hitherto waning fortunes. Washington has baffled the enemy in his retreat from New York. He has pounced on the Hessians like an eagle upon a hen and is safe once more on his side of the river. If he does nothing more, he will live in history as a great military commander.

His daring plan having been brilliantly executed, Washington withdrew across the Delaware into Pennsylvania. The minor victory had raised the drooping spirits of his men. It roused the fury of the British. Unwisely, Washington decided upon another adventure. He recrossed the river and reoccupied Trenton, as Sergeant R— described in his narrative:

Three or four days after the victory at Trenton, the American army recrossed the Delaware into New Jersey. At this time our troops were in a destitute and deplorable condition. The horses attached to our cannon were without shoes, and when passing over the ice they would slide in every direction, and could advance only by the assistance of the soldiers. Our men too, were without shoes or other comfortable clothing; and as traces of our march towards Princeton, the ground was literally marked with the blood of the soldiers' feet. Though my own feet did not bleed, they were so sore that their condition was little better.

While we were at Trenton, on the last of December, 1776, the time for which I and most of my regiment had enlisted expired. At this trying time General Washington, having now but a little handful of men and many of them new recruits in which he could place but little confidence, ordered our regiment to be paraded, and personally addressed us, urging that we should

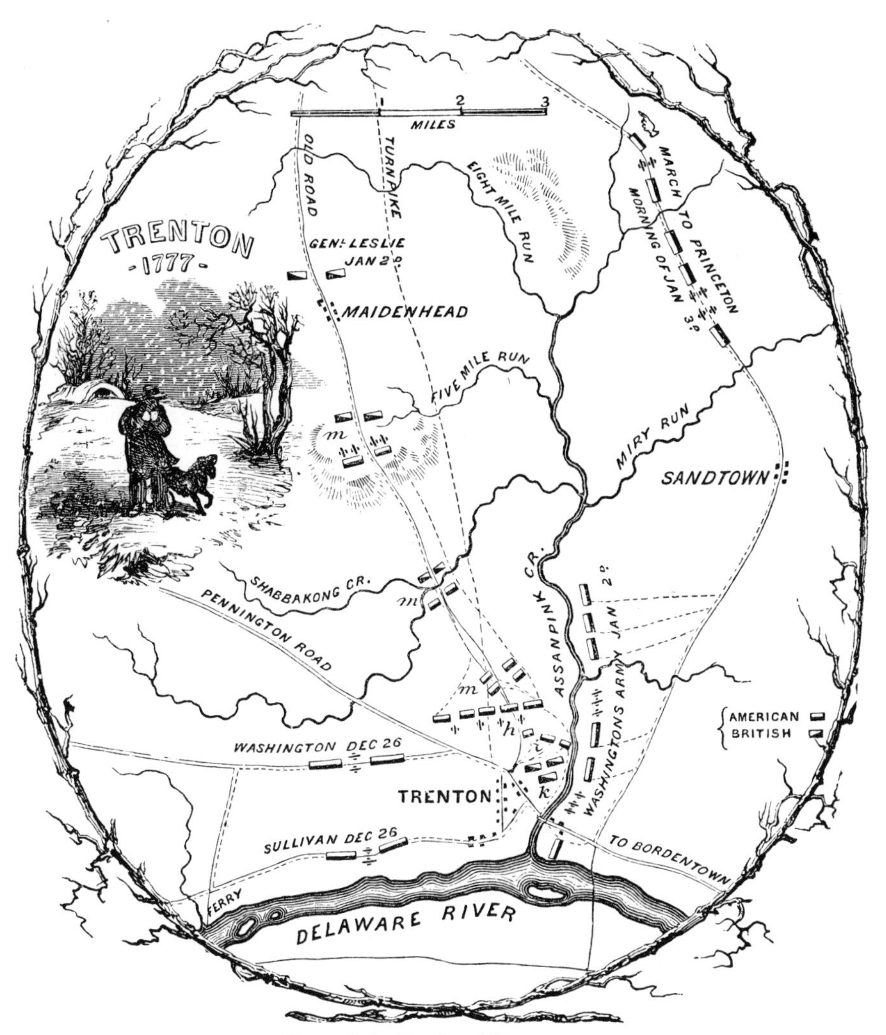

Plan of the Battle of Trenton

Explanation of the plan.—This map shows the country around Trenton, and the military operations there at the close of 1776 and commencement of 1777. *h* shows the position of Hand's rifle corps on the 26th of December, where they stopped the retreat of the Hessians; *i,* the Virginia troops; *k,* the Hessians; *m, m, m,* skirmishes, January 2d; *n, n,* Cornwallis, January 3d.

stay a month longer. He alluded to our recent victory at Trenton; told us that our services were greatly needed, and that we could now do more for our country than we ever could at any future period; and in the most affectionate manner entreated us to stay. The drums beat for volunteers, but not a man turned out. The soldiers, worn down with fatigue and privations, had their hearts fixed on home and the comforts of the domestic circle, and it was hard to forego the anticipated pleasures of the society of our dearest friends.

"Men who will volunteer in such a case as this need no enrollment to keep them to their duty."

The General wheeled his horse about, rode in front of the regiment, and addressing us again said, "My brave fellows, you have done all I asked you to do, and more than could be reasonably expected; but your country is at stake, your wives, your houses, and all that you hold dear. You have worn yourselves out with fatigue and hardships, but we know not how to spare you. If you will consent to stay only one month longer, you will render that service to the cause of liberty, and to your country, which you probably never can do under any other circumstances. The present is emphatically the crisis, which is to decide our destiny." The drums beat the second time. The soldiers felt the force of the appeal. One said to another, "I will remain if you will." Others remarked, "We cannot go home under such circumstances." A few stepped forth, and their example was immediately followed by nearly all who were fit for duty in the regiment, amounting to about two hundred volunteers. An officer enquired of the General if these men should be enrolled. He replied, "No! men who will volunteer in such a case as this need no enrollment to keep them to their duty."

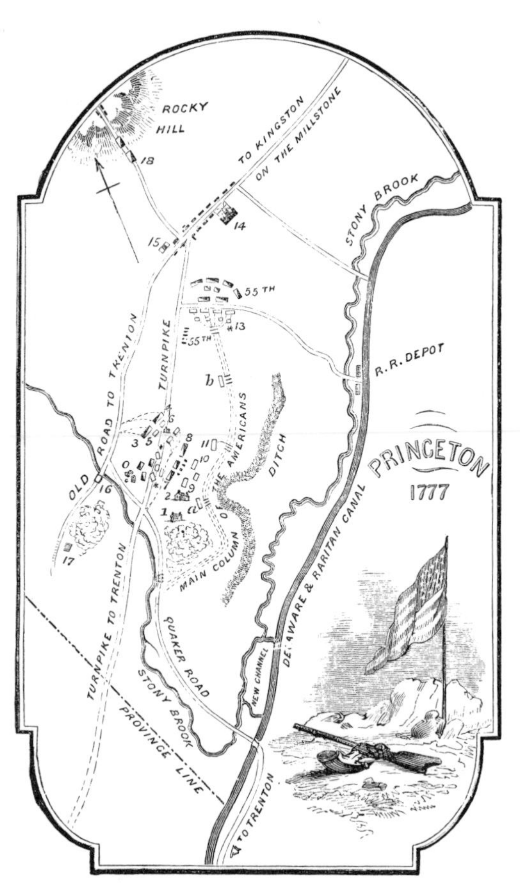

Plan of the Battle of Princeton

Explanation of the map.—a, head of the American column when first seen by the British; *b,* head of column after Mercer's engagement; *o,* retreat of the British; **, pursuit of the Americans; 1, Quaker meeting-house; 2, Clark's house, where Mercer died; 3, 4, the British seventeenth regiment; 5, 6 Mercer beginning the battle; 7, 8, the seventeenth attempting to dislodge Moulder; 9, 10, Pennsylvania militia under Washington; 11, Hitchcock's regiment; 13 display of Continentals; 14, Nassau Hall, or Princeton College, in the village; 15, Richard Stockton's residence, and Cornwallis's headquarters for a time; 16, Worth's Mill, on Stony Brook; 17, Millett's, the position of the seventeenth regiment at sunrise; 18, the fortieth and fifty-fifth regiments of the British retreating, after the action, toward Rocky Hill. The rail-way station is seen upon the Delaware and Raritan Canal, southeast of Princeton village.

As Washington might have expected, the British struck back to recover the lost post and to avenge the defeat of their Hessian allies. As Lord Cornwallis advanced, the Americans retreated behind Assanpink Creek. They were in great peril, for the British could cut their line of retreat. "At last we have run down the old fox," exclaimed Cornwallis, "and we will bag him in the morning." But he delayed his move, allowing Washington to slip away in the direction of Princeton. "Leaving our fires burning, we decamped," said Sergeant R–.

"We were observed by a lone horseman, who wheeled and galloped out of reach."

Marching in great silence, the colonial army reached the outskirts of Princeton a little before daybreak. "We were observed," said Sergeant R– "by a lone horseman, who wheeled and galloped out of reach." The Americans had run into two British regiments who were on march to Trenton. Knox spotted them:

> You may judge of their surprise when they saw such large columns marching up. They could not possibly suppose it was our army, for that, they took for granted, was cooped up near Trenton. They could not possibly suppose it was their own army returning by a back road; in short, I believe they were as much astonished as if an army had dropped perpendicularly upon them. However, they had not much time for consideration. We pushed a party to attack them. This they repulsed with great spirit, and advanced upon another column just then coming out of a wood, which they likewise put in some disorder; but fresh troops coming up, and the artillery beginning to play, they were, after a smart resistance, put totally to the rout.

Shortly after he had seen the horseman, said Sergeant R–:

> We were descending a hill through an orchard, when a party of the enemy who were entrenched behind a bank and fence rose and fired upon us. Their first shot passed over our heads, cutting the limbs of the trees under which we were marching. At this moment we were ordered to wheel. As the platoon which I commanded were obeying the order, the corporal who stood at my left shoulder, received a ball and fell dead on the spot. He seemed to bend forward to receive the ball which might otherwise have ended my life. We formed, advanced, and fired upon

the enemy. They retreated eight rods to their packs, which were laid in a line. I advanced to the fence on the opposite side of the ditch which the enemy had just left, fell on one knee, and loaded my musket with ball and buckshot. Our fire was most destructive; their ranks grew thin and the victory seemed nearly complete, when the British were reinforced. Many of our brave men had fallen, and we were unable to withstand such superior numbers of fresh troops.

He heard Colonel Mercer call, in a voice of distress, "Retreat!" He fell, mortally wounded. Sergeant R. discharged his musket and ran for a wood. At this critical moment, General Washington appeared at the head of his whole army. He called to the fugitives, "Parade with us, my brave fellows, there is but a handful of the enemy, and we will have them directly."

Colonel Hugh Mercer
–From a pencil drawing
by Colonel John Trumbull

"The horror of the scene"

The Sergeant rejoined the main body. The ground, he said, was frozen, and all the blood which had been shed lay on the surface which "added to the horror of the scene."

The British were unable to resist this attack, and retreated into the College, where they thought themselves safe. Our army was there in an instant, and cannon were planted before the door, and after two or three discharges, a white flag appeared at the window, and the British surrendered. They were a haughty, crabbed set of men, as they fully exhibited while prisoners, on their march to the country. In this battle, my pack, which was made fast by leather strings, was shot from my back, and with it went what little clothing I had. It was, however, soon replaced by a pack which had belonged to a British officer, and was well furnished. It was not mine for long, for it was stolen shortly afterwards.

An unidentified 85-year-old resident of Princeton watched the battle:

The battle was plainly seen from our door. Before any gun was heard a man was seen to fall and immediately the report and smoke of a gun was seen and heard, and the guns went off so quick and many together that they could not be numbered. We presently went down into the cellar to keep out of the way of the shot. There was a neighbor woman down in the cellar with us that was so affrighted that she imagined that the field was covered with blood, and when we came out of the cellar she called earnestly to us to look out and see how all the field was quite red with blood, when none was to be seen at that distance. This I mention only to show into what strange mistakes sudden frights with the fear of death may put us.

Almost as soon as the firing was over our house was filled and surrounded with Gen. Washington's men, and himself on horseback at the door. They brought with them on their shoulders two wounded Regulars; one of them was shot in at his hip and the bullet lodged in his groin, and the other was shot through his body just below his short ribs. He was in great pain and bled much out of both sides, and often desired to be removed from one place to another, which was done accordingly, and he died about three o' afternoon.

Immediately after the battle Gen. Washington's men came into our house. Though they were hungry and thirsty some of them were laughing outright, others smiling, and not a man among them but showed joy in his countenance. It really animated my old blood with love to those men that but a few minutes before had been courageously looking death in the face in ravages of a bold and daring enemy. By the joy that I felt myself, I cannot help but be of the opinion that the most strict of them all against bearing arms in our own defense (if they have any love for their bleeding country) must in some degree or other rejoice with the rest of their neighbors and others for that day's happy relief that it pleased God to bless us with.

Word came that the British were hurrying from Trenton, according to Knox "in a most infernal sweat—running, puffing, blowing, and swearing at being so outwitted." Washington had intended to march on the British base at Brunswick but, stated Knox, "The men having been without rest, rum, or provisions for two nights and days were unequal to the task of marching seventeen miles further." He determined to retreat to Morristown. About an hour after the Americans had left Princeton, laden with their spoils, the British entered the town, and believing that the Americans were on their way to Brunswick, marched there. Once again Washington had outwitted his enemy. In his official report he praised the militiamen who "have undergone more fatigues and hardships than I expected militia, especially citizens, would have done at this inclement season." He told the President of Congress that he would put his ill-clad and barefoot army under cover at Morristown.

Howe withdrew to the comfort of New York.

Howe withdrew most of his soldiers to the comfort of New York, where he himself wintered, diverting himself, as the indignant loyalist, Judge Thomas Jones, recorded in his History, "in feasting, banquetting, and in the arms of Mrs. Loring, the wife of a complacent commissioner." Both Generals had problems. Howe considered his next move and Washington tried to guess what it might be. Probably neither General heard of the small incident which Frank Moore recorded in 1777:

March 20th. This morning a young woman passing an evacuated house in Woodbridge, New Jersey, saw through the window a drunken Hessian soldier, who had straggled from his party. There being no men within less than a mile of the town, she went home, dressed herself in man's apparel, and armed with an old firelock, returned to the house, entered it, and took the Hessian prisoner, whom she soon stripped of his arms and was leading off, when she fell in with the patrol guard of a New Jersey regiment, stationed near Woodbridge, to whom she delivered her prisoner.

The little story, had they heard it, might have made the British less confident. They still failed to understand that they were up against a nation roused to fight to the death. The events of 1777 partly convinced them.

THE LAKES

Scene of Arnold's naval battle

During the eventful months when Generals Howe and Washington were having their series of engagements, there were other actions involving the regular British forces and the colonial rebels. Leaving the generals to their deliberations, agonies, and festivities, we need to step back six months.

Following his withdrawal from Canada in the spring of 1776, Benedict Arnold halted at Fort Ticonderoga on Lake Champlain. There he built a fleet to halt or delay the expected British advance from Montreal. The Americans surmised that, sooner or later, the British would attempt to divide the colonies by advancing simultaneously from Montreal and New York City, by the waterway provided by Lakes Champlain and George and the Hudson River. General Horatio Gates was appointed by Congress to command the Northern Department at Ticonderoga where the survivors of the Canadian expedition assembled, "a mob and not an army," as John Trumbull described them to his father.

At Montreal, Sir Guy Carleton was joined by General John Burgoyne, who, following his role as a spectator at the battle of Bunker Hill, had returned to England from where, now, he brought considerable reinforcements, including a number of German mercenaries. Forced, like Arnold, to create a navy, Carleton delayed his advance southwards until October, by which time Arnold had collected a squadron of seventeen nondescript vessels. He was expressly ordered by Gates not to risk them in a naval battle.

Carleton swept down Lake Champlain, his army protected by thirty armed ships, mounting seventy guns. He caught Arnold at Valcour Island, halfway down the lake.

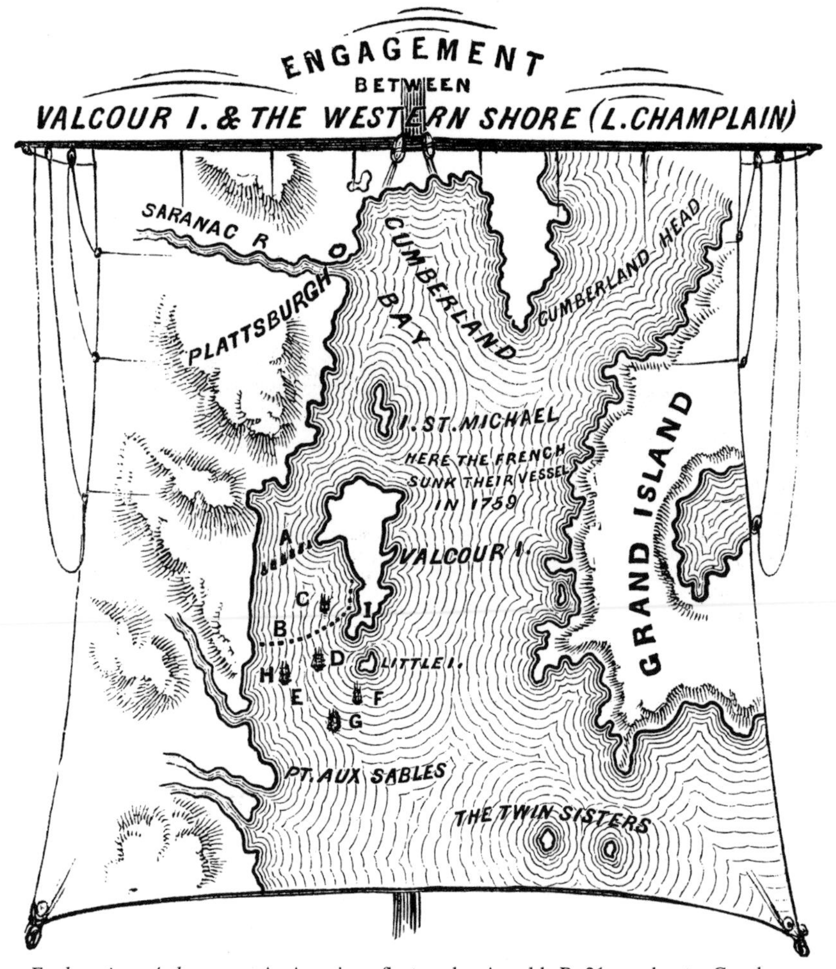

Explanation of the map.—A, American fleet under Arnold; B, 21 gun-boats; C, schooner Carleton, 12 six pounders; D, ship Infiexible, 18 twelve pounders; E, anchorage of the British fleet during the night, to cut off the Americans' retreat; F, radeau Thunderer, 6 twenty-four pounders and 12 six pounders; G, gondola *Loyal Convert,* 7 nine pounders; H, schooner *Maria,* 14 six pounders, with General Carleton on board; I, the place where the American schooner *Royal Savage,* of 8 six pounders and 4 four pounders, was burned. This plan is copied from *Brasrier's Survey of Lake Champlain,* edition of 1779.

Whether Arnold by disobeying orders, lost his fleet, or succeeded in delaying the British southward thrust for another year, has been argued by his detractors and supporters. Never loath to extol his own virtues, he described the action in a letter he wrote to Gates on October 12:

> Dear General: Yesterday morning at eight o'clock, the enemy's fleet, consisting of one ship mounting sixteen guns, one scow mounting the same number, one schooner of fourteen guns, two of twelve, two sloops, a bomb-ketch and a large vessel (that did not come up), with fifteen or twenty flat-bottomed boats or gondolas, carrying one twelve or eighteen-pounder in their bows, appeared off Cumberland Head. We immediately prepared to receive them. The galleys and *Royal Savage* were ordered under way; the rest of our fleet lay at an anchor. At eleven o'clock they ran under the lee of Valcour and began the attack. The schooner, by some bad management, fell to leeward and was first attacked; one of her masts was wounded, and her rigging shot away. The captain thought prudent to run her on the point of Valcour, where all the men were saved. They boarded her, and at night set

fire to her. At half-past twelve the engagement became general and very warm. Some of the enemy's ships and all her gondolas beat and rowed up within musket-shot of us. They continued a very hot fire with round and grapeshot until five o'clock when they thought proper to retire to about six or seven hundred vards distance, and continued the fire until dark. The *Congress* and *Washington* have suffered greatly; the latter lost her first lieutenant killed, captain and master wounded. The *New York* lost all her officers, except her captain. The *Philadelphia* was hulled in so many places that she sunk in about one hour after the engagement was over. The whole killed and wounded amounts to about sixty. The enemy landed a large number of Indians on the island and each shore, who kept an incessant fire on us, but did little damage. The enemy had, to appearance, upwards of one thousand in batteaux, prepared for boarding. We suffered much for want of seamen and gunners. I was obliged myself to point most of the guns on board the *Congress*, which I believe did good execution. The *Congress* received seven shot between wind and water, was hulled a dozen times, had her mainmast wounded in two places and her yard in one. The *Washington* was hulled a number of times, her mainmast shot through, and must have a new one. Both vessels are very leaky and want repairing.

On consulting with General Waterbury and Colonel Wigglesworth, it was thought prudent to return to Crown Point, every vessel's ammunition being nearly three-fourths spent. At seven o'clock, Colonel Wigglesworth, in the *Trumbull*, got under way, the gondolas and small vessels followed, and the *Congress* and *Washington* brought up the rear. The enemy did not attempt to molest us. Most of the fleet in this minute come to anchor. The wind is small to the southward. The enemy's fleet is under way to leeward and beating up. As soon as our leaks are stopped, the whole fleet will make the utmost dispatch to Crown Point, where I beg you will send ammunition and your further orders for us. On the whole, I think we have had a very fortunate escape and have great reason to return our humble and hearty thanks to Almighty God for preserving and delivering so many of us from our more than savage enemies.

"The times that tried men's souls"

Their command of the waterway now undisputed, the British sailed to Ticonderoga. The excitement of the moment remained vividly depicted in the mind of the Pennsylvanian Captain, John Lacey:

On the morning of the 28th of October, word was brought by our scouts and lookout boats on the lakes that the enemy were approaching both by land and water. A general alarm was fired, and everyone hurried to his post. All was bustle; the whole camp presented a terrific blaze of fire arms issuing from every quarter to prepare for battle, which was momently expected to commence. Collem after collem [column] presented their fronts along the lines, with fixed bayonet, whose glissining firearms reflecting the bright raise of the sun presented a luster from their tablits more radient than the sun itself. What mind could resist a flash like this! The sounds of the drums to arms, the reports of the alarm cannon, and the crye of the sergeants to the men hurrying them from their tents of "Turn out! Turn out!" would make even a coward brave. These were, however, the times that tried men's souls, and here only the sunshine and summer soldier shrunk from the expected conflict.

I will throw a vail over some names, who but the evening before boasted over a glass of grog what feats they intended to do on the approach of the enemy, now drunk with sickning apathy within the cover of their tents and markees, never appeared to head their men; leaving that task to their subalterns to perform. On finding at last the enemy had made a halt, and that this movement was only to cover a reconitering from them, they came out as bold soldiers as ever, complaining only of a little sick headake.

Catherine Schuyler, wife of the General

Carleton did not attack Ticonderoga. Deeming it too strong to assault, and knowing that the terrible Canadian winter was at hand, he withdrew to Montreal. Burgoyne went to London. There he proposed his plan for the subjugation of the colonists. Commissioned to put it into effect, he returned to Canada in May 1777. Learning of his arrival, the American generals tried to fathom the British plan.

Sir William Howe at New York with 25,000 soldiers was one of the forces to be reckoned with in the future. Burgoyne, who had replaced Carleton as military commander, stood at Montreal with 10,000 men. This latter force held the fulcrum by which perhaps the British could divide the colonies, an undertaking which Washington thought to be beyond their capacity. Like most Americans, he believed Fort Ticonderoga to be impregnable, a view in which he was supported by Anthony Wayne, who had commanded the fort during the winter. He told Washington that all was well there, and that it "could never be carried, without much loss of blood." Schuyler superseded Gates as Yankee commander in the north, and Washington stayed in New Jersey, wondering whether Howe would strike at Philadelphia, or move up the Hudson to support Burgoyne.

Major General Philip Schuyler

Ticonderoga was vulnerable.

Underestimating British audacity, or foolhardiness, the Americans failed to strengthen Fort Ticonderoga, which was in a dilapidated condition, and they remained blind to its major defect, specifically, that it was vulnerable to a bombardment from the hill to the west, which the garrison was too weak to occupy. When, in May, Colonel Arthur St. Clair was sent to command the fort, less than 3,000 men were available to guard its 2,000-yard perimeter.

To the south, American General Schuyler commanded only 700 men. After a visit to Ticonderoga, he described the garrison as "barefoot, all were ragged and the supplies were insufficient to hold the fort against a prolonged siege." Only a miracle could save the fort, believed its twenty-one-year-old adjutant, James Wilkinson. On June 30, the British fleet swept into view, three miles above the fort.

FROM A WATER-COLOR SKETCH BY KAY SMITH

Fort Chambly on the Richelieu River the waterway between Lake Champlain and the Saint Lawrence River in Canada which during the colonial period was a vital supply and communication route from European and Canadian seaports.

Construction of Fort Ticonderoga was begun in 1755 by the French, employing as many as 2000 men at one time to clear and level the ground. It was strategically situated at the south end of Lake Champlain controlling the portage into Lake George. Oak timbers were first used for the walls but within two years stone was used to replace the timbers. In July 1758, the largest army ever seen up to that time on the American continent—15,000 troops consisting of 6000 British regulars and the rest provincials from New York, New Jersey, and New England—attacked, but after a furious battle, Montcalm and his fighting French defenders held the fort. In 1759, the French, under pressure from Colonial forces commanded by General Jeffery Amherst, abandoned the fort and blew it up with a delayed fuse into the powder magazine. From 1759 to 1775, the fort was used by the British as a storehouse for military supplies. On May 10, 1775, American troops under Ethan Allen surprised the British garrison and captured the fort. The cannon and other supplies taken helped to equip Washington's army at Cambridge. On July 5, 1777, the British under General Burgoyne drew a battery of guns to the top of Mount Defiance, from which it was possible to shell the interior of Fort Ticonderoga. The Americans under General Arthur St. Clair withdrew from the fort suffering a serious defeat, losing 324 men killed and wounded. After Burgoyne's defeat at Saratoga the British burned the houses and barracks at Ticonderoga and abandoned the fort. In 1783, General George Washington, Governor Clinton, Colonel Alexander Hamilton and others visited here on a tour of inspection. After many years of neglect and plunder by the public, the fort has been authentically restored to its once awesome status as a key fort on the waterway between the colonies and the Saint Lawrence River.

FROM A WATER-COLOR PAINTING BY KAY SMITH

FROM A WATER-COLOR SKETCH BY KAY SMITH

Freeman's Farm on the Saratoga battlefield in New York where the action on September 19, 1777, four years before the British surrender at Yorktown, developed into a confused struggle which lasted until nightfall, with General Burgoyne losing half of his force and having nothing to show for it, while the Americans fought with "courage and obstinacy" to the astonishment of everyone because they were fighting a large force of well trained British regulars who felt they could rout the inexperienced colonials with little difficulty.

Viewing Fort Ticonderoga from the top of Mount Defiance across the bay

Perceiving Ticonderoga's weakness, the British landed cannon, dragging several pieces up the precipitous slopes of Mount Defiance, the 800-foot hill to the west which dominated the old fort. A shot from a gun alerted St. Clair to the danger. Calling a council of officers, he declared his opinion that, to save the garrison, the fort must be evacuated immediately. His brave decision earned him great unpopularity, because, to the Americans, Ticonderoga was a symbol. They called it the "Gibraltar of the North," and its evacuation came as a shattering blow. During the night of July 4, the majority of the garrison withdrew to the Vermont shore. Another party sailed down Lake George, believing that the log-barrier across the narrows protected them from pursuit. The British warships smashed through it in less than an hour. Sending the Light Infantry, the Grenadiers and the Germans to chase Colonel St. Clair, General Burgoyne sailed down the lake.

Dr. James Thacher sailed with the water-borne contingent, blissfully unaware that the British ships were close behind. "The sun burst forth in the morning," he recalled, "with uncommon luster, the day was fine, the water's surface serene and unruffled." Among the hospital stores he found many dozens of choice wines, which cheered the hearts of the fugitives. Confident that they had outstripped their pursuers, they landed at Skenesboro (now Whitehall), completely unaware of their peril.

The Hubbardton battlefield

Explanation of the Map.—A, advanced corps of General Fraser, attacked at B; C, position of the corps while it was forming; D, Earl of Balcarras detached to cover the right wing; E, the vanguard and Brunswick company of Chasseurs coming up with General Reidesel; F, position of the Americans after Riedesel arrived. The lines extending downward show the course of the retreat of the Americans over the Pittsford Mountains. H, position of the British after the action; I, house where the wounded were carried, mentioned in the description of the picture on page 144; O, position of the Americans previous to the action. This map is a reduced copy of one drawn by P. Gerlach, Burgoyne's deputy quartermaster general.

The discharge of cannon abruptly awakened them to their plight.

> The officers of our guard now attempted to rally the men, and form them in battle array, but this was found impossible; every effort proved unavailable and in the utmost panic they were seen to fly in every direction for personal safety. In this desperate condition, I perceived our officers scampering for their baggage. I ran to the batteaux, seized my chest, carried it a short distance, took from it a few articles, and instantly followed in the train of our retreating party. We took the route to Fort Ann through a narrow defile in the woods, and were so closely pressed by the pursuing enemy that we frequently heard calls from the rear to "march on, the Indians are at our heels."

"The enemy is upon us."

Giving his 850 Light Infantrymen and Grenadiers no time for rest, Brigadier Simon Fraser caught the American rearguard at Hubbardton. St. Clair, with the main body, had reached Castleton, a few miles north, from where he ordered Colonel Seth Warner, with his regiment of Green Mountain Boys, Colonel Nathan Hale, who commanded the 2nd New Hampshire regiment, and Colonel Ebenezer Francis, with his 11th Massachusetts regiment, to follow. They left too late and were caught napping. Bivouacking by a stream, the 360 New Hampshire men were breakfasting when the British reached the valley. "The enemy is upon us," cried Ebenezer Fletcher who scurried into the woods with the rest of the regiment.

From their vantage point on the hill above, Warner and Francis watched the British swarming up the slopes. The small battle of Hubbardton was fought on July 7. Though outnumbered, Simon Fraser did not hesitate. He sent Lord Balcarres with the Light Infantry to oust the Massachusetts regiment and Major Acland with his Grenadiers to scale Mount Zion, the precipitous and craggy hill which dominated the road to Castleton. To General Von Riedesel and his Hessians, he sent word that he was committing his whole force to battle, urging him to hasten.

Colonel Francis, "that gallant and brave man," as the British diarist Lieutenant Digby called him, brought his men to the crest of the ridge. Into the ranks of the climbers they poured their deadly fire. Stumbling and tumbling, the Light Infantry retreated down the hill. On the right, Acland gained his objective. Warner sent two companies to dislodge him, as British Lieutenant Anbury described:

> During the battle the Americans were guilty of such a breach of all military rules as could not fail to exasperate our soldiers. The action was chiefly in woods, interspersed with a few open fields. Two companies of grenadiers, who were stationed in the skirts of the wood, close to one of these fields, to watch that the enemy did not outflank the 24th Regiment, observed a number of the Americans to the amount of near sixty, coming across the field with their arms clubbed, which is always considered to be a surrender as prisoners of war. The grenadiers were restrained from

General John Burgoyne addressing the Indians

> firing, commanded to stand with their arms, and show no intention of hostility; when the Americans had got within ten yards, they in an instant turned round their muskets, fired upon the grenadiers, and ran as fast as they could into the woods; their fire killed and wounded a great number of men, and those who escaped immediately pursued them and gave no quarter.

The survivors of the American "strategem" threw themselves across the Castleton road, cutting their enemies' line of retreat. Again the Light Infantry assaulted the ridge. Realizing the danger, Francis threw his men down the slope, pouring point blank fire upon the climbers. They were saved by the timely arrival of the Germans who outflanked the Massachusetts soldiers who fell back in disarray. Francis was killed.

The action had lasted forty-five minutes. The British suffered 150 casualties, the Germans 24. Exhausted by their climb, they were unable to pursue St. Clair who, learning that Burgoyne had reached Fort Ann, made a wide detour. He reached Fort Edward on the Hudson with his garrison largely intact. It would form the nucleus of the army which gathered to bar General Burgoyne's path.

The General was full of confidence. He had captured the "impregnable" Fort Ticonderoga, almost without a blow. He led a large and well-equipped army. He brought many boats by which to navigate the Hudson to Albany where he expected support from the south. Sir William Howe would keep Washington occupied, and prevent him from going north.

"Desertion prevails"

Ahead of Burgoyne the New Yorkers, led by Philip Schuyler, threw up obstacles, felling trees and digging ditches. They delayed him for twenty precious days. But there seemed to be little chance of halting Burgoyne's triumphal progress. Schuyler despaired. "Desertion prevails," he warned Washington, "nor is it to be wondered at, for we have neither tents, houses, barns, boards of any shelter except a little brush; every rain that falls – and we have it in great abundance almost every day – wets the men to the skin. We are besides in great want of every kind of necessaries, provision excepted. Camp kettles we have so few, that we cannot afford one to twenty men." A third of his troops were, "Boys, negroes and aged men, not fit for the field, and many of the officers would be a disgrace to the most contemptible troop that ever was collected."

He had only thirty cannon and no carts by which to move them. The British were only twenty miles away and "a very great proportion of the inhabitants are taking protection from General Burgoyne, as most of those in this quarter are also willing to do." Schuyler despaired of holding Burgoyne "who is bending his course this way." He begged Washington for reinforcements.

The American Commander had none to send. He debated which course to follow: to hurry north to crush Burgoyne and return quickly to defend Philadelphia, or to watch and follow Howe who, he believed, might either sail up the Hudson or go to Philadelphia. Washington's mind was made up for him. About twenty percent of his soldiers had no shoes, and two forced marches over rough roads were impossible. He remained in New Jersey. In the north, the road to Albany lay open.

An atrocity that outraged the colonists

A tiny, tragic incident turned the scales in the Americans' favor. The rebels needed a "Yankee Joan of Arc," Tom Paine had declared. Jane McCrea, a tragic victim, fulfilled the role. She was murdered and scalped by one of Burgoyne's Indians. As the atrocity story spread throughout New England, thousands of farmers, shopkeepers, artisans, and even sailors abandoned their callings to "go against Burgoyne." Unaware of the fury he had aroused, Burgoyne launched his boats on the Hudson. In the next few weeks he suffered two serious blows which had a fatal effect on his campaign.

Jane McCrea tree at Fort Edward

General John Burgoyne

BENNINGTON

The small force, commanded by Colonel St. Leger, which had been sent from Montreal to surprise the rebels in the rear by crossing Lake Ontario and ascending the Mohawk valley to Albany, failed to capture Fort Stanwix, and was forced to retreat. This denied Burgoyne a reinforcement of one thousand soldiers. Meanwhile, he had suffered a far more serious disaster, one which contributed to his eventual downfall.

Burgoyne had been told incorrectly that the area around Bennington, a town twenty miles away, was "teeming" with the horses he badly needed. Believing that opposition would be small he dispatched Lieut.Col. Frederick Baum with his German regiment to get the horses. Seth Warner, who, following the battle of Hubbardton, had remained in Vermont, learned "that a considerable body of the enemy will attempt to penetrate to Bennington." John Stark, a famed Indian fighter, was sent by the General Court of New Hampshire to "check Burgoyne." How he mobilized a force is described by the historian of Concord:

> As soon as it was decided to raise volunteer companies and place them under the command of Gen. Stark, Col. Hutchins (delegate from Concord) mounted his horse, and traveling all night with all possible haste, reached Concord on Sabbath afternoon, before the close of public service. Dismounting at the meeting-house door, he walked up the aisle of the church while Mr. Walker was preaching. Mr. Walker paused in his sermon, and said, "Col. Hutchins, are you the bearer of any message?" "Yes," replied the Colonel, "General Burgoyne, with his army, is on his march to Albany. Gen. Stark has offered to take the command of the New Hampshire men; and, if we all turn out, we can cut off Burgoyne's march." Whereupon Rev. Mr. Walker said, "My hearers, those of you who are willing to go, better leave at once." At which word all men in the meeting house rose and went out. Many immediately enlisted. The whole night was spent in preparation, and a company was ready to march next day.

That Sunday, 419 men were recruited in the town of Concord and sufficient numbers mobilized elsewhere to enable Stark to send 700 volunteers to aid Warner. He, himself, marched to Manchester, New Hampshire, with 300 more.

Unaware of the forces gathering ahead, the Germans marched resolutely but in no special rush. Then, learning that

1800 of the rebels had collected at Bennington, Baum sent a message to Burgoyne, who ordered Lieutenant Colonel von Breymann to go to Baum's aid. He, too, traveled slowly, his wagons and artillery sticking and overturning in the mud.

That night Stark received a visitor. Among the militia who had answered his call came a contingent from the town of Pittsfield, Massachusetts, commanded by their minister, Parson Thomas Allen. He entered Stark's cabin and demanded to be allowed to attack the enemy which, previously, he and his men had not been permitted to do. "Would you go out on this dark and rainy night?" inquired Stark, who told the warlike minister, "Go back to your people, and tell them to get some rest if they can, and if the Lord gives us some sunshine, and I do not give you fighting enough, I will never ask you to come out again."

"We'll beat them today or by night Molly Stark's a widow!"

Lieutenant Colonel Baum, seventeen miles ahead of von Breymann, occupied a convex-shaped hill, known to this day as "Hessian Hill," overlooking the Walloomsac River. He spread his small force in detachments on the low ground, un-

aware that he was surrounded by 2,000 men commanded by the redoubtable Stark who, according to legend, joked, "We'll beat them today or by night Molly Stark's a widow!" Pretending to be Tories, some of his men infiltrated Baum's camp where their homespun clothes disguised their true identity. An aged veteran of the battle told his story, which was published in 1852:

> To a man they wore small-clothes, coming down and fastening just below the knee, and long stockings with cowhide shoes ornamented by large buckles, while not a pair of boots graced the company. The coats and waistcoats were loose and of huge dimensions, with colors as various as the barks of oak, sumach, and other trees of our hills and swamps could make them, and their shirts were all made of flax and, like every other part of the dress, were homespun. On their heads was worn a large round-top and broad-brimmed hat. Their arms were as various as their costume. Here an old soldier carried a heavy Queen's Arm, with which he had done service at the conquest of Canada twenty years previous, while by his side walked a stripling boy, with a Spanish fusee not half its weight or calibre, which his grandfather may have taken at the Havana, while not a few had old French pieces that dated back to the reduction of Louisburg. Instead of the cartridge box, a large powder horn was slung under the arm, and occasionally a bayonet might be seen bristling in the ranks. Some of the swords of the officers had been made by our Province blacksmiths, perhaps from some farming utensil; they looked serviceable, but heavy and uncouth.

Firing from the flanks notified the infiltrators that the moment had come to throw off their masks. Raising their muskets, they shot down the unsuspecting Germans and Tories whom they had duped.

The Germans threw down their arms and fled into the woods. The Tory contingent stood their ground. Their post by the river was attacked by a party led by the fiery Parson Allen. Recognizing some of the Tories who came from his own district, Allen went forward, stood on a log and exalted them in his best pulpit manner to defect to the American cause. "There's Parson Allen. Let's pot him," came the cry from the redoubt. His neighbor's volley failed to harm Allen, who led the rush over the breastwork. Tory Captain Peters described the fight:

"An old schoolmate and playfellow, and a cousin of my wife . . . I felt regret at being obliged to destroy him."

> A little before the Loyalists gave way, the rebels rushed with a strong party on the front of the Loyalists which I commanded. As they were coming up, I observed a man fire at me, which I returned. He loaded again as he came up, and discharged again at me, crying out, "Peters, you d-n Tory, I have got you." He rushed on me with his bayonet, which entered just below my left breast but was turned by my bones. By this time I was loaded and saw it was a rebel Captain, Jeremiah Post by name,

FROM A WATER-COLOR SKETCH BY KAY SMITH

Sherburne House, Portsmouth, New Hampshire, built between 1695 and 1703, reflects the style of colonial New Hampshire.

FROM A WATER-COLOR SKETCH BY KAY SMITH

William Pitt Tavern, Portsmouth, New Hampshire, used at various times by such distinguished guests as John Hancock, Elbridge Gerry, Edward Rutledge, William Whipple, and Matthew Thornton, all signers of the Declaration of Independence.

The Bennington battlefield

an old schoolmate and playfellow, and a cousin of my wife. Though his bayonet was in my body I felt regret at being obliged to destroy him.

The Tories were forced from the redoubt and made prisoner. Colonel Baum had fallen, mortally wounded. "The battle," Stark told General Gates, "represented one clap of thunder. Our martial courage proved too much for them."

A "Memorable Day"

Warner's regiment reached the scene at five in the afternoon, in time to complete the victory. Pushing ahead, he attacked von Breymann who was within four miles of the battle, unaware of the action. Only darkness saved him from sharing Baum's fate. "We pursued them until dark," recalled Stark. "Had daylight lasted one hour longer, we should have taken the whole body." His victory had been prodigious. The Germans had lost 207 men killed and 700 prisoners. Of Baum's 375 soldiers, only nine escaped. The American casualties numbered 30 killed and 40 wounded. "Saturday, August 16" was a "Memorable Day" remarked Almons Remembrancer.

To Burgoyne, the disaster at Bennington was a staggering blow. The losses reduced his effective troops to 4,500 men. Howe, he learned, had gone to Philadelphia and could not aid him. Many of his Indians had deserted and the recruitment of Tories had proved disappointing. He decided to push on, unaware that the rebels were mobilizing to bar his path.

FREEMAN'S FARM

Thaddeus Kosciusko, Polish engineer

Elated by the recent victories, and infuriated by the murder of Jane McCrea, the New England militias converged on Albany where Schuyler had been relieved by Horatio Gates. His army numbered 4,500 men. Within a few days he was reinforced by the arrival of 500 frontiersmen from Pennsylvania, Maryland, and Virginia, commanded by Daniel Morgan, a veteran of the battle of Quebec. Morgan was a legendary hero and his men were armed with the Kentucky rifle, which, with its 200-yard range and great accuracy, enabled them to adopt "frontier tactics," sharpshooting from cover.

On September 8, Gates moved north, towards Burgoyne, reaching Bemis Heights on the bluffs overlooking and commanding the west bank of the Hudson. There the Polish engineer, Thaddeus Kosciusko, had constructed fortifications. To reach Albany, Burgoyne needed to drive Gates from his fortified base. He moved his army that included, as a witness, Fredericka von Riedesel, the little blue-eyed wife of the Commander of the German mercenaries. She traveled in a carriage with her three small daughters and described her experience as follows:

> We made only small day's marches, and were very often sick; yet always contented at being allowed to follow. I had still the satisfaction of daily seeing my husband. A great part of my baggage I had sent back, and had kept only a small summer wardrobe. In the beginning all went well. We cherished the sweet hope of a sure victory, and of coming to the "promised land;" and when we passed the Hudson river, and General Burgoyne said, "The English never lose ground," our spirits were greatly exhilarated. But that which displeased me was, that the wives of all the officers belonging to the expedition, knew beforehand everything that was to happen; and this seemed the more singular to me, as I had observed, when in the armies of the Duke Ferdinand (of Brunswick), during the Seven Years War (1754–1763), with how much secrecy everything was conducted. But here, on the contrary, the Americans were apprised beforehand of all our intentions; so that at every place where we came they already awaited us; a circumstance which hurt us exceedingly.

The action developed into a confused struggle which lasted until nightfall.

On September 19, 1776, Burgoyne led three quarters of his army on to the plateau overlooking the west bank of the Hudson, to search out the enemy's position and, if possible, to turn their left flank. Though he learned from his scouts of the British advance, Gates was disinclined to move. Arnold persuaded him to send out Morgan's 500 riflemen and Major Dearborn's 250 sharpshooters to seek the enemy. They advanced along the wagon-track which ran northwards through thick woods from Bemis Heights. The encounter with the British, stated James Wilkinson, was "perfectly accidental." The two forces clashed in the small clearing around Freeman's Farm, where the action developed into a confused struggle which lasted until nightfall. On the excuse that he needed to gain information, Wilkinson rode out of the camp:

> I put spurs to my horse, and directed by the sound, had entered the wood about a hundred rods, when the fire suddenly ceased: I however pursued my course, and the first officer I fell in with was Major Dearborn who, with great animation and not a little warmth, was forming thirty or forty file of his infantry; I exchanged a few words with him, passed on and met Major Morris alone, who was never so sprightly as under a hot fire; from him I learnt that the corps was advancing by files in two lines, when they unexpectedly fell upon a picket of the enemy, which they almost instantly forced, and pursuing the fugitives, their front had as unexpectedly fallen in with the British line; that several officers and men had been made prisoners, and that to save himself, he had been obliged to push his horse through the ranks of the enemy, and escaped by a circuitous route.
>
> To show me where the action commenced, he leaped a fence into the abandoned field of Freeman, choked up with weeds, and led me to the cabin which had been occupied by the British picket, but was then almost encircled with dead; he then cautioned me to keep a look out for the enemy, who, he observed, could not be far from us; and as I never admired exposition from which neither advantage nor honor could be derived, I crossed the angle of the field, leapt the fence, and just before me on a ridge discovered Lieutenant Colonel Butler with three men, all *tree'd;* from him I learnt that they had "caught a Scotch prize," that having forced the picket, they had closed with the British line, had been instantly routed, and from the suddenness of the shock and the nature of the ground, were broken and scattered in all directions; he repeated Morris's caution to me, and remarked that the enemy's sharpshooters were on the opposite side of the ravine, and that being on horseback, I should attract a shot.
>
> We changed our position, and the Colonel inquired what were Morgan's orders, and informed me that he had seen a heavy column moving towards our left. I then turned about to regain the camp, and report to the General, when my ears were saluted by an uncommon noise, when I approached, and perceived Colonel Morgan attended by two men only, who with a *turkey call,* (an instrument for decoying the wild turkey) was collecting his dispersed troops. The moment I came up to him, he burst into tears, and exclaimed, "I am ruined, by G—d! Major Morris ran on so rapidly with the front, that they were beaten before I could get up with the rear, and my men are

General Philip Schuyler and Baroness Fredericka von Riedesel

scattered God knows where." I remarked to the Colonel that he had a long day before him to retrieve an inauspicious beginning, and informed him where I had seen his field offiers, which appeared to cheer him, and we parted.

As the result of the information brought back by his aide, Gates sent out, successively, seven more regiments, to support the riflemen and sharpshooters who came into conflict with Simon Fraser's Light Infantrymen. They suffered severely from the marksmanship of the Americans, being unable to fire effectively in return against their elusive opponents, many of whom had perched themselves in trees where, against the autumn foliage, the frontier-shirts of Morgan's men were indistinguishable. In face of this fire, the British retreated slowly across the clearing, rallying again and again to drive back their pursuers who, stated the Earl of Balcarres "behaved with great obstinacy and courage." As more and more American reinforcements came up, the action extended to the right and left of the clearing, as Lieutenant Anbury described:

We heard a most tremendous firing upon our left, when we were attacked in great force, and the very first fire Lieutenant Don of the 21st Regiment received a ball through his heart. I am sure it will never be erased from my memory; for when he was wounded, he sprang from the ground nearly as high as a man. The party that had attacked us were again driven in by our cannon, but the fire raged most furiously on our left, and the enemy were marching to turn their right flank, when they met the advanced corps, posted in wood, who repulsed them. From that time, which was about three o'clock, till after sunset, the enemy, who were continually supplied with fresh troops, most vigorously attacked the British line: the stress lay upon the 20th, 21st and 62nd Regiments, most part of which were engaged for near four hours without intermission.

"The contest terminated on the spot where it began."

If not an active participant, Wilkinson was another eyewitness who recorded his observations:

The theater of action was such that although the combatants changed ground a dozen times in the course of the day, the contest terminated on the spot where it began. This may be explained in a few words. The British line was formed on an eminence in a thin pine wood, having before it Freeman's farm, an oblong field stretching from the center towards its right, the ground in front sloping gently down to the verge of this field, which was bordered on the opposite side by a close wood; the sanguinary scene lay in the cleared ground, between the eminence occupied by the enemy and the wood just described; the fire of our marksmen from this wood was too deadly to be withstood by the enemy in line, and when they gave way and broke, our men rushing from their covert, pursued them to the eminence, where, having their flanks protected, they rallied, and charging in turn drove us back into the wood, from whence a dreadful fire would again force them to fall back; and in this manner did the battle fluctuate, like waves of a stormy sea, with alternate advantage for four hours without one moment's intermission.

The British artillery fell into our possession at every charge, but we could neither turn the pieces upon the enemy, nor bring them off; the wood prevented the last, and the want of a match the first, as the lint stock was invariably carried off, and the rapidity of the transitions did not allow us time to provide one. The slaughter of this brigade of artillerists was remarkable, the captain and thirty-six men being killed or wounded out of forty-eight. It was a gallant conflict, in which death by familiarity lost its terrors, and certainly a drawn battle, as night alone terminated it; the British army keeping its ground in rear of the field of action, and our corps, when they could no longer distinguish objects, retiring to their own camp.

Sergeant Lamb, British medical orderly, also saw the battle:

Here the conflict was dreadful; for four hours a constant blaze of fire was kept up, and both armies seemed to be determined on death or victory. Men, and particularly officers, dropped every moment on each side. Several of the Americans placed themselves in high trees, and as often as they could distinguish a British officer's uniform, took him off by deliberately aiming at his person. Reinforcements successively arrived and strengthened the American line.

"On this Day has been fought one of the Greatest Battles that Ever was fought in America."

The battle swayed to and fro across the clearing. That night Colonel Dearborn noted in his diary, "On this Day has been fought one of the Greatest Battles that Ever was fought in America, and I trust we have Convinced the British Butchers that the Cowardly yankees Can, and when there is a Call for it, will, fight."

The American General Glover, on the other hand, found both sides equally courageous:

> Both armies seemed determined to conquer or die. One continual blaze without any intermission till dark, when by consent of both parties it ceased. During which time we several times drove them, took the ground, passing over great numbers of their dead and wounded. Took one fieldpiece, but the woods and brush were so thick, and being close pushed by another party of the enemy coming up, was obliged to give up our prize. The enemy in turn sometimes drove us. They were bold, intrepid, and fought like heroes, and I do assure you, Sirs, our men were equally bold and courageous and fought like men fighting for their all.

Writing at the end of the day, Anbury remarked:

> Notwithstanding the glory of the day remains on our side, I am fearful the real advantages resulting from this hard fought battle will rest with the Americans, our army being so much weakened by this engagement as not to be of sufficient strength to venture forth and improve the victory, which may, in the end, put a stop to our intended expedition, the only apparent benefit gained is that we keep possession of the ground where the engagement began.
>
> The courage and obstinacy with which the Americans fought were the astonishment of everyone, and we now become fully convinced they are not that contemptible enemy we had hitherto imagined them, incapable of standing a regular engagement, and that they would only fight behind strong and powerful works.

Major General Horatio Gates of the American forces

Burgoyne had lost half his force and had gained nothing. Gates remained secure within his fortifications. He needed only to remain there to win a great victory. That night Burgoyne received a message, carried by an officer who had penetrated the American lines, stating that General Clinton (whom Howe had left at New York) would attempt to push up the Hudson to relieve pressure on Burgoyne. As a result, Burgoyne postponed renewal of the attack on Bemis Heights. Clinton penetrated the Highlands, captured forts Clinton (named after the American General of that name) and Montgomery, and sailed up the Hudson as far as Esopus. He got within eighty miles of Burgoyne but was forced to retreat.

BEMIS HEIGHTS

Despairing of aid from the south, Burgoyne renewed his attack on Bemis Heights on October 7, 1776. Leaving the bulk of his diminished army to guard his camp, he took 1,500 men on to the plateau, with the forlorn hope of turning the left flank of the Yankee line. He advanced to two small clearings, about halfway between Freeman's farm and Bemis Heights. The presence of the British was quickly reported to Gates, who sent Wilkinson out to observe and report. He returned to say that the British were drawn up in the clearings. Gates ordered Morgan's forces into action. Morgan announced his plan, to attack the British simultaneously from right, front, and left. During the afternoon, Gates sent out more than 9,000 men.

The engagement began in midafternoon. Gaining the height to the north, Morgan's Riflemen and Dearborn's Light Infantry poured down, in Wilkinson's words "like a torrent" onto the British right wing, attacking it in front and rear. American General Poor engaged Major Acland's Grenadiers on the left, as had been planned, before Yankee General Learned assaulted Von Riedesel's Hessian troops at the center of the British line. Within a few minutes, the whole British-German line of 1,500 men was under assault by five or six times their number.

"Our cannon were surrounded and taken."

General Poor led his New Yorkers and New Hampshire men up the slope in face of a deadly volley of musket fire and a fusilade of grape-shot, his troops holding their fire until they reached the crest. Then they fired at point-blank range, mowing down the Grenadiers standing shoulder to shoulder. They charged with a great shout, sweeping over the British guns, hurling back the Grenadiers. "Our cannon were surrounded and taken," said British Lieutenant Digby. Their capture gave the enemy "additional spirits and they rushed with loud shouts, when we drove them back a little with so great a loss to ourselves, that it evidently appeared a retreat was the only thing left for us. They still advanced under a storm of grape-shot."

Captain Pausch, in command of the German cannon, saw his compatriots form themselves into a half-circle:

> At this junction, our left wing retreated in the greatest possible disorder, thereby causing a similar rout among our Germand command, which was stationed behind the fence in line of battle. They retreated—or to speak more plainly—they left their position without informing me, although I was but fifty paces in advance of them. Each man for himself, they made for the bushes. Without knowing it, I kept back the enemy for a while with my unprotected cannon loaded with shells. How long before this the infantry had left its position, I cannot tell, but I saw a great number advance towards our now open left wing within a distance of about 300 paces. I looked back towards the position still held, as I supposed, by our German infantry, under whose protection I, too, intended to retreat—but not a man was to be seen. Their right wing was thus in front of the house I have so often mentioned, but all was in disorder, though they still fought the enemy which continued to advance.

"I have dipt my hands in British blood."

A sidearm from the Saratoga battlefield

Poor's amateur soldiers had broken the elite of the British army. The experience so excited the courageous Colonel Cilley, that he sat himself astraddle the brass twelve-pounder, exalting in its capture, a show of exuberance which was as much applauded by Wilkinson, who sharply rebuked the barbarism of a surgeon, a man "of great worth," who was dressing the wounds of one of the British officers. Raising his blood-besmeared hands in a frenzy of patriotism, he exclaimed "Wilkinson, I have dipt my hands in British blood."

The rout of the British grenadiers, and the loss of the guns, exposed the left flank of Von Riedesel's Brunswickers, who, simultaneously with the British grenadiers, had been under assault during the fifty-two minutes this phase of the battle lasted. The conflict extended along the whole line. On the right, Morgan and Dearborn fell upon the British 24th regiment which, although temporarily rallied by Lord Balcarres, retreated, exposing the center where Von Riedesel's 300

Germans bravely resisted the assault of General Learned's five regiments. Ebeneazer Matton, an artillery officer, described this part of the fight:

Site of the first meeting between Generals Gates and Burgoyne

> In a few minutes, Captain Furnival's company of artillery, in which I was lieutenant, was ordered to march towards the fire, which had now opened upon our pickets in front, the picket consisting of about 300 men. While we were marching, the whole line, up to our picket in front, was engaged. We advanced to a height of ground which brought the enemy in view, and opened our fire. But the enemy's guns, eight in number, and much heavier than ours, rendered our position untenable.
>
> We then advanced into the line of infantry. Here Lieutenant M'Lane joined me. In our front there was a field of corn, in which the Hessians were secreted. On our advancing towards the corn field, a number of men rose and fired upon us. M'Lane was severely wounded. While I was removing him from the field, the firing still continued without abatement.
>
> During this time, a tremendous firing was heard on our left. We poured in upon them our canister shot as fast as possible, and the whole line, from left to right, became engaged. The smoke was very dense, and no movements could be seen; but as it soon arose, our infantry appeared to be slowly retreating, and the Hessians slowly advancing, their officers urging them on with their hangers.
>
> The troops continuing warmly engaged, Colonel Johnson's regiment, coming up, threw in a heavy fire and compelled the Hessians to retreat. Upon this we advanced with a shout of victory. At the same time Lord Acland's corps gave way. We proceeded but a short distance before we came upon four pieces of brass cannon, closely surrounded with the dead and dying; at a few yards further we came upon two more. Advancing a little further we were met by a fire from the British infantry, which proved very fatal to one of Colonel Johnson's companies, in which were killed one sergeant, one corporal, fourteen privates—and about twenty were wounded.
>
> They advanced with a quick step, firing as they came on. We returned them a brisk fire of canister shot, not allowing ourselves time even to sponge our pieces. In a short time they ceased firing and advanced upon us with trailed arms. At this juncture Arnold came up with a part of Brooke's regiment, and gave them a most deadly fire, which soon caused them to face about and retreat with a quicker step than they advanced.

"That gallant officer is General Fraser. I admire him, but it is necessary that he should die."

Flushed by victory, Morgan's riflemen closed in on the 24th regiment and Light Infantry which, alone of the British line, retained some semblance of order. They were rallied by Simon Fraser, a conspicuous figure on his splendid horse. At that moment Benedict Arnold reached the scene of action. Spotting the General, Arnold called to Morgan, "that officer upon a grey horse is of himself a host, and must be disposed of—direct the attention of some of the sharp-shooters amongst your riflemen to him." Morgan, nodding assent, went over to his riflemen, and pointing to Fraser said, "That gallant officer is General Fraser. I admire him, but it is necessary that he should die; do your duty."

Traditionally, an Irishman named Tim Murphy, a famous Indian fighter and a crack-shot, climbed a tree and aimed at Simon Fraser. The first rifle bullet cut the crupper of the horse, the next passed through its mane, a little back of the ears. An aide urged the General to retire and not to expose himself longer. Murphy's third bullet penetrated Fraser's abdomen and he fell to the ground, mortally wounded. Lieutenant Digby claimed that Fraser's fall helped "to turn the fate of the day." He was the only wounded man "we were able to carry off."

The British, abandoning the clearing, fell back on the two redoubts they had built near Freeman's farm. Hard on their heels came their pursuers led by Arnold. Galloping across the line, and flourishing his sword, Arnold, "exposing himself with great folly" (according to Wilkinson) led the assault on the redoubt held by von Breymann.

"Don't hurt him, he is a fine fellow. He only did his duty."

A wounded German, lying on the ground, seeing an American officer on a horse charging down upon him, raised his rifle and shot the horse at point blank range. The charger rolled over pinioning Arnold to the ground, and breaking his leg, the one that had been broken previously at Quebec. At this moment Colonel Brooks and his men mounted the works. When a soldier aimed to kill the wounded German, Arnold cried out, "Don't hurt him, he is a fine fellow. He only did his duty." Arnold was carried back to the camp on a litter.

The victors returned to Bemis Heights, carrying their spoils, six captured cannon and 240 prisoners. It had been a "Memorable Day" remarked Ralph Cross in his journal. Burgoyne had lost half his force and many distinguished officers; von Breymann was dead, and Simon Fraser was dying in the house, where Madam von Riedesel sat, surrounded by her three children, anxiously awaiting news of her husband:

> Finally, toward evening, I saw my husband coming, upon which I forgot all my sufferings and thanked God that he had spared him to me. He ate in great haste with me, and his adjutant, behind the house. We had been told that we had gained an advantage over the enemy, but the sorrowful and downcast faces which I beheld, bore witness to the contrary, and before my husband again went away, he drew me on one side and told me that everything might go very badly and that I must keep myself in constant readiness for departure, but by no means to give anyone the least inkling of what I was doing. I therefore pretended that I wished to move into my new house the next morning, and had everything packed up.

At the British camp, Anburey watched the return of the troops. He judged the situation to be very serious.

Burgoyne's encampment on the western shore of the Hudson River in September, 1777
—From a print published in London in 1779

SARATOGA

Burgoyne knew that the game was up. He had failed to force the American lines. His only hope lay in retreat. The day following the battle, he ordered his exhausted troops to break camp and march. Madam von Riedesel told the story of her own experience:

I did not wish to set out before the troops. The wounded Major Harnage, although he was so ill, dragged himself out of bed, that he might not remain in the hospital, which was left behind protected by a flag of truce. As soon as he observed me in the midst of danger, he had my children and maid servants put into the calashes [carriages], and intimated to me that I must immediately depart. As I still begged to be allowed to remain, he said to me, "Well, then your children at least must go, that I may save them from the slightest danger." He understood how to take advantage of my weak side. I gave it up, seated myself inside with them, and we drove off at eight o'clock in the evening.

The greatest silence had been enjoined; fires had been kindled in every direction; and many tents left standing, to make

Cannon overlooking the valley at Saratoga battlefield
—Sketch by Kay Smith

> the enemy believe that the camp was still there. We traveled continually the whole night. Little Frederica was afraid, and would often begin to cry. I was, therefore, obliged to hold a pocket handkerchief over her mouth, lest our whereabouts should be discovered.

By the time the British had retreated to the village of Saratoga, the modern Schuylersville, they were surrounded by 16,000 Americans, a situation about which Madam von Riedesel is our best informant:

> I was wet through and through by the frequent rains, and was obliged to remain in this condition the entire night, as I had no place whatever where I could change my linen. I, therefore, seated myself before a good fire, and undressed my children; after which, we laid ourselves down together upon some straw. I asked General Phillips who came up to where we were, why

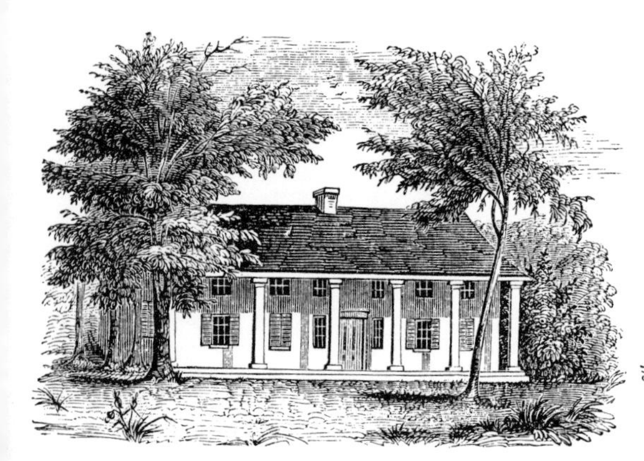

General Schuyler's home

General Schuyler's mill in Saratoga

we did not continue our retreat while there was yet time, as my husband had pledged himself to cover it, and bring the army through. "Poor woman," answered he, "I am amazed at you! Completely wet through, have you still the courage to wish to go further in this weather? Would that you were only our commanding general! He halts because he is tired and intends to spend the night here and give us a supper." In this latter achievement, especially, General Burgoyne was very fond of indulging. He spent half the nights in singing and drinking, and amusing himself with the wife of a commissary, who was his mistress, and who, as well as he, loved champagne.

The von Riedesel house in Saratoga

Burgoyne knew the danger.

The wife of Burgoyne's German officer may have been too critical. Self-indulgent as he undeniably was, Burgoyne knew the danger in which he stood. Believing that he could still escape the net which was closing in around him, he sent a column to open the road to Ticonderoga. It was intercepted and thrown back. "The whole army clamored for a retreat," wrote Madam von Riedesel. Day and night it was under fire:

We were finally obliged to take refuge in a cellar in which I laid myself down in a corner not far from the door. My children laid down on the earth with their heads upon my lap, and in this manner we passed the entire night. A horrible stench, the cries of the children, and yet more than all this, my own anguish, prevented me from closing my eyes.

Burgoyne called his officers to a council, "You have brought me to this pass," Burgoyne accused Skene, "Now tell me how to get out of it." The resourceful Tory leader had an answer. "Scatter your baggage, stores and everything that can be spared, at proper distances," he told Burgoyne, "and the colonial militiamen will be so busy plundering them that you and the troops will get clean off."

The state of the army, said Anburey, was "truly calamitous."

Worn down by a series of incessant toils and stubborn actions; abandoned in our utmost distress by the Indians; weakened by the desertion and disappointed as to the efficacy of the Canadians and Provincials (Tories); the regular troops reduced, by the late heavy losses of many of our best men and distinguished officers, to only 3,500 effective men, of which number there were not quite 2,000 British:—in this state of weakness, no possibility of retreat, our provisions nearly exhausted, and invested by an army of four times our number that almost encircled us, who would not attack us from a knowledge of our situation, and whose works could not be assaulted in any part. In this perilous situation the men lay continually upon their arms, the enemy incessantly cannonading us, and their rifle and cannon shot reaching every part of our camp.

Capitulation with honors

With no other course open, Burgoyne decided to surrender, and a flag of truce was sent to Gates. To Wilkinson's surprise, he accepted the British terms, allowing Burgoyne's army to "capitulate" rather than surrender. They would be allowed to march out with full honors of war and be evacuated to England, on the promise that the soldiers would not serve again in America.

On October 17, the British and German soldiers marched out of camp, as Digby recorded, "with drums beating and the honors of war, but the drums seemed to have lost their inspiring sound, and though we beat the Grenadiers March, which not long before was so animating, yet then it seemed by its last effort, as if almost ashamed to be heard on such an occasion." He was almost in tears, and if he had been alone, "I could have burst to give myself vent."

Accompanied by his staff, Burgoyne rode to Gates's camp, under Wilkinson's guidance:

> General Gates, advised of Burgoyne's approach, met him at the head of his camp, Burgoyne in a rich royal uniform, and Gates in a plain blue frock. When they had approached nearly within sword's length, they reigned up and halted. I then named the gentleman, and General Burgoyne, raising his hat most gracefully, said, "The fortunes of war, General Gates, has made me your prisoner," to which the conqueror returning a courtly salute, promptly replied, "I shall always be ready to bear testimony that it has not been through any fault of your Excellency." Major General Phillips then advanced, and he and Gates saluted, and shook hands with the familiarity of old acquaintances. (They had known each other when Gates served in the British army.) The Baron Riedesel and the other officers were introduced in their turn.

The Saratoga fields where the British capitulated

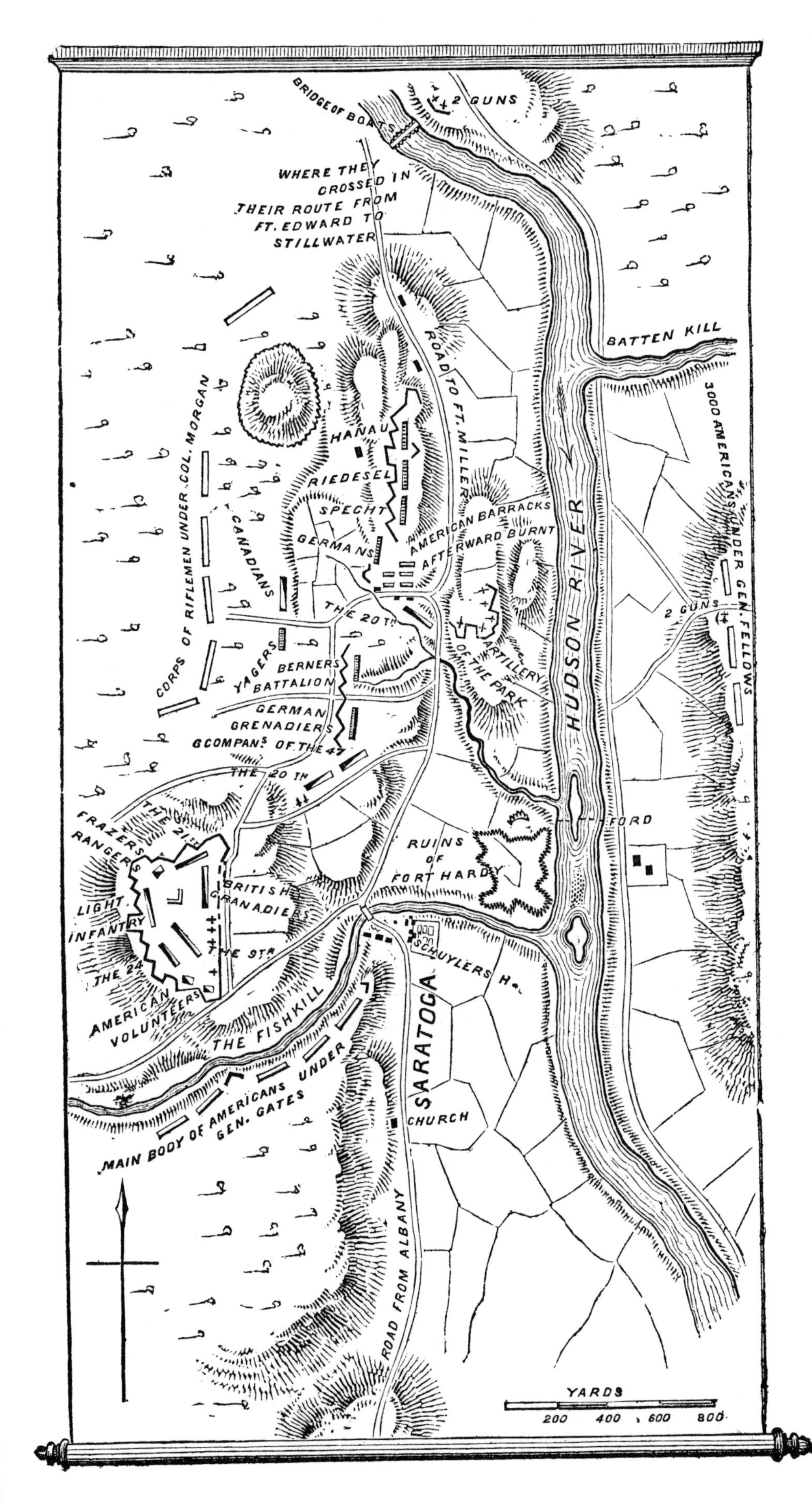

The plan of the Battle of Saratoga

Digby, who was present, found the meeting between Burgoyne and Gates well worth watching, for "Gates paid Burgoyne almost as much respect as if he was the conqueror; his noble air, tho' prisoner, seemed to command attention and respect from every person."

Observed only by Gates's officers, the British and German soldiers paraded in the meadow by the Fishkill Creek, where they laid down their arms. They then marched into captivity, passing the massed ranks of their enemy. A band struck up *Yankee Doodle*. As the soldiers marched away, Burgoyne and Gates turned to face each other. Burgoyne drew his sword and offered it to Gates who, equally courteously, bowed and returned it. The ceremony was conducted according to 18th century manners. It gave the diarists little to record. Ralph Cross remarked, "The Grand Army of General Burgoyne capitulated and agreed to be all Prisoners of War, as Grand a Sight as ever was beheld by Eye of Man in America." Henry Dearborn was equally terse, "This Day the Great Mister Burgoyne with his whole army surrendered themselves as Prisoners of War with all their Publick Stores," which he called the "Greatest Conquest ever known."

The "Convention Army," as it became known, marched to Massachusetts and was billeted at Cambridge. Madam von Riedesel went too. Her journey to Boston was marked by considerable hardship:

> I know not whether it was my carriage that attracted the curiosity of the people to it—for it certainly had the appearance of a wagon in which they carry around rare animals—but often I was obliged to halt, because the people insisted upon seeing the wife of the German general with her children. For fear that they would tear off the linen coverings from the wagon in their eagerness to see me, I very often alighted, and by this means got away more quickly. However, I must say that the people were very friendly, and were particularly delighted at my being able to speak English, which was the language of their country.

Madam Fredericka von Riedesel

A guinea for a pair of boots

She lost neither her frolicsomeness nor her spirits, despite her husband's depression, and she retained her capability of observation:

> Some of their generals who accompanied us were shoemakers; and upon our halting days they made boots for our officers, and also mended nicely the shoes of our soldiers. They set a great value upon our money coinage, which, with them, was scarce. One of our officers had worn his boots entirely into shreds. He saw that an American general had on a good pair, and said to him jestingly, "I will gladly give you a guinea for them." Immediately the general alighted from his horse, took the guinea, gave up his boots, and put on the badly worn ones of the officer, and again mounted his horse.

Hannah Winthrop, a resident of Cambridge, watched the captives come into the town:

Last Thursday, which was a very stormy day, a large number of British troops came softly through the town via Watertown to Prospect Hill. On Friday we heard the Hessians were to make a procession in the same route. We thought we should have nothing to do with them, but view them as they passed. To be sure, the sight was truly astonishing. I never had the least idea that the Creation produced such a sordid set of creatures in human figures—poor, dirty, emaciated men, great numbers of women, who seemed to be the beasts of burden, having a bushel basket on their back, by which they were bent double; the contents seemed to be pots and kettles, various sorts of furniture, children peeping through gridirons and other utensils, some very young infants who were born on the road, the women barefoot, clothed in dirty rags; such effluvia filled the air while they were passing, had not they been smoking all the time, I should have been apprehensive of being contaminated by them.

After a noble-looking advance guard, General Johnny Burgoyne headed this terrible group on horseback. The other generals, also clothed in blue coats, Hessians, Anspachers, Brunswickers, etc., etc., etc., followed on. The Hessian General gave us a polite bow as they passed. Not so the British.

Commemorative medal struck for General Gates and his army

Burgoyne was permitted to return to England. His soldiers were not so fortunate. They were sent to Virginia, and few, if any, returned to their homes. The von Riedesels were eventually repatriated, and they returned home to Germany where the Baroness wrote her "Memoirs."

The turning point of the Revolution

The battle of "Saratoga," as it is named, was the turning point of the Revolution. The Americans had won a prodigious victory, far greater than they realized at the time. The threat to divide the colonies had been put down. The American northern army had taken prisoner 7 generals, 300 other officers, 3,379 British and 2,202 German soldiers, and had captured all the cannon and military stores that remained. During the campaign, the British and Germans had lost 1,429 men, killed or wounded. On November 8, the British garrison evacuated Ticonderoga and retreated to Canada.

The rebels had gained far more than a local success. The news of Burgoyne's surrender reached Paris on December 5, and the next day King Louis XVI declared his recognition of the United States. On February 6, 1778, he signed the formal Treaty of Alliance, which turned the family quarrel into a world-wide conflict.

When he heard of Burgoyne's surrender, General Washington called it a most important event which exceeded "our most sanguine expectations." The news of the American victory came at a particularly opportune moment because he had suffered two reverses.

Headquarters of Marquis de Lafayette at Brandywine
–Reproduced in halftone from a water-color sketch by Kay Smith

BRANDYWINE

Howe, instead of aiding Burgoyne, whereby he might have ended the war, embarked 15,000 troops at New York on July 23, 1777, and landed them four weeks later at the head of Chesapeake Bay, fifty-five miles south of Philadelphia. Washington, who had been "puzzled and embarrassed" by his failure to divine Howe's intentions, now knew the direction of his campaign. He marched his army, which numbered about 16,000 men, to Philadelphia, reaching the city ahead of the British. There he met the nineteen-year-old Marquis de Lafayette, the most distinguished of the French officers who had volunteered to fight for American liberty.

Lafayette had arrived at Charleston, from where on June 19 he wrote:

> I will now tell you about the country and its inhabitants. They are as agreeable as my enthusiasm had painted them. Simplicity of manners, kindness, love of country and of liberty, and a delightful equality everywhere prevail. The wealthiest man and the poorest are on a level; and, although there are some large fortunes, I challenge anyone to discover the slightest difference between the manners of these two classes respectively towards each other. I first saw the country life at the house of Major Huger. I am now in the city, where everything is very much after the English fashion, except that there is more simplicity, equality, cordiality, and courtesy here than in England. The city of Charleston is one of the handsomest and best built, and its inhabitants among the most agreeable that I have ever seen.
>
> The American women are very pretty, simple in their manners, and exhibit a neatness, which is everywhere cultivated even more studiously than in England. What most charms me is that all the citizens are brethren. In America, there are no poor, nor even what we call peasantry. Each individual has his own honest property, and the same rights as the most wealthy landed proprietor.
>
> The inns are very different from those of Europe; the host and hostess sit at table with you, and do the honors of a comfortable meal; and, on going away, you pay your bill without higgling. When one does not wish to go to an inn, there are country-houses where the title of a good American is a sufficient passport to all those civilities paid in Europe to one's friend.

An impressive parade

Captivated by the boy, Washington invited him to watch the parade of the army which, on August 24, marched through Philadelphia on its way to meet the British invaders. Among the spectators was John Adams who described the scene in a letter to his wife, Abigail:

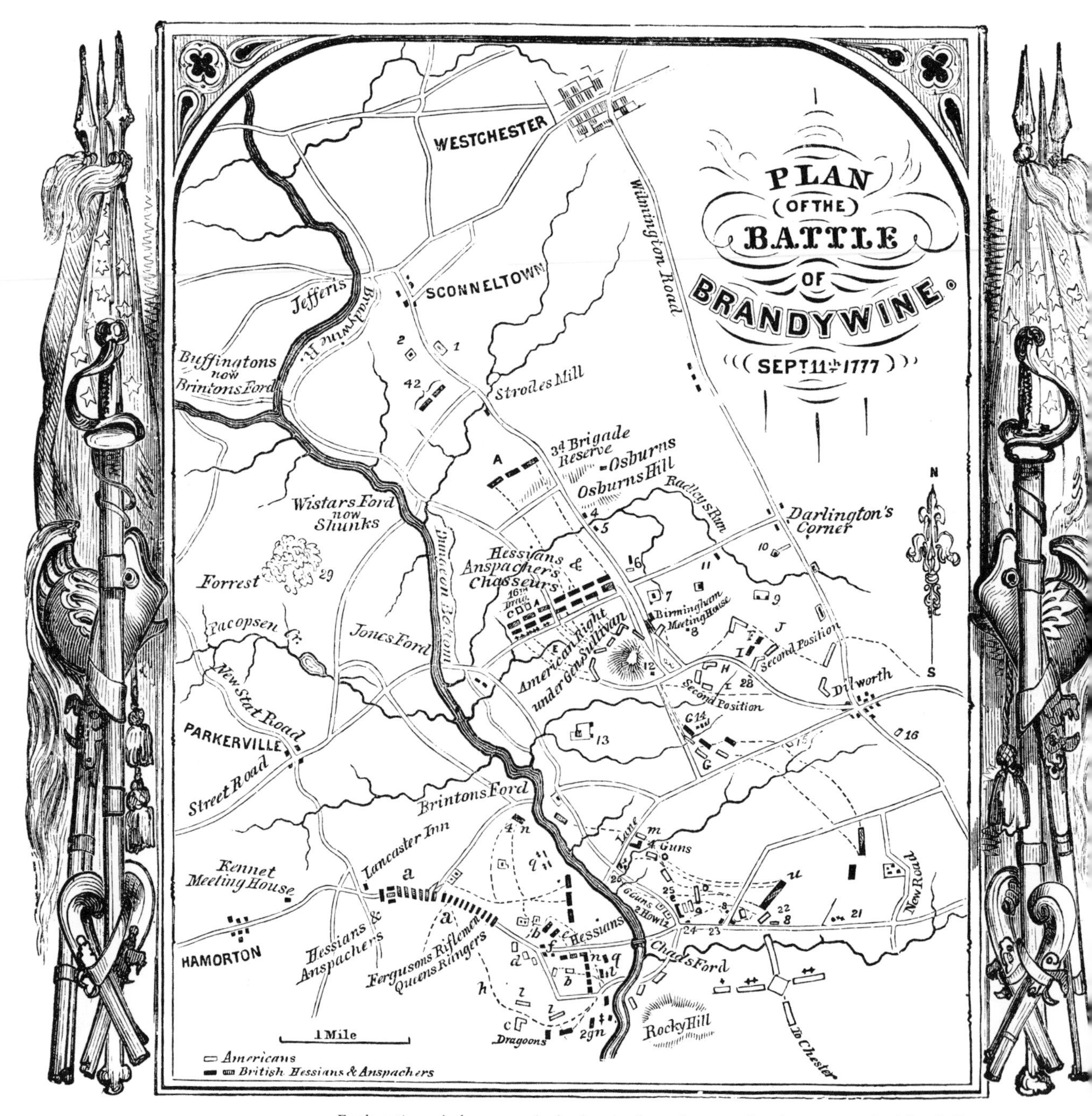

Explanation of the map.—A A, denote the column under the command of Lord Cornwallis, after having crossed the forks of the Brandywine. C, two squadrons of dragoons, which were not employed in the action. E E, the first general attack of the enemy's guards and grenadiers. F, Deborre's brigade, on the right, forced by the enemy. G, G, the British and Hessian grenadiers entangled in a wood. H H, march of the enemy toward and beyond Dilworth. The position of the Americans when the battle commenced is named on the plan. I, indicates the ravine or difile where Greene checked the enemy until night. No. 28 denotes the site of a blacksmith's shop which stood near the defile, but now destroyed.

The rain ceased, and the army marched through the town between seven and ten o'clock. The wagons went another road. Four regiments of light horse, Bland's, Baylor's, Sheldon's, and Moylan's. Four grand divisions of the army, and the artillery with the attached infantrymen. They marched twelve deep, and yet took about two hours in passing by General Washington and the other general officers with their aides on horseback. The colonels and other field officers on horseback. We have now an army well appointed between us and Mr. Howe and this army will be immediately joined by ten thousand militia, so that I feel as secure as if I were at Braintree [his home in Massachusetts], but not so happy. My happiness is nowhere to be found but there.

After viewing this fine spectacle and firm defense, I went to Mr. Duffield's meeting to hear him pray, as he did most fervently, and I believe he was most sincerely joined by all present for its success.

The army, upon an accurate inspection of it, I find to be extremely well armed, pretty well clothed, and tolerably disciplined. There is such a mixture of the sublime and the beautiful together with the useful in military discipline, that I wonder every officer we have is not charmed with it. Much remains to be done. Our soldiers have not quite the air of soldiers. They don't step exactly in time. They don't hold up their heads quite erect, nor turn out their toes so exactly as they ought. They don't all of them cock their hats, and such as do, don't all wear them the same way.

Abigail Adams, wife of John Adams

From the landing place, Howe moved his army up the western bank of the Delaware River, reaching Brandywine Creek on September 11. At Chad's Ford, Washington waited to repel the British army and protect Philadelphia, the colonial capital.

He drew up his troops – 8,000 volunteers and 3,000 militia – along the northern bank of Brandywine Creek, concentrating behind Chad's Ford, the best crossing place. Greene commanded the center, Sullivan the right, and a small force of militiamen covered Pyle's Ford to the south. American Brigadier General Maxwell, with 800 men, crossed the creek, taking position on the approach road to Chad's Ford. They received the first British onslaught, the attack on the American center led by General Knyphausen. From an eminence on the farther bank of the creek, Ebenezer Elmer saw the Hessians "hove in sight" about eight o'clock in the morning. With the Hessians came the Queen's Rangers, among them Sergeant Stephen Jarvis (who rose later to the rank of Colonel):

We came in sight of the enemy at sunrise. The first discharge of the enemy killed the horse of Major Grymes, who was leading the column, and wounded two men in the Division directly in my front, and in a few moments the Regiment became warmly engaged and several of our officers were badly wounded. None but the Rangers and Ferguson's Riflemen were as yet engaged; the enemy retired, and there was a cessation for a short time, to reconnoiter the enemy, who had taken up their position in a wood which skirted the road that led down to the River. The

Colonel Timothy Pickering

Rangers were ordered to advance, and drive the enemy from that position. We marched from the right of Companys, by files, entered the wood, and drove the enemy from it, into an open field where there was a large body of the enemy formed. Major Wymes, who commanded the Rangers, ordered the Regiment to halt and cover themselves behind the trees, but the right of the Regiment was hotly engaged with the enemy, and Captain Dunlap came to Major Wymes, and requested him to let the Regiment charge or the two Companies would be cut off.

The Major then ordered the Adjutant (Ormand), who being glad of the opportunity to lead the troops in our rear to support him, ordered the Regiment to charge. At this instant, my pantaloons received a wound, and I don't hesitate to say that I should have been very well pleased to have seen a little blood also. The enemy stood until we came near to bayonet points, then gave us a volley and retired across the Brandywine. Captain Williams and Captain Murden were killed, and many of the officers were wounded in this conflict. The Brandywine of each side was skirted with wood, in which the Rangers took shelter, whilst our artillery were playing upon a half moon battery on the other side of the River which guarded the only fording place where our Army could cross. In this position we remained waiting for General Howe to commence his attack on the right flank of General Washington's main Army.

Defending the middle

Maxwell's men forded the creek and took position on the left of the American center which now came under a heavy cannonade from the Hessians who had reached the creek. The Massachusetts Colonel, Timothy Pickering, thought that they were only trying to "amuse us." The delay in crossing might have warned Washington that Howe was adopting his usual tactic, a flank movement to take the enemy in the rear. After sending Knyphausen to engage the American center, the British commander had directed Lord Cornwallis with half the army to cross the Brandywine six miles higher up, where the fords were unprotected. Washington received several contradictory reports. About eleven o'clock, a messenger from Colonel Moses Hazen, on the extreme right, informed him that the British were circling, which General Sullivan, Hazen's Commander, denied. Fearing that the main assault might still come at Chad's Ford, Washington ordered Colonel Bland, who led a squadron of horse, to ride northwards to reconnoiter the enemy's action.

An hour later, Washington was still without definite news. At one o'clock he was told by Bland that the British were crossing the creek above its forks. Uncertain still whether the British move was only a feint, Washington hesitated to wheel his center in that direction. His doubts were increased by an elderly farmer who rode up to say that he had heard firing around the Birmingham meeting house, behind the American right wing.

"Push along, old man."

Washington decided to see for himself, and sought a guide to take him to the meeting house by the shortest and speediest route, as William Darlington learned later:

> He found a resident of the neighborhood, named Joseph Brown, and asked him to go as guide. Brown was an elderly man, and extremely loath to undertake the duty. He made many excuses, but the occasion was too urgent for ceremony. One of Washington's staff dismounted from a fine charger and told Brown if he did not instantly get on his horse and conduct the General by the nearest and best route to the place of action, he would run him through on the spot.
>
> Brown thereupon mounted and steered his course direct towards Birmingham Meeting House with all speed—the General and his attendants being close at his heels. He said the horse leapt all the fences without difficulty, and was followed in like manner by the others. The head of General Washington's horse, he said, was constantly at the flank of the one on which he was mounted; and the General was continually repeating to him, "*Push along, old man—push along old man.*"

Brown told Darlington that "the bullets were flying so thick that he felt very uncomfortable, and as Washington no longer required nor paid attention to his guide, the latter embraced the first opportunity to dismount and make his escape."

A colonial scene in Newcastle, Delaware

Washington was accompanied by Lafayette, who was later struck in the leg by a bullet.

Ebenezer Elmer, a surgeon with the New Jersey Continental regiment, went to join General Sullivan at Birmingham Meeting House:

> We marched on some distance till we Came in Sight of the Enemy who had Crossed the river & were coming down upon us; we formed about four o'clock on an Eminence, the right being in ye woods. Presently a large Column Came on in front playing ye Grenediers March & Now the Battle began which proved Excessive severe. The Enemy Came on with fury; our men stood firing upon them most amazingly, killing almost all before them for near an hour till they got within six rods of each other, when a Column of the Enemy came upon our right flank which caused them to give way which soon extended all along ye line; we retreated & formed on ye first ground and gave ym another fire & so continued on all ye way, but unfortunately for want of a proper Retreat, three or four of our pieces were left on ye first ground.

A retreat exposing the middle

The flight of Sullivan's troops exposed the American center which was simultaneously attacked by Hessians and the Queen's Rangers who had crossed the creek at Chad's Ford. "The water," related Sergeant Jarvis, "took us up to our breasts and was much stained with blood." He landed on the farther bank and took position on a small hill from where "we saw our brave comrades cutting them up in great style."

"After an obstinate engagement with our artillery," said Colonel Pickering, Anthony Wayne's division, which, with Maxwell's men had held the ford, retreated. They "swept off great numbers of the enemy," stated Joseph Clark, a surgeon who collected accounts from officers who were concerned in that part of the action:

> The enemy must have suffered very much from our people before they broke, though, indeed, our people suffered much in this action, and would have suffered more if General Greene had not been detached to their assistance, by whose timely aid they made a safe retreat of the men, though we lost some pieces of artillery; he, however, got up too late to form in a proper line and give our party that was broken time to recover. Notwithstanding this repulse, which was the most severe upon the 3d Virginia Regiment, who, through mistake, was fired upon by our own men, our whole body got off with but an inconsiderable loss in men, though something considerable in artillery.

The rout of the right wing

The collapse of the center, following the rout of the right wing, left Washington with no alternative but to order a retreat to Chester. About sunset Joseph Clark, "saw the fate of the day:"

> His Excellency I saw within 200 yards of the enemy, with but a small party about him, and they drawing off from their station,

FROM A WATER-COLOR SKETCH BY KAY SMITH

Fort Mifflin on the Delaware River, Philadelphia, located on what was then Mud Island, where the Americans delayed the British to buy precious time in November of 1777 before leaving the fort in flames after enduring heavy naval bombardment.

Mrs. André, wife of Major John André,
dressed in ladies' formal attire of the Revolutionary period,
in a sketch drawn by her talented husband,
who, with Benedict Arnold, conspired to capture West Point,
was captured in civilian dress, and was convicted
and executed as a British spy.

FROM A WATER-COLOR SKETCH BY KAY SMITH

The legend of Betsy Ross and how she came to make the first official United States flag in this house in Philadelphia, Pennsylvania, in June 1777, to the specifications of a committee headed by George Washington is one of the very pleasant stories of American history.

FROM A WATER-COLOR SKETCH BY KAY SMITH

Washington's headquarters at Valley Forge during the brutal winter of 1777 and 1778 when more than 3000 men died as a result of privation and disease—a period crucial to future success in the war because at Valley Forge the training under Baron von Steuben created a more disciplined fighting corps that formed the basis of the army that eventually won the war.

The headquarters of General Washington at Brandywine
—From a black and white sketch by Kay Smith

our army broke at the right, and night coming on, adding a gloom to our misfortunes, amidst the noise of cannon, the hurry of people, and wagons driving in confusion from the field, I came off with a heart full of distress. In painful anxiety I took with hasty step the gloomy path from the field, and traveled 15 miles to Chester, where I slept two hours upon a couple of chairs.

The private soldier, Elisha Stevens, summed up the battle in a few terse words:

The Battel was at Brandy wine it Began in the morning and Held til knight with out much seasation of arms Cannon Roaring muskets Cracking Drums Beating Bombs flying all round; men a dying wounded's Horred Grones which would Greave the Heardest of Hearts to See Such a Sorriful Sight as this to see our Fellow Creators Slain in Such a manner as this.

The Americans fled in disorder. They had suffered a thousand casualties and the British only half that number. Within the next few days, Washington withdrew most of his army north of Philadelphia across the Schuylkill River. He left a small detachment commanded by Anthony Wayne at Paoli, where at midnight on September 21, it was surprised by three battalions commanded by British Major General Charles Grey.

The Paoli massacre

The Paoli massacre, as it became known, was described by Major Samuel Hay, an eyewitness, as a "scene of butchery," unsurpassed in the annals of the age. All was confusion. The several British accounts of the night attack, which caught Wayne's men asleep around their campfires, seem to have been derived from the first-hand story recorded by Major John André:

> No soldier was suffered to load; those who could not draw their pieces took out the flints. We knew nearly the spot where the Rebel corps lay, but nothing of the disposition of their camp. It was represented to the men that firing discovered us to the enemy, hid them from us, killed our friends and produced a confusion favorable to the escape of the Rebels and perhaps productive of disgrace to ourselves. On the other hand, by not firing we knew the foe to be wherever fire appeared and a charge ensured his destruction; that amongst the enemy those in the rear would direct their fire against whoever fired in front, and they would destroy each other.
>
> General Grey's detachment marched by the road leading to the White Horse (tavern) and took every inhabitant with them as they passed along. About three miles from camp they turned to the left and proceeded to the Admiral Warren (tavern), where, having forced intelligence from a blacksmith, they came in upon the out sentries, pickets, and camp of the Rebels. The sentries fired and ran off to the number of four at different intervals. The piquet was surprised and most of them killed in endeavoring to retreat. On approaching the right of the camp we perceived the line of fires, and the Light Infantry being ordered to form to the front, rushed along the line putting to the bayonet all they came up with, and overtaking the main herd of the fugitives, stabbed great numbers and pressed on their rear till it was thought prudent to order them to desist.
>
> Near 200 must have been killed, and a great number wounded. Seventy-one prisoners were brought off; forty of them badly wounded were left at different houses on the road. A major, a captain, and two lieutenants were amongst the prisoners. We lost Captain Wolfe killed and one or two private men; four or five were wounded, one an officer, Lieut. Hunter of the 52d Light Company.
>
> It was about one o'clock in the morning when the attack was made, and the Rebels were then assembling to move towards us, with the design of attacking our baggage.

"A dreadful scene of havoc"

An unknown British officer, whose MSS journal was later captured by Americans, described the final stage of the attack:

> We then saw their wigwams, or huts, partly by almost extinguished light of their fires and partly by the light of a few stars, & the frightened wretched rebels endeavoring to form. We then charged. For two miles we drove them, now and then firing scatteringly from behind trees, fences, &c. The flashes of the pieces had a fine effect in the night—then followed a dreadful scene of havoc. The light dragoons came on, sword in hand. The shrieks, groans, shouting, imprecations, deprecations, the clashing of swords and bayonets, &c. &c. (no firing from us & little from them except now and then—a few as I said before, scattering shots) were more expressive of horror than is the thunder of artillery, &c. on the day of action.

A Hessian sergeant, boasting of his exploits that night, recalled "we killed three hundred of the rebels with the bayonet. I stuck them myself like so many pigs, one after another, until the blood ran out of the touch-hole of my musket."

Samuel Hay escaped and returned the next day:

> The 22d I went to the ground to see the wounded. The scene was shocking—the poor men groaning under their wounds, which were all by stabs of bayonets and cuts of Light-Horsemen's swords. Colonel Grier is wounded in the side by a bayonet, superficially slanting to the breast bone. Captain Wilson's stabbed in the side, but not dangerous, and it did not take the guts or belly. He got also a bad stroke on the head with the cock nail of the locks of a musket. Andrew Irvine was run through the fleshy part of the thigh with a bayonet. They are all lying near David Jones' tavern. I left Captain McDowell with them, to dress and take care of them, and they are all in a fair way of recovery. Major La Mar, of the 24th Regiment, was killed, and some other inferior officers. The enemy lost Captain Wolf, killed, and four or five Light-Horsemen, and about 20 privates, besides a number wounded.

"Cold-blooded cruelty"

Robert Morton, a fifteen-year-old resident of Philadelphia, who had begun to keep a diary, described the Paoli massacre as "British barbarity" and "cold-blooded cruelty."

Chad's house

GERMANTOWN

Cheered from the rooftops by the royalist sympathizers, Lord Cornwallis marched through Philadelphia on September 25, 1777. Leaving 3,000 soldiers in the city, Howe advanced seven miles to Germantown with the bulk of his army of 9,000 men. He encamped north of the Schuylkill River, but did not fortify his position. Washington decided that the opportunity to take the British by surprise was too good to miss. He planned an attack by three columns at dawn following a night march. The feasibility of this strategy was doubted by his adjutant, Colonel Timothy Pickering:

> This disposition appears to have been well made; but to execute such a plan requires great exactness in the officers conducting the columns, as well as punctuality in commencing the march, to bring the whole to the point of action at once; and for this end it is absolutely necessary that the length and quality of the roads be perfectly ascertained, the time it will take to march them accurately calculated, and guides chosen who are perfectly acquainted with the roads. It is also necessary to assign proper halting places, if either column would arrive before the appointed hour.

Writing up his journal on October 3, Pickering described the dispositions:

> The troops were got ready for marching, it being intended to make an attack upon the enemy the next morning. In the evening, about eight o'clock, the troops were on the march, in the following disposition: General Sullivan, commanding the right wing, was to move down, with his and Wayne's divisions, on the direct road to Germantown, preceded by Conway's brigade, which was to take off the enemy's picket, file off to the right, and fall upon the enemy's left flank and rear, while Sullivan's and Wayne's divisions attacked them in front. Maxwell's and the North Carolina brigades were to form a second line in rear of Sullivan and Wayne. General Greene, with the left wing, was to move down the North Wales road to attack the enemy's right, the front line of this wing being composed of Greene's and McDougall's divisions, and the second line, of Stephen's; while Smallwood, with his Maryland, and Forman, with his Jersey militia, were to attack them on their right flank and rear. At the same time General Armstrong, with his division of Pennsylvania militia, was to move down the old Egypt or Schuylkill road, and take off a Hessian picket posted there, and attack the enemy's left wing and rear. The attack was to begin upon every quarter at five in the morning.

Marching through the night on roads separated by rough country, the columns lost contact with other units. The guide on the left wing mistook the way and the right wing attacked the enemy too soon. The first Sir William Howe knew of "Washington marching against us, was by his attacking us at daybreak," stated Lieutenant Martin Hunter, who was on picket duty at Biggenstown:

> General Wayne commanded the advance, and expected to be fully revenged for the surprise that we had given him. When the first shots were fired at our pickets, so much had we all Wayne's affair in remembrance, that the battalion was out and under arms in a minute. At this time the day was just broke; but it was a very foggy morning, and so dark that we could not see a hundred yards before us. Just as the battalion had formed, the pickets came in and said that the enemy were advancing in force.
>
> They had hardly joined the battalion when we heard a loud cry of, "Have at the bloodhounds; revenge Wayne's affair!" and they immediately fired a volley. We gave them one in re-

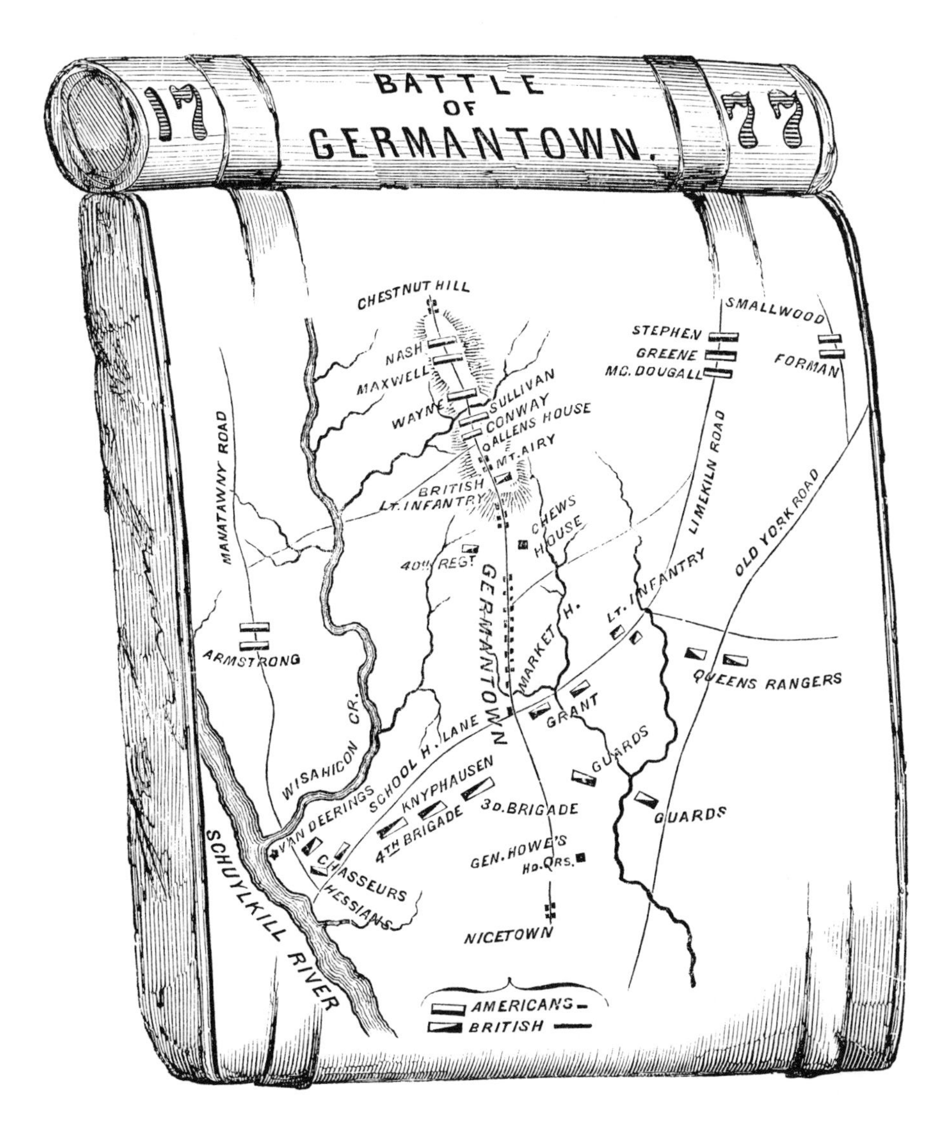

Market square and church in Germantown

turn, cheered, and charged. As it was near the end of the campaign, it was very weak. It did not consist of more than three hundred men, and we had no support nearer than Germantown, a mile in our rear. On our charging they gave way on all sides, but again and again renewed the attack with fresh troops and greater force. We charged them twice, till the battalion was so reduced by killed and wounded, that the bugle was sounded to retreat; indeed, had we not retreated at the very time we did, we should have all been taken or killed, as nearly two columns of the enemy had nearly got around our flank. But this was the first time we had retreated before the Americans, and it was with great difficulty we could get our men to obey our orders.

The enemy were kept so long in check that the two brigades had advanced to the entrance of Biggenstown, when they met our battalion retreating. By this time General Howe had come up, and seeing the battalion retreating, all broken, he got into a passion and exclaimed, "For shame, light infantry! I never saw you retreat before. Form! Form! It's only a scouting party." However, he was soon convinced it was more than a scouting party, as the heads of the enemy columns soon appeared. One coming through Biggenstown, with three pieces of cannon in their front, immediately fired at the crowd that was standing with General Howe under a large chestnut tree. I think I never saw people enjoy a discharge of grape before, but we really all felt pleased to see the enemy make such an appearance, and to hear the grape rattle about the Commander-in-Chief's ears, after he had accused the battalion of having run away from a scouting party. He rode off immediately full speed, and we joined the two brigades that were now formed a little way in our rear; but it was not possible for them to make any stand against Washington's whole army, and they all retreated to Germantown, except Colonel Musgrave, who, with the 40th Regiment, nobly defended Chew's house till we were reinforced from Philadelphia.

So far the action had gone well for the Americans; the British had retreated, leaving a pocket of resistance in the enemy's rear.

The Chew house in Germantown, a British bulwark

Colonel Pickering rode up with General Washington who came to investigate the firing. "I am afraid General Sullivan is throwing away his ammunition," the General remarked. He ordered his adjutant to "ride forward and tell him to preserve it." Pickering had no idea that some of the enemy were to his rear until he learned it from the whizzing of musket shells. Turning his eyes to the right he saw the blaze of muskets from the windows of a large stone house standing back about a hundred yards from the road. "This house of Chew's was a strong stone building and exceedingly commodious, having windows on every side, so that you could not approach it without being exposed to a severe fire; which, in fact, was well directed and killed and wounded a great many of our officers and men."

The Hessian officer, Captain Frederick Ernest von Munchhausen, who reached the scene at this time, praised Colonel Musgrave's "well planned and boldly executed movement," which delayed the Americans who "took so much time in waiting for guns with which to drive him out."

Washington, it seems, was persuaded by Colonel Knox, his chief artilleryman, to batter down the house by cannon fire, and thereby valuable time was lost.

Pickering came upon some American artillery who were firing very obliquely on the front of the house:

> I remarked to them, that in that position their fire would be unavailing, and that the only chance of their shot making any impression on the house would be by moving down and firing directly on its front.
>
> Then immediately passing on, I rejoined General Washington who, with General Knox and other officers, was in front of a stone house (nearly all the houses in Germantown were of stone), next northward of the open field in which Chew's house stood. I found they were discussing, in Washington's presence, this question: whether the whole of our troops then behind should immediately advance, regardless of the enemy in Chew's house, or first summon them to surrender. General Knox strenuously urged the sending of a summons. Among other things he said, "It would be unmilitary to leave a castle in our rear." I answered, "Doubtless that is a correct general maxim, but it does not apply in this case. We know the extent of this castle (Chew's house), and to guard against the danger from the enemy sallying and falling on the rear of our troops, a small regiment may be posted there to watch them, and if they sally, such a regiment will take care of them. But to summon them to surrender will be useless. We are now in the midst of battle, and its issue is unknown. In this state of uncertainty, and so well secured as the enemy find themselves, they will not regard a summons—they will fire on your flag." However, a flag was sent with a summons. Lieutenant Smith of Virginia, my assistant in the office of adjutant general, volunteered his service to carry it. As he was advancing, a shot from the house gave him a wound of which he died. When poor Smith was brought off wounded, Major Gibbs, who was in the General's family, (i.e. staff), said to me, "While you were absent, I offered to carry the flag; and bless my stars that it was not accepted."

We hear of Colonel Musgrave's defense of the house from an unknown British officer who seems to have been present:

> The light infantry defended themselves for some time with great spirit, but the fog was so thick that they could not distinguish what was opposed to them. The 40th Regiment came to their support, and they together, by well timed and heavy discharges, contrived to advance a great way upon the enemy, who retired, not being aware of the small party that attacked them. However, no reinforcement appearing, and the light infantry ammunition being almost expended, Colonel Musgrave, who commanded the 40th Regiment and had been sparing of his ammunition, told the light infantry that he would cover their retreat,

The Chew house in Germantown where the British held off the attack of the Americans

which he did in a most masterly manner, till he arrived at his old encampment.

The light infantry were by this time secure, but the rebels were in the encampment of the 40th Regiment, and Colonel Musgrave found himself entirely surrounded, and all means of retreating cut off. Without being embarrassed, he immediately ordered his regiment to get into a large stone house (which had been his quarters) with the greatest expedition possible, but the rebels pressed so close upon their heels, that they must inevitably have entered the house at the same time, if he had not faced the regiment about and given them a fire which checked them enough for him to have time to get his regiment into the house and shut the door.

Musgrave ordered all the window shutters of the ground floor to be shut, as the enemy's fire would otherwise have been too heavy there. He placed, however, a certain number of men at each window, and at the hall doors, with orders to bayonet everyone who should attempt to come in. He disposed of the rest in the two upper stories, and instructed them to cover themselves, and direct their fire out of the window. He then told them "their only safety was in the defence of that house; that if they let the enemy get into it, they would undoubtedly every man be put to death; that it would be an absurdity for anyone to think of giving himself up with hopes of quarter; that their situation was nevertheless by no means a bad one, as there had been instances of only a few men defending a house against numbers; that he had no doubt of their being supported and delivered by our army; but that at all events they must sell themselves as dear as possible to the enemy."

FROM A WATER-COLOR SKETCH BY KAY SMITH

Cliveden, the Chew House. More than 200 years old, this historic estate in Germantown, Pennsylvania, was a focal point in the Battle of Germantown, October 4, 1777, when it was used by the British troops as a headquarters in which they barricaded themselves and succeeded in turning back a contingent of 3000 American soldiers led by General Washington.

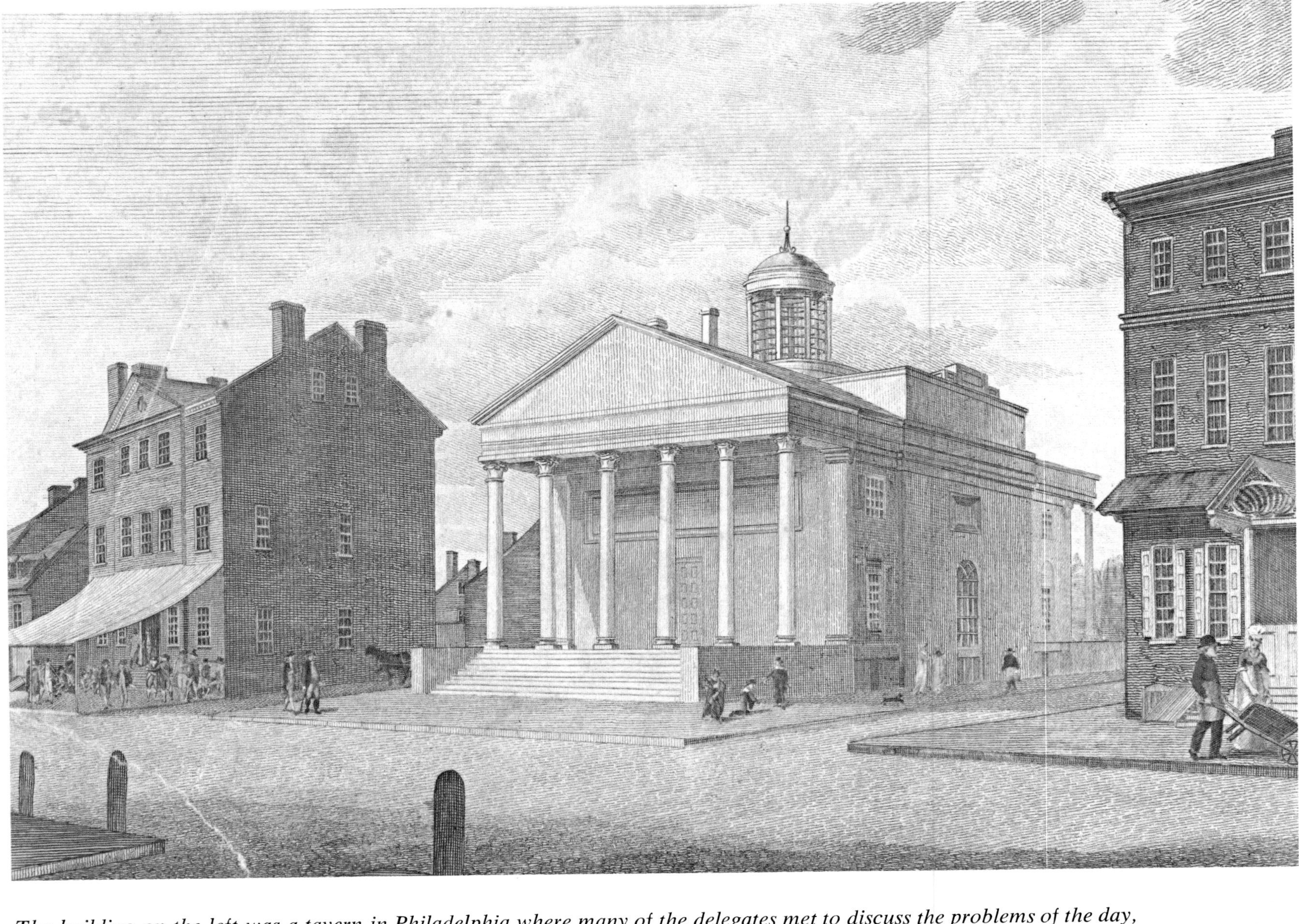

The building on the left was a tavern in Philadelphia where many of the delegates met to discuss the problems of the day, including the questions related to drafting the Declaration of Independence. This scene from a W. Birch & Son print shows Philadelphia as it appeared about 1800. The impressive building in the middle is the Bank of Pennsylvania, which was on South Second Street.

> By this time the rebels had brought up four pieces of cannon (three-pounders) against the house, and with the first shot they burst open the hall doors, and wounded some men with the pieces of stone that flew from the wall. Captain Hains, a brave intelligent officer, who commanded on the ground floor, reported to Colonel Musgrave what had happened, and that he had thrown chairs, tables and any little impediments he could before the door, and that he would endeavor to keep the enemy out as long as he had a single man left. He was very soon put to the test, for the rebels directed their cannon (sometimes loaded with round, sometimes with grape shot) entirely against the upper stories, and sent some of the most daring fellows from the best troops they had, to force their way into the house under cover of their artillery. To do them justice, they attacked with great intrepidity, but were received with no less firmness. The fire from the upper windows was well directed and continued. The rebels, nevertheless, advanced and several of them were killed with bayonets getting in at the windows and upon the steps, attempting to force their way in at the door.

The house, stated American General John Armstrong, who described the engagement in a letter he wrote five days later to Horatio Gates, "proved too strong for the metal of our field-pieces." The delay to storm the house was ill judged, he thought, for it impeded the troops in their pursuit of the enemy, who, other than at Chew's house, had retreated before the American advance.

The attack on Chew's house had drawn the attention of ten times the number of men who should have been sufficient to occupy its small garrison. What then happened has never been exactly decided. After some artillery had been brought to play upon opposite sides of the house, stated William Heth, a Continental officer, "each party took the other for the enemy," whereby he meant that, in the heavy fog and smoke, some American troops fired upon their comrades. Attempting to assess where the fault lay, General Armstrong conjectured, "The morning was foggy and so far unfavorable. It's said ours took the maneuvers of part of our own people for large reinforcements of the enemy and thereby took fright at themselves or at one another. Some unhappy officer is said to have called out, 'We are surrounded, we are surrounded!'"

A surprise retreat

The firing ceased, said Pickering and "soon the enemy advanced, and our troops gave way on all sides and retired with precipitation." The retreat surprised everybody for all "supposed victory was nearly secured in our favor." He attributed the disaster chiefly to "the fog and smoke, which, from the stillness of the air, remained a long time, hanging low and undissipated. But, on the other hand, it must be remembered that the fog blinded the enemy as well as ourselves, though it certainly injured us most."

Thomas Paine

Heth thought, "The heavy smoke, added to a thick fog, was of vast injury to us. It undoubtedly increased the fear of some to fancy themselves flanked and surrounded, which like an electrical shock seized some thousands, who fled in confusion, without the appearance of an enemy."

General Armstrong said that having driven the enemy back for a space of two miles, "some unhappy spirit of insubordination seized our troops almost universally whereby they began to retreat and fled in wild disorder—that is, without any orders from the command. Thus, a victory—a glorious victory fought for and eight-tenths won—was mysteriously lost, for to this moment no one man can, or at least will, give any good reason for the flight."

Thomas Paine, a witness

Thomas Paine witnessed the retreat, which he described six months later in a letter to Benjamin Franklin: "I never could and cannot now learn, and I believe no man can inform truly the cause of that day's miscarriage. The retreat was extraordinary. Nobody hurried themselves. Everyone marched at his own pace."

The true answer is not difficult to assess. Washington had attempted too much. His soldiers were tired, and they lacked the experience for a dawn attack, at the end of a long night march. Instead of following their appointed routes, the two wings converged at Chew's house, delayed too long, and became confused in the fog and smoke. Washington felt that the miscarriage of his plan was "rather more unfortunate than injurious." He had lost more than a thousand men, and the British half that number. American Colonel Heth took an optimistic view: "Though we gave away a complete victory, we have learned this valuable truth: to beat them by vigorous exertion, and that we are far superior in respect to swiftness. We are in high spirits. Every action of our troops reflects fresh vigor and a greater opinion of their own strength."

Next day, young Robert Morton rode out to inspect the scene of the action, in order, if possible, to secure a true account. The Americans, he heard, came up to the windows of Chew's house, "with unusual firmness." It was too strongly barricaded to enter. "One of the Americans went up to a window on the north side of the house to set fire to it, and just as he was putting the torch to the window he rec'd a Bayonet thro' his mouth, which put an end to his existence."

Dismissal for cause

Following the engagement, Colonel Adam Stephen was charged with being drunk, having fired upon Anthony Wayne's men, and ordering a retreat, and he was dismissed from the army.

Following the battle, Howe withdrew his army to Philadelphia. He could not settle there for the winter until he had cleared the Delaware River of the obstructions the Americans had created to block the channel. He also needed to capture two forts which prevented him from bringing up his transports and store-ships. The Americans had sunk sharp-pointed wooden stakes across the channel at Billingsport and had constructed similar chevaux-de-frise between Forts Mercer, on the Jersey shore, and Mifflin on the Pennsylvania side. The former was held by the Rhode Island Colonel Christopher Greene, and the latter by Colonel Simeon Thayer, who had with him the French artilleryman, the Vicomte de Fleury. A number of American vessels were anchored higher up the river.

Joseph Plumb Martin joined in the defense of Fort Mercer. He had missed the battle of Brandywine, and his company had not become engaged at Germantown. Soon after that affair, the Continental regiments were ordered to march to the Delaware forts. As usual, Martin was cold and hungry, and he and his companions marched until they could proceed no further:

> We halted about one o'clock at night, in a village and were put into houses of the inhabitants, much, I suppose, to their contentment, especially at that time of night. Sleep took such strong hold of me and most of the others, that we soon forgot our wants. Not so with some five or six of our company, who were determined not to die of hunger that night, if any means could be devised to prevent it. They, therefore, as soon as all was still, sallied out on an expedition. They could not find anything eatable but the contents of a beehive, which they took the liberty to remove from the beehouse to a place which they thought more convenient. I had no hand in the battle and consequently no share in the spoil. One man who belonged to this foraging party had rather an uncouth visage; he had very thick lips, especially the upper one, a large flat nose, and quite a wide mouth, which gave him, as the Irishman said, really an open countenance. One of the inhabitants of the city he had helped to sack, not quite forgetting his resentment for the ill-usage he had received from this paragon of beauty and his associates in the outrage, gave him a severe wound directly in the middle of the upper lip, which added very much to its dimensions. In the morning, when we came to march off, O, the woeful figure the poor fellow exhibited! A minister in his pulpit would have found it difficult to have kept his inclination to laugh in due subjection. To see him on the parade endeavoring to conceal his face from the men, and especially from the officers, was ludicrous in the extreme, and as long as it lasted it diverted our thoughts from resting on our own calamities.

"Sally forth and endeavor to procure something by foraging."

Martin crossed the Delaware to New Jersey, halting for the night at Burlington, where he procured some carrion beef. On the next night he had nothing to eat, which led him and his companions to contrive how they might get what he termed "belly-timber."

> At length, after several plans had been devised, many "resolves proposed and all refused a passage," it was finally determined

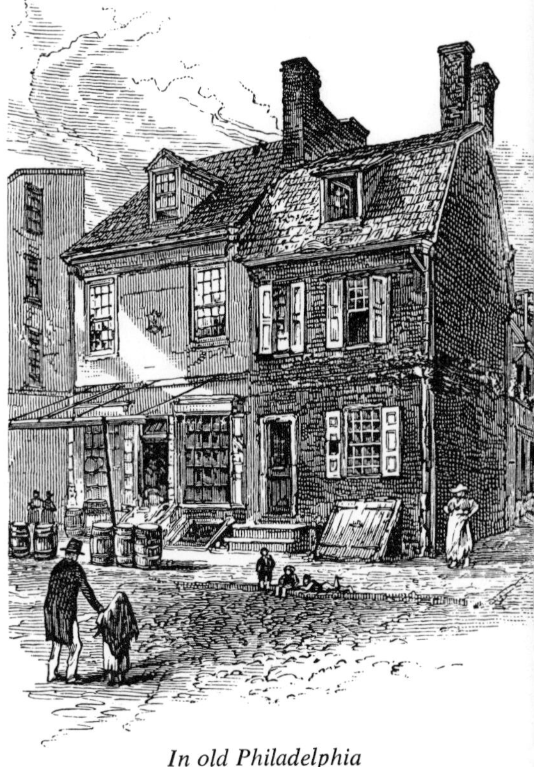

In old Philadelphia

that two or three of the most expert at the business should sally forth and endeavor to procure something by foraging. Accordingly, two of the club went out and shortly after returned with a Hissian, a cant word with the soldiers for a goose. The next difficulty was how to pluck it; we were in a chamber and had nothing to contain the feathers. However, we concluded at last to pick her over the fire and let that take care of the feathers. We dressed her and then divided her amongst us. If I remember rightly, I got *one wing*. Each one broiled his share and ate it, as usual without bread or salt. After this sumptuous repast, I lay down and slept as well as a gnawing stomach would permit. In the morning we found a sad witness to our overnight's adventure to testify against us; the whole funnel of the chimney was stuck full of feathers from top to bottom, and it being a very calm night the street opposite the house was as full of them as the chimney. We would have set the chimney on fire, but having nothing to do it with, we concluded to let the chimney and street unite in their testimony against us if they pleased; but as we marched off early in the morning we heard no more about the goose.

Fort Mercer had already been attacked by a force of 2,000 Hessians. The assault, which was led by Colonel Carl von Donop, ended in failure, and his capture and death. According to Martin, Donop had begged the favor of the command for "the privilege of cutting the throats of about five hundred brave Rhode Island Yankees." Their Colonel, a cousin of General Nathanael Greene, so overwhelmed the enemy that "they threw their cannon into a creek, left their provisions behind and fled for their lives." The garrison lost 24 men, killed and wounded. Colonel William Bradford told a more circumstantial story:

The 22d instant about four o'clock, the enemy to the number of about 1,500 appeared before the fort at Red Bank, and immediately began a most furious cannonade, for about 15 minutes, when they rushed on with great resolution to storm the fort, and got into the upper part of the old works which were not finished, and gave three cheers, thinking all was their own, but were received so warmly that they were glad to get out. They endeavored to force thro' the abatis that were before the fort, and some even got over the ditch and were killed within the pickets; after about 40 minutes action they took to their heels and ran off with great precipitation.

"Enough hardship to kill half a dozen horses"

Martin entered Fort Mifflin, situated on Mud Island. Here, he recalled, he "endured enough hardship to kill half a dozen horses."

Let the reader only consider for a moment and he will be satisfied if not sickened. In the cold month of November, without provisions, without clothing, not a scrap of either shoes or stockings to my feet or legs, and in this condition to endure a siege, in such a place as that, was appalling in the highest degree.

In confirmation of what I have here said, I will give the reader a short description of the pen that I was confined in. Confined I was, for it was next to impossible to have got away from it, if I had been so disposed. Well, the island, as it is called, is nothing more than a mud flat in the Delaware, lying upon the west side of the channel. It is diked around the fort, with sluices so constructed that the fort can be laid under water at pleasure, (at least, it *was* so when I was there, and I presume it has not grown much higher since). On the eastern side, next the main river, was a zig-zag wall built of hewn stone, built, as I was informed, before the Revolution at the king's cost. At the southeastern part of the fortification (for fort it could not with propriety be called) was a battery of several long eighteen-pounders. At the southwestern angle was another battery with four or five twelve and eighteen-pounders and one thirty-two pounder. At the northwestern corner was another small battery with three twelve-pounders. There were also three blockhouses in different parts of the enclosure, but no cannon mounted upon them, nor were they of any use whatever to us while I was there. On the western side, between the batteries, was a high embankment, within which was a tier of palisades. In front of the stone wall, for about half its length, was another embankment, with palisades on the inside of it, and a narrow ditch between them and the stone wall. On the western side of the fortification was a row of barracks, extending from the northern part of the works to about half the length of the fort. On the northern end was another block of barracks which reached nearly across the fort from east to west. In front of these was a large square two-story house, for the accommodation of the officers of the garrison. Neither this house nor the barracks were of much use at this time, for it was as much as a man's life was worth to enter them, the enemy often directing their shot at them in particular. In front of the barracks and other necessary places were parades and walks; the rest of the ground was soft mud. I have seen the enemy's shells fall upon it and sink so low that their report could not be heard when they burst, and I could only feel a tremulous motion of the earth at the time. At other times, when they burst near the surface of the ground, they would throw the mud fifty feet in the air.

The British brought up several warships and erected land batteries from which they shelled the fort incessantly. The garrison replied, firing one 18-pounder, striking and blowing up the *Augusta*, a vessel mounting 64 guns, which Colonel Bradford found a "glorious sight."

An early farm in Germantown

Day by day the British guns leveled the American fortifications; the garrison repaired them at night. De Fleury, the engineer in the fort, Martin described as "an austere man who kept us constantly employed day and night; there was no chance of escaping his vigilance."

De Fleury also kept a journal. On November 10 he wrote: "It is probable that the enemy will undertake to carry this place by storm." Late that night he added, "Our garrison diminishes, our soldiers are overwhelmed with fatigue—they spend nights in watching and labor without doing much on account of their weakness."

The eastern side of the surrounding wall was the only place Martin could find safety from the flying splinters broken off the palisades by the enemy's shot:

> We would watch an opportunity to escape from the vigilance of Colonel Fleury, and run into this place for a minute or two's respite from fatigue and cold. When the engineer found that the workmen began to grow scarce, he would come to the entrance and call us out. He had always his cane in his hand, and woe betide him he could get a stroke at. At his approach I always jumped over the ditch and ran down on the other side, so that he could not reach me, but he often noticed me and as often threatened me, but threatening was all. He could never get a stroke at me, and I cared but little for his threats.
>
> It was utterly impossible to lie down to get any rest or sleep on account of the mud, if the enemy's shot would have suffered us to do. Sometimes some of the men, when overcome with fatigue and want of sleep, would slip away into the barracks to catch a nap of sleep, but it seldom happened that they all came out again alive. I was in this place a fortnight and can say in sincerity that I never lay down to sleep a minute in all that time.

"The grapeshot came down like a shower of hail."

The British gunners, said Martin, learned about this "place of safety." Knowing that they could not reach behind the wall, they fired elevated grape-shot. When the sentries cried "Shot," seeing no missile, the soldiers became careless. "The grapeshot came down like a shower of hail about our ears."

The garrison, stated Martin, possessed no shot for their 32-pounder, and were unable to retaliate against the equivalent caliber gun the British had mounted. It was so fixed as to rake the parade in front of the barracks, the only place the garrison could pass up and down the fort:

> The artillery officers offered a gill of rum for each shot fired from that piece, which the soldiers would procure. I have seen from twenty to fifty men standing on the parade waiting with impatience the coming of the shot, which would often be seized before its motion had fully ceased and conveyed off to our gun to be sent back again to its former owners. When the lucky fellow who had caught it had swallowed his rum, he would return to wait for another, exulting that he had been more lucky or more dexterous than his fellows.

On November 14, at dawn, a number of warships, including six "64's," came to attack the fort, which de Fleury claimed could not be taken by fire alone. "It may kill us men, but this is the fortune of war. And all their bullets will not render them masters of the island, if we have courage enough to remain on it." The ruins were the garrison's breastwork, and they would defend the ground inch by inch. The enemy would pay dearly for every step gained, he asserted. "Our blockhouses are in a pitiful condition, but with fascines I hope to cover two pieces in each lower story which will be sufficient to flank us, I say again the enemy's fire will not take our fort, If they attempt to storm we shall still have a little parapet to oppose to them, but we must have men to defend it."

The British soon began firing, recorded Martin, who expected them to land under the fire of their cannon and attempt to storm the fort:

> Some of our officers endeavored to ascertain how many guns were fired in a minute by the enemy, but it was impossible; the fire was incessant. In the height of the cannonade it was desirable to hoist a signal flag for some of our galleys that were lying above us to come down to our assistance. The officers inquired who would undertake it. As none appeared willing for some time, I was about to offer my services. I considered it no more exposure of my life than it was to remain where I was. The flagstaff was of easy ascent, being an old ship's mast, having shrouds to the ground, and the round top still remaining, While I was hesitating, a sergeant of the artillery offered himself. He accordingly ascended to the round top, pulled down the flag to affix the signal flag to the halyard, upon which the enemy, thinking we had struck, ceased firing in every direction and cheered. "Up with the flag!" was the cry of our officers in every part of the fort. The flags were accordingly hoisted, and the firing was immediately renewed. The sergeant then came down and had not gone half a rod from the foot of the staff when he was cut in two by a cannon shot. This caused me some serious reflections at the time. He was killed!

"If I had been at the same business, I might have been killed instead," reflected Martin. But it had been decided otherwise by Divine Providence. "The enemy's shot cut us up. I saw five artillerists belonging to one gun cut down by a single shot, and I saw men who were stooping to be protected by the works, but not stooping low enough, split like fish to be broiled."

The cannonade continued all day, and every gun in the fort was silenced. The men were cut up like cornstacks. Even the courageous de Fleury despaired. With the embrasures and blockhouses battered to the ground:

> We are not secured against storm. If the enemy attempt it, I fear they will succeed in penetrating a circumference of 1,200 paces defended only by 450 men and half ruined palisades. A boat which this day deserted from the fleet will have given the enemy sufficient intimation of our weakness—they will probably attack us or attempt a lodgment on the island which we cannot prevent with our present strength.

Old houses in Philadelphia

To Martin, the fort exhibited a picture of desolation:

The whole area of the fort was as completely ploughed as a field. The buildings of every kind hanging in broken fragments, and the guns all dismounted, and how many of the garrison sent to the world of spirits, I knew not. If ever destruction was complete, it was here.

Major de Fleury was wounded by a piece of flying timber; the Lieutenant standing at his side was killed.

"We will give it to the damned rebels in the morning."

Observing British preparations to land a detachment of soldiers, the fort's Commander, Colonel Thayer, decided to evacuate the garrison under cover of night. Martin was one of the last men to leave:

I happened to be left with a party of seventy or eighty men to destroy and burn all that was left in the place. I was in the northwest battery just after dark when the enemy were hauling their shipping on that side higher up to a more commanding position. They were so nigh that I could hear distinctly what they said on board the sloop. One expression of theirs I well remember. "We will give it to the d–d rebels in the morning." The thought that then occupied my mind I as well remember, "The d–d rebels will show you a trick which the devil never will; they will go off and leave you." After the troops had left the fort and were embarking at the wharf, I went to the waterside to find one of my messmates to whom I had lent my canteen in the morning, as there were three or four hogsheads of rum in the fort, the heads of which we were about to knock in, and I was desirous to save a trifle of their contents. There being nothing to eat, I thought I might have something to drink. I found him, indeed, but lying in a long line of dead men who had been brought out of the fort to be conveyed to the main, to have the last honors conferred upon them which it was in our power to give. Poor young man! He was the most intimate associate I had in the army, but he was gone, with many more as deserving of regard as himself.

Before the survivors embarked, the fort was completely in flames, which lit up the water as though it had been broad daylight. Almost the whole enemy fire seemed to be directed at the boat in which Martin escaped:

Sometimes our boat seemed almost thrown out of the water, and at length a shot took the sternpost of the rear boat. We had then to stop and take the men from the crippled boat into the other two, and now the shot and water flew merrily, but by the assistance of a kind Providence we escaped without any further injury and landed, a little after midnight, on the Jersey shore.

"When I awoke I was as crazy as a goose shot through the head."

Martin marched with the others into the pine woods where they found the troops who had reached there earlier:

They had made up some comfortable fires and were enjoying the warmth, and that was all the comfort they had to partake of, except rest, for victuals was out of the question. I wrapped myself up in my blanket and lay down upon the leaves and soon fell asleep and continued so till past noon, when I awoke from the first sound sleep I had had for a fortnight. Indeed, I had not laid down in all that time. The little sleep I had obtained was in cat naps, sitting up and leaning against the wall, and I thought myself fortunate if I could do that much. When I awoke I was as crazy as a goose shot through the head.

Martin ended his story of the defense of Fort Mifflin with an amusing anecdote:

We left one man in the fort who had taken too large a dose of "the good creature." He was a deserter from the German forces in the British service. The British took him to Philadelphia, where, not being known by them, he engaged again in their service, received two or three guineas bounty, drew a British uniform, and came back to us again at Valley Forge.

Some months later, Martin read Tom Paine's comment on the defense of the fort: "They had nothing but their bravery and good conduct to cover them." Probably he did not hear of Ambrose Serle's statement: "They certainly defended it with a spirit they have shown nowhere else to an equal degree during the war."

The evacuation of Fort Mifflin caused the Americans to abandon Fort Mercer. With the Delaware open, Howe settled his army in winter quarters within Philadelphia. Washington withdrew his army twenty miles away to Valley Forge.

Explanation of the Map.—This shows the main operations upon the Delaware between the middle of October and the close of November, 1777. Fort Mifflin is seen on the lower end of Mud Island. A, B, two British transports; C, the *Experiment;* D, the *Vigilant* frigate; E, the Fury sloop; F, a passage opened through the stockadoes at Billingsport; G, American fleet burned at Gloucester; H, the village of Woodbury and Cornwallis's encampment on the 21st of November, 1777; I, camp on the 24th, between the branches of Timber Creek; J, a battery of two eighteen pounders and two nine pounders; K, fort at Billingsport, Colonel Stirling's corps, and Cornwallis's camp on the 18th of November; L, redoubt on Carpenter's Island; M, on Province Island, to cover the bridge in the direction of Philadelphia; N, a battery of six twenty-four pounders, one eight-inch howitzer, and one eight-inch mortar; O, a battery with one eight-inch howitzer and one eight-inch mortar; P, a battery with one thirteen-inch mortar; *n,* two twelve pounders; *o,* one eighteen pounder; S, stockadoes in the channel in front of Fort Mifflin; *a,* a small vessel; *b,* wreck of the *Merlin; c,* the *Liverpool; d, Cornwallis* galley; *e,* the *Pearl; f,* the *Somerset; g,* the *Roebuck; h,* wreck of the *Augusta; i,* the *Iris; j,* ship sunk; *k,* the *Vigilant; l,* the *Fury;* W, the Whitall house, just below Fort Mercer. The parallelograms around Fort Mercer denote the attack by Donop, on the 22d of October. The small island between Red Bank Island and the Jersey shore is Woodbury Island, on which the Americans erected a small battery. The creek, just below Fort Mercer, is Woodbury Creek, a deep and sluggish stream near the Delaware.

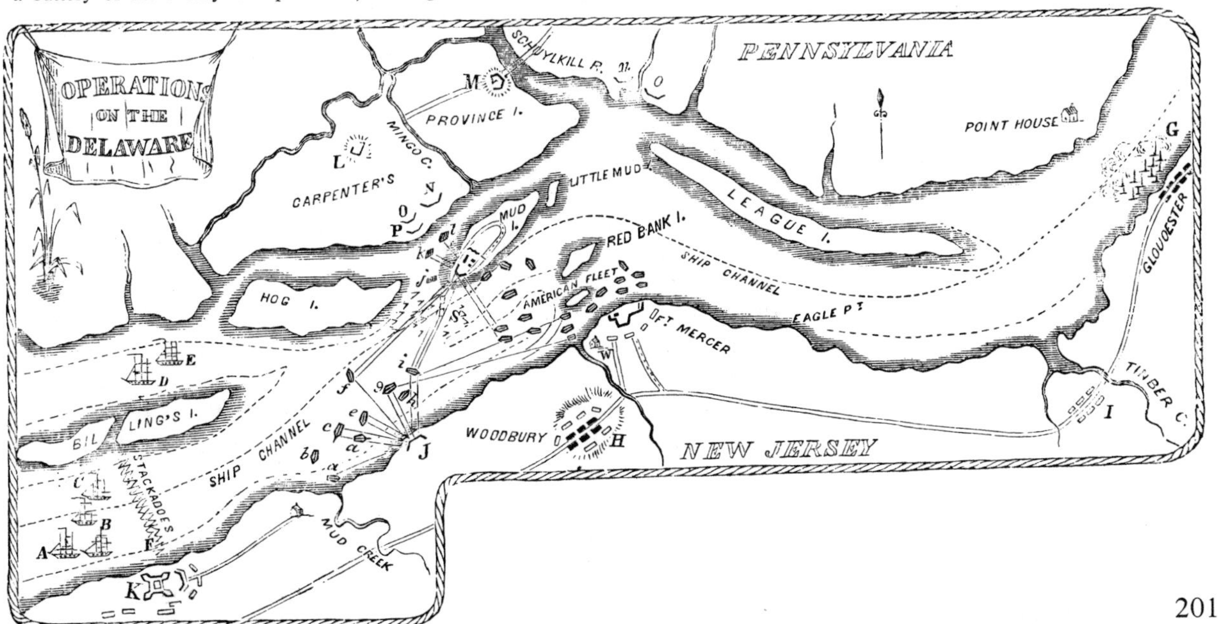

Christ Church, where many American patriots worshiped

PHILADELPHIA

Howe had captured the rebel capital, a place of no strategic importance. He had failed to bring Washington to decisive battle, and he had failed to support Burgoyne. The British had undertaken a near-impossible task. They were forced to ferry their troops and supplies across 3,000 miles of turbulent ocean, and campaign in a rough, trackless country unsuited to European military tactics. Furthermore, they dared not utterly crush the rebels for that would defeat their purpose, the eventual reconciliation of mother and daughter. To overcome their difficulties, they relied on the support of the loyalists. This proved disappointing. Even in Philadelphia (which had been described to Howe as a "hot-bed of loyalism") the response was meager. Some Quaker women had the audacity to sing the popular ballad lampooning Burgoyne's defeat under the noses of the British soldiers. Others, less patriotic, reveled in the unaccustomed novelty of the gay life. Falling in love with a redcoat was called "scarlet fever." The Quaker belle, Peggy Shippen, of whom we shall hear again, became very friendly with the handsome Major André.

Fashionable social life

Nineteen-year-old Rebecca Franks enjoyed herself, as she told her friend Nancy Pacca, who had fled to Baltimore with her Congressman husband. Rebecca subsequently married her "very smart beau," Colonel Sir Henry Johnson:

> You may see the above is not in my writing. A very smart beau, I assure you wrote it, but not being acquainted with your disposition was afraid to go on.
>
> I expected ere this to have had an answer to the letter I wrote by Betty Tilghman. What is your excuse. I hope 'tis want of opportunity and not inclination.
>
> You can have no idea of the life of continued amusement I live in. I can scarce have a moment to myself. I have stole this while everybody is retired to dress for dinner. I am but just come from under Mr. J. Black's hands and most elegantly am I dressed for a ball this evening at Smith's where they have one every Thursday. You would not know this room 'tis so much improv'd.
>
> I wish to Heaven you were going with us this evening to judge for yourself. I spent Tuesday evening at Sir William Howe's where we had a concert and Dance. I asked his leave to send you a Handkerchief to show the fashions. He very politely gave me permission to send anything you wanted, tho' I

told him you were a Delegate's Lady. I want to get a pair of Buckles for your Brother Joe.

If I can't, tell him to be in the fashion he must get a pair of Harness ones. The Dress is more ridiculous and pretty than anything that ever I saw—great quantity of different colored feathers on the head at a time besides a thousand other things. The Hair dress'd very high in the shape Miss Vining's was the night we returned from Smiths—the Hat we found in your Mother's Closet wou'd be of a proper size. I have an afternoon cap with one wing—tho' I assure you I go less in the fashion than most of the Ladies—not being dress'd without a hoop. B. Bond makes her first appearance tonight at the rooms.

No loss for partners, even I am engaged to seven different gentlemen, for you must know 'tis a fix'd rule never to dance but two dances at a time with the same person. Oh how I wish Mr. P. wou'd let you come in for a week or two—tell him I'll answer for your being let to return. I know you are as fond of a gay life as myself—you'd have an opportunity of raking as much as you choose either at Plays, Balls, Concerts or Assemblys. I've been but three evenings alone since we mov'd to town. I begin now to be almost tired. Tell Mrs. Harrison she has got a gentleman in her house who promises me not to let a single thing in it be hurt and I'm sure he'll keep his word—the family she left in it still remain. I had a long conversation about you the other evening with John Saunders. He is just the same as when you knew him—two or three more of your old acquaintances are in town such as Prideaux & Jock De-Lancy they often ask after you. Is Mrs. White with you? I long to hear all that concerns you. Do pray try to get an opportunity. The clock is now striking four, and Moses is just going out to dinner—quite the Congress hours. Moses wrote to your Mother about her house six weeks ago. Did she get the letter? All your Philadelphia friends well and desire their loves—Mine to all in Maryland.

When you see the Miss Tilghmans, tell them I never hear a new song or piece of music that I don't wish them to hear it. I must go finish dressing as I'm engaged out to tea.

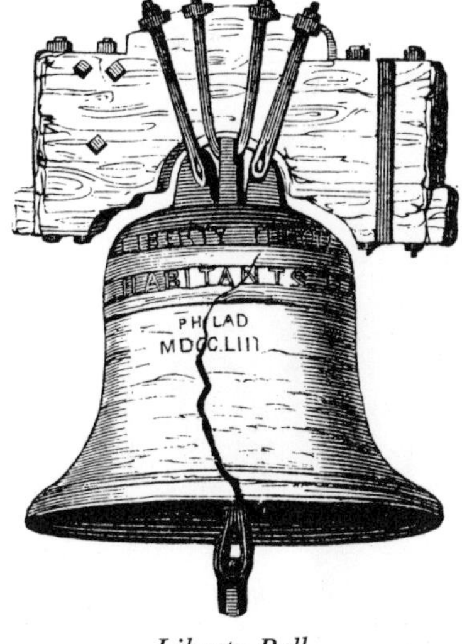

Liberty Bell

Other residents were not above "taking-in" the gullible foreigners. Writing to his family in Germany, the Hessian Captain, John Heinricks, gravely informed them: "Nowhere have I seen so many *mad* people as here. Only yesterday, as I was dining with a Gentleman, a third person came into the room, and he whispered in my ear: *Take care, this gentleman is a madman.* Frequently, the people are cured, but almost all have a quiet madness, a derangement of mind which proceeds from sluggish, not active blood."

The battle of the kegs

Lacking normal means of annoying the British, the patriots again employed David Bushnell's submarine, as the correspondent of the Boston *Continental Journal and Weekly Advertiser* reported (February 19):

This city has lately been entertained with a most astonishing instance of the activity, bravery and military skill of the Royal Navy of Great Britain.

EARLY PHILADELPHIA SCENES

The old court house and Friends' meeting house

High Street prison and marketplace

The Swedes' Church and the residence of Sven Sen

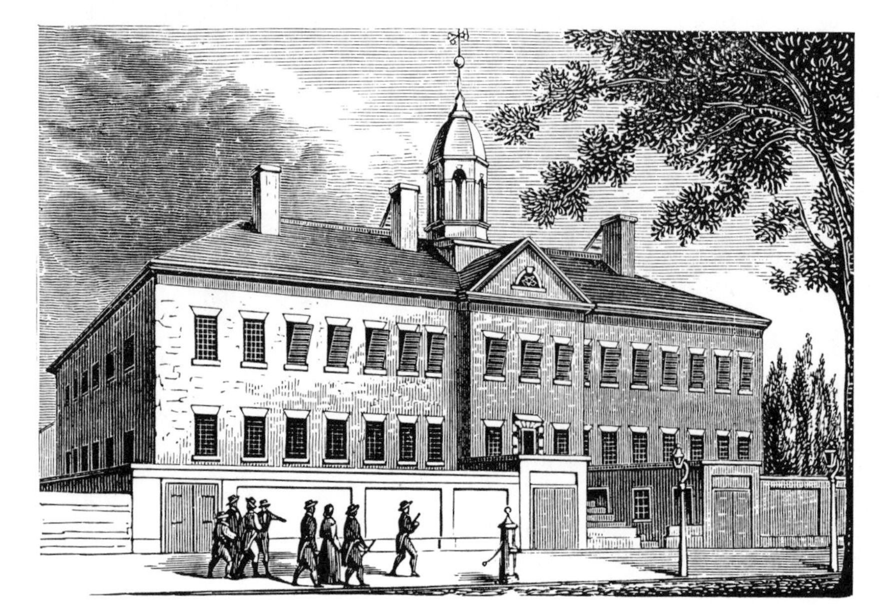

Walnut Street prison

Carpenter's mansion

The Arch Street bridge at Front Street

Friends' Bank meeting house

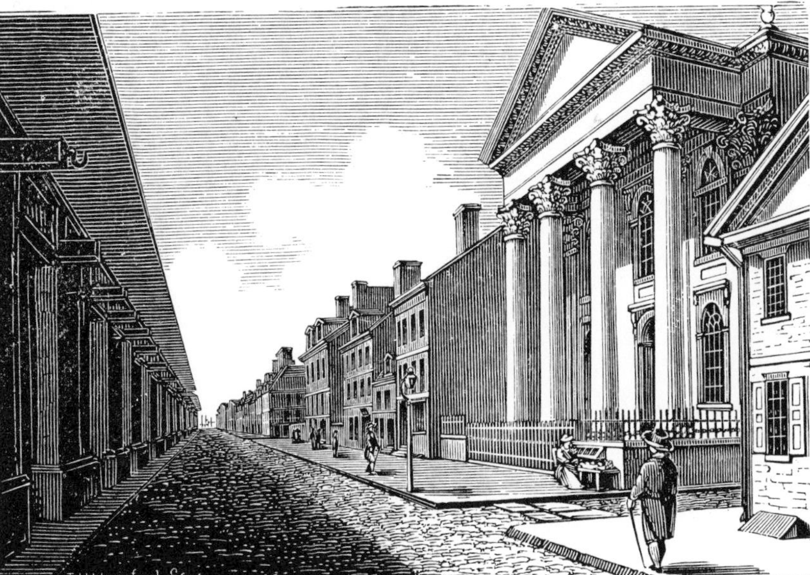

First Presbyterian Church on High Street

Some time last week two boys observed a keg of a singular construction floating in the river opposite to the city. They got into a small boat, and attempting to take up the keg, it burst with a great explosion and blew up the unfortunate boys.

On Monday last several kegs of a like construction made their appearance. An alarm was immediately spread through the city. Various reports prevailed, filling the city and the royal troops with unspeakable consternation. Some reported that these kegs were filled with armed rebels, who were to issue forth in the dead of night, as the Grecians did of old from their wooden horse at the siege of Troy, and take the city by surprise, asserting that they had seen the points of their bayonets through the bung-holes of the kegs. Others said they were charged with the most inveterate combustibles to be kindled by secret machinery and, setting the whole Delaware in flames, were to consume all the shipping in the harbor; whilst others asserted that they were constructed by art magic, would of themselves ascend the wharves in the night time and roll all flaming through the streets of the city, destroying everything in their way.

Be this as it may, certain it is that the shipping in the harbor and all the wharves of the city were fully manned. The battle begun and it was surprising to behold the incessant blaze that was kept up against the enemy, the kegs.

Both officers and men exhibited the most unparalleled skill and bravery on the occasion, whilst the citizens stood gazing as solemn witnesses of their prowess. From the *Roebuck* and other ships of war whole broadsides were poured into the Delaware. In short, not a wandering chip, stick, or drift log befell the vigor of British arms.

Carpenter's Hall in Philadelphia,
where the First Continental Congress met in September 1774
(also shown in color in a sketch by Kay Smith)

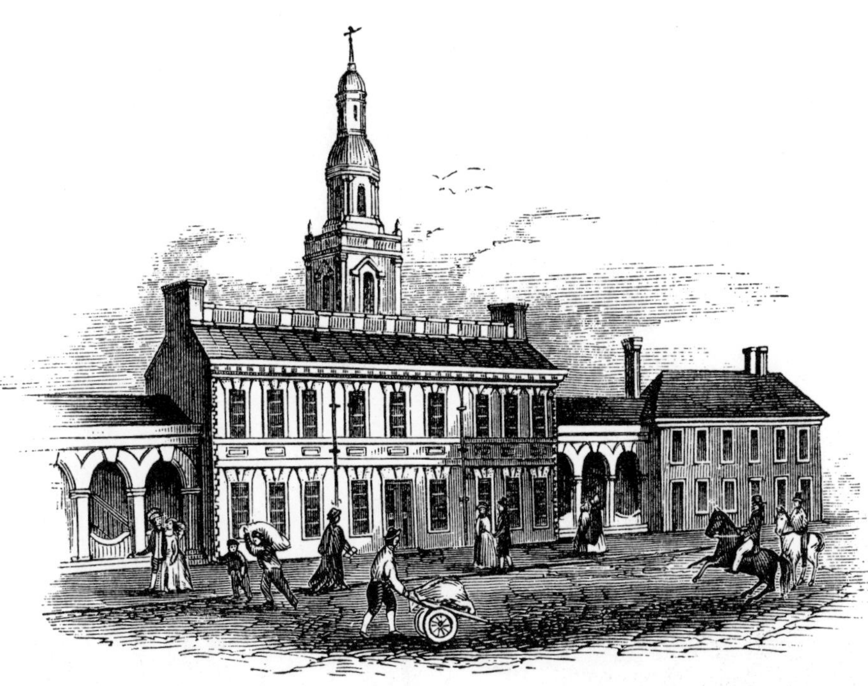

The State House, now known as Independence Hall, as it appeared in 1774

The action begun about sunrise and would have been completed with great success by noon had not an old market woman, coming down the river with provisions, unfortunately let a small keg of butter fall overboard, which (as it was the ebb) floated down to the scene of action. At the sight of this unexpected reinforcement of the enemy, the battle was renewed with fresh fury; the firing was incessant till the evening closed the affair.

The kegs were either totally demolished or obliged to fly, as none of them have shown their *heads* since. It is said his Excellency, Lord Howe has dispatched a swift sailing packet with an account of this victory to the court of London. In a word, Monday, the fifth of January, 1778, must ever be distinguished in history for the memorable BATTLE OF THE KEGS.

Another wit, Francis Hopkinson, lampooned the British in a ballad appropriately entitled *The Battle of the Kegs.* The point of the jibe was reserved for the seventh verse:

Sir William, he, snug as a flea,
Lay all this time a-snoring;
Nor dreamed of harm, as he lay warm
In bed with Mrs. Loring.

Mrs. Loring, or the "Sultana," as she was called, was the wife of the Commissary whom Howe had picked up in New York.

Howe relieved of his command

At his own request Howe was recalled to England, and his place as Commander-in-Chief was taken by Sir Henry Clinton who came to Philadelphia on May 8, 1778. His officers gave Howe a convivial farewell, putting on a pageant which was called the *Mischianza*, an Italian word meaning "medley." It

Sir Henry Clinton, British Commander in Chief who succeeded General Howe

The great Mischianza celebration in Philadelphia

was organized by André, who selected Philadelphia's fourteen prettiest girls to grace the parade. One of the chosen beauties, Peggy Shippen, stayed at home. Her Quaker father disapproved of the flimsy costume she was expected to wear.

The lavish display displeased many of the spectators. The loyalist lady, Mrs. Henry Drinker, called it "folly and vanity" at such a time. She and her friends knew that the British intended to depart and abandon them to their bitter enemies. When the patroits returned, they hanged the Tory who had guided Howe at Brandywine and they staged a mock parade in parody of the *Mischianza*, with a notorious prostitute as its star.

Howe took ship to England where he defended his actions in Parliament.

"A fatal blow to the existence of the army"

Washington was also forced to defend himself against his critics who pointed to his lack of success in striking contrast to Gates's notable victory at Saratoga. A powerful clique had the temerity to suggest that Horatio Gates would make a better Commander-in-Chief. On November 27, Congress appointed the victor of Saratoga, President of the Board of War. Two weeks later it commissioned Thomas Conway, an Irish volunteer and the youngest brigadier in the army, Major General and elevated him to the rank of Inspector General, which

FROM A WATER-COLOR SKETCH BY KAY SMITH

Christ Church, Philadelphia, Pennsylvania, where members of the Continental Congress—including George Washington, Thomas Jefferson, Benjamin Franklin, and many other famous Americans—have worshiped.

Company Street, Valley Forge. Washington put his troops to work building huts to accommodate twelve men— "dimensions 14 by 16 feet, sides, ends and roof made of logs,

FROM A WATER-COLOR PAINTING BY KAY SMITH

the roof made light with split slabs, the sides made tight with clay, the fireplaces made of wood and secured with clay in the inside eighteen inches thick, the fireplace to be in the rear of the hut, the door to be in the end next to the street."

FROM A WATER-COLOR SKETCH BY KAY SMITH

Hospital at Valley Forge. This was the second schoolhouse built in the colonies, and during the long winter of 1777 and 1778 this building was converted to use as a hospital.

Washington called "as unfortunate a measure as was ever adopted," and a "fatal blow to the existence of the army."

Conway, a braggart and an officer of no merit, who was hated by Washington's officers, encouraged Gates's aspirations. Gates, a sycophant and intriguer, referred to Washington as a "weak general." Supported by his officers, Washington scotched the conspiracy, the "Conway Cabal," as it became known, which had weakened the army at its most perilous moment.

Facsimile of a ticket for the Mischianza

Headquarters of Frederick von Steuben at Valley Forge
–From a black and white sketch by Kay Smith

VALLEY FORGE

On December 12, 1777, Washington moved his army across the Schuylkill River to Gulph Mills and Valley Forge, into the "wooded wilderness, a desert," as the German officer, the Baron Johann de Kalb, called it. The village comprised a few scattered houses and a ruined forge. From the river, into which flowed Valley Creek, a densely wooded slope rose to a low hill. It had advantages as a place to winter in, thought the Connecticut surgeon, Albigence Waldo, for there was plenty of wood and water and few families for the soldiers to steal from. The valley was the best winter quarters that could be found, Washington told his troops. Although it lay only twenty-two miles northwest of Philadelphia, it was secure from surprise.

It was already bitterly cold. Waldo was "prodigious sick," and could find no relief for his stomach positively refused to entertain beef, and if he could not obtain beef he would starve:

> Sun Set—We are order'd to march over the River—It snows—I'm Sick—eat nothing—No Whiskey—No Baggage—Lord—Lord—Lord. The Army were 'till Sun Rise crossing the River—some at the Wagon Bridge & some at the Raft Bridge below. Cold & Uncomfortable.

"I am Sick—my feet lame—my legs are sore"

Washington put his men to building huts, "on the warm side of the hill," as Waldo described:

> The Army who have been surprisingly healthy hitherto—now begin to grow sickly from the continued fatigues they have suffered this Campaign. Yet they still show spirit of Alacrity & Contentment not to be expected from so young Troops. I am Sick—discontented—and out of humor. Poor food—hard lodging—Cold Weather—fatigue—Nasty Cloaths—nasty Cookery—Vomit half my time—smok'd out of my senses—the Devil's in't—I can't Endure it—Why are we sent here to starve and freeze? What sweet Felicities have I left at home: a charming Wife—pretty Children—Good Beds—good food—good Cookery—all agreeable—all harmonious. Here, all Confusion—smoke Cold—hunger & filthyness—A pox on my bad luck—Here comes a bowl of beef soup—full of burnt leaves and dirt, sickish enough to make a hector spue, away with it Boys—I'll live like the Chamelon upon Air. Poh! Poh! crys Patience within me—you talk like a fool. Your being sick Covers your mind with a Melancholic Gloom, which makes everything about you appear gloomy. See the poor Soldier, when in health with what

Cheerfulness he meets his foes and encounters every hardship—if barefoot—he labors thro' the Mud & Cold with a Song in his mouth extolling War & Washington—if his food be bad—he eats it notwithstanding with seeming content—blesses God for a good Stomach—and Whistles it into digestion. But harkee Patience—a moment. There comes a Soldier—his bare feet are seen thro' his worn out Shoes—his legs nearly naked from the tatter'd remains of an only pair of stockings—his Breeches not sufficient to cover his Nakedness—his Shirt hanging in Strings—his hair disheveled—his face meager. His whole appearance pictures a person forsaken & discouraged. He comes, and cries with an air of wretchedness & Despair—I am Sick—my feet lame—my legs are sore—my body covered with this tormenting Itch—my Cloaths are worn out—my Constitution is broken—my former Activity is exhaused by fatigue, hunger & Cold. I fail fast—I shall soon be no more! and all the reward I shall get will be—"Poor Will is dead."

"No meat—no meat!"

Four nights later, Waldo secured and roasted a pig, to celebrate "Universal Thanksgiving." He felt much better:

Rank & Precedence make a good deal of disturbance and confusion in the American Army. The Army are poorly supplied with Provision, occasioned, it is said, by the Neglect of the Commissary of Purchases. Much talk among Officers about discharges. Money has become of too little consequence.

Dec. 21st. Preparations made for huts. Provisions scarce. Mr. Ellis went homeward—sent a Letter to my Wife. Heartily wish myself at home—my Skin & eyes are almost spoiled with continual smoke.

A general cry thro' the Camp this Evening among the Soldiers—"No meat—no meat!" the Distant vales Echo'd back the melancholy sound—"No meat! No meat!" Imitating the noise of Crows & Owls, also, made a part of the confused Musick.

What have you for our Dinners, Boys? "Nothing but Fire Cake & Water, Sir." At night—"Gentlemen the Supper is ready." What is your Supper, Lads? "Fire Cake & Water, Sir."

Dec. 22d. Lay excessive Cold & uncomfortable last Night—my eyes are started out from their Orbits like a Rabbit's eyes, occasioned by a great Cold—and Smoke.

What have you got for Breakfast, Lads? "Fire Cake & Water, Sir." The Lord send that our Commissary of Purchases may live on Fire Cake & Water.

He was tempted, he was ashamed to say, to steal fowls, or even a whole hog ("for I feel as if I could eat one"), but there were none to steal.

"Starvation," remarked Joseph Plumb Martin, "rioted in its glory." He had had nothing to eat for two or three days before the sumptuous Thanksgiving which had been ordained by Congress to "close the year of high living we had now nearly seen brought to a close:"

Well, to add something extraordinary to our present stock of provisions, our country ever mindful of its suffering army, opened her sympathizing heart so wide, upon this occasion, as

Blacksmith shop and cannon of General Knox's artillery at Valley Forge
--From a black and white sketch by Kay Smith

to give us something to make the world stare. And what do you think it was, reader? Guess. You cannot guess, be you as much of a Yankee as you will. I will tell you; it gave each and every man *half a gill* of rice and a *tablespoonful* of vinegar!

"A leg of nothing and no turnips"

Martin's Thanksgiving Dinner consisted of "a leg of nothing and no turnips:"

The army was now not only starved but naked. The greatest part were not only shirtless and barefoot but destitute of all other clothing, especially blankets. I procured a small piece of raw cowhide and made myself a pair of moccasins, which, while they lasted, kept my feet from the frozen ground, although as I well remember, the hard edges so galled my ankles, while on a march, that it was with much difficulty and pain that I could

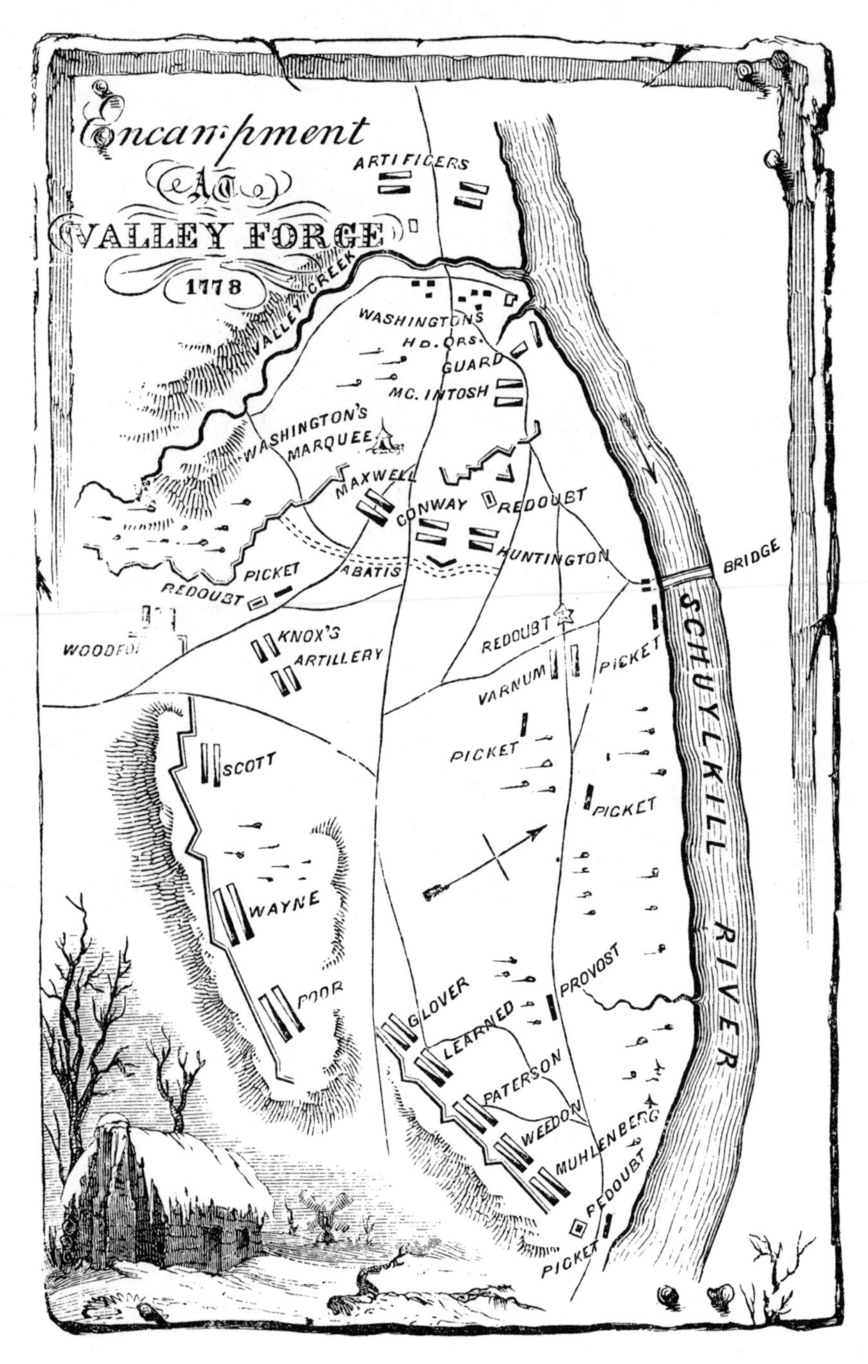

The Valley Forge encampment

wear them afterwards; but the only alternative I had was to endure this inconvenience or to go barefoot as hundreds of my companions had to, till they might be tracked by their blood upon the rough frozen ground. But hunger, nakedness, and sore shins were not the only difficulties we had at that time to encounter; we had hard duty to perform and little or no strength to perform it with.

The prospect was dreary:

In our miserable condition, to go into the wild woods and build us habitations to *stay* (not to *live*) in, in such a weak, starved

> and naked condition, was appalling in the highest degree, especially to New Englanders, unaccustomed to such kind of hardships at home. However, there was no remedy, no alternative but this or dispersion. But dispersion, I believe, was not thought of; at least, I did not think of it. We had engaged in the defense of our injured country and were willing, nay, we were determined to persevere as long as such hardships were not altogether intolerable. I had experienced what I thought sufficient of the hardships of a military life the year before, although nothing in comparison to what I had suffered the present campaign, and therefore expected to meet with rubbers. But we were now absolutely in danger of perishing, and that too, in the midst of a plentiful country. We then had but little and often nothing to eat for days together; but now we had nothing and saw no likelihood of any betterment of our condition.

Martin was fortunate. He spent most of the winter away from camp on foraging expeditions, and consequently he ate well.

Thanksgiving Day

"This is Thanksgiving Day thro' the whole Continent of America," laconically remarked Colonel Henry Dearborn (who had brought his regiment of sharpshooters from the north, following Burgoyne's surrender):

> . . . but God knows We have very Little to keep it with, this being the third Day we have been without flour or bread—and Living on a high uncultivated hill, in huts & tents Laying on the Cold Ground; upon the whole, I think all we have to be thankful for is that we are alive & not in the Grave with many of our friends. We had for Thanksgiving breakfast some Exceeding Poor beef which has been boiled & Now warmed in an old short-handled frying pan in which we were Obliged to Eat it, having no other Platter. I Dined & sup'd at General Sullivan's today & so Ended thanksgiving.

"Starve, dissolve or disperse"

The army, Washington informed the President of Congress on December 23, must inevitably be reduced to one or other of three things, "Starve, dissolve or disperse, in order to obtain sustenance in the best manner they can." The Commissariat Department had not a single hoof of any kind to slaughter, and only twenty-five barrels of flour. "What then is to become of the army this winter?" he asked:

> Soap, Vinegar, and other Articles allowed by Congress we see none of, nor have seen, I believe, since the battle of Brandywine. The first indeed we have now little occasion of, few men having more than one Shirt, many only the Moiety of one, and Some none at all; in addition to which as a proof of the little benefit received from a Cloathier General and at the same time as a further proof of the inability of an Army under the circumstances of this, to perform the common duties of Soldiers (besides a number of Men confined to Hospitals for want of Shoes, and others in farmers' Houses on the same account) we have, by a field return this day, made no less than 2,898 Men

now in Camp unfit for duty because they are barefoot and otherwise naked, and by the same return it appears that our whole strength in Continental Troops (including the Eastern Brigades which have joined us since the surrender of General Burgoyne), exclusive of the Maryland Troops sent to Wilmington, amount to no more than 8,200 in Camp fit for duty from the hardships and exposures they have undergone, particularly on account of Blankets (numbers being obliged to set up all Night by fires, instead of taking comfortable rest in a natural way) we have decreased near 2,000 Men.

The huts, each 14 feet by 16 feet, were completed by January 14, the soldiers laboring, as Tom Paine described following his visit to the army, "like a family of beavers; everyone busy; some carrying logs, others mud, and the rest fastening

Bake shop at Valley Forge
–From a black and white sketch by Kay Smith

them together." Washington offered a reward of a hundred dollars for anyone who could discover anything better than boards for roofing. None did. The whole army, wrote Benjamin Tallmadge, was "in great want of the most necessary articles of clothing, and many of them had no shoes to their feet, so that they could be tracked by the blood which they left on the ground as they entered their huts."

"No bread, no soldier!"

Writing his *Autobiography* many years later, the French volunteer, Pierre Etienne du Ponceau, recalled seeing "the soldiers popping their heads out of the miserable huts and calling out in an undertone, "No bread, no soldier!" Their condition he thought "truly pitiful" and their courage and perseverance "beyond praise."

Du Ponceau did not know what could be done about clothing "but it is certain that half the army are half naked, and almost the whole army go barefoot." The men were infected with the itch, "a matter which attracts very little attention either at the hospitals or in camp." They were covered over and over with scab. All things seemed to contribute "to the ruin of our cause."

Though more cheerful, Dr. Waldo was no less pessimistic:

Dec. 24th. Huts go on Slowly—Cold & Smoke make us fret. But mankind are always fretting, even if they have more than their proportion of the Blessings of Life. We are never Easy—always repining at the Providence of an Allwise & Benevolent Being—Blaming our Country—or faulting our Friends. But I don't know of anything that vexes a man's Soul more than hot smoke continually blowing into his Eyes—and when he attempts to avoid it, being met by a cold and piercing Wind.

Dec. 25th. Christmas. We are still in Tents—when we ought to be in huts—the poor Sick suffer much in Tents this cold Weather—but we now treat them differently from what they used to be at home, under the inspection of Old Women & Doct. Bolus's Linctus. We give them Mutton & Grogg—and a Capital Medicine once in a While—to start the Disease from its foundation at once. We avoid—Piddling Pills, Powders, Bolus's Linctus—Cordials—and all such insignificant matters whose powers are Only render'd important by causing the Patient to vomit up his money instead of his disease. But very few of the Sick Men Die.

"Ye who eat Pumpkin Pie and Roast Turkies" and yet curse their luck, Waldo advised to curse her no more, "lest she reduce your allowance of her favors to a bit of Fire Cake and a draught of Cold Water."

"I am alive. I am well."

Waldo spent the last day of the year being "learned" how to darn stockings, but he built a "genteel chimney" to his hut "undirected." On New Year's Day he recorded the miraculous feat, "I am alive. I am well."

Colonel Dearborn was given leave and set off for Massachusetts, hoping for "a happy sight of my friends." Captain Joseph Hodgkins, from Ipswich in that State, thought of his family. On his arrival at Valley Forge he had been given the Regulation Plan for constructing huts:

> Dimensions 14 by 16 feet, Sides Ends & Roof made of Logs, the Roof made light with Split Slabs, the sides made tight with Clay; the fireplaces made of wood & secured with Clay in the Inside 18 Inches thick, this fireplace to be in the rear of the hut, the door to be in the end next to the Street. Side walls 6½ feet high, the Officers' Huts to form a line in the rear of the Whole.

Each cabin was occupied by twelve men; the officers had a hut to themselves.

"This winter's campaign beats all for fatigue and hardships"

Hodgkins received a letter from his wife announcing the birth of a daughter. She begged him to return home. He hoped, he replied, to get leave in about a month:

> But I am not stating I shall Be sucksesfull in my attemptes; therefore I would not have you Depend too much on it for if you should, and I should fail of Coming, the Disappointment would be the Grater But I will Tell you the Gratest incoredgement that I have of getting home is that I intend to Pertishion to the Genl. for Liberty to go to New England to Take the small Pox & if this Plan fails me I shall have But Little or no hope. I Believe I have as grate a Desire to Come home as you can Posibly have of having me for this winter's campaign beats all for fatigue and hardships that Ever I went through. But I have Been Carried through it thus far & Desire to Be thankful for it. We have got our huts almost Done for the men.

His scheme to be sent home for vaccination misfired, for he and his men were immunized in camp.

He wanted to see her very much, he told his wife whom he asked to send some winter shirts, otherwise "I must go naked for I can get nothing here." He wrote again on February 22:

> I must just inform you that what our soldiers have suffred this Winter is Beyond Expression as one half has Been Bare foot & almost Naked all winter the other half Very Badly on it for Clothes of all sorts and to Compleat our misery Very shorte on it for Provision not Long since our Brigade drue But a half Day's allowance of Meat in Eight Days But these Deficeltis the men Bore with a Degree of fortitude Becoming soldiers. But I must say one word to the people at home who I fear have lost all Bowles of Compassion if they Ever had any, for the Contry Towns have Provided Clothing for there men and Brought them to Camp But as there has Ben none from the seeport Towns I fear they have Lost all there Publick Spirit. I would beg of them to Rouse from there stupedity and Put on som humanity and stir themselves Before it is too Late. I would not have them think hard of maintaining there soldiers for what the soldiers has sufferd this past year Desarves a Penshon During Life.

Hodgkins obtained leave in May and spent two months with his wife.

The Knox covered bridge at Valley Forge
—From a black and white sketch by Kay Smith

"Nothing but virtue," kept the army together, stated the Massachusetts Colonel, John Brooks. "For a week past," he told a friend on January 5, "we have had snow, and as cold weather as I almost ever knew at home. To see our poor brave fellows living in tents, bare-footed, bare-legged, bare-breeched etc. etc. in snow, in rain, on marches, in camp, and on duty, without being able to supply their wants is really distressing."

He did not know where the fault lay. The soldiers were equally lacking in food and money. He mentioned these things to give an idea of the soldiers' life. Yet, no men ever showed more spirit. "There has been that great principle, the love of our country, which first called us into the field, and that only to influence us." But he feared that it would not last always.

"I would cherish these dear ragged Continentals,
whose patience will be the admiration of future ages."

De Kalb told Colonel John Laurens that no European army would have withstood the hardships Washington's soldiers were asked to bear. Nonetheless, as Laurens informed his father, hunger and privation had nearly brought mutiny. But, he said, "I would cherish these dear ragged Continentals, whose patience will be the admiration of future ages, and I glory in bleeding with them." There were many desertions. Washington estimated that nine out of ten deaths were due to malnutrition and exposure.

The winter was not all gloom and misery. Martha Washington came to visit her husband who had taken over Deborah Hewes's house by the creek. She entertained the foreign officers, the French and Polish volunteers, and the wives of General Greene, Colonel Knox, and Lord Stirling. Catherine Greene, "a handsome, elegant and accomplished woman," as she was described by Du Ponceau, spoke schoolgirl French, but her spelling was weak. Her blacksmith husband cautioned her to be careful in the presence of Mrs. Knox who, as the wife of a bookseller, might detect her imperfections. These people often met at each other's quarters, recalled Du Ponceau, "the evenings were spent in conversation over a dish of tea or coffee. There were no levees, or formal soirees, no dancing, card-playing, or amusements of any kind, except singing. Every gentleman or lady who could sing was called upon in turn for a song."

Baron Frederick von Steuben volunteers

Early in January, Washington received a letter that pleased him. From Portsmouth, New Hampshire, where he had recently arrived, the Baron Frederick von Steuben wrote offering his services as a "volunteer," rather than be the subject of discontent to "such deserving officers as had already distinguished themselves." The many status-hungry European officers who had flocked to America usually demanded ranks higher than those enjoyed by her native sons. The Baron had served, twenty-five years before, on the staff of Frederick the Great of Russia. Although the Baron was little more than an adventurer, Washington welcomed him as "a man of military knowledge and well acquainted with the world." He appointed von Steuben acting Inspector-General of the army and put him in charge of training his troops in maneuver and discipline, a task at which the Baron "toiled with the zeal of a lieutenant anxious for promotion," stated John Laurens, who, with the young Alexander Hamilton, acted as his aides. Although unable to speak English, von Steuben quickly learned to understand the American character, as he explained to a friend in Germany:

> In the first place, the genius of this nation is not in the least to be compared with that of the Prussians, Austrians, or French.

You say to your soldier, "Do this," and he doeth it, but I am obliged to say, "This is the reason why you ought to do that," and then he does it.

Von Steuben also possessed a sense of humor, as his aide explained:

We who lived in good quarters did not feel the misery of the times so much as the common soldiers and the subaltern officers, yet we had more than once to share our rations with the sentry at the door. We put the best face we could upon the matter. Once with the Baron's permission, his aides invited a number of young officers to dine at our quarters, on condition that none should be admitted that had on a whole pair of breeches. This was understood of course as *pars pro toto*, but torn clothes were an indispensable requisite for admission and in this the guests were very sure not to fail. The dinner took place; the guests clubbed their rations, and we feasted sumptuously on tough beefsteaks and potatoes with hickory nuts for our desert. In lieu of wine, we had some kind of spirits with which we made *Salamanders;* that is to say, after filling our glasses, we set the liquor on fire, and drank it up flame and all. Such a set of ragged and, at the same time, merry fellows were never before brought together.

The Baron loved to speak of that dinner, and of his *sans-culottes*, as he called us. Thus the denomination was first invented in America, and applied to the brave officers and soldiers of our revolutionary army, at a time when it could not be foreseen that the name which honored the followers of Washington would afterwards be assumed by the satellites of a Marat and a Robespierre.

Von Steuben succeeded in winning the esteem and even the affection of the raw soldiers whom he turned into veterans. Struggling with the difficulties of language, he was helped by Captain Benjamin Walker, who thought "his fits of passion were comical and rather amused the soldiers."

"What a beautiful, what a happy country this is!"

"I was received with more marks of distinction than I expected," Von Steuben wrote on July 4, at the conclusion of his term of duty as drillmaster. He would cheerfully die for the nation that had so honored him, he told his friend. He was raised to the rank of major general and commanded a wing at the battle of Monmouth. He hoped, one day, his friend would dine with him in America:

What a beautiful, what a happy country this is! Without kings, without prelates, without blood-sucking farmer-generals, (Tax-Collectors) and without idle barons! Here everybody is prosperous. Poverty is an unknown evil. Indeed, I should become too prolix were I to give you an account of the prosperity and happiness of these people.

The six foreign officers, von Steuben observed, caused more trouble to him—

. . . than two hundred American ones; and indeed most of the foreigners have so utterly lost their credit, that it is daily becoming more difficult to employ foreign officers. A large number of German barons and French marquises have already sailed away; and I am always nervous and apprehensive when a baron or a marquis announces himself. While here we are in a republic; and Mr. Baron does not count a farthing more than Mister Jacob or Mister Peter. Indeed, German and French noses can hardly accustom themselves to such a state of things! Our general of artillery (Knox), for instance, was a bookbinder in Boston. He is a worthy man, thoroughly understands his trade, and fills his present position with much credit.

He would finish the war, unless it finished him first. Von Steuben did not expect that England could continue it but two years longer, by when he would have been pensioned and rewarded.

Another officer who reached Valley Forge in the spring was not as welcome, although Washington thought that "no event was ever received with more heartfelt joy." Following his capture at Basking Ridge, Major General Charles Lee had spent a year in New York as the honored guest of Sir William Howe. Some of Washington's officers believed that Howe had won Lee's loyalty. Whether or not Lee was a traitor, as has been claimed, he was exchanged for the British General Richard Prescott, who had been captured in embarrassing circumstances at Providence, Rhode Island, on July 12, 1777.

She "gave him to the foe—without his breeches."

A rebel raiding party got into Prescott's quarters undiscovered (as Frederick MacKenzie recorded) and found him in bed with a nymph who, according to the rhyme composed by a local wit, "gave him to the foe—without his breeches."

Lee's exchange was arranged by Elias Boudinot, the American Commissary of Prisoners, as he described in his journal:

When the day arrived the greatest preparations were made for his reception. All the principal Officers of the Army were drawn up in two lines, advanced of the Camp about 2 miles toward the Enemy. Then the troops with the inferior Officers formed a line quite to head Quarters. All the Music of the Army attended. The General with a great number of principal Officers and their Suites, rode about four miles on the road towards Philadelphia and waited till Gen. Lee appeared. Gen. Washington dismounted & rec'd Gen. Lee as if he had been his brother. He passed thro' the lines of Officers & the Army, who all paid him the highest military Honors to Head Quarters, where Mrs. Washington was, and there he was entertained with an Elegant Dinner, and the Music Playing the whole time. A Room was assigned him, back of Mrs. Washington's Sitting Room, and all his Baggage was stowed in it. The next morning he lay very late, and Breakfast was detained for him. When he came out, he looked as dirty as if he had been in the Street all night. Soon after I discovered that he had brought a miserable dirty hussy with him from Philadelphia (a British Sergeant's Wife) and had actually taken her into his Room by a Back Door and she had slept with him that night.

Monument to the New Jersey Brigade of the Continental Army under Brigadier General William Maxwell at Valley Forge

—From a black and white sketch by Kay Smith

Lee informed Boudinot that he "found the army in worse condition than he expected" and that the General was "not fit to command a sergeant's guard," opinions which boded ill for the future. Despite several warnings of Lee's untrustworthiness, Washington reappointed him second-in-command of the army.

Alliance with France

The coming of spring reinvigorated the army which had (in the words of the recent historian of the Revolution, Richard Alden) undergone the "Gethsemane" of Valley Forge. The striving and starving army had miraculously survived and, better trained and disciplined than before, it was determined to fight to the death. More than 2,000 men had died or had deserted. Yet the army was now stronger, the men more determined. In May came the great news of the French alliance. George Ewing described how it was celebrated:

> *May 6th. 1778*. This day we fired a grand *feu de joie* on account of the news brought by Mr. Simeon Dean in the *La Sensible* from our Plenepotentiary at the Court of France, the purport of which was that the Courts of France and Spain had declared the United States of America to be free and independent States and had ceded to us all the territories on the continent of America which formerly belonged to the Crown of Great Britain, and also the Island of Bermuda, and also to assist us in carrying on this just and necessary war with no other conditions on our part but that we should not in any treaty of peace with England give up our independency.
>
> In consequence of this intelligence this day was set apart for a day of rejoysing throughout the whole army. Accordingly at ten o'clock A.M. a cannon was fired as a signal for the whole to parade, and after a discourse suited to the subject by the chaplains of each brigade a second cannon fired a signal for each brigade to repair to their respective post. Thirteen six-pounders were drove to a height in the rear of Conway's brigade. After the troops were posted the flag on the fort was dropt and the third cannon fired at the park when the 13 cannon fired on the height, after which a fire of musquetry began on the right of the front line and proceeded to the left of the same, and then instantly beginning on the left of the rear line proceeded to the right of the same. After this firing was over a fourth cannon from the park was the signal for the three cheers and "Long Live the King of France," after this thirteen more cannon and musquetry as aforesaid the signal and three cheers and a shout of "God save the friendly powers of Europe." The third cannon and musquetry as aforesaid signal and cheers and a shout of "God Save the American States." As soon as this was concluded the troops marched to their respective quarters. No accident happened during this day. After the *feu de joie* was over and the troops dismissed, his Excellency invited the officers of the army to assemble under a booth that was prepared for the purpose and partake of a cold collation which was prepared for them, where he did us the honor to eat and drink with us, where many patriotic toasts were drank and the celebration concluded with harmless mirth and jollity.

More soberly, Nathanael Greene wrote, "God grant we may never be brought to such a terrible condition again."

The army had survived the winter. It had nearly disintegrated. Now the rebellious colonists had a great and powerful ally.

MONMOUTH COURT HOUSE

Obeying orders from London, Sir Henry Clinton (who had replaced Howe as Commander-in-Chief) abandoned Philadelphia on June 18, 1778. Sending 3,000 loyalists, with their goods and chattels, ahead by sea, Clinton set out to march his army through New Jersey to New York. As the British rear guard left, Benedict Arnold, still limping on the leg he had broken at Bemis Heights, marched in leading an American detachment.

Washington, (as General Greene said "People expect something from us and our strength demands it") went in pursuit of Clinton, to harass and delay his long column, which, with 1,500 wagons and carts, stretched over twelve miles of road. The army that had wintered at Valley Forge now numbered 11,000 men. The soldiers were fresh and eager for a fight.

On June 25, Washington sent Lafayette ahead in command of the advance guard with orders to give the enemy "every degree of annoyance." At the same time, Generals Morgan, Wayne, and Dickinson harried their flanks.

At the council of war when these decisions were made, Charles Lee, as Second-in-Command of the army, had been invited to lead the advance. He declined, declaring that he was well pleased to be freed from all responsibility for a plan which he was sure would fail. Now, however, he demanded to be given his rightful command. Washington agreed, making the condition that Lee should not interfere with any plan already put into operation by Lafayette. On Lee's arrival at the scene of action, the young Frenchman gracefully bowed to his superior's orders.

Early in the morning of June 28, Washington learned that the British were preparing to leave Monmouth Court House on the last stage of their march to Sandy Hook where ships were waiting to ferry them to New York. Washington ordered Lee to strike at the vulnerable rear guard which was commanded by Lord Cornwallis. In the stifling heat (the temperature was 96°F at noon), and on roads churned to mud by the recent rains, the British and Hessians moved slowly, impeded by their heavy clothing, tons of baggage, and their loot. The rear guard straggled over four miles of road, presenting a wonderful target for an aggressive army.

Sandy Hook from the shipping channel

Lee did not attack as ordered, thus dissipating an unusual opportunity to destroy many British troops and quantities of

Battlefield at Monmouth

supplies. Instead of culminating in an American victory, the battle of Monmouth ended in disorderly retreat and near disaster.

Shortly after eight in the morning, the American wings closed round the British rear which was on the point of leaving the Court House. Wayne sent Colonel Butler to cut their retreat. Seeing the danger, Cornwallis ordered the Dragoons to attack Butler on Briar Hill, and he formed his rear guard obliquely across the road. What then happened is still a matter of controversy. Instead of supporting his wings, Lee retreated, leaving his commanders in confusion and without orders. They were forced to fall back across the road which ran from the Court House to Perth Amboy. By 11:30 A.M. the retreat had degenerated into a rout and, according to Lieutenant Colonel Laurens, "all this disgraceful retreating passed without the firing of a musket, over ground which might have been disputed inch by inch."

Colonel Henry Dearborn described this stage of the battle in his journal:

> Haveing Intiligence this morning before sun Rise, that the Enimy were mooving, we ware Ordered, together with the Troops Commanded by the Marquis & Genl. Lee (in the whole about 5000) to march towards the Enimy & as we thought to Attack them. At Eleven o'clock A.M. after marching about 6 or 7 miles we arriv'd on the Plains Near Monmouth Court House, Where a Column of the Enimy appear'd in sight. A brisk Cannonade Commens'd on both sides. The Column which was advancing towards us Halted & soon Retired, but from some moovements of theirs we ware Convinced they Intended to fight us, shifted our ground, formed on very good Ground & waited to see if they Intended to Come on. We soon Discovered a Large Column Turning our Right & another Coming up in our Front With Cavalry in front of both Columns. Genl. Lee was on the Right

of our Line who Left the ground & made Tracks Quick Step towards English Town. Genrl Scott's Detachment Remain'd on the ground we formed on until we found we ware very near surrounded—& ware Obliged to Retire, which we Did in good order altho' we ware hard Prest on our Left flank, the Enimy haveing got a mile in Rear of us before we began to Retire and ware bearing Down on our Left as we went off—Confin'd by a Morass on our Right.

General Charles Lee was court-martialed.

General Charles Lee was subsequently court-martialed. Part of the testimony as given by Lieutenant Colonel Richard Harrison follows:

When we came to where the roads forked, His Excellency [Washington] made a halt for a few minutes, in order to direct a disposition of the army. The wing under General Greene was then ordered to go to the right to prevent the enemy's turning our right flank.

After order was given in this matter, and His Excellency was proceeding down the road, we met a fifer, who appeared to be a good deal frighted. The General asked him whether he was a soldier belonging to the army, and the cause of his returning that way; he answered that he was a soldier, and that the Continental troops that had been advanced were retreating. On this answer the General seemed to be exceedingly surprised and rather more exasperated, appearing to discredit the account, and threatened the man, if he mentioned a thing of the sort, he would have him whipped.

We then moved on a few paces forward (perhaps about fifty yards), where we met two or three more persons on that road; one was, I think, in the habit of a soldier. The General asked them from whence they came and whether they belonged to the army; one of them replied that he did and that all the troops that had been advanced, the whole of them, were retreating. His Excellency still appeared to discredit the account, having not heard any firing except a few cannon a considerable time before. However, the General, or some gentleman in company, observed that, as the report came from different persons, it might be well not wholly to disregard it.

Harrison went ahead, encountering Colonel Mathias Ogden, who told him, "My God, they are flying from a shadow:"

I fell in immediately after with Captain Mercer, who is an aide-de-camp to Major-General Lee, and, expecting to derive some information from him, I put the same question to him. Captain Mercer seemed, by the manner of his answer (as I addressed myself to him, saying "For God's sake, what is the cause of this retreat?"), to be displeased; his answer was, "If you will proceed, you will see the cause; you will see several columns of foot and horse." I replied to Captain Mercer that I presumed that the enemy was not in greater force than when they left Philadelphia, and we came to that field to meet columns of foot and horse.

The next field-officer I met was Lieutenant Colonel Rhea of New Jersey, who appeared to be conducting a regiment. I

Boot worn by a Hessian Dragoon of the Riedesel's Forces

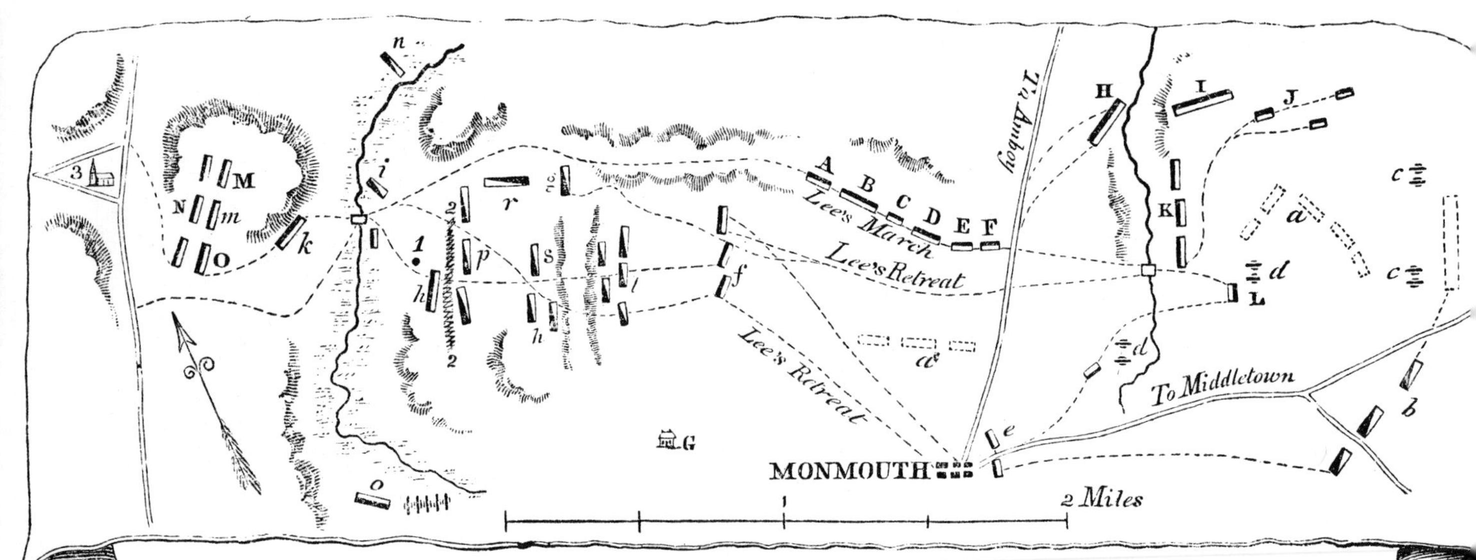

Plan of the Battle of Monmouth

Explanation of the plan.—a a, position occupied by the British army the night before the battle. *b,* British detachment moving toward Monmouth. *c c,* British batteries. *d d,* Colonel Oswald's American batteries. *e,* American troops formed near the court-house. *f,* first position taken by General Lee in his retreat. *g,* attack of a party of the British in the woods. *h h,* positions taken by General Lee. *i,* a British detachment. *k,* last position of the retreating troops on the west side of the marsh. *m,* army formed by General Washington after he met Lee retreating. *n,* British detachment. *o,* American battery. *p,* place of the principal action near the parsonage. *r,* first position of the British after the action. *s,* second position. *t,* place where the British passed the night after the battle. 1, the spot where Washington met Lee retreating. 2, a hedgerow. 3, the Freehold meeting-house, yet standing. A, Maxwell's brigade; B, Wayne's; C, Varnum's; D, Scott's. E and F, Jackson's and Grayson's regiments. G, Carr's house. H, I, and J, the brigades of Maxwell and Scott, with the regiments of Grayson and Jackson, marching to the attack. K and L, Greene and Varnum. M, Lord Stirling. N, La Fayette; and O, Greene, with Washington.

asked him uniformly the same question for information, and he appeared to be very much agitated, expressed his disapprobation of the retreat, and seemed to be equally concerned (or perhaps more) that he had no place assigned to go where the troops were to halt.

About this time I met with General Maxwell; and, agreeable to the General's directions to get intelligence, I asked him the cause. He appeared to be as much at a loss as Lieutenant Colonel Rhea or any other officer I had met with; and intimated that he had received no orders upon the occasion and was totally in the dark what line of conduct to pursue.

Putting spurs to his horse, Washington galloped to the bridge over the middle ravine, where he met Lee. Whether or not, as tradition states, he called Lee "a damned poltroon," he peremptorily demanded an explanation for the retreat. Nor is Lee's answer certain. According to some witnesses, he said that the British counter-attack had brought about a confusion he could not control, and to the ears of others he stated that his troops were unable to meet the British Grenadiers.

He expected his orders would have been obeyed.

He did say, however, that the whole plan of attack had been against his expressed opinion, which brought from Washington the heated reply that whatever his opinions might have been, he expected his orders would have been obeyed. Washington countermanded his orders, relieved him of his command, and ordered the army to resist the British onslaught. Lafayette watched the General rally his army:

> Never was General Washington greater in war than in this action. His presence stopped the retreat; his dispositions fired the victory; his fine appearance on horseback, his calm courage, roused to animation by the vexations of the morning, gave him the air best calculated to excite enthusiasm.

Washington "rode along the lines, amidst the cheers of the soldiers, cheering them by his voice and example and restoring to our standard the fortunes of the fight. I thought then, as now, that never had I beheld so superb a man."

Both Dearborn and Joseph Plumb Martin participated in the fight for the western ravine, the former describing it in his usual terse, factual style:

"I think that was the finest musick I Ever heard."

> After Retireing about 2 miles we met his Excelency Genl. Washington who after seeing what Disorder Genl. Lee's Troops ware in appeer'd to be at a Loss whether we should be able to make a stand or not; however, he ordered us to form on a Heighth, & Indevour to Check the Enimy. We form'd & about 12 pieces of Artillery being brought on to the hill with us: the Enimy at the same time advancing very Rappedly finding we had form'd, they form'd in our front on a Ridge & brought up their Artillery within about 60 Rods of our front. Then came *the briskest Cannonade on both sides* that I Ever heard. Both Armies ware on Clear Ground, & if anything Can be Call'd Musical where there is so much Danger, I think that was the finest musick I Ever heard—*however*, the agreeableness of the musick was very often Lessen'd by the balls Coming too near. Our men being very much beat out with Fateague & heat which was very Intense, we ordered them to sit Down & Rest themselves—from the time we first met the Enimy until we had form'd as above mentioned several sevear scurmishes happened at Different Places & Times—Soon after the Cannonade became serious a Large Collum of the Enimy began to Turn our Left—Some Part of our Artillery Play'd upon them very Briskly & they finding their main Body ware not advancing, halted—the Cannonade Continued about 2½ hours & then the Enimy began to Retire from their Right.
>
> Genl. Washington being in front of our Regt. when the Enimy began to Retire on their Right, he ordered Col. Cilley & me with abt. 300 men to go & attack the Enimies Right wing which then was Passing thro' an orchard, but when they found we ware about to attack them they form'd & stood Redy to Receive us, when we arriv'd within 200 yards of them we form'd Battallion & advanc'd but having two Rail fences to take Down as we advanced (the Last of which was within 60 yards of the Enimy), we Could advance but slowly. The Enimy when we ware takeing Down the Last fence give us a very heavy fire which we Did not Return. After takeing Down the Last fence we march'd on with armes shouldered Except 20 men who we

sent on their Right to scurmish with them while we Passed the fences.

The Enimy finding we ware Determined to Come to Close quarter, fil'd off from the Left & Run off upon our Right into a swamp & form'd in the Edge of it. We Wheel'd to the Right & advanc'd towards them. They began a heavy fire upon us. We ware Desending toward them in Open field, with shoulder'd armes until we had got within 4 Rods of them when our men Dress'd very Coolly & we then gave them a very heavy fire from the whole Batallion. They had two Pieces of artillery across a small Run which Play'd with grape very briskly upon us but when they found we ware Determin'd to Push upon them they Retreated to their main body which was giving way & ware Persued by some Parties from our Line. We Persued until we got Possession of the field of Battle, where we found 300 dead & a Considerable number of wounded. Among the Dead was Col. Mungton & a number of other officers. The Enimy Retired across a Morass & formed. Our men being beat out with heat & fateague, it was thought not Prudent to Persue them.

Great numbers of the Enimy Died with heat & some of ours. We Remain'd on the field of Battle & ware to attact the Enimy Early Next morning but they Prevented us by a Precipitate Retreet in the middle of the night.

The battlefield at Monmouth
—From a painting by George Washington Parke Custis, Esq.

"The weather was almost too hot to live in."

Martin, now a member of the Light Infantry, had marched in support of the left wing, when he learned that Lee was retreating. He took refuge behind a fence, where a sharp conflict ensued:

These troops maintained their ground, till the whole force of the enemy that could be brought to bear had charged upon them through the fence, and after being overpowered by numbers and the platoon officers had given orders for their several platoons to leave the fence, they had to force them to retreat, so eager were they to be revenged on the invaders of their country and rights.

As soon as the troops had left this ground the British planted their cannon upon the place and began a violent attack upon the artillery and our detachment, but neither could be routed. The cannonade continued for some time without intermission, when the British pieces being mostly disabled, they reluctantly crawled back from the height which they had occupied and hid themselves from our sight.

Before the cannonade had commenced, a part of the right wing of the British army had advanced across a low meadow and brook and occupied an orchard on our left. The weather was almost too hot to live in, and the British troops in the orchard were forced by the heat to shelter themselves from it under the trees. We had a four-pounder on the left of our pieces which kept a constant fire upon the enemy during the whole contest. After the British artillery had fallen back and the cannonade had mostly ceased in this quarter, and our detachment had an opportunity to look about us, Colonel Joseph Cilly of the New Hampshire Line, who was attached to our detachment, passed along in front of our line, inquiring for General Warnum's men, who were the Connecticut and Rhode Island men belonging to our command. We answered, "Here we are." He did not hear us in his hurry, but passed on. In a few minutes he returned, making the same inquiry. We again answered, "Here we are." "Ah!" said he, "you are the boys I want to assist in driving those rascals from yon orchard."

"We pursued them without order."

Martin joined a corps of about 500 men. They marched towards the enemy's right wing and formed line in open fields. The British retreated and, said Martin, "we pursued them without order." They overtook the British in a bushy meadow:

When within about five rods of the rear of the retreating foe, I could distinguish everything about them. They were retreating in line, though in some disorder. I singled out a man and took my aim directly between his shoulders. (They were divested of their packs.) He was a good mark, being a broad-shouldered fellow. What became of him I know not; the fire and smoke hid him from my sight. One thing I know, that is, I took as deliberate aim at him as ever I did at any game in my life. But after all, I hope I did not kill him, although I intended to at the time.

By this time our whole party had arrived, and the British had obtained a position that suited them, as I suppose, for they returned our fire in good earnest, and we played the second part of the same tune. They occupied a much higher piece of ground than we did, and had a small piece of artillery, which the soldiers called a grasshopper. We had no artillery with us. The first shot they gave us from this piece cut off the thigh bone of a captain, just above the knee, and the whole heel of a private in the rear of him. We gave it to poor Sawney (for they were Scotch troops) so hot that he was forced to fall back and leave the ground they occupied. When our commander saw them retreating and nearly joined with their main body, he shouted, "Come, my boys, reload your pieces, and we will give them a set-off." We did so, and gave them the parting salute, and the firing on both sides ceased. We then laid ourselves down under the fences and bushes to take breath, for we had need of it.

"Molly Pitcher"

One little incident happened during the heat of the cannonade, to which Martin was a witness, and which he thought would be unpardonable not to mention:

> A woman whose husband belonged to the artillery and who was then attached to a piece in the engagement, attended with her husband at the piece the whole time. While in the act of reaching a cartridge and having one of her feet as far before the other as she could step, a cannon shot from the enemy passed directly between her legs without doing any other damage than carrying away all the lower part of her petticoat. Looking at it with apparent unconcern, she observed that it was lucky it did not pass a little higher, for in that case it might have carried away something else, and continued her occupation.

The woman, Mary Ludwig Hayes, was the wife of a Pennsylvania private, who had been assigned to a gun battery. She won immortal fame in the name of "Molly Pitcher," due to her service in carrying pitchers of water to the parched soldiers. Her gallantry was rewarded by a Sergeant's warrant which entitled her to that rank's pay and allowances. Her tombstone in the old Carlisle Cemetery, Pennsylvania, describes her as "The Heroine of Monmouth." She died in 1832 at the age of seventy-nine.

Several other heroic, unusual, and even comic incidents occurred.

Captain Henry Fauntleroy of the Fifth Virginia regiment, stopped to drink at a well. Seeing himself surrounded by parched soldiers, he waived his turn and unselfishly stood aside. A round shot struck his side, throwing him to the ground badly mangled and dying. Washington's superb white horse collapsed and died from heat prostration. His body-servant, Billy Lee, galloped up a little hill with a party of servants to view the battle. Drawing out the General's spyglass, he surveyed the scene, attracting the attention of the enemy. "See those fellows collecting on yonder height," Washington remarked to his staff, "the enemy will fire on them to a certain-

Map published about 1780

ty." A shot from a British six-pounder rattled the branches of the tree beneath which the servants stood. Even in that hour of anxiety, Washington laughed.

"Steady, steady, then pick out the King's birds"

Late in the day, Lieutenant Colonel Henry Monckton led the British Grenadiers in a spirited attack on the rail-fence defended by General Anthony Wayne. "Steady, steady," Wayne called to his men, ordering them to wait for the word and "then pick out the King's birds," meaning the officers. One rifleman shot Monckton, who fell dead close to the fence. Both sides made a rush to retrieve his body. The red-coated Grenadiers who loved their Colonel, and the shirt-sleeved Pennsylvanians fought over it, before the latter carried it off. After the battle, they buried the gallant Colonel's body with full military honors, in the churchyard of the old Tennent Church. Years later a local resident raised a monument to the subject of Great Britain who "sleeps in an unknown grave."

By late afternoon, the Americans were strong enough to counterattack and drive the British back. By six o'clock they were in full retreat. Clinton reached New York, his army depleted by the loss of 1,500 men, chiefly from heat-stroke and by desertion. Washington wrote that "from an unfortunate and bad beginning, it turned out a glorious and happy day." The "Capital army of Britain defeated and obliged to retreat before the Americans," observed Colonel Knox.

The achievement of Washington's army had been great. Thrown back in disorder it had put up a disciplined resistance. Thanks to von Steuben, it was no longer a rabble in arms.

Baron Frederick von Steuben

The engagement on Rhode Island, August 29, 1778
—From a print in the Gentleman's Magazine, 1778

RHODE ISLAND AND STONY POINT

At New York, Clinton learned that a French fleet had been sighted on June 8 off the Virginia Capes. Count D'Estaing had eluded the British blockade and escaped from Toulon. The entry of France changed the war for the British. The subjugation of the rebellious colonists became a secondary issue. Faced by her old rival, eager to regain the possessions she had lost in the previous war, Britain was forced to fight in European waters, across the Atlantic and in the Caribbean.

D'Estaing sailed to New York, where his powerful ships of the line outnumbered and outgunned the fleet commanded by Lord Howe. But, warned by local pilots against entering the harbor, D'Estaing sailed to Rhode Island, where the British garrison was under siege from General Sullivan.

D'Estaing missed the opportunity to deal a decisive blow. He landed his troops to assist Sullivan. When the British fleet, which had been reinforced by the arrival of a squadron from England, hove in sight, he re-embarked his soldiers and stood out to sea. Both fleets were scattered by a severe gale, and D'Estaing went to Boston to refit. Sullivan was furious. He indulged in passionate denunciation of D'Estaing, writing to Henry Laurens:

> This movement has raised every voice against the French nation, revived all those ancient prejudices against the faith and sincerity of that people, and inclines them most heartily to curse the new alliance. These are only the first sallies of passion, which will in a few days subside.

He resented the conduct of the Count which had stranded him on the island without means of retreat:

> I begged the Count to remain only twenty-four hours, and I would agree to dismiss him, but in vain. He well knew that the original plan was for him to land his own troops with a large detachment of mine within their lines, under fire of some of his ships, while with the rest I made an attack in front, but his departure has reduced me to the necessity of attacking their works in front or of doing nothing. They have double lines across the island in two places, at near quarter of a mile distance.

The outer line is covered in front by redoubts within musket-shot of each other; the second in the same manner by redoubts thrown up between the lines. Besides this, there is an inaccessible pond which covers more than half of the first line. A strong fortress on Tomminy Hill overlooks and commands the whole adjacent country.

At Boston, the French sailors became involved in a "violent affray" with the citizens. Several lives were lost, including that of a French officer. The riot engendered great hostility between the two allies.

General Sullivan, recalled Major John Trumbull, was left to pursue the enterprise on his own:

The enemy shut themselves up in Newport, while he advanced to the town in admirable order, and the place was invested in form.

It soon became evident that the attempt was vain, so long as the enemy could receive supplies and reinforcements by water, unmolested, so as soon as it was ascertained that the French fleet would not resume its station, the enterprise was abandoned—on the night between the 28th and 29th of August, the army was withdrawn, and reoccupied their former position on Butts' Hill, near Howland's ferry, at the north end of the island.

Soon after daybreak the next morning, the rear guard, commanded by that excellent officer, Col. Wigglesworth, was attacked on Quaker, otherwise called Windmill Hill; and Gen. Sullivan, wishing to avoid a serious action on that ground, sent me with orders to the commanding officer to withdraw the guard. In performing this duty I had to mount the hill by a broad smooth road, more than a mile in length from the foot to the summit, where was the scene of the conflict, which, though an easy ascent, was yet too steep for a trot or a gallop. It was necessary to ride at a leisurely pace, for I saw before me a hard day's work for my horse, and was unwilling to fatigue him.

Nothing can be more trying to the nerves, than to advance thus deliberately alone and into danger. At first I saw a round shot or two drop near me and pass bounding on. Presently, I met poor Col. Tousard, who had just lost one arm, blown off by the discharge of a fieldpiece, for the possession of which there was an ardent struggle. He was led off by a small party. Soon

View northward from Butts' Hill

He traveled to Philadelphia to consult with Congress. What he saw there increased his gloom. "Our affairs," he wrote on December 18, "are in a more depressed, ruinous, and deplorable condition than they have been since the commencement of the war. Idleness, dissipation, extravagance, peculation, and an insatiable thirst for riches seem to have taken hold of everyone."

Lamenting the lack of great men, he returned to Morristown, where the army, still badly clothed and lacking food, endured a more severe winter than in the previous year. It did not lack gaiety. Many officers had brought their wives to share their discomforts. At one ball, Washington danced with Colonel Knox's wife, Lucy. At another, Mrs. Nathanael Greene, according to her husband, "danced upwards of three hours without sitting down." He described the occasion to a friend as "a pretty little frisk."

A near mutiny

Martin (who had transferred to the Continental Line) wintered in Connecticut, arriving there in January, a "very stormy month, a good deal of snow," and "it was a mere chance if we got anything to eat at all." The condition of his regiment became "insupportable," and the soldiers concluded "we could not or would not bear it any longer." One evening after roll call the men mustered but without their arms. Realizing that they faced a near mutiny, the officers came in front of the regiment, "expressing a deal of sorrow for the hardships we were compelled to undergo, but much more for what they were pleased to call our mutinous conduct." Their officers' concern served only to exasperate the men, who were persuaded by an abundance of fair promises to return to their quarters:

> But hunger was not to be so easily pacified, and would not suffer many of us to sleep. We were therefore determined that none others should sleep. Martial law was very strict against firing muskets in camp. Nothing could, therefore, raise the officers' "lofty ideas" sooner, or more, than to fire in camp; but it was beyond the power or vigilance of all the officers to prevent the men from "making void the law" on that night. Finding they were watched by the officers, they got an old gun barrel which they placed in a hut that was unfinished. This they loaded a third part full and putting a slow match to it, would then escape to their own huts, when the old barrel would speak for itself, with a voice that would be heard. The officers would then muster out, and some running and scolding would ensue; but none knew who made the noise, or where it came from. This farce was carried on the greater part of the night; but at length the officers, getting tired of running so often to catch Mr. Nobody, without finding him, that they soon gave up the chase, and the men, seeing they could no longer gull the officers, gave up the business likewise.

For a few days the soldiers fared better "but the old system soon returned." Martin obtained leave and walked the thirty

Explanation of the map.—This map shows the relative position of Verplanck's and Stony Points, and the forts in the time of the Revolution. A represents the position and form of the fort on Stony Point; B, General Wayne's right column, and C his left column, when he stormed the ramparts and fort; and D shows the site of Fort Fayette, on the east side of the river.

miles to his home at Milford, to visit his grandparents. In the early summer he went to Peekskill on the Hudson.

The war moved to the southern states. In the north, Clinton ascended the Hudson and took possession of Verplanck's Point and Stony Point, the two forts which defended the passage through the Highlands, the natural barrier that protected the upper part of the state. The British advance posed a dangerous threat to the American base at West Point, higher up the river. To protect that fort, Washington stationed General Anthony Wayne behind the Dunderberg mountain. Clinton returned to New York, leaving garrisons to hold the two river forts.

"I'll storm hell if you will only plan it"

Wayne proposed and Washington approved an attack on the forts which stood opposite each other, jutting out a mile into the water. Positioned on the neck formed by Haverstraw bay, near Peekskill, Stony Point on the west bank was the stronger of the two. On the river side, it was protected by the *Vulture* warship anchored in the bay. On the land side, it was surrounded by marshes, crossed by a narrow causeway. "Will you lead the assault?" asked Washington. "I'll storm hell if you will only plan it," replied Wayne. He sent Captain Allan McLane to spy out the fort's strength. Joining a party of women carrying provisions, he discovered "the unfinished state of the works." It was garrisoned by 700 soldiers, commanded by Colonel Henry Johnson.

A reward of five hundred dollars to the first man to enter the fort.

Setting out on the night of July 15, Wayne led his Pennsylvania and Virginia riflemen to the attack. Each man was directed to place a piece of white paper in his hat, to distinguish him from the enemy, and they were ordered to use their bayonets only. Wayne told them, "If any soldier presume to take his musket from his shoulder, attempt to fire, or begin the battle till ordered by his proper officer, he shall be instantly put to death." When one man forgot, he was stabbed through the heart. A reward of five hundred dollars was offered to the first man to enter the fort.

By eight o'clock on the 16th, Wayne's force had reached within a mile and a half of Stony Point. Wayne himself went to the right, Colonel Butler to the left. Light Horse Harry Lee came up behind with reinforcements. Each column was led by a picked force of one hundred men who were directed to surprise and kill the sentries. Another detachment was ordered to make a feint attack along the causeway, six minutes ahead of other columns. Silently, the soldiers waded through the marsh. The silence was broken by the crack, crack of muskets. Spotting the decoy force, the sentries fired, drawing the garrison to the causeway.

Admiral Sir George Collier described the assault from the British viewpoint:

> The rebel troops, under a General Wayne, formed two attacks with fixed bayonets and unloaded arms during the darkness and silence of the night; it was said that they had taken the precaution to kill every dog two days before that was within some miles round the post, to prevent their approach being discovered by their barking. They began to march from their camp, eleven miles off, soon after dusk, proceeding with celerity and silence; and soon after midnight fell in with the British piquets, whom they surprised, and bayonetted a number of them; the rest hastily retreated, keeping up a straggling fire, though to very little purpose, for the rebels followed close at their heels. Their forlorn hope consisted of forty men, and they were followed by a party with hooks on long poles to pull aside the abatis and thereby give an entrance to the column behind.

Gold medal awarded by Congress to General Wayne

"Keep on, keep on, remember Paoli!"

The two flank columns crept through the marsh, amidst flying bullets and cannon balls. They reached the abatis. Colonel Johnson, a young man but "a brave and good officer for his years," hurried there. "Come on, you damned rebels! Come on!" cried the guards. They fired into the darkness. Wayne was hit in the head. He fell to the ground crying, "Keep on, keep on, remember Paoli." Colonel Feberger, the Danish volunteer, took the lead. Shouting, "Paoli, Paoli!" the soldiers climbed over the abatis. On the left, Butler led his men up the jagged rocks. Johnson heard the cry, "The fort is ours." Twenty minutes had elapsed since the attack began.

"The whole business was done with fixed bayonets."

"The whole business was done with fixed bayonets," stated General Greene. "The rebels," said Collier, "made the attack with a bravery they never before exhibited, and they showed at this moment a generosity and clemency which during the course of the rebellion had no parallel. There was light sufficient after getting up the heights to show them many of the British troops with arms in their hands; instead of putting them to death, they called to them "to throw their arms down if they expected any quarter." It was too late then to resist; they submitted, and the strong post of Stony Point fell again into possession of the rebels." He called the enterprise "a really gallant one, and as bravely executed."

Wayne was only slightly wounded. The Americans had lost ninety men killed and wounded. The British loss was small other than in prisoners and of valuable cannon.

The Americans, having destroyed its fortifications, abandoned Stony Point, which they could not hold. Their victory was psychological. They had shown themselves capable of disciplined night attack, and in the use of the bayonet. And they had avenged Paoli. Wayne, already famous, became the hero of the hour, a man no longer deserving of Washington's lukewarm praise, "brave and nothing else."

Harry Lee, who had earned a considerable reputation as a partisan leader, was piqued by Wayne's success. He gained Washington's consent for a raid on the British port at Paulus Hook, now the site of Jersey City, opposite New York. On the night of August 18, Allan McLane led his men across the swamps and over the ditch. Using their bayonets, the Americans routed the 200-man garrison. Threatened by the relief force, they withdrew with their prisoners.

In the north, the year 1778 proved disappointing to both sides, for neither was strong enough to make a decisive move. This stalemate gave Washington the opportunity to launch an enterprise which he had long wished to undertake. From the frontier came reports of Indian massacres.

NEWTOWN

In June, 1778, Colonel John Butler, leading a force of 500 Tory Rangers and 500 Seneca Indians, swept from Fort Niagara on Lake Ontario into the Wyoming valley in western Pennsylvania, burning, plundering, scalping and murdering, and carrying off its 2,000 peaceful settlers. At Lackawanna, the settlers took refuge in a stockade. When the enemy approached, 582 men went out and advanced boldly on the Indians, who retreated, leading them into an ambush. For a time the settlers held their ground until the Indians, throwing down their muskets, rushed in wielding their tomahawks and spears. The settlers received the first onslaught with undaunted courage; rushing in again with redoubled fury, the Indians put them to flight. The survivors plunged into the river with the hope of reaching the farther bank. Being naked their pursuers overtook and killed them. Only 33 men escaped the massacre.

Joseph Brant

It was seen and heard by the families sheltering within the stockade—those too old to fight, the women and children, the widows and orphans—who could now expect the same fate. When they had finished their scalping, the Indians demanded entrance. Lacking means to resist and hoping for clemency, the defenders, if such they may be called, opened the gates. The Indians rushed in, brandishing their bloody weapons and exhibiting their gory trophies. The women knelt, their children clustering around them, entreating mercy. The miracle happened. The savages ignored them. They burned the stockade, all the houses and barns in the valley, and drove off the stock.

The survivors of the massacre abandoned the valley, trekking back to the safe country from which they had emigrated, spreading their tale of despoilation and murder. The Indians returned to Niagara, led by their chief, Thayendanegea, who is better known by his adopted name of Joseph Brant, his men laden with 250 scalps, leaving the once fertile valley a desolate wasteland.

Two months later, Brant raided the Mohawk valley and in November wiped out settlements in the Cherry valley, reaching to within fifty miles of Albany on the Hudson.

An appeal to Congress

The terrified settlers on the frontier appealed to Congress; that body urged Washington to punish the offending Indian tribes, those of the Six Nations, the powerful Confederacy

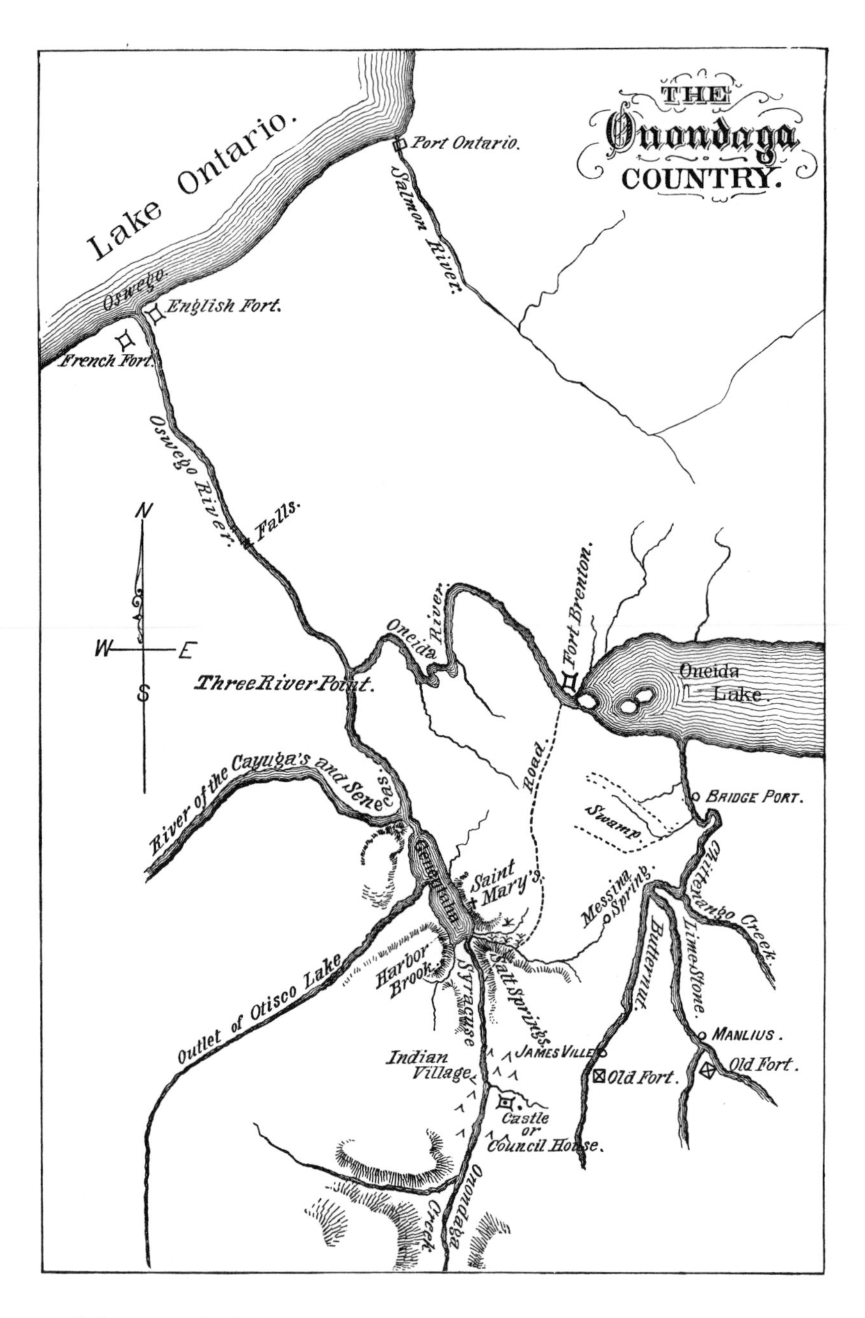

which occupied the area bounded on the east by the Catskill mountains, on the south by the Susquehanna River and on the north by Lake Erie. These Indians had remained loyal to British rule. They depended upon Canada for their supplies and for the sale of their pelts and furs.

Washington brought General John Sullivan from Rhode Island and put him in command of the punitive expedition comprising 4,000 soldiers. He moved up the Delaware and Susquehanna rivers and James Clinton, the brother of General George Clinton, with part of the army, ascended the Hudson. He turned into the Mohawk valley, and struck westward to the Susquehanna. The two columns joined at Tioga on August 22. Forsaking the river, Sullivan marched overland, as Clinton informed his brother:

> Being encumbered with a train of artillery and wagons and the roads being very bad, owing to a heavy rain the preceding day, together with other circumstances attending the first day's movements, we did not march more than three miles and encamped. Friday we proceeded on our march about eight o'clock in the morning, but my brigade, which formed the rear or second line of the army, had not marched from their ground more than two miles before the infantry in front halted at a narrow defile formed by the jutting out of the mountain to the river. This defile, which was near half a mile in length and would at first sight have been judged impassible, particularly to artillery etc., detained the army so long that it was near ten o'clock at night before the rear of the main body, consisting of Poor's and Maxwell's brigades had passed. As it was then dark, and as the cattle had not yet passed it, I judged it most proper not to attempt it that night, but marched back about a mile and encamped on tolerable good ground. Saturday I decamped and joined the army at Chemung about twelve o'clock. This town, which is about twelve miles from Tioga, had been destroyed by Gen. Sullivan immediately on his arrival at Tioga, together with a large quantity of corn, beans, etc., preserving only one field, consisting of about forty acres, for the use of the army on their arrival, and which they effectually consumed and destroyed.
>
> Altho' we had every reason to expect the enemy would have attempted to prevent our progress and retard our march, from the amazing advantages Nature had liberally furnished them with, yet they never gave us the least opposition, or ever made their appearance, except a small party who fired upon and killed and wounded a few of Gen. Hand's advanced guard on the former attempt to destroy the settlement.

Lieutenant William Barton recalled in his journal the march to the Indian settlement at Newtown:

> *Sunday 29th.* Proceeded very slowly two miles, occasioned by the roughness of the way, which we had to clear for the artillery, baggage etc. to pass. Here we halted for one hour and a half, until the artillery, etc. should raise a difficult height, at which time an advanced party of our riflemen discovered the enemy throwing up some works on the other side of a morass, and a difficult place through which we had to pass. It appears this was intended for an ambuscade, it being on a small height, where some logs, etc. were laid up, covered with green bushes; which extended half a mile. On the right was a small town which they had destroyed themselves, making use of the timber, etc. in the above works. After the ground was well reconnoitred, the artillery was advanced on their left. At the same time Gen'l Poor with his brigade was endeavoring to gain their rear around their left; Gen'l Hand's brigade was following in rear of Poor. Our brigade was kept as a reserve, also Gen'l Clinton's, until their rear should be gained; but they having a party posted on a very considerable height, over which our right flank had to pass, we were discovered by them.

About 9:00 A.M., stated Clinton, the scouts brought intelligence that the enemy was about five miles ahead, near Newtown. The magnitude of their fires indicated a considerable

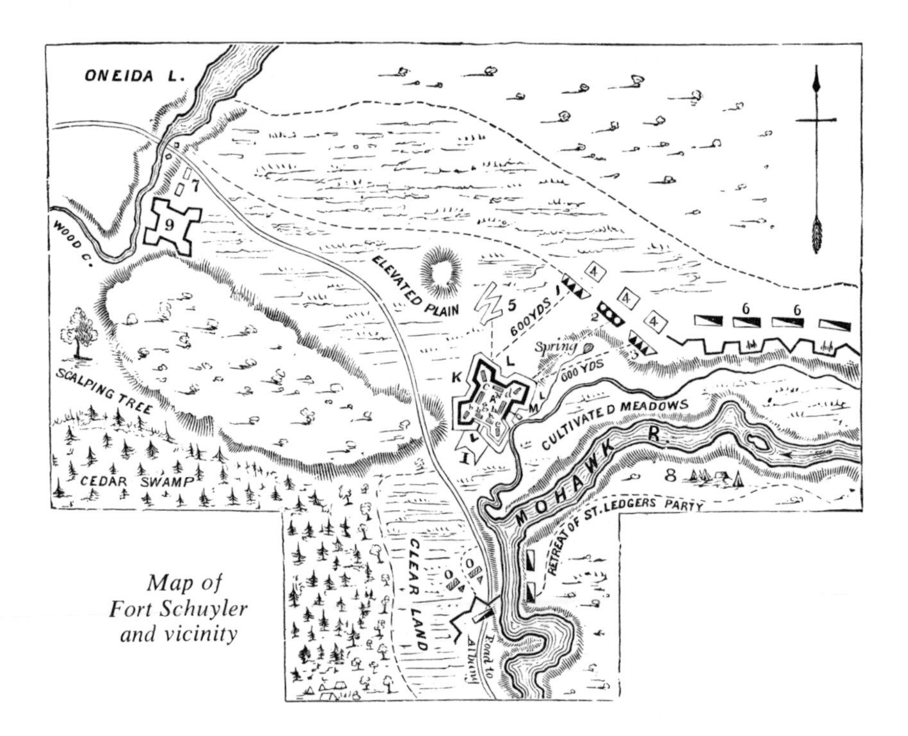

Map of Fort Schuyler and vicinity

force. The scouts had heard the sound of axes which suggested that the Indians were preparing an ambuscade:

> This, in fact, appeared to be their intention, and if we had proceeded as they expected, in all probability we should have been very severely handled. About ten o'clock a scattering fire commenced between some of their scouts and a few of our riflemen and volunteers, when the former gave way, and the latter proceeded until they plainly discovered their works which were very extensive, tho' not impregnable. As our design was not to drive them, but to surround or bring them to a fair open action, the army halted, and a council being called, it was concluded that the artillery, supported by Gen. Hand with the infantry and rifle corps. should commence the action, previously allowing sufficient time for Poor's and my brigade to gain their right flank, while Maxwell's and the covering party under Col. Ogden might gain their left.

Two columns marched to outflank the Indians while the artillery pounded their fortifications. Lieutenant Robert Parker was with the guns:

> We began the attack by opening upon them two 5½ Irish howitzers and six three-pounders, when a pleasing piece of music ensued. But the Indians, I believe, did not admire the sound so much, nor could they be prevailed upon to listen to the music, although we made use of all the eloquence we were masters of for that purpose. But they were deaf to our entreaties and turned their backs upon us in token of their detestation for us.

Barton observed the results of the bombardment:

> Some shells and round shot were thrown among them in their works, which caused them to give several yells, and doubtless intimidated them much. But at this discovery they gave a most hideous yell and quit their works, endeavoring to prevent Gen'l Poor's ascending the height by a loose scattering fire.

General George Clinton

Clinton commanded one flank column:

> About one o'clock Col. Proctor commenced a very warm cannonade upon their works, which continued near two hours, in which time we attempted to complete our march upon their flanks, but from the very thick swamps and rough country thro' which we were to pass we were in some measure prevented. The enemy, finding their situation in their lines rather uncomfortable and finding we did not intend to storm them, abandoned them some time before the infantry discovered it, and immediately proceeded to join the remaining half of the force who were posted on a hill, and attack our right flank as we expected.
>
> Gen. Poor, who was near a quarter of a mile on the left of my front, had ascended a considerable mountain about half way, which was very steep, when he discovered them and received their fire accompanied by the war whoop, but tho' his troops were considerably fatigued with ascending the mountain under their heavy packs, yet they pushed up in the face of their fire, driving them from tree to tree until they fled with the utmost precipitation, leaving their pack and blankets behind them, etc. in order to take off their dead and wounded, which must be very considerable, as they left nine Indians on the field whom they could not carry off. My brigade, which had just reached the foot of the hill when the firing commenced, pushed up with such ardor that many of them almost fainted and fell down with excessive heat and fatigue, for the ground was so steep that no person could ride up.

Yet another diarist, Nathan Davis, saw the Indians race up the hill on their left and take cover behind its many trees:

> When our front had advanced within a short distance of them, they commenced a fire from behind every tree and at the same time gave the war whoop. Not all the infernals of the prince of darkness, could they have been let loose from the bottomless pit, would have borne any comparison to these demons of the forest.

As the soldiers advanced, withholding their fire;

> The Indians kept up an incessant fire upon us from behind the trees, firing and retreating back to another tree, loading and firing again, still keeping up the war whoop. They continued this mode of warfare until we had driven them half way up the hill, when we were ordered to charge bayonets and rush on. No sooner said than done. We then in our turn gave our war whoop in the American style, which completely silenced the unearthly voice of their stenorian throats.

"Our troops," said Barton:

> pressing forward with much vigor, made them give way, leaving their dead behind (amounting to eleven or twelve), which were scalped immediately. We likewise took one white man, who appeared to be dead, and was stripped, when an officer came up and examined him, said he was not wounded, gave him a stroke and bade him get up; he immediately rose up and implored mercy, and was kept a prisoner some time. In the evening a Negro was taken. Their number wounded not known. Two or

An early sketch of Niagara Falls

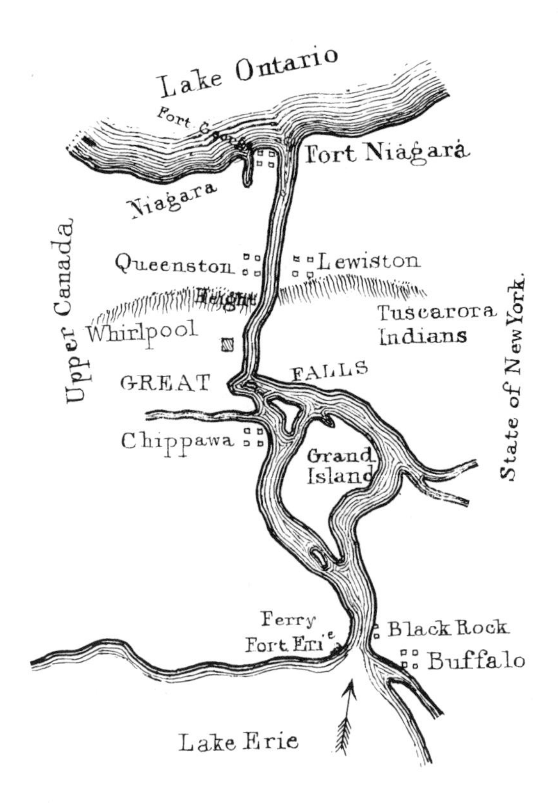

three of ours killed, and thirty-four or five wounded. Among the latter Major Titcomb, Capt. Cloise, and Lt. Allis.

At half after three the firing ceased, and the army proceeded one mile and a half to a considerable town consisting of about twenty huts. The number of the enemy uncertain, but from the best intelligence from the prisoners, the whites were about two hundred, the Indians five. They were commanded by Butler and Brant, who had been waiting some days for our approach. It appears their expectations were great, from their numbers, situation, etc. The prisoners likewise inform us they had been kept on an allowance of seven ears of corn per day each although there is a very great abundance of corn, beans, potatoes, squashes, etc. for several miles on the creek, upon which our whole army has subsisted for days. We had nevertheless to destroy some hundred bushels. Here was found a deal of plunder of theirs, such as blankets, brass kettles etc.

The whole action, noted Clinton, had lasted, from first to last, near six hours. Colonel Butler and Joseph Brant escaped.

Sullivan continued his march northwards, burning many Indian villages. At one, a party led by Lieutenant Thomas Boyd (as Barton related) killed and scalped an Indian. Learning that others had been seen hurrying away, Boyd led his men in pursuit. They killed another Indian: "The men then went to scalp him, which caused some dispute who should have it, at the same instant the enemy rose up from their ambuscade, when the action commenced, but they being much superior in numbers, caused him and one or two others to surrender, though not until the rest were all killed and got off." The next day, Lieutenant Enkuries Beatty entered the town:

We found the body of Lt. Boyd and another rifleman in a most terrible mangled condition. They were both stripped naked and their heads cut off, and the flesh of Lt. Boyd's head was entirely taken off and his eyes punched out. The other man's head was not there. They was stabbed, I suppose, in 40 different places in the body with a spear and great gashes cut in their flesh with knives, and Lt. Boyd's privates was nearly cut off and hanging down, his finger and toe nails was bruised off, and the dogs had eat part of their shoulders away; likewise a knife was sticking in Lt. Boyd's body. They was immediately buried with the honors of war.

At another village Barton encountered "a white woman with a young child, who was almost starved, having made her escape two or three nights before from the enemy." She told Barton she had been taken from the Wyoming valley, where her husband had been killed.

Another punitive expedition

Another punitive expedition, commanded by Colonel Daniel Brodhead, starting from Fort Pitt, moved up the Allegheny River, burned Indian villages, and returned thirty-three days later without suffering the loss of a man.

The Indians were soon again active. In 1780, Brant again ravaged the Mohawk valley, where he was joined by a force of

Tories commanded by Sir John Johnson (whose father had dominated the valley) and Colonel Butler. Collecting a force of New York militia, Colonel Marinus Willett, the defender of Fort Stanwix in 1777, met and defeated them at Johnstown, pursuing the survivors, as he informed Governor Clinton:

> I am just returned from a most fatiguing pursuit of the enemy and tho' it has not been in my power to take or kill the whole of the detachment that lately made their appearance in this quarter, yet I flatter myself they are little better off, as those that are not among the killed and taken are in a famishing situation, scattered throughout the wilderness on the route to Buck Island, where any of them that may arrive will have tales of horror only to relate.

It took the Americans to the end of 1781 to clear New York state of Indians and Tories.

A spirited dissenter
—Sketch by Kay Smith

MORRISTOWN

Washington's headquarters in Morristown

The war fluctuated in the south, now the principal campaign area. Washington remained in the north, to watch Clinton; the two armies clashed in the spring of 1780 in New Jersey, at Springfield and the village of Connecticut Farms, which the Hessians looted and burned, incensing the inhabitants. Otherwise, the war in the north stagnated. Neither army was strong enough to challenge the other.

Again, keeping his army in being was Washington's principal task. The winters of 1779–80 and 1780–81 were particularly severe, and both were marked by dangerous mutinies. They threatened the army's existence.

Joseph Plumb Martin called the winter of 1779–80 the "hard winter," one of those times that "tried men's souls." At Morristown, New Jersey, he said that "we were absolutely, literally starved." For four days he did not put a single morsel of victuals into his mouth except "a little black birch bark" which he gnawed off a stick of wood. He saw men roast their shoes and eat them. By May, they were still attended by "the monster Hunger." The Connecticut men became exasperated and saw no alternative "but to starve to death, or break up the army, give all up and go home." What was to be done?

> Here was the army starved and naked, and there their country sitting still and expecting the army to do notable things while fainting from sheer starvation. All things considered, the army was not to be blamed. Reader, suffer what we did and you will say so, too.

It was more than human nature could endure. On parade, the soldiers growled, snapping at their officers and acting contrary to orders. One man spoke to an officer who said something which did not altogether accord with the soldier's sense of propriety. The man retorted; the officer called him a mutinous rascal. Stamping the butt of his musket in passion, the soldier called "Who will parade with me?" The whole regiment fell in immediately. Three other regiments joined in. When he attempted to prevent other regiments from parading with their arms, Colonel Jonathan Meigs received a bayonet wound in his side. Other officers seized a man, dragging him from the ranks, but "the bayonets of the men pointing at their breasts, as thick as hatchet teeth, compelled them quickly to relinquish their hold of him." The men refused to disperse. Eventually, the mutiny fizzled out, but "our stir did us some good in the end, for we had provisions directly after, so we had no great cause for complaint for some time."

The Military Journal kept by Dr. James Thacher (whom we met first on his escape from Ticonderoga) shows that the soldiers, during these terrible winters, had cause for complaint:

> But the sufferings of the poor soldiers can scarcely be described. While on duty they are unavoidably exposed to all the inclemency of storm and severe cold. At night they now have a bed of straw on the ground and a single blanket to each man. They are badly clad and some are destitute of shoes.

The snow was four to six feet deep, and so obstructed the roads that no provisions could be brought to camp:

> For the last ten days we have received but two pounds of meat a man, and we are frequently for six or eight days entirely destitute of meat, and then as long without bread. The consequence is, the soldiers are so enfeebled from hunger and cold as to be almost unable to perform their military duty or labor in constructing their huts. It is well known that General Washington experiences the greatest solicitude for the sufferings of his army and is sensible that they in general conduct themselves with heroic patience and fortitude.

Mutiny at Princeton, New Jersey

The minor mutiny of the Connecticut regiments in May, 1780, was followed in January, 1781, by the far more serious mutiny of the Pennsylvanian Line at Princeton, New Jersey. Their uniforms hung in rags, they were underfed, they lacked liquor, their pay was in arrears, and they were mostly men of Irish-Scotch descent. Their commanding officer, the popular Anthony Wayne, warned the State Council in December that trouble was brewing.

> Neither officers nor soldiers have received a single drop of spirituous liquors from the public magazines since the 10th of October last, except one gill per man some time in November; this, together with the old worn out coats and tattered linen overalls, and what was once a poor substitute for a blanket (now divided among three soldiers), is but very wretched living and sheltering against the winter's piercing cold, drifting snows, and chilling sleets.

The example of their officers standing "for hours every day exposed to wind and weather, among the poor naked fellows," and sharing every vicissitude with them, prevented their murmuring in public. Only an immediate supply of cash could alleviate the situation, but he feared it was too late.

The men had enlisted early in 1777 for a term of three years at a stipulated pay. Their enlistments expired on December 31, 1780. Wayne felt it in his bones, as he put it, that there was going to be a bad storm and somebody was going to get lost at sea. On New Year's Day the camp was ominously still. Wayne and his officers spent the evening playing cards, "as cheerfully as you could wish," related Lieutenant Enos Reeves. About ten o'clock, they were disturbed by the huzzas of the soldiers. Wayne, followed by his officers, rushed out. Reeves saw numbers of men clustered in small groups, whispering and "busily running up and down the line." On the right, a gun fired; it was answered by another on the left. From the center rose a skyrocket "which was accompanied by a general huzza throughout the line, and the soldiers running out with their arms, accoutrements and knapsacks." Reeves realized it was a mutiny. The thirteen hundred men, comprising six regiments, announced that they were determined to march to Philadelphia to demand from Congress the money owing to them.

> The officers in general exerted themselves to keep the men quiet, and keep them from turning out. Each applied himself to his own company, endeavored to keep them in their huts and

A view of the battlefield near Princeton

lay by their arms, which they would do while we were present, but the moment we left one hut to go to another, they would be out again. Their excuse was they thought it was an alarm and the enemy coming on.

Next they began to move in crowds to the Parade, going up to the right which was the place appointed for their rendezvous. Lieut. White of our regiment, in endeavoring to stop one of those crowds, was shot through the thigh, and Capt. Samuel Tolbert, in opposing another party, was shot through the body, of which he is very ill. They continued huzzaing and firing in a riotous manner, so that it soon became dangerous for an officer to oppose them by force. We then left them to go their own way.

Hearing a confused noise to the right, between the line of huts and Mrs. Wicks, curiosity led me that way, and it being dark in the orchard I mixed among the crowd and found they had broken open the magazine and were preparing to take off the cannon.

In taking possession of the cannon, they forced the sentinel from his post and placed one of their own men. One of the mutineers coming officiously up to force him away (thinking him to be one of our sentinels) received a ball through the head and died instantly.

A dispute arose among the mutineers about firing the alarms with the cannon, and continued for a considerable time—one party alleging that it would arouse the timid soldiery; the other objected because it would alarm the inhabitants. For a while, I expected the dispute would be decided by the bayonet, but the gunner in the meantime slipped up to the piece and put a match to it, which ended the affair. Every discharge of the cannon was accompanied by a confused huzza and a general discharge of musketry.

"If you mean to kill me, shoot me at once—here's my breast!"

Wayne, accompanied by several officers, pistols in hand, approached "the mob," as he called it. He demanded that the men lay down their arms. A hundred men stepped from the ranks, leveling their bayonets at his breast. Several platoons fired their muskets over his head.

The General called out: "If you mean to kill me, shoot me at once—here's my breast!" opening his coat. They replied that it was not their intention to hurt or disturb an officer of the line (two or three individuals excepted); that they had nothing against these officers, and they would oppose any person that would attempt anything of the kind.

They only wanted justice, they said. They had been wronged and were determined to see themselves righted. Taking no further notice of Wayne, the mutineers marched away, shouting, cursing, and firing their muskets. He dashed to headquarters, where he mobilized a still faithful regiment. At its head, he led it up the road ahead of the mutineers. According to Enos Reeves, the loyal regiment refused to fire, and its officers were forced to retreat. One captain was killed.

General Anthony Wayne

> About twelve o'clock they sent parties to relieve or seize the old camp guard, and posted sentinels all around the camp. At one o'clock they moved off towards the left of the line with the cannon and when they reached the center they fired a shot. As they came down the line, they turned the soldiers out of every hut, and those who would not go with them were obliged to hide till they were gone. They continued huzzaing and a disorderly firing till they went off, about two o'clock with drums and fifes playing, under command of the sergeants, in regular platoons, with a front and rear guard.
>
> General Wayne met them as they were marching off and endeavored to persuade them back, but to no purpose; he then inquired which way they were going, and they replied either to Trenton or Philadelphia. He begged them not to attempt to go to the enemy. They declared it was not their intention, and that they would hang any man who would attempt it, and for that, if the enemy should come out in consequence of this revolt, they would turn back and fight them. "If that is your sentiment," said the General, "I'll not leave you, and if you won't allow me to march in your front, I'll follow in your rear."

Wayne, on the other hand, stated that he stood in front of the mutineers and ordered them to halt. When they fired again and marched on, he ordered his loyal soldiers to fire their cannon. The grapeshot killed a number of the rioters. Realizing it was suicide to resist, they filed slowly back to camp, muttering and threatening.

The mutiny threw the whole country into panic. Joseph Reed, the President of the Pennsylvania Council, hurried to the camp. He promised the men better clothing and their full back pay. "Thus," wrote General John Sullivan, "has this surprising affair been brought to a happy issue." He took solace from the fact that the mutineers had returned to duty as soon as their reasonable demands had been met.

The British in New York learned of the mutiny within two days, as Lieutenant Mackenzie described, remarking hopefully;

> The country is in great confusion, and the persons in authority under Congress dread the effects of this revolt, as the people in general are tired of the oppression and difficulties they suffer and earnestly wish for a return of peace and the old Government.

If they laid down their arms, they would be pardoned.

Emissaries were sent to assure the mutineers that "in this struggle for their rights and liberties" they would be assisted by a body of British troops. If they laid down their arms, they would be pardoned. They disdained these blandishments "with a firmness" which Sullivan thought worthy of ancient Romans. Three months after their mutiny, the Pennsylvanians were ordered to march southwards, to reinforce the army in Virginia. On May 19, the day before the march, twelve men stepped from the ranks and shouted that they would not march a step until their money had been paid in full. Wayne ordered out a firing squad. "Fire!" he called. Eleven mutineers fell dead. The twelfth writhed on the ground badly wounded. Wayne ordered a man to kill him with his bayonet. The soldier refused. Wayne held his pistol to the soldier's head. White-faced and trembling, he ran his comrade through the heart. The regiment marched to Virginia.

The story of these terrible winters—and the mutinies the men's hardships caused—has carried us ahead of other important events, one in particular.

Following the reoccupation of Philadelphia, Benedict Arnold had been appointed military governor of the city, and there he married the Tory belle, the one-time friend of Major John André, Peggy Shippen. Washington, who admired Arnold's military skill, offered him an active command. Pleading his lameness, Arnold requested and was given command of the fort at West Point on the Hudson. He reached the fort in the spring of 1780.

Mrs. Benedict Arnold (Peggy Shippen)

FROM A WATER-COLOR SKETCH BY KAY SMITH

Louis XV of France presented this 650-pound bronze bell, cast in 1741, to Kaskaskia for the French Jesuits, traders, and soldiers quartered in that area, and it was this bell—eleven years older than the Liberty Bell in Independence Hall, Philadelphia—that called the people to hear George Rogers Clark the night of July 4, 1778, through the intercession of Father Gibault, the French parish priest.

FROM A WATER-COLOR SKETCH BY KAY SMITH

This brick building in Ste. Genevieve, Missouri, near Kaskaskia, is of special interest in that it is believed to have been built about 1800 as the first brick structure west of the Mississippi River in a community that was inhabited years before the American Revolution.

KENTUCKY

First State House at Kaskaskia, Illinois

Kentucky also suffered the depredations of the Indians who were mobilized from the British fort at Detroit by Colonel Henry Hamilton. His nickname, the "hair-buyer," reveals the fear and hatred in which he was held on the frontier. His offer to buy American scalps was not, however, the immediate cause of the expedition organized in 1779 by George Rogers Clark.

Clark, a twenty-five-year-old surveyor and frontiersman, went to Virginia to enlist support for his plan to conquer the British held northwest, the territory stretching from the Ohio River to the Great Lakes. The towns of Kaskaskia, Vincennes and Detroit were the chief centers of British power. From these military stations, they supplied the arms and ammunition which stimulated the Indian raids which "drenched the land in blood." The Virginia assembly approved Clark's plan, gave him £1,200 sterling, and commissioned him to raise seven companies of militia.

Leading 120 men, Clark set off from Redstone on June 24, 1779. The Monongahela and Ohio rivers provided transport to Fort Massac. An overland march of 120 miles brought the expedition to within three miles of Kaskaskia, a town comprising 250 houses and a stone fort. En route, Clark was joined by a number of French settlers who brought his numbers to 175 men. Recalling the march, when he composed his Journal in 1796, Clark observed:

> Nothing remarkable on this route, The weather was favorable; in some parts water was scarce as well as game; of course we suffered drought and hunger, but not to excess. On the third day, John Saunders, our principal guide, appeared confused, and we soon discovered that he was totally lost, without there was some other cause of his present conduct. I asked him various questions and from his answers could scarcely determine what to think of him, whether or not he was sensible that he was lost or that he wished to deceive us. The cry of the whole detachment was that he was a traitor. He begged that he might be suffered to go some distance into a plain that was in full view, to try to make some discovery whether or not he was right. I told him he might go but that I was suspicious of him from his conduct.

After a search, Saunders found the way and "we discovered that fellow had been, as they call it, bewildered."

Clark reached Kaskaskia on July 4. The inhabitants, he believed, suspected nothing:

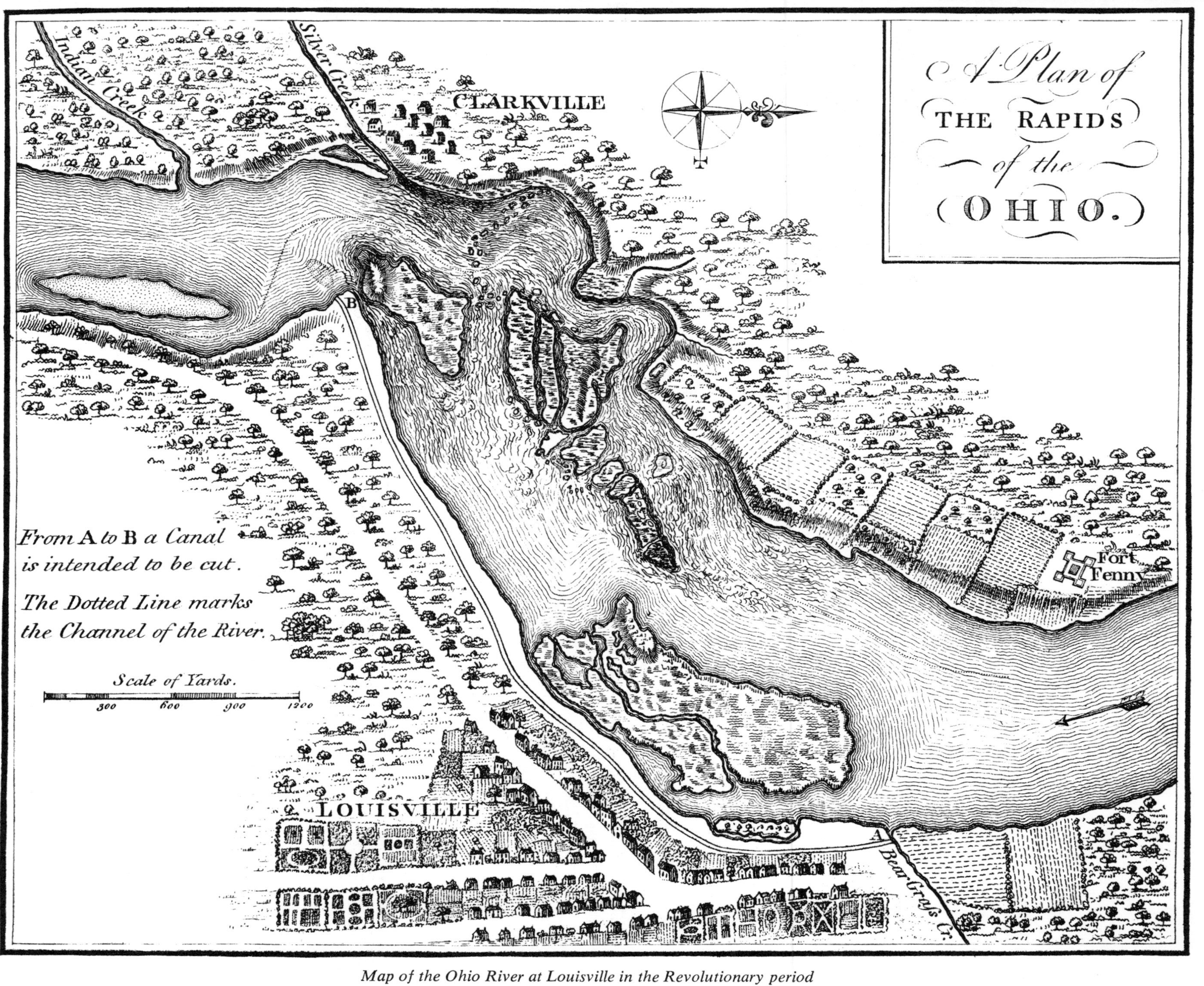

Map of the Ohio River at Louisville in the Revolutionary period

With one of the divisions, I marched to the fort and ordered the other two into different quarters of the town. If I met with no resistance, at a certain signal a general shout was to be given, and certain parts were to be immediately possessed, and the men of each detachment who could speak the French language were to run through every street and proclaim what had happened, and inform the inhabitants that every person who appeared in the streets would be shot down. This disposition had its desired effect. In a very little time we had complete possession, and every avenue was guarded to prevent any escape to give the alarm to the other villages, in case of opposition. Various orders had been issued not worth mentioning. I don't suppose greater silence ever reigned among the inhabitants of a place than did at present; not a person to be seen, not a word to be heard from them for some time; but, designedly, the greatest noise kept up by our troops through every quarter of the town, and patrols continually the whole night round it, as intercepting any information was a capital object, and in about two hours the whole of the inhabitants were disarmed, and informed that if one was taken attempting to make his escape, he would be immediately put to death.

The French-Canadian inhabitants of Kaskaskia took the oath of allegiance to the United States.

Kaskaskia had been captured without firing a shot. From the inhabitants Clark learned that the Indians had been recruited by the British and that "the sound of war was universal among them; scarcely a nation but had declared it and received the bloody belt and hatchet."

Vincennes was the next objective. The French priest at Kaskaskia, Father Gibault, told Clark that it was very strong and to capture it required "other means than that of guns." Gibault undertook to win the loyalty of its inhabitants. "He gave me to understand that although he had nothing to do with temporal business, he would give them such hints in the spiritual way that would be very conducive to the business."

The people of Vincennes took the oath of allegiance to the United States.

Father Gibault was completely successful. The people of Vincennes took the oath of allegiance to the United States, and displayed the American flag. Now citizens of the new Republic, the inhabitants informed the Indians that their old father:

. . . the king of France, was come to life again, had joined the big knife, and was mad at them for fighting for the English; that they would advise them to make peace with the Americans as soon as they could, otherwise they might expect the land to be very bloody, etc. The Indians began to think seriously. Throughout the country this was now the kind of language they generally got from their ancient friends of the Wabash and Illinois.

The good news of the capitulation of Vincennes was brought to Kaskaskia on August 1. Clark sent Captain Leonard Helm to take command at Vincennes, while he set out to win the allegiance of the Indian tribes, and the loyalty of the Peankeshaw Chief named "Tobacco's Son," whom the Indians called "The Grand Door of the Wabash," meaning that he controlled that region, for "nothing of consequence was to be undertaken without his consent." Captain Helm carried Clark's letter:

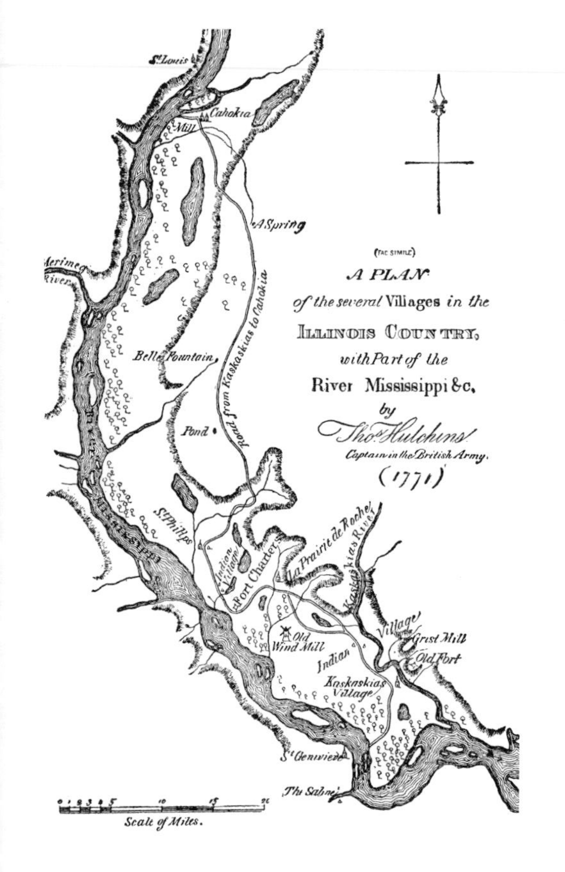

> After having it read, he informed the captain that he was happy to see him, one of the big knife chiefs, in this town—it was here that he had joined the English against him—but he confessed that he always thought that they looked gloomy; that as the contents of the letter was a matter of great moment, he could not give an answer for some time; that he must collect his counselors on the subject, and was in hopes that the captain would be patient. In short, he put on all the courtly dignity that he was master of, and Captain Helm, following his example, it was several days before this business was finished, as the whole proceeding was very ceremonious. At length the captain was invited to the Indian council and informed by the Tobacco that they had maturely considered the case in hand and had got the nature of the war between the English and us explained to their satisfaction; that, as we spoke the same language, and appeared to be the same people, he always thought he was in the dark as to the truth of it, but now the sky was cleared up; that he found that the big knife was in the right; that, perhaps, if the English conquered, they would serve them in the same manner that they intended to serve us; that his ideas were quite changed, and that he would tell all the red people on tne Wabash to bloody the land no more for the English. He jumped up, struck his breast; called himself a man and a warrior; said that he was now a big knife, and took Captain Helm by the hand. His example was followed by all present, and the evening was spent in merriment. Thus ended this valuable negotiation and the saving of much blood.
>
> This man proved a zealous friend to the day of his death, which happened two years after this, when he desired to be buried among the Americans.

In December, Clark learned from his spies that Governor Hamilton had marched from Detroit with thirty soldiers, fifty French volunteers and four hundred Indians, had retaken Vincennes, and expected reinforcements in the spring.

A critical situation

The situation was critical for, by a junction of the northern and southern Indians, Hamilton could command such a force "that nothing in this quarter could withstand his arms." Kentucky must immediately fall. Clark believed that by the time he could raise sufficient force, it would be too late:

> We saw but one alternative, which was to attack the enemy in their quarters. If we were fortunate, it would save the whole; if otherwise it would be nothing more than what would certainly be the consequence if we should not make the attempt.

George Rogers Clark

Encouraged by the idea of the greatness of the consequences that would attend our success—the season of the year being also favorable—as the enemy could not suppose that we should be so mad as to attempt to march eighty leagues through a drowned country in the depths of winter; that they would be off their guard and probably would not think it worth while to keep out spies; that, probably, if we could make our way good, we might surprise them, and if we fell through, the country would not be in a worse situation than if we had not made the attempt. These, and many other similar reasons, induced us to resolve to attempt the enterprise, which met with the approbation of every individual belonging to us.

Clark made his preparations:

The whole country took fire at the alarm and every order was executed with cheerfulness by every description of the inhabitants—preparing provisions, encouraging volunteers, etc.—and, as we had plenty of stores, every man was completely rigged with what he could desire to withstand the coldest weather.

The Wabash River, Clark knew, would be "overflowed to five or six miles wide," which would require a wide detour. Dispatching forty-six men in a long boat, he set out in February on a march of 240 miles through "I suppose one of the most beautiful countries in the world, but at this time in many parts flowing with water and exceedingly bad marching. My greatest care was to direct the men as much as possible in order to keep up their spirits. The difficulties," said Clark, "would have been enough to have stopped any set of man that was not in the same temper that we were."

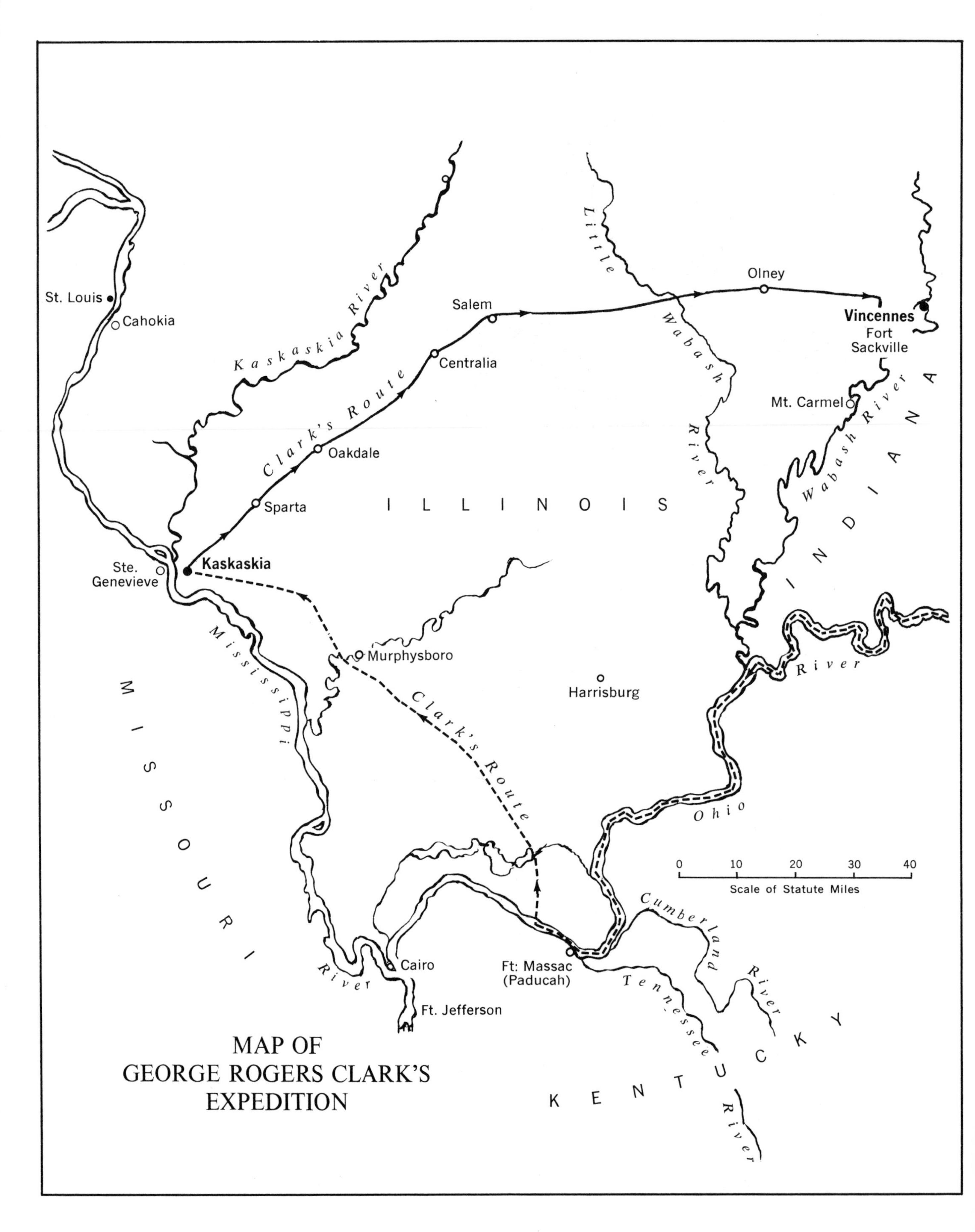

MAP OF
GEORGE ROGERS CLARK'S
EXPEDITION

By ferrying his horses, troops, and baggage over the waterlogged lowlands, Clark brought his men, "to our inexpressible joy" on the evening of February 23, to within three miles of Vincennes. He took a prisoner from whom he obtained all the intelligence he wished for, and he sent the man to warn the inhabitants to keep indoors. A thousand ideas flashed through his head. If he took too long to besiege the fort, a superior number of Englishmen, whom he learned were on the river to the north, commanded by Captain Lamothe, might come against him. He resolved to appear as daring as possible, so that "the enemy might conceive by our behavior that we were very numerous and probably discourage them. We were flinging ourselves into certain destruction or success." There was no middle course.

> We had but little to say to our men, except in calculating an idea of the necessity of obedience, etc. We knew they did not want encouraging, and that anything might be attempted with them that was possible for such a number—perfectly cool, under proper subordination, pleased with the prospect before them, and much attached to their officers. They all declared that they were convinced that an implicit obedience to orders was the only thing that would ensure success, and hoped that no mercy would be shown the person who should violate them—he should be immediately put to death. Such language as this from soldiers to persons in our station must have been exceedingly agreeable. We moved on slowly in full view of the town; but, as it was a point of some consequence to us to make ourselves appear formidable, we, in leaving the covert that we were in, marched and countermarched in such a manner that we appeared numerous.

When they approached the town there was "no hostile appearance." Even when the Americans fired on the fort, the British did not believe it was an enemy, "as drunken Indians frequently saluted the fort at night." The death of a sentry awakened them to their peril. "The drums now sounded and the business fairly commenced on both sides. Reinforcements were sent to the attack of the garrison." The inhabitants were warned to keep out of the way:

> We now found that the garrison had known nothing of us; that, having finished the fort that evening, they had amused themselves at different games, and had retired just before my letter arrived, as it was near roll-call. The placard being made public, many of the inhabitants were afraid to show themselves out of the houses for fear of giving offence, and not one dare give information.
>
> Our friends flew to the commons and other convenient places to view the pleasing sight, which was observed from the garrison and the reason asked, but a satisfactory excuse was given; and, as a part of the town lay between our line of march and the garrison, we could not be seen by the sentinels on the walls.

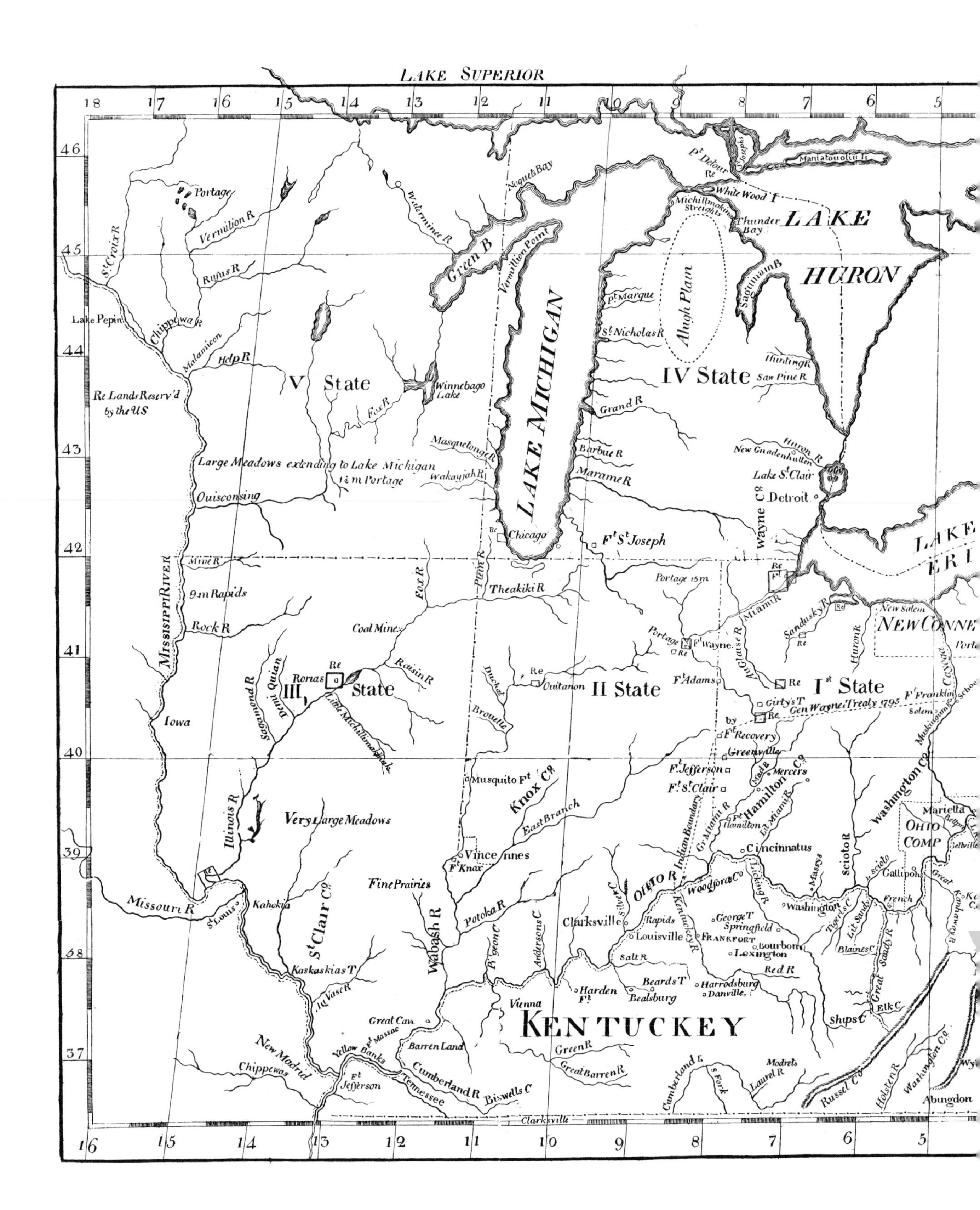
LAKE SUPERIOR
LAKE MICHIGAN
LAKE HURON
V State
IV State
III State
II State
Ist State
KENTUCKEY
Missisippi River
Chicago
Detroit
Louisville
Lexington
Cincinnatus
Vincennes
Green B
Winnebago Lake
Large Meadows extending to Lake Michigan
Very Large Meadows
Fine Prairies
Ohio R
Wabash R
Illinois R
Missouri R
Knox Co.
St Clair Co.
Wayne Co.
Hamilton Co.
Washington Co.

QUEBECK
DISTRICT of MAINE
VERMONT
NEW HAMPSHIRE
MASSACHUSETTS
RHODE ISLAND
CONNECTICUT
NEW YORK
NEW-JERSEY
PENNSYLVANIA
MARYLAND
DELAWARE
LAKE ONTARIO
ATLANTIC OCEAN
Explanation
Re Reserve
CH Court House
MAP of the Northern Part of the UNITED STATES of AMERICA
By Abraham Bradley Junr

The friendly citizens succeeded in sending a messenger into the fort to warn Captain Helm (who was held prisoner) of his approaching deliverance:

> The Tobacco's Son being in town with a number of warriors, immediately mustered them, and let us know that he wished to join us, saying that by the morning he would have a hundred men. He received for an answer that we thanked him for his friendly disposition, and, as we were sufficiently strong ourselves, we wished him to desist and that we would counsel on the subject in the morning; and, as we knew that there were a number of Indians in and near the town who were our enemies, some confusion might happen if our men should mix in the dark, but hoped that we might be favored with his counsel and company during the night, which was agreeable to him.

The fort was completely surrounded.

The fort was completely surrounded and the firing continued without intermission:

> The cannons of the garrison were on the upper floors of strong block-houses, at each angle of the fort, eleven feet above the surface, and the ports so badly cut that many of our troops lay under the fire of them within twenty or thirty yards of the walls. They did no damage, except to the buildings of the town, some of which they much shattered, and their musketry, in the dark, employed against woodsmen covered by houses, palings, ditches, the banks of the river, etc. was but of little avail and did no damage to us, excepting wounding a man or two, and as we could not afford to lose men, great care was taken to preserve them sufficiently covered and to keep up a hot fire in order to intimidate the enemy as well as to destroy them. The embrasures of their cannon were frequently shut, for our riflemen, finding the true direction of them, would pour in such volleys when they were open that the men could not stand to the guns—seven or eight of them in a short time got cut down.
>
> Our troops would frequently abuse the enemy in order to aggravate them to open their ports and fire their cannons, that they might have the pleasure of cutting them down with their rifles, fifty of which, perhaps, would be leveled the moment the port flew open, and I believe that if they had stood at their artillery the greater part of them would have been destroyed in the course of the night, as the most of our men lay within thirty yards of the wall, and in a few hours were covered equally to those within the walls and much more experienced in that mode of fighting. The flash of our guns detected them, perhaps, the instant the man moved his body. The moment there was the least appearance at one of their loop-holes, there would probably be a dozen guns fired at it.

Clark became concerned lest the garrison hold out long enough for the fort to be relieved:

> The Indians of different tribes that were inimical had left the town and neighborhood. Captain Lamothe continued to hover about it, in order, if possible, to make his way good into the fort. Parties attempted in vain to surprise him. A few of his party were taken, one of which was Maisonville, a famous Indian

> partisan. Two lads, who captured him, tied him to a post in the street, and fought from behind him as a breastwork—supposing that the enemy would not fire at them for fear of killing him, as he would alarm them by his voice. The lads were ordered, by an officer who discovered them at their amusement, to untie their prisoner and take him off to the guard, which they did, but were so inhuman as to take part of his scalp on the way. There happened to him no other damage. As almost the whole of the persons who were most active in the department of Detroit were either in the fort or with Captain Lamothe, I got extremely uneasy for fear that he would not fall into our power, knowing that he would go off if he could not get into the fort in the course of the night.

Believing that "without some unforeseen accident, the fort must inevitably be our's," Clark allowed Lamothe to enter the fort, preferring to have his twenty men within rather than hovering in his rear.

> The firing immediately commenced on both sides with double vigor, and I believe that more noise could not have been made by the same number of men—their shouts could not be heard for the fire-arms; but a continual blaze was kept around the garrison, without much being done, until about daylight, when our troops were drawn off to posts prepared for them, from about sixty to a hundred yards from the garrison. A loophole then could scarcely be darkened but a rifle-ball would pass through it. To have stood to their cannon would have destroyed their

Map of the Northwestern Territory

men without a probability of doing much service. Our situation was nearly similar. It would have been imprudent in either party to have wasted their men, without some decisive stroke required it.

Clark sent a flag of truce to Hamilton, inviting him to surrender. He replied that the garrison was not disposed to be awed into anything unbecoming to British subjects:

The firing then commenced warmly for a considerable time, and we were obliged to be careful in preventing our men from exposing themselves too much, as they were now much animated, having been refreshed during the flag. They frequently mentioned their wishes to storm the place and put an end to the business at once. This would at this time have been a piece of rashness. Our troops got warm.

The firing was heavy, through every crack that could be discovered in any part of the fort, with cross shot. Several of the garrison got wounded, and no possibility of standing near the embrasures. Towards the evening a flag appeared.

Tomahawked in full view of the garrison

Hamilton offered to surrender, but Clark refused to accept his terms, which as a "man of barbarity," Hamilton did not deserve. In light of his sentiments, Clark adopted a remarkable expedient. He caused two Indian prisoners to be tomahawked in full view of the garrison. Their murder had the desired effect. Hamilton accepted Clark's terms of surrender. After the fort's capitulation, a "remarkable circumstance," as Clark called it, happened.

An Indian prisoner, who had been sentenced to death, was put in the charge of an old French man, named St. Croix, one of the volunteers who had joined Clark. Seeing the tomahawk raised to give him the fatal stroke, the man, raising his eyes as if to make his last address to heaven, cried in English "Save me!" St. Croix recognized the voice of his son, whom the Indian war paint disguised. Clark granted his life.

Hamilton was sent to Virginia as a prisoner because Clark feared his dangerous influence with the Indians. Released at the end of the war, he returned to Canada and was appointed Lieutenant Governor of Quebec.

Denied the reinforcements he had hoped for, Clark failed to capture Detroit, the source of British power. Although he failed to achieve his major objective, the subjugation of the northwest, he had saved Kentucky from the Indians, a heroic achievement and one of the most remarkable episodes of the war. Clark died in 1818. In 1893, a monument was erected to his memory in Indianapolis.

WEST POINT

The lone horseman in "a deep reverie in contemplation of his future glory," as Elias Boudinot imaginatively described him, halted at the crossroads early in the morning of September 24, 1780. One road led directly to New York City, the other to Tarrytown on the Hudson River. Lost in thought, the rider left the way to his horse. It had been bred at Tarrytown and naturally took that road. A mile north of town, the horseman, dressed in fine clothes, was spotted by three marauders, partisans who hunted in that area of "no man's land," hoping for plunder. One man wore a stolen British red-coat. Rushing from the wood where they lay concealed, the three seized the horse, bringing it to a halt. At this critical moment, as Colonel Alexander Hamilton afterwards related, the rider's presence of mind foresook him. He held a pass from no less a person than General Arnold, the Commander of the district:

> Instead of producing this pass, which would have extricated him from our parties and could have done him no harm with his own, he asked the militiamen if they were in the *upper* or *lower* party—descriptive appellations known among the enemy's refugee corps. The militiamen replied they were of the lower party, upon which he told them he was a British officer and pressed them not to detain him, as he was upon urgent business. This confession removed all doubts, and it was in vain he afterwards produced his pass.

By the "lower party" Hamilton described the partisans who operated on the American side. Suspicious of the rider, the three partisans took him to the nearest American post where:

> After a careful search, there were found concealed in the feet of his stockings several papers of importance, delivered to him by Arnold. Among these were a plan of the fortifications of West Point; a memorial from the engineer on the attack and defense of the place; returns of the garrison, cannon and stores; copy of the minutes of a council of war held by General Washington a few weeks before.

The man, who said his name was John Anderson, was sent to Washington's headquarters at Old Salem; his papers were delivered to Lieutenant Colonel Jameson, the local commander at North Castle. Boudinot said that Jameson was thunderstruck at finding the papers in the handwriting of General Arnold, his superior officer. He considered them to be a forgery. He sent an officer to take them to Washington, who was out on

Major John André —From a pen and ink sketch by himself

a tour of inspection. "Through an ill-judged delicacy," as Hamilton described it, Jameson sent Arnold a message, informing him of the spy's capture.

Arnold's sudden departure

Washington, with whom rode Lafayette and Hamilton, was on his way to West Point, to breakfast with Arnold and his pretty wife, of whose beauty the young Frenchman had heard. While Washington loitered to inspect the new fortifications, Lafayette and Hamilton went on to Arnold's house. While they were breakfasting, Arnold received a message. He read it, rose from the table, and with perfect composure asked to be excused. He told the messenger to wait for an answer, ordered his horse to be saddled, and sent a soldier to order his barge's crew to man his boat. He then called his wife, whom he told that he must fly to save his life; there was no time to explain.

Washington reached the house to find Mrs. Arnold hysterical—screaming and weeping. The arrival of the papers found on the rider and the story of the man's capture cleared up the mystery.

Arnold told the story of his escape to the British officer, Andrew Elliott:

> Just as he set off, an armed boat from West Point came to the landing (supposed to be ordered by Washington to carry off Arnold). General Arnold called to them to go up to the house to get refreshment and tell his Excellency when he arrived that he would be back before dinner. He was not three hundred yards from the wharf when he saw the armed vessel put off after him, but having new sails, got soon from them. When he was as far as Stony Point he told his men that particular business from

His Excellency to the Captain of the *Vulture* obliged him to go on board. He promised them two gallons of rum and they rowed on, but never were men so surprised when they found their general was to stay, and that they were prisoners.

Hamilton tried to intercept Arnold's boat, and, according to Boudinot, "Arnold rose and with a pistol in each hand, swore he would put the first man to death who would stop his oar, and soon passed out of reach of the fort." The British warship *Vulture* was anchored at Verplanck's Point. Arnold was taken to New York to meet General Clinton with whom he had been in clandestine correspondence for more than a year.

Major Benjamin Tallmadge was at headquarters when the prisoner Anderson was brought in:

> As soon as I saw Anderson, and especially after I saw him walk (as he did almost constantly) across the floor, I became impressed with the belief that he had been *bred to arms*. I communicated my suspicion to Lieut. Col. Jameson, and requested him to notice his gait, especially when he turned on his heel to retrace his course across the room.
>
> It was deemed best to remove the prisoner to Salem, and I was to escort him. I was constantly in the room with him, and he soon became very conversable and extremely interesting. It was very manifest that his agitation and anxiety were great. After dinner on the 24th, perhaps by three o'clock, he asked to be favored with a *pen, and ink and paper*, which I readily granted, and he wrote a letter to General Washington, dated "Salem, 24th September, 1780," which is recorded in most of the histories of this eventful period. In this letter he disclosed his true character to be *Major John André, Adjutant General to the British Army.*

"The guilty traitor had escaped."

Alexander Hamilton, who knew André, confirmed the identification. "By this time," related Tallmadge, "the plot was all discovered and the guilty traitor had escaped."

Before he left the *Vulture*, Arnold had the effrontery to write to General Washington asking for his clothes to be sent to him. His wife and his staff had been entirely ignorant of his proceedings and intentions, which he now sought to justify:

> The heart which is conscious of its own rectitude cannot attempt to palliate a step which the world may censure as wrong; I have ever acted from a principle of love to my country since the commencement of the present unhappy contest between Great Britain and the Colonies; the same principle of love to my country actuates my present conduct, however it may appear inconsistent to the world, who very seldom judge right of any man's actions.
>
> I have no favour to ask for myself. I have too often experienced the ingratitude of my country to attempt it; but from the known humanity of your Excellency, I am induced to ask your protection of Mrs. Arnold from every insult and injury that the mistaken vengeance of my country may expose her to. It ought to fall only on me; she is good and as innocent as an angel, and

is incapable of doing wrong. I beg she may be permitted to return to her friends in Philadelphia, or to come to me as she may choose; from your Excellency I have no fears on her account, but she may suffer from the mistaken fury of the country.

I have to request that the enclosed letter may be delivered to Mrs. Arnold and she be permitted to write to me.

I have also to ask that my clothes and baggage, which are of little consequence, may be sent to me; if required, their value shall be paid in money.

John Anderson—the identity Major John André had adopted

André (who may have been suggested as an intermediary by Mrs. Arnold) had been corresponding in code with Arnold for months. Arnold had disclosed Washington's plans for an attack on New York and he had offered to hand over the American fort at West Point for the sum of £20,000 sterling, which he called "a cheap price for an object of so much importance." A personal interview with a British officer was absolutely necessary, he declared. André reached the *Vulture* on September 20. A farmer named Joseph Smith brought a flag of truce from Arnold and a pass made out in the name of John Anderson, the identity André had adopted in their correspondence. In the statement he made, André said, "I went into the boat, landed and spoke to Arnold." He proceeded to Smith's house where Arnold gave André the papers which he hid between his stockings and feet:

> Whilst he did it, he expressed a wish in case of any accident befalling me, that they should be destroyed, which I said, of course would be the case, as when I went into the boat I should have them tied about with a string and a stone. Before we parted, some mention had been made of my crossing the river, and going by another route; but, I objected much against it, and thought it was settled, in that in the way I came I was also to return.

Elliott stated that Arnold—

> Thought it would be dangerous for John Anderson to return by water, as they had spyboats always plying on the river when our armed vessels were advanced from their usual station (but if Anderson had been taken by them he would have been brought directly to Arnold, and as papers were *necessary* to be sent, they could have easily been sunk). Whether it was a desire of doing too much, or fate, it was therefore determined that André, still as John Anderson, should pass the river and go by land to Kingsbridge, with a pass from General Arnold, Mr. Smith (who all this time Arnold declares knew nothing of his plan) to conduct him and pass him over the new bridge on Croton River and there leave him, all of which was happily effected, and Smith returned.
>
> André, before he set out by land, had at the express desire of General Arnold, changed his clothes, left his uniform at Smith's, was there furnished with other clothes, and a horse and saddle from Arnold.

Map showing the scene of Arnold's treason

Captured within enemy territory out of uniform, a crime warranting death

He had been expressly ordered by General Clinton not to quit his uniform, stated André. Nevertheless, he had been captured within enemy territory out of uniform, a crime warranting death, as observed Major Tallmadge, who, in common with all American officers, grieved that such must be the fate of the young officer they regarded with affection and admiration.

André fully understood his painful situation, as he explained to General Washington:

What I have as yet said concerning myself was in the justifiable attempt to be extricated; I am too little accustomed to duplicity to have succeeded.

I beg your Excellency will be persuaded, that no alteration in the temper of my mind, or apprehension for my safety, induces me to take the step of addressing you, but that it is to rescue myself from an imputation of having assumed a mean character for treacherous purposes or self-interest; a conduct incompatible with the principles that actuate me, as well as with my condition in life.

It is to vindicate my fame that I speak, and not to solicit security.

The person in your possession is Major John André, Adjutant General to the British army.

The influence of one commander in the army of his adversary is an advantage taken in war. A correspondence for this purpose I held; as confidential (in the present instance) with his Excellency Sir Henry Clinton.

To favor it, I agreed to meet upon ground not within the posts of either army, a person who was to give me intelligence. I came up to the *Vulture* man-of-war for this effect, and was fetched by a boat from the ship to the beach. Being there, I was told that the approach of day would prevent my return, and that I must be concealed until the next night. I was in my regimentals and had fairly risked my person.

Against my stipulation, my intention, and without my knowledge beforehand, I was conducted within one of your posts. Your Excellency may conceive my sensation on this occasion, and will imagine how much more must I have been affected by a refusal to reconduct me back the next night as I had been brought. Thus become a prisoner, I had to concert my escape. I quitted my uniform, and was passed another way in the night, without the American posts, to neutral ground, and informed I was beyond all armed parties and left to press for New York. I was taken at Tarrytown by some volunteers.

Thus, as I have the honor to relate, was I betrayed (being Adjutant General of the British army) into the vile condition of an enemy in disguise within your posts.

Having avowed myself a British officer, I have nothing to reveal but what relates to myself, which is true on the honor of an officer and a gentleman.

The request I have to make to your Excellency, and I am conscious I address myself well, is, that in any rigor policy may dictate, a decency of conduct towards me may mark that, though unfortunate, I am branded with nothing dishonorable, as no motive could be mine but the service of my King, and as I was involuntarily an impostor.

Another request is, that I may be permitted to write an open letter to Sir Henry Clinton, and another to a friend for clothes and linen.

I take the liberty to mention the condition of some gentlemen at Charleston, who, being either on parole or under protection, were engaged in a conspiracy against us. Though their situation

The capture of Major John André

is not similar, they are objects who may be set in exchange for me, or are persons whom the treatment I receive might affect.

It is no less, Sir, in a confidence of the generosity of your mind, than on account of your superior station, that I have chosen to importune you with this letter. I have the honor to be, with great respect, Sir, your Excellency's most obedient humble servant.

John André, Adjutant General

Sir Henry Clinton and Benedict Arnold interceded with Washington to spare André's life; Clinton on the ground that at the time of his capture André carried a pass signed by an American general, and Arnold in typical vein. He threatened, should André be executed, to "retaliate on such unhappy persons of your army as may fall within my power." If Washington suffered the unjust sentence to proceed, "I call heaven and earth to witness that your Excellency will be justly answerable for the torrent of blood that may be spilt in consequence." In his reply to Clinton, Washington pointed out:

From these proceedings it is evident Major André was employed in the execution of measures very foreign to the Objects of Flags of truce and such as they were never meant to authorize or countenance in the most distant degree; and this Gentle-

Washington's headquarters at Tappan

man confessed with the greatest candor in the course of his examination, "that it was impossible for him to suppose he came on shore under the sanction of a Flag."

He did not reply to Arnold, and Clinton, quite properly, rejected Hamilton's clandestine suggestion that he should hand over Arnold in return for André.

"Some compassionate minds were ready to wish for his pardon"

André's fate, stated Boudinot, was sincerely deplored throughout the army and "some compassionate minds were ready to wish for his pardon." His execution, on October 1, was witnessed and described by three eyewitnesses, Tallmadge, Hamilton, and Dr. James Thacher. Tallmadge wrote:

> As I was with him most of the time from his capture, and walked with him as he went to the place of execution, I never discovered any emotions of fear respecting his future destiny before I reached Tappan, nor of emotion when his sentence was made known to him. When he came within sight of the gibbet, he appeared to be *startled*, and inquired with some emotion whether he was not to be shot. Being informed that the mode first appointed for his death could not consistently be altered, he exclaimed, "How hard is my fate!" but immediately added, "it will soon be over." I then shook hands with him under the gallows and retired.

Tallmadge stated that he had become deeply attached to André, and that many of the spectators were reduced to tears.

The young Alexander Hamilton, Washington's devoted aide, expressed his feelings to Colonel John Laurens: "Never, perhaps, did man suffer death with more justice, or deserve it less."

When brought before the board of officers he met with every mark of indulgence, and was required to answer no interrogatory which could even embarrass his feelings. On his part, while he carefully concealed everything that might involve others, he frankly confessed all the facts relating to himself; and, upon his confession, without the trouble of examining a witness, the board made their report. The members of it were not more impressed with the candor and firmness mixed with a becoming sensibility which he displayed, than he was penetrated with their liberty and politeness. He acknowledged the generosity of the behavior towards him in every respect, but particularly in this, in the strongest terms of manly gratitude. In a conversation with a gentleman who visited him after his trial, he said he flattered himself he had never been illiberal, but if there were any remains of prejudice in his mind, his present experience must obliterate them.

In one of the visits I made to him (and I saw him several times during his confinement), he begged me to be the bearer of a request to the General, for permission to send an open letter to Sir Henry Clinton. "I foresee my fate," said he, "and though I pretend not to play the hero, or to be indifferent about life, yet I am reconciled to whatever may happen, conscious that misfortune, not guilt, has brought it upon me. There is only one thing that disturbs my tranquillity. Sir Henry Clinton has been too good to me; he has been lavish of his kindness. I am bound to him by too many obligations, and love him too well, to bear the thought that he should reproach himself, or that others should reproach him, on the supposition of my having conceived myself obliged by his instructions to run the risk I did. I would not for the world leave a sting in his mind that should imbitter his future days." He could scarce finish the sentence, bursting into tears in spite of his efforts to suppress them, and with difficulty collected himself enough afterwards to add, "I wish to be permitted to assure him I did not act under this impression, but submitted to a necessity imposed upon me, as contrary to my own inclination as by his orders." His request was readily complied with, and he wrote the letter annexed, with which I dare say you will be as much pleased as I am, both for the diction and sentiment.

When his sentence was announced to him, he remarked that since it was his lot to die, there was still a choice in the mode, which would make a material difference in his feelings, and he would be happy, if possible to be indulged with a professional death. He made a second application, by letter, in concise but persuasive terms. It was thought this indulgence, being incompatible with the customs of war, could not be granted, and it was therefore determined, in both cases, to evade an answer, to spare him the sensations which a certain knowledge of the intended mode would inflict.

"I am reconciled to my fate but not to the mode"

In going to the place of execution, he bowed familiarly as he went along to those with whom he had been acquainted in his confinement. A smile of complacency expressed the serene fortitude of his mind. Arrived at the fatal spot, he asked with some emotion, "Must I then die in this manner ?" He was told that it had been unavoidable. "I am reconciled to my fate," said he, "But not to the mode." Soon, however, recollecting himself, he added, "It will be but a momentary pang," and, springing upon the cart, performed the last office to himself with a composure that excited the admiration and melted the hearts of the beholders. Upon being told that the final moment was at hand, and asked if he had anything to say, he answered: "Nothing but to request you will witness to the world that I die like a brave man." Among the extraordinary circumstances that attended him, in the midst of his enemies, he died universally esteemed and universally regretted.

Dr. James Thacher was explicit in detail:

October 2d. 1780. Major André is no more among the living. I have just witnessed his exit. It was a tragical scene of the deepest interest. During his confinement and trial, he exhibited those proud and elevated sensibilities which designate greatness and dignity of mind. Not a murmur or a sigh ever escaped him, and the civilities and attentions bestowed on him were politely acknowledged. Having left a mother and two sisters in England, he was heard to mention them in terms of the tenderest affection, and in his letter to Sir Henry Clinton he recommended them to his particular attention.

The principal guard officer, who was constantly in the room with the prisoner, relates that when the hour of his execution was announced to him in the morning, he received it without emotion, and while all present were affected with silent gloom, he retained a firm countenance, with calmness and composure of mind. Observing his servant enter the room in tears, he exclaimed, "Leave me till you can show yourself more manly ! " His breakfast being sent to him from the table of General Washington, which had been done every day of his confinement, he partook of it as usual and having shaved and dressed himself, he placed his hat on the table and cheerfully said to the guard officers, "I am ready at any moment, gentlemen, to wait on you."

The fatal hour having arrived, a large detachment of troops was paraded and an immense concourse of people assembled; almost all our general and field officers, excepting His Excellency and his staff, were present on horseback; melancholy and gloom pervaded all ranks, and the scene was affectingly awful. I was so near during the solemn march to the fateful spot as to observe every movement and participate in every emotion which the melancholy scene was calculated to produce. Major André walked from the stone house in which he had been confined between two of our subaltern officers, arm in arm. The eyes of the immense multitude were fixed on him, who, rising superior to the fears of death, appeared as if conscious of the dignified deportment which he displayed. He betrayed no want of fortitude, but retained a complacent smile on his countenance, and politely bowed to several gentlemen whom he knew, which was respectfully returned.

It was his earnest desire to be shot, as being the mode of death most comfortable to the feelings of a military man, and he had indulged the hope that his request would be granted. At the

West Point in 1780

moment, therefore, when suddenly he came in view of the gallows, he involuntarily started backwards and made a pause.

"Why this emotion, sir?" said an officer by his side.

Instantly recovering his composure, he said, "I am reconciled to my death, but I detest the mode."

"It will be but a momentary pang"

While waiting and standing near the gallows, I observed some degree of trepidation: placing his foot on a stone and rolling it over, and choking in his throat as if attempting to swallow. So soon, however, as he perceived that things were in readiness, he stepped quickly into the wagon, and at this moment he appeared to shrink, but instantly elevating his head with firmness, he said, "It will be but a momentary pang," and taking from his pocket two white handkerchiefs, the provost marshal, with one, loosely pinioned his arms, and with the other, the victim, after taking off his hat and stock, bandaged his own eyes with perfect firmness, which melted the hearts and moistened the cheeks, not only of his servant, but of the throng of spectators.

The rope being appended to the gallows, he slipped the noose over his head and adjusted it to his neck, without the assistance of the awkward executioner. Colonel Scammel now informed him that he had an opportunity to speak, if he desired it. He raised the handkerchief from his eyes, and said, "I pray you to bear me witness that I meet my fate like a brave man." The wagon being now removed from under him, he was suspended, and instantly expired; it proved indeed "but a momentary pang." He was dressed in his royal regiments and boots, and his remains, in the same dress, were placed in an ordinary coffin and interred at the foot of the gallows; and the spot was consecrated by the tears of thousands.

"By a misguided zeal he became a devoted victim"

Thus died, in the bloom of life, the accomplished Major André, the pride of the Royal Army, and the valued friend of

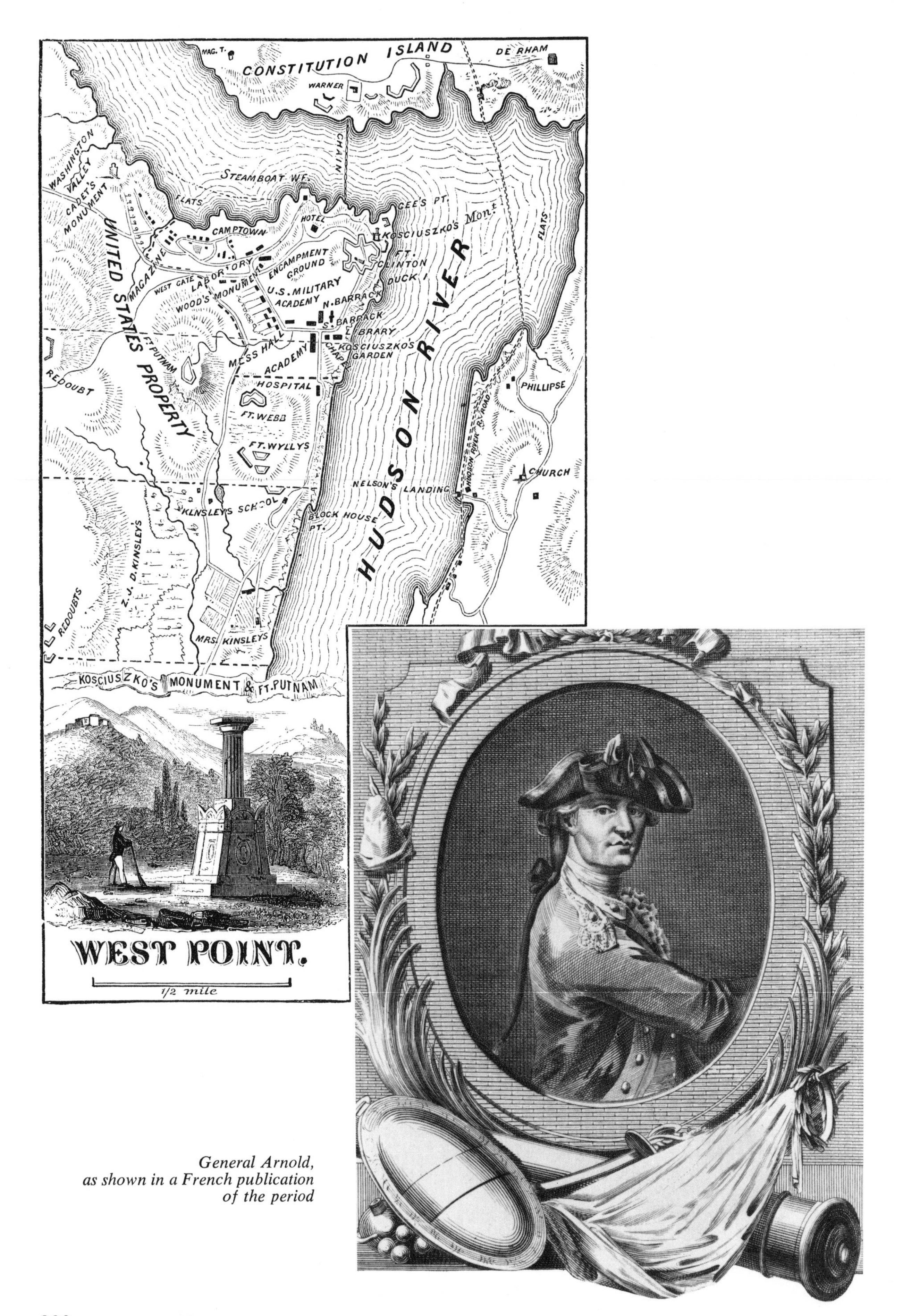

*General Arnold,
as shown in a French publication
of the period*

Sir Henry Clinton. He was about twenty-nine years of age, in his person well proportioned, tall, genteel, and graceful. His mien respectable and dignified. His countenance mild, expressive and prepossessing, indicative of an intelligent and amiable mind. His talents are said to have been of a superior cast, and, being cultivated in early life, he had made very considerable proficiency in literary attainments. Military glory was the mainspring of his actions, and the sole object of his pursuits, and he was advancing rapidly in the gratification of his ambitious views till by a misguided zeal he became a devoted victim.

A soldier, an artificier in Colonel Jeduthan Baldwin's regiment, called the execution a "shocking sight." Lafayette wept openly. Even the hardy Wayne was deeply affected. Washington retired to his house and closed the shutters tight, unable to endure the scene.

Arnold, they execrated. General Greene called his act, "Treason of the blackest dye." Wayne thought his "dirty, dirty acts" beggared all description. "Whom can we trust now?" he asked Lafayette. He attributed his treason to the pernicious influence of his wife, the Tory hellcat, Peggy Shippen. General Greene took comfort from the thought, "Happily the scheme (to deliver up the fort) was timely discovered to prevent the final misfortune." The providential circumstances were proof, he declared, that "the liberties of America are an object of divine protection."

Edward Shippen, father of Arnold's wife

"You will shudder at the danger we have run and be astonished at the miraculous chain of accidents and circumstances by which we have been saved," Lafayette told his friend, the Chevalier de la Luzerne:

> I cannot describe to you, M. le Chevalier, to what degree I am astounded by this piece of news. In the course of a revolution such as ours it is natural that a few traitors should be found, and every conflict which resembles a civil war of the first order must necessarily bring to light some great virtues and some great crimes. Our struggles have brought forward some heroes (General Washington for instance) who would otherwise have been merely private citizens. They have also developed some great scoundrels who would otherwise have remained merely obscure rogues. But that an Arnold, a man who, although not so highly esteemed as has been supposed in Europe, had nevertheless given proof of talent, of patriotism, and especially of the most brilliant courage, should at once destroy his very existence and should sell his country to the tyrants whom he had fought against with glory, is an event, M. le Chevalier, which confounds and distresses me, and, if I must confess it, humiliates me to a degree that I cannot express. I would give anything in the world if Arnold had not shared our labors with us, and if this man, whom it still pains me to call a scoundrel, had not shed his blood in the American cause.

The Shippen residence

The treason of Benedict Arnold was never fully explained.

Arnold's treason has never been fully explained. Why did the captor of Ticonderoga and the hero of the march to

The Hudson highlands near Forts Clinton and Montgomery

Quebec change sides? His excuse that he disapproved of the French alliance does not bear examination. Arnold, it seems, had grown resentful of imagined slights; he had been passed over in promotion and at Philadelphia he had been court-martialed and censured for aiding the escape of Tory sympathizers and using army wagons for private purposes. He was convinced of his own superiority and he was probably influenced by his wife. He gained little by his treachery. Commissioned a brigadier general in the British army, he led a raid into Connecticut, burning to the ground the town of New London, after plundering and killing its inhabitants, his old neighbors. He was given a command in the south, where we shall hear of him again. The Americans were well rid of him.

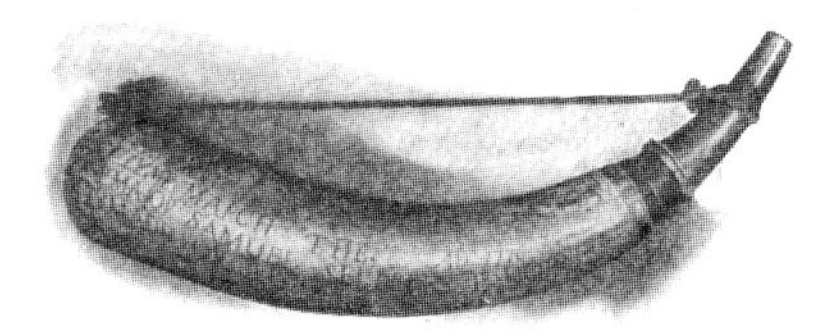

AT SEA

The shortages from which the soldiers suffered, and which caused the grumbles and mutinies, derived from the British blockade which the Americans could do little to counter. The Royal Navy dominated the coastline. The Americans retaliated as best as they could. During the war, their few naval vessels and their host of privateers captured or sunk nearly one thousand enemy vessels. As many as 60,000 seamen engaged in privateering. In the eastern states, according to Robert Morris, the Philadelphia banker, "They are so intent on privateering that they mind little else." There were many famous fights and encounters, none more stirring than the battle between the *Bonhomme Richard* and the *Serapis*.

Close action between the Richard and Serapis

John Paul Jones, a naval officer, had been active from the start of the war, raiding British commerce in the West Indies and on the coast of Nova Scotia. Robert Morris urged him to take the war to the coasts of Britain, an adventure which became possible in 1778 when the French opened their ports to American warships. Sailing to Europe that summer, Jones raided the English, Scottish, and Irish coasts, taking many prizes and striking terror in the seaports. The British newspapers called him a pirate and clamored for his blood.

Leading a small fleet composed of both American and French ships, Jones swept down the east coast in September, 1779. His flagship, the *Bonhomme Richard* (named after Benjamin Franklin, who had adopted the pen name of "Poor Richard"), mounted 40 guns; the *Alliance*, commanded by the treacherous Frenchman, Pierre Landais, 36; the *Pallas*, 32; the *Revenge*, 12; *Le Grand*, 14 and a cutter.

On September 23, Jones sighted forty merchantmen off Scarborough, escorted by the 44-gun *Serapis*, and the 28-gun frigate, the *Countess of Scarborough*. Four eyewitnesses–Jones, the British Captain Pearson, the American Lieutenant Richard Dale, and midshipman Nathaniel Fanning–wrote accounts of the action in which they engaged. Dale stood on the quarterdeck and Fanning was stationed in the maintop, an advantageous position from where he saw the action clearly; in his narrative he called Jones's ship the *Goodman Richard*.

Robert Morris, financier of the American Revolution

When he saw the two ships of war, Jones made disposition for battle. Only the *Alliance* paid no attention to his signals. Earnest as he was for action, it was seven o'clock in the evening before he came within pistol shot of the *Serapis*. Fanning, who made it "eight o'clock," recalled that "the moon was rising with majestic appearance, the weather being clear, the surface of the great deep smooth, even as a millpond." "What ship is that?" hailed the *Serapis*. "Come a little nearer, and I will tell you," answered someone of the *Bonhomme Richard:*

> The next question was, by the enemy, in a contemptuous manner, "What are you laden with?" The answer returned was, if my recollection does not deceive me, "Round, grape, and double-headed shot." And instantly, the *Serapis* poured her range of upper and quarterdeck guns into us.

"We returned the enemy's fire, and thus the battle began," wrote Fanning.

"Every method," said Jones, "was practiced on both sides to gain an advantage and take each other":

> I must confess that the enemy's ship, being much more manageable than the *Bonhomme Richard*, gained thereby several times an advantageous situation, in spite of my best endeavors to prevent it. As I had to deal with an enemy of greatly superior force, I was under the necessity of closing with him, to prevent the advantage which he had over me in point of maneuver. It was my intention to lay the *Bonhomme Richard* athwart the enemy's bow; but as that operation required great dexterity in the management of both sails and helm, and some of our braces being shot away, it did not exactly succeed to my wish.

Lieutenant Dale explained this maneuvering in greater detail:

> Our position being to windward of the *Serapis* we passed ahead of her, and the *Serapis* coming up on our larboard quarter, the action commenced abreast of each other. The *Serapis* soon passed ahead of the *Bonhomme Richard*, and when he thought he had gained a distance sufficient to go down athwart the fore foot to rake us, found that he had not enough distance, and that the *Bonhomme Richard* would be aboard him, put his helm alee, which brought the two ships on a line, and the *Bonhomme Richard*, having head way, ran her bows into the stern of the *Serapis*.

A dreadful havoc among our crew

Dale may have been too occupied in navigating the ship to know what was happening below-deck, as Fanning observed or learned:

> At this first fire, three of our starboard lower-deck guns burst, and killed most of the men stationed at them. As soon as Captain Jones heard of this circumstance, he gave orders not to fire the other three eighteen-pounders mounted upon that deck; but that the men stationed to them should abandon them. Soon after this we perceived the enemy, by their lanthorns, busy in running out their guns between decks, which convinced us the *Serapis* was a two-decker, and more than our match. She had by this time got under our stern, which we could not prevent. And now she raked us with whole broadsides, and showers of musketry. Several of her eighteen-pound shot having gone through and through our ship, on board of which, she made a dreadful havoc among our crew.

John Paul Jones

An artist's sketch of hand-to-hand combat on the deck of the Serapis

Both sides of a gold medal presented to John Paul Jones

The *Serapis*, gaining by her greater mobility and "outsailing us by two feet to one," kept under the American ship's stern, "raking us fore and aft."

The enemy's bowsprit came over the *Bonhomme Richard's* poop by the mizzenmast, stated Jones:

> I made both ships fast together in that situation, which, by the action of the wind on the enemy's sails, forced her stern close to the *Bonhomme Richard's* bow, so that the ships lay square alongside each other, the yards being all entangled, and the cannon of each ship touching the opponent's.

The *Bonhomme Richard* had received sundry eighteen-pound shots below the water line, and began to leak:

> My battery of twelve-pounders, on which I had placed my chief dependence, being commanded by Lieutenant Dale and Colonel Weibert, and manned principally with American seamen and French volunteers, was entirely silenced and abandoned.

The French Colonel, de Chamillard, who commanded a party of twenty sailors on the poop, finding almost all his men slain, quit his station and came to the quarterdeck, from where Dale continued to fire the two remaining cannon, both nine-pounders. The purser, M. Mease, who commanded them, had been wounded, and Jones had great difficulty in rallying sufficient men to serve them. "The tops alone seconded the fire of this battery, and held out bravely during the whole of the action." Captain Jones gave special praise to Lieutenant Stack who commanded the main-top. Fanning stood there:

> All this time our tops kept up an incessant and well-directed fire into the enemies' tops which did great execution. The *Serapis* continued to take a position, either under our stern, or athwart our bow; gauled us in such a manner that our men fell in all parts of the ship by *scores*. At this juncture it became necessary on the part of our commander, to give some orders to extricate us from this scene of bloody carnage; for, had it lasted one half an hour longer, in all human probability the enemy would have slain nearly all our officers and men; consequently we should have been compelled to strike our colors and yield to superior force.
>
> Accordingly, Captain Jones ordered the sailing master, a *true blooded Yankee*, whose name was Stacy, to lay the enemies' ship on board; and as the *Serapis* soon after passed across our fore-foot, our helm was put hard aweather, the main and mizzen topsails, then braced aback, were filled away, a fresh flaw of wind swelling them at that instant, which shot our ship quick ahead, and she ran her jib boom between the enemies' starboard mizzen shrouds and mizzen vang. Jones at the same time cried out, "Well done, my brave lads, we have got her now; throw on board the grappling irons, and stand by for boarding," which was done, and the enemy soon cut away the chains, which were affixed to the grappling irons; more were thrown on board, and often repeated. And as we now hauled the enemies' ship snug alongside of ours, with the tailings to our grappling-irons, her jib-stay was cut away aloft and fell upon our ship's poop, where Jones was at the time, and where he assisted Mr.

Stacy in making fast the end of the enemies' jib-stay to our mizzenmast. The former here checked the latter for swearing, by saying, "Mr. Stacy, it is no time for swearing now, you may by the next moment be in eternity; but let us do our duty." A strong current was now setting in towards Scarborough, the wind ceased to blow, and the sea became as smooth as glass.

During this time the fire from the tops had been kept up without intermission, with "musketry, blunderbusses, cowhorns, swivels and pistols." Jones saw that the enemy's decks had been cleared. Their tops fell silent, except, stated Fanning, for one man in the foretop:

> . . . who would, once in a while peep out from behind the head of the enemies' foremast and fire into our tops. As soon as I perceived this fellow, I ordered the marines in the main top to reserve their next fire, and the moment they got sight of him to level their pieces at him and fire; which they did, and we soon saw this skulking tar, or marine, fall out of the top upon the enemies' forecastle.

The men stationed in the maintop took possession of the maintop of the *Serapis*, which gave them command of her decks. Fanning expected her captain to strike. He described the "farcical piece" that was acted on the *Bonhomme Richard.*

Both ships on fire in several places

Both captains seemed to think that the other was ready to strike; both ships were on fire in several places. The American's flagstaff had been shot away and the Stars and Stripes had fallen into the sea:

> It seems that a report was at this time circulated among our crew between decks, and was credited among them, that Captain Jones and all his principal officers were slain; the gunners were now the commanders of the ship; that the ship had four or five feet of water in her hold; and that she was then sinking; they therefore advised the gunner to go upon deck, together with the carpenter, and master at arms, and beg of the enemy quarters, in order, as they said, to save their lives. These three men being thus delegated, mounted the quarterdeck and bawled out as loud as they could, "Quarters, quarters, for God's sake, quarters! Our ship is sinking!" and immediately got upon the ship's poop with a view of hauling down our colors.
>
> Hearing this in the top, I told my men that the enemy had struck and was crying out for quarters, for I actually thought that the voices of these men sounded as if on board of the enemy; but in this I was soon undeceived. The three poltroons, finding the ensign, and ensign-staff gone, they proceeded upon the quarterdeck and were in the act of hauling down our pendant, still bawling for "quarters" when I heard our commodore say, in a loud voice, "what d—d rascals are them—shoot them—kill them!" He was upon the forecastle when these fellows first made their appearance upon the quarterdeck where he had just discharged his pistols at some of the enemy. The carpenter, and the master-at-arms, hearing Jones's voice, skulked below, and the gunner was attempting to do the same,

Esek Hopkins,
Commodore of the American Sea Forces

when Jones threw both of his pistols at his head, one of which struck him in the head, fractured his skull, and knocked him down at the foot of the gangway ladder, where he lay till the battle was over.

"The enemy," Fanning said, "now demanded of us if we had struck, as they had heard the three poltroons halloo for quarters. "If you have," said they, "why don't you haul down your pendant?" as they saw our ensign was gone. "Ay, ay," said Jones, "we'll do that when we can fight no longer, but we shall see yours come down the first; for you must know, that Yankees do not haul down their colors till they are fairly beaten."

"I have not yet begun to fight!"

Fortunately, Lieutenant Dale recalled and recorded the exact words of the interchange:

> We had remained in this situation but a few minutes when we were again hailed by the *Serapis*, "Has your ship struck?" To which Captain Jones answered, "I have not yet begun to fight!"

Jones explained that the carpenter had expressed fears that the ship would sink and the other two under-officers ran to the poop, without his knowledge, to strike the colors. Both ships took fire again, as Fanning experienced:

> And on board of our ship it communicated to, and set our main top on fire, which threw us into the greatest consternation imaginable for some time, and it was not without some exertions and difficulty that it was overcome. The water which we had in a tub, in the fore part on the top, was expended without extinguishing the fire. We next had recourse to our clothes, by pulling off our coats and jackets, and then throwing them upon the fire, and stamping upon them, which in a short time smothered it. Both crews were also now, as before, busily employed in stopping the progress of the flames, and the firing on both sides ceased.

The two ships were lying head-to-stern, so close that the seamen were unable to sponge and reload the guns:

> In this situation, the enemy, to prevent (as they told us afterwards) our boarding them, leaped on board of our ship, and some of them had actually got upon the fore part of our quarter-deck; several were there killed, and the rest driven back on board of their own ship, whither some of our men followed them, and were most of them killed. Several other attempts to board were made by both parties in quick succession, in consequence of which many were slain upon the two ships' gangways, on both sides.

Of the other ships of the squadron, Fanning saw only the two brigs, neither of which dared to come to the assistance of the *Bonhomme Richard.* So far she had sustained the action alone, explained Jones:

> At last, at half-past 9 o'clock, the *Alliance* appeared, and I now thought the battle at an end; but to my utter astonishment, he discharged a broadside full into the stern of the *Bonhomme Richard.* We called to him: "For God's sake to forbear firing

into the *Bonhomme Richard!*" Yet he passed along the offside of the ship and continued firing. There was no possibility of his mistaking the enemy's ship for the *Bonhomme Richard*, there being the most essential difference in their appearance and construction; besides, it was then full moonlight, and the sides of the *Bonhomme Richard* were all black, while the sides of the prizes (the two British warships) were yellow. Yet, for the greater security I showed the signal of our reconnaissance by putting out three lanthorns, one at the head, another at the stern, and the third in the middle in a horizontal line. Every tongue cried that he was firing into the wrong ship, but nothing availed. He passed round, firing into the *Bonhomme Richard's* head, stern and broadside, and by one of his volleys killed several of my best men and mortally wounded a good officer on the forecastle.

Following the battle, Jones complained "loudly" of Captain Landars' conduct. It did not change the situation as Fanning recalled:

The enemy's tops being entirely silenced, the men in ours had nothing to do but to direct their whole fire down upon the enemy's decks and forecastle; this we did, and with so much success that in about twenty- five minutes more we had cleared her decks so that not a man on board the *Serapis* was to be seen. However, they still kept up a constant fire with four of their foremost bow guns on the starboard side; viz. two eighteen-pounders upon the lower gun-deck, and two nine-pounders upon her upper gun-deck; these last were mounted upon her forecastle, under cover from our fire from our tops; her cannon upon the larboard side, upon the quarterdeck and forecastle, from the position of both ships, were rendered altogether useless; her four guns which she could manage, annoyed us very much, and did our ship considerable damage.

About this time the enemy's light sails, which were filled on to the *Serapis*'s cranes over her quarterdeck sails caught fire; this communicated itself to her rigging and from thence to ours; thus were both ships on fire at one and the same time; therefore the firing on both sides ceased till it was extinguished by the contending parties, after which the action was renewed again. By this time, the top-men in our tops had taken possession of the enemy's tops, which was done by reason of the *Serapis*'s yards being locked together with ours, that we could with ease go from our main top into the enemy's fore top, and so on from our fore top in to the *Serapis*'s main top. Having knowledge of this, we transported from our own into the enemy's tops, stink pots, flasks, hand grenades, &c., which we threw in among the enemy whenever they made their appearance.

John Paul Jones raising the first American flag ever displayed on a United States warship

The fires, having been extinguished, the battle recommenced with renewed vigor:

. . . with what cannon we could manage; hand grenades, stink pots, &c., but principally, towards the closing scene, with lances and boarding pikes. With these the combatants killed each other through the ship's portholes, which were pretty large; and the guns that had been run out at them becoming useless, as before observed, had been removed out of the way.

Commodore (Lieutenant) Dale

A really deplorable situation

"My situation was really deplorable," remarked Jones. The leak was gaining on the pumps, and his treacherous master-at-arms had released the prisoners (the 500 seamen who had been taken from captured ships) from the hold. Some of his officers wanted him to strike; he refused to give up. Dale and Fanning saw the final act in the drama. The fire from the main top, noticed Dale, had forced every man on the quarterdeck of the *Serapis* to go below; "not even under the shelter of the deck were they more secure." The powder-monkeys, the boys who brought up the guncharges, finding no officer to receive them, threw them on the deck where some of them broke. Fanning takes over the story:

> And at thirty-five minutes past 12 at night, a single hand-grenade having been thrown by one of our men out of the main top of the enemy, designing it to go among the enemy, who were huddled together between her gun decks, it on its way struck on one side of the combings of her upper hatchway, and rebounding from that, it took a direction and fell between their decks, where it communicated to a quantity of loose powder scattered about the enemy's cannon; and the hand grenade bursting at the same time, made a dreadful explosion, and blew up about twenty of the enemy.

The effect, stated Dale, was tremendous; he noticed that the survivors of the explosion "stood only with the collars of their shirts upon their bodies." Captain Pearson, who placed the incident earlier in the action, recorded that this unfortunate accident rendered his guns useless. To Fanning "this closed the scene:"

> The enemy now in their turn, (notwithstanding the gasconading of Capt.Pearson) bawled out "Quarters, quarters, quarters, for God's sake!" It was, however, some time before the enemy's colors were struck. The captain of the *Serapis* gave repeated orders for one of his crew to ascend the quarterdeck and haul down the English flag, but no one would stir to do it. They told the Captain they were afraid of our riflemen, believing that all our men who were seen with muskets were of that description.

The encounter between the two captains

Jones reported that the *Serapis* struck at half past ten o'clock. Fanning watched Captain Pearson ascend the quarterdeck and personally haul down the flag which he had nailed to the mast before the battle began, and which he had sworn never to strike to "that infamous pirate J. P. Jones." Lieutenant Dale climbed aboard the *Serapis*, accompanied by a few men, several of whom were inadvertently killed by the English sailors who were unaware that their ship had surrendered. Fanning saw and heard the encounter between the two captains:

> The officers, headed by the captain of the *Serapis*, now came on board of our ship; the latter, (Captain Pearson) enquired for Captain Jones, to whom he was introduced by Mr. Mase, our

purser. They met, and the former accosted the latter, in presenting his sword, in this manner: "It is with the greatest reluctance that I am now obliged to resign you this, for it is painful to me, more particularly at this time, when compelled to deliver up my sword to a man, who may be said to fight *with a halter around his neck!*" Jones, after receiving his sword, made this reply; "Sir, you have fought like a hero, and I make no doubt that your sovereign will reward you in a most ample manner for it." Captain Pearson then asked Jones what countrymen his crew principally consisted of; the latter said, "Americans." "Very well," said the former, "it has been *diamond cut diamond* with us."

Fanning learned of a remarkable incident which happened on the *Serapis:*

One circumstance relative to the first lieutenant, by the name of Stanhope, is so singular, that I am induced to relate the fact; it was this, early in the action he hung himself down by one of the *Serapis*'s stern ladders into the water, so that his body was immersed in water; in this situation he hung with only his head above water during the remainder of the action. It was noticed by one of our officers when Stanhope surrendered among his brother officers, and came on our quarterdeck, that he appeared to be entirely wet, and the question was put to him how his clothes came to be wet. He said he had just before the *Serapis* struck, attempted to sound her pump-well to see how much water she had in her, and fell into it. But the petty officers of the *Serapis* declared to us, that the fact was as above stated, and was also confirmed by several of the English sailors belonging to that ship.

I do hereby certify that John Paul Jones was duly commissioned and appointed to command the armed ~~continental~~ Sloop called the Providence and ~~that~~ this Sloop is now employed in the Service of the thirteen United States of North America Witness my Hand October 29th 1776

John Hancock Presid

Richard Dale summed up the action thus:

From the commencement to the termination of the action, there was not a man on board the *Bonhomme Richard* ignorant of the superiority of the *Serapis*, both in weight of metal and in the qualities of the crews. The crew of that ship was picked seamen, and the ship itself had only been a few months off the stocks, whereas the crew of the *Bonhomme Richard* consisted of part Americans, English and French, and a part of Maltese, Portuguese, and Malays, these latter contributing by their want of naval skill and knowledge of the English language to depress rather than to elevate a just hope of success in a combat under such circumstances.

Neither the consideration of the relative force of the ships, the fact of the blowing up of the gundeck above them by the bursting of two of the 18-pounders, nor the alarm that the ship was sinking, could depress the ardor or change the determination of the brave Captain Jones, his officers and men. Neither the repeated broadsides of the *Alliance*, given with a view of sinking or disabling the *Bonhomme Richard*, the frequent necessity of suspending the combat to extinguish the flames, which several times were within a few inches of the magazine, nor the liberation by the master-at-arms of nearly 500 prisoners, could change or weaken the purpose of the American commander.

At the moment of the liberation of the prisoners, one of them, a commander of a 20-gun ship taken a few days before, passed through the ports on board the *Serapis* and informed Captain Pearson that if he would hold out only a little while longer, the ship alongside would either strike or sink, and that all the prisoners had been released to save their lives. The combat was accordingly continued with renewed ardor by the *Serapis*.

Fanning thought that the battle could be ranked, with propriety, as "the most bloody, the hardest fought, and the greatest scene of carnage, ever fought between two ships of war of any nation under heaven."

The Americans had lost in the battle 165 officers, men, and boys killed and 137 wounded and missing. A great many of the wounded died, due to the unskillfulness of the surgeons, and they were thrown overboard. Of the crew of the *Serapis* 137 were killed and about 67 wounded.

Enemies more formidable than the British—fire and water

With the battle ended, Captain Jones had two enemies to encounter far more formidable than the British, fire and water:

The *Serapis* was attacked only by the first, but the *Bonhomme Richard* was assailed by both; there were five feet of water in the hold, and though it was moderate from the explosion of so much gun-powder, yet the three pumps that remained could with difficulty only keep the water from gaining. The fire broke out in various parts of the ship, in spite of all the water that could be thrown in to quench it, and at length broke out as low as the powder magazine, and within a few inches of the powder. In that dilemma, I took out the powder upon deck, ready to be

The battle of September 23, 1779, between the Bonhomme Richard and the Serapis, as painted by Sir Richard Patten
—UPI Compix

thrown overboard at the last extremity, and it was ten o'clock the next day, the 24th, before the fire was entirely extinguished.

With respect to the situation of the *Bonhomme Richard*, the rudder was cut entirely off, the stern frame and transoms were almost entirely cut away, and the timbers by the lower deck, especially from the mainmast towards the stern, being greatly decayed with age, were mangled beyond my power of description, and a person must have been an eyewitness to form a just idea of the tremendous scene of carnage, wreck, and ruin which everywhere appeared. Humanity cannot but recoil from the prospect of such finished horror, and lament that war should be capable of producing such fatal consequences.

To his inexpressible grief the old ship sank the next day. "No lives were lost with the ship, but it was impossible to save the stores of any sort whatever. I lost even the best part of my clothes, books and papers; and several of my officers lost all their clothes and effects."

Jones and his crew had transferred to the other ships of the squadron, one ship of which, the *Pallas*, had taken the *Countess of Scarborough*. Had the Captain of the *Alliance* obeyed orders, believed Fanning, the whole fleet must have been captured. As it was, the merchantmen escaped to port. The action which had lasted for four hours had been watched in the bright moonlight by fifteen hundred spectators on shore. Jones conveyed his prizes to the Texel in Holland.

Other American captains achieved remarkable successes. Captain James Nicholson, the commander of the naval frigate *Trumbull*, fought an obstinate and bloody, though inconclusive action with the British privateer *Watt*, north of Bermuda on June 2, 1780. A year later he was forced to strike to the British frigate *Iris*. The exploits of Captain John Barry became nearly as legendary as those of John Paul Jones, the great American naval hero of the war. Their cruises forced the British to retain in European waters ships which were badly needed on the American coast where, for a time, French naval superiority forced the British Commander-in-Chief to limit his operations.

SAVANNAH

Believing that strong loyalist support would be forthcoming, and being stalemated in the north, Sir Henry Clinton, late in 1778, projected the war to the southern states. In the fall, he sent Lieutenant Colonel Archibald Campbell with thirty-five hundred soldiers to invade Georgia, and ordered General Augustine Prevost to move northwards from St. Augustine in Florida with two thousand troops. Before he arrived, Campbell had captured Savannah, and the two armies in combination quickly dominated the state. Congress sent General Benjamin Lincoln (who had commanded the right wing at Bemis Heights) to retrieve the situation. His army, composed chiefly of militia, was defeated at Briar Creek; fifty miles above Savannah. During the lull caused by the summer heat, Prevost withdrew his army to Savannah where, in the fall of 1779, he was besieged by Lincoln and Admiral D'Estaing who came from the West Indies with four thousand French soldiers on board his fleet.

General Benjamin Lincoln

The French landed on September 16. D'Estaing's hope to reduce the town by siege operations was soon blighted. Anxious to return home, and "covetous of glory," as one of his officers described him, D'Estaing persuaded Lincoln to join a direct assault at dawn on October 9. Thirty-five hundred French troops, six hundred Continentals and three hundred South Carolina militia were ordered to storm the lines. During the night, an American sergeant named Curry deserted to the enemy, informing the garrison that the allied troops would concentrate on the key position, the British battery on Spring Hill.

One of the actors in the drama, Major Thomas Pickney, from South Carolina, described the dispositions for the assault:

> The French troops were to be divided into three columns, the Americans into two, the heads of which were to be posted in a line, with proper intervals at the edge of the wood adjoining the open space of five or six hundred yards between it and the enemy's line, and at four o'clock in the morning, a little before daylight, the whole was, on a signal being given, to rush forward and attack the redoubts and batteries opposed to their front.
>
> The American column of the right, which adjoined the French, were to be preceded by Pulaski, with his cavalry and the cavalry of South Carolina, and were to follow the French until they approached the edge of the wood, when they were to break off and take their position.

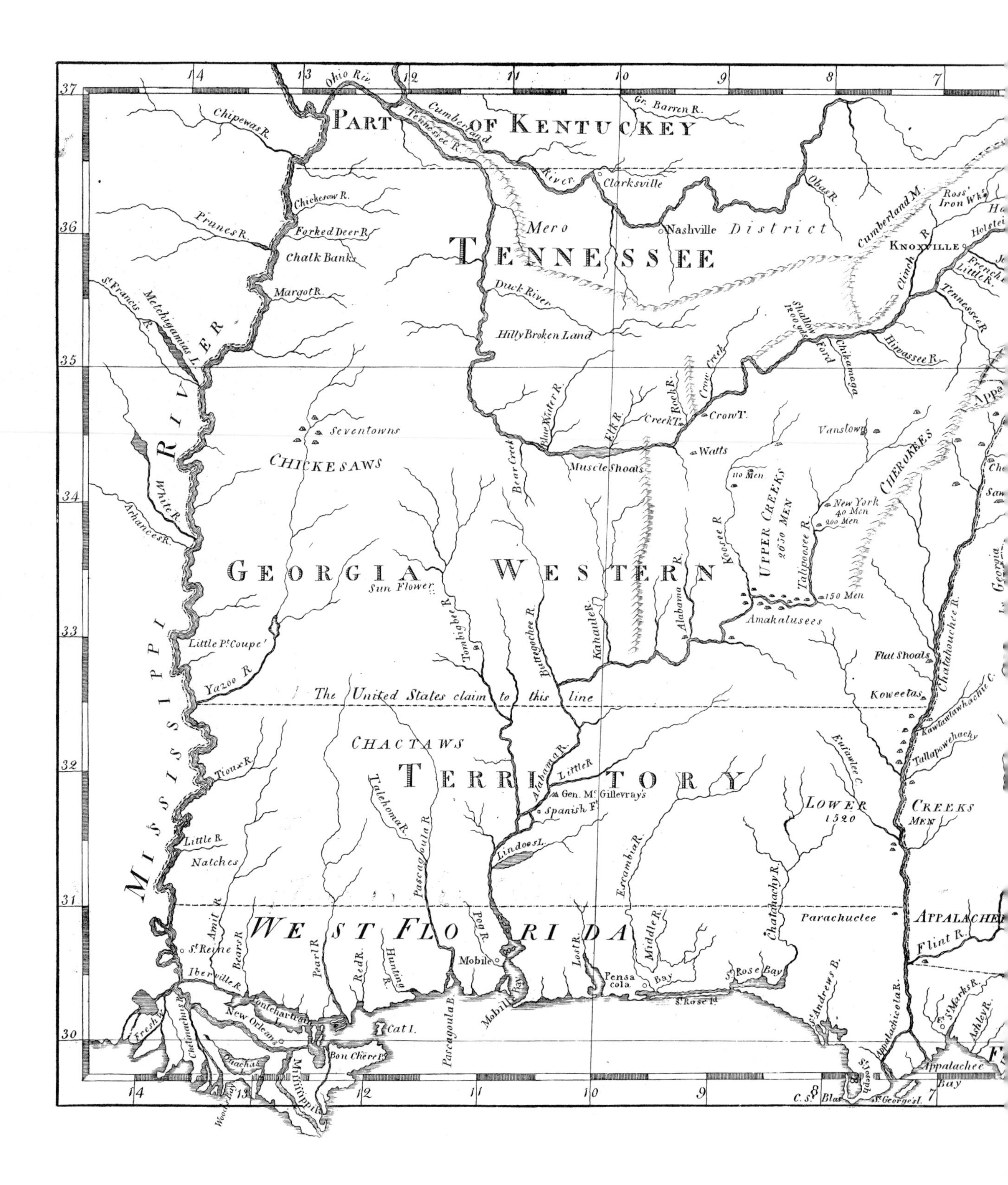
PART OF KENTUCKEY
TENNESSEE
Mero District
Nashville
Clarksville
KNOXVILLE
CHICKESAWS
Seventowns
GEORGIA WESTERN TERRITORY
The United States claim to this line
CHACTAWS
UPPER CREEKS 2650 MEN
CHEROKEES
LOWER CREEKS 1520 MEN
Amakalusees
Muscle Shoals
Gen. Mc Gillevray's
Spanish Ft
WEST FLORIDA
MISSISSIPPI RIVER
Mobile
Pensacola
New Orleans
Natches
Parachuclee
APPALACHEE
Hilly Broken Land
Sun Flower
Koweetas
Flat Shoals

MAP
of the
Southern Parts
of the
UNITED STATES
OF
AMERICA
By
Abraham Bradley jun.r
PART OF VIRGINIA
NORTH CAROLINA
SOUTH CAROLINA
GIA
Scale
C.H. CourtHouse
Longitude calculated from Wafhington.
RALEIGH
COLUMBIA
CHARLESTON
Savannah
Augusta
LOUISVILLE
Wilmington
Newbern
Fayetteville
Camden
Norfolk
Portsmouth
Ocrecock Inlet
Albemarle Sound
Pamlicoe Sd
Ekanfanoka Swamp

Savannah before the Revolution

Without waiting for the American troops to come up, D'Estaing, placing himself at the head of his soldiers, led them to the attack.

Among the Frenchmen was an officer, whose name was unrecorded:

> The Admiral (D'Estaing) now orders an advance at double quick, to shout *Vive le Roi*, and to beat the charge. The enemy opens upon us a very brisk fire of artillery and musketry which, however, does not prevent the vanguard from advancing upon the redoubt, and the right column upon the entrenchments. The ardor of our troops and the difficulties offered by the ground do not permit us long to preserve our ranks. Disorder begins to prevail. The head of the column penetrates within the entrenchments but, having marched too quickly, is not supported by the rest of the column which, arriving in confusion, is cut down by discharges of grape shot from the redoubts and batteries, and the musketry fire from the entrenchments. We are violently repulsed at this point; and, instead of moving to the right, this (Dillon's) column and the vanguard fall back toward the left. Count D'Estaing receives a musket shot almost within the redoubt, and M. Betizi is here several times wounded.

Pickney was an eyewitness to the Frenchmen's discomfiture:

> But this body was so severely galled by the grape shot from the batteries as they advanced, and by both grape shot and musketry when they reached the abatis, that, in spite of the effort of the officers, the column got into confusion and broke away to their left toward the wood in that direction; the second and the third French columns shared successively the same fate, having the additional discouragement of seeing, as they marched to the attack, the repulse and loss of their comrades who had preceded them.

Major General Charles Cotesworth Pinckney

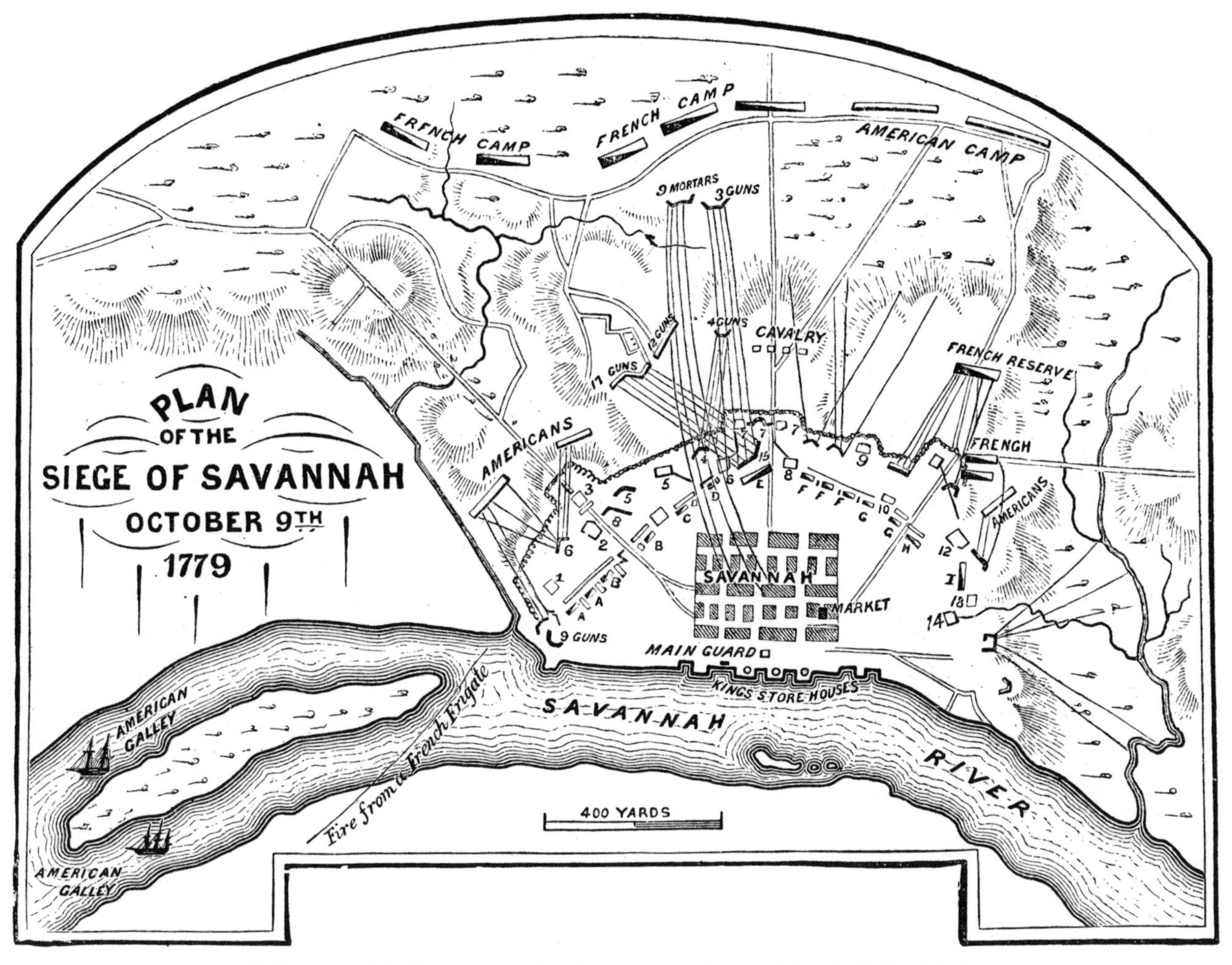

Explanation of the Plan—1, Georgia volunteers, under Major Wright. 2, Picket of the 71st. 3, First battalion of Delancey's corps, under Lieutenant-colonel Cruger. 4, Georgia militia. 5, Third battalion Jersey volunteers, under Lieutenant-colonel Allen. 6, Georgia militia. 7, Picket of the line and armed negroes. 8, General's quarters; convalescents of the line. 9, South Carolina Royalists. 10, Georgia militia and detachment of the fourth battalion of the 60th, Lieutenant-governor Graham. 11, Fourth battalion 60th dismounted dragoons and South Carolina Royalists, Captain Taws. 12, North Carolina Loyalists, Lieutenant-colonel Hamilton, Governor Sir James Wright. 13, 14, King's rangers, Lieutenant-colonel Brown. A, First battalion of the 71st, Major M'Arthur. B, Regiment of Trombach. C, Second battalion Delancey's corps, Lieutenant-colonel Delancey. D, New York volunteers, Major Sheridan. E, Light infantry, Major Graham. F, Weisenbach's regiment. G, Second battalion 71st, Major M'Donald. H, 60th Grenadiers, three companies and one of marines, Lieutenant-colonel Glazier. I, North Carolina Loyalists, under Colonel Maitland. The working of the artillery during the siege was under the direction of Captain Charlton.

Two South Carolina officers, Lieutenants Bush and Holmes, reached the redoubt before they were killed. Sergeant Jasper raised the American flag on the embankment. He was mortally wounded, but he and Lieutenant Gray managed to rescue the colors before they died. Colonel Moultrie from Charleston, saw this stage of the action:

> Our troops were so crowded in the ditch upon the beam, that they could hardly raise an arm, and while they were in this situation, huddled up together, the British loaded and fired deliberately, without any danger to themselves.

The Polish volunteer, Count Pulaski, riding at full gallop at the head of 200 cavalrymen, attempted to get into the town between the British redoubts. One of his field officers, Major Rogowski, described the charge:

Admiral Charles Henry D'Estaing

For half an hour the guns roared and blood flowed abundantly. Seeing an opening between the enemy's works, Pulaski resolved, with his Legion and a small detachment of Georgia cavalry, to charge through, enter the city, confuse the enemy, and cheer the inhabitants with good tidings. General Lincoln approved the daring plan. Imploring the help of the Almighty, Pulaski shouted to his men "Forward," and we, two hundred strong, rode at full speed after him, the earth resounding under the hoofs of our chargers.

For the first two minutes all went well. We sped like Knights into the peril. Just, however, as we passed the gap between the two batteries, a cross fire, like a pouring shower, confused our ranks. I looked around. Oh, sad moment, ever to be remembered! Pulaski lies prostrate on the ground. I leaped towards him, thinking possibly his wound was not dangerous, but a *canister shot* had pierced his thigh, and the blood was also flowing from his breast, probably from a second wound. Falling on my knees I tried to raise him. He said in a faint voice, Jesus! Maria! Joseph! Further, I knew not, for at that moment a musket ball grazing my scalp blinded me with blood, and I fell to the ground in a state of insensibility.

Death of Count Pulaski

The wounded Count was carried on board the United States brig, the *Wasp*, where the efforts of the most skillful surgeons failed to save his life.

To Lincoln's consternation, D'Estaing called off the assault and "no argument could dissuade him" from re-embarking his soldiers and leaving the coast. He sailed to France, leaving the Americans to count the cost of yet another allied failure. Their casualties had been severe – 800 Frenchmen and 457 Americans killed or wounded. The British loss was small – 40 killed and 63 wounded.

D'Estaing's short visit to the American coast brought Sir Henry Clinton hurrying from New York with reinforcements to support the British attempt to subjugate the southern states.

The British fleet leaving New York harbor

CHARLESTON

Lincoln took his army to Charleston where he was in turn besieged by Clinton and by Admiral Mariot Arbuthnot, who attempted the feat which Sir Hyde Parker, early in the war, had failed to accomplish—to silence Fort Moultrie on Sullivan's Island and force an entrance into the inner harbor.

Lord Rawdon

To protect his escape route, should he need to evacuate the town, Lincoln stationed a mixed force of cavalry, commanded by General Isaac Huger and Colonel William Washington (no relation to the General), at Monck's Corner, at the head of the Cooper River, thirty miles north of Charleston.

Early in April, 1780, both armies were reinforced. Lord Rawdon brought 2,000 British soldiers from New York and General William Woodford arrived with 750 Virginia and North Carolina militia, having completed a march of 500 miles in thirty days. His feat increased Lincoln's numbers to 2,000 Continentals and a similar number of militiamen.

Clinton pushed his siege craft up the narrow neck between the Ashley and Cooper rivers which protected the town. The garrison attempted to delay the advance by artillery fire. William Moultrie, who in 1775 had successfully defended Sullivan's Island, was watching and reported:

> The women walked out from the town to the lines with all the composure imaginable to see us cannonade the enemy, but I fancy when the enemy begin they will make themselves pretty scarce.

Admiral Arbuthnot weighed anchor on April 8. The Hessian officer, Captain Johann Heinrichs, saw the fleet sail into the harbor area:

> This afternoon our men-of-war passed Fort Moultrie. At four o'clock they came out of Five Fathom Hole with a splendid wind and a strong tide, and aided by fog. The Admiral went ahead in a jolly boat and piloted each ship. (Heinrichs was wrong—Arbuthnot was on the *Roebuck*.) Sir Andrew Snape Hammond led the vanguard with the *Roebuck*. At half-past four he passed the fort, which belched fire out of forty pieces, most of them 24-pounders. As soon as this ship in all her glory came under the fort she defiantly replied with a broadside and then sailed by without loss and without delay. After crossing below the city she cast anchor at Fort Johnson. Then followed the *Richmond*, which had come from Cork. She lost her fore-topmast. The *Renown* formed the rear guard, and when she arrived at the fort she lay-to, took in her sails, and gave such an unre-

A view of the busy southern city of Charleston, South Carolina, from the harbor in 1774, with the Provost prominently displayed as the most impressive of all the buildings. (This same building appears in a sketch by Kay Smith in the following color insert.)

Lieutenant-colonel Banastre Tarleton

lenting, murderous fire that the whole ship seemed to flare up. Thus she covered the rear of the squadron. One transport ran aground and was so shot to pieces that the sailors had to set her afire and abandon her. Several cannon balls went through the ships without doing any damage. By half-past six our ships lay at anchor on this side, having seven killed and one midshipman and thirteen men wounded, most of whom were on the *Renown*.

What a trifling loss under so enormous a fire! The enemy suddenly stopped firing, and filled with amazement, saw the proud Briton, the master of the sea, meet and overcome every danger, every obstacle, with scorn and disdain. Horror, astonishment, fear, despondency, and shattered hopes seemed to befog their eyes, ears, and hearts to such an extent that they did not fire a single shot at our men, who had jumped upon the parapets of the works!

Fort Moultrie had been allowed to fall into disrepair, and it was no longer the obstacle it had formerly presented.

The presence of the warships above the forts sealed Charleston's fate. The garrison could still escape. To forestall Lincoln, Clinton sent the Dragoon officer, Colonel Banastre Tarleton at the head of his Tory Legion to cut the escape corridor. Writing in the third person, Tarleton recalled his exploit:

Tarleton moved in the evening, with his own and Ferguson's corps, towards Monck's Corner, as had been previously concerted with the commander in chief, in order, if possible, to surprise the Americans encamped at that place. An attack in the night was judged most advisable, as it would render the superiority of the enemy's cavalry useless, and would, perhaps, present a favorable opportunity of getting possession of Biggin bridge, on Cooper River, without much loss to the assailants. Profound silence was observed on the march.

From a prisoner, Tarleton learned the American dispositions:

At three o'clock in the morning, the advanced guard of dragoons and mounted infantry, supported by the remainder of the legion and Ferguson's corps, approached the American post. A Watchword was immediately communicated to the officers and soldiers, which was closely followed by an order to charge the enemy's grand guard on the main road, there being no other avenue open, owing to the swamps upon the flanks, and to pursue them into their camp. The order was executed with the greatest promptitude and success. The Americans were completely surprised. Major Vernier of Pulaski's legion, and some other officers and men who attempted to defend themselves, were killed or wounded; General Huger, Colonels Washington and Jamieson with many officers and men, fled on foot to the swamps, close to their encampment, where, being concealed by the darkness, they effected their escape. Four hundred horses belonging to officers and dragoons, with their arms and appointments, (a valuable acquisition for the British cavalry in their present state) fell into the hands of the victors. About one hundred officers, dragoons and hussars, together with fifty wagons, loaded with arms, clothing, and ammunition, shared the same fate.

FROM A WATER-COLOR SKETCH BY KAY SMITH

The Provost, Charleston, South Carolina, British dungeon of the American Revolution, erected as an Exchange and Custom House in 1767 but converted to use as a jail during the war.

FROM A WATER-COLOR SKETCH BY KAY SMITH

Madison Square scene of one of the early Revolutionary War battles in Savannah, Georgia.

A shameful surprise

Moultrie called the surprise of the detachment "shameful."

Leaving a force of infantry to guard the corridor, Tarleton returned to Charleston, his men mounted on the four hundred captured horses.

The siege of the town progressed slowly. The British, with their Hessian allies, fought their way into town. Captain Heinrichs reached the second parallel of trenches:

> The enemy had built counter approaches between their front redoubt and their abatis and manned them with riflemen, with whom we exchanged many shots in the course of the day. Into our parallel fell seventeen grapeshot, nineteen 18-pound balls from their left front redoubt, and thirteen shells, 6 to 10 inches, from the right front redoubt. Two shells burst among us in the trench and five others on the parapet. The rest failed to explode. We had no loss, none whatever, except one broken rifle, and all of us covered with earth. I caused several traverses to be made. Our batteries did not support us well. Two of my light infantrymen were wounded by the enemy's small-arms fire. They threw their shells in a masterly manner.

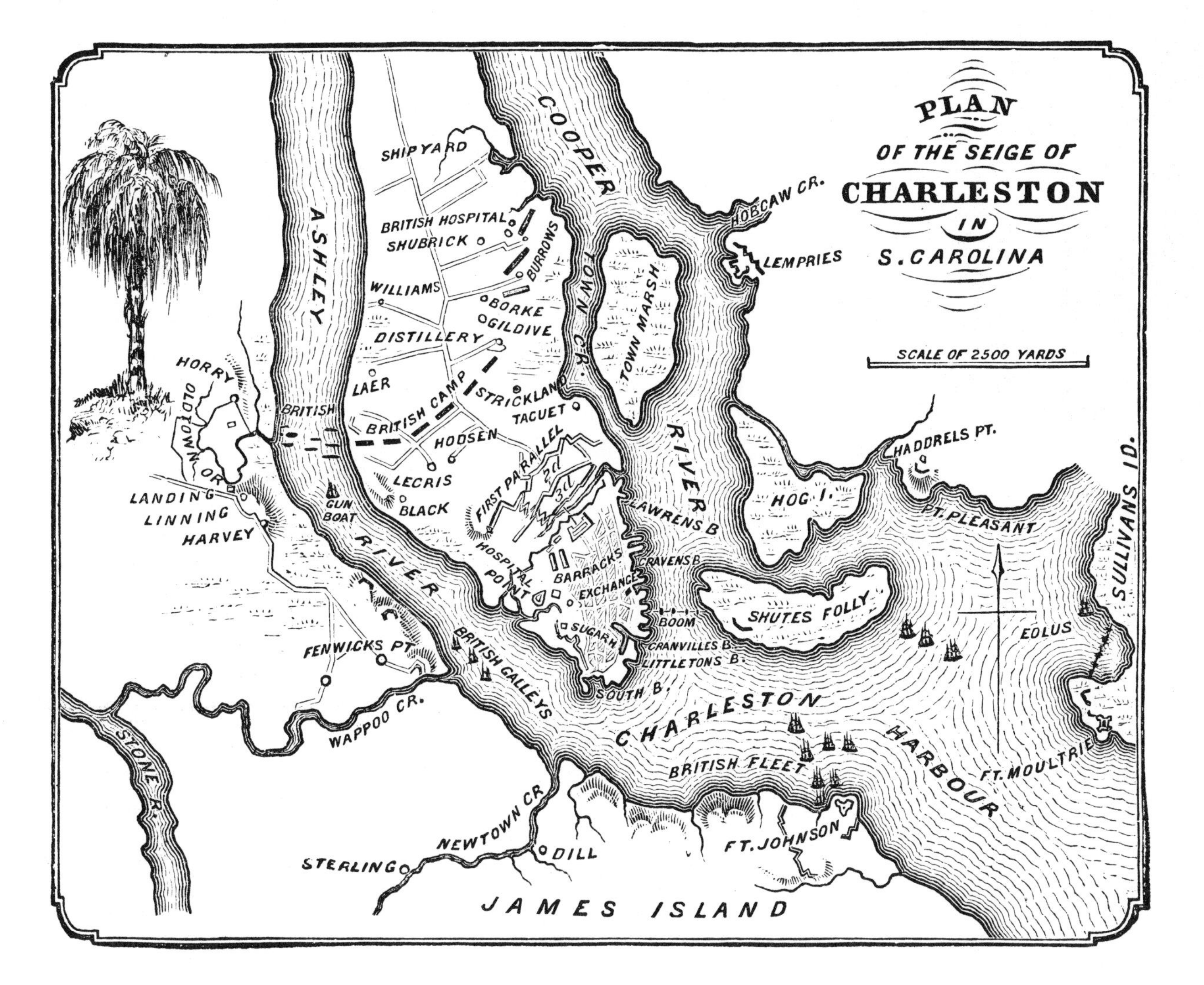

Major General William Moultrie

A few hundred yards away, Moultrie stood within one of the redoubts which protected the town:

> Mr. Lord and Mr. Basquin, two volunteers, were sleeping upon a mattress together, when Mr. Lord was killed by a shell falling upon him, and Mr. Basquin at the same time, had the hair of his head burnt, and did not wake till he was called upon. The fatigue in that advance redoubt was so great, for want of sleep, that many faces were so swelled they could scarcely see out of their eyes. I was obliged to relieve Major Mitchell, the commanding officer; they were constantly upon the lookout for the shells that were continually falling among them. It was by far the most dangerous post on the lines. On my visit to this battery, not having been there for a day or two, I took the usual way of going in, which was a bridge that crossed our ditch, quite exposed to the enemy. In the meantime, they had advanced their works within seventy or eighty yards of the bridge, which I did not know of; as soon as I had stepped upon the bridge, an uncommon number of bullets whistled about me. On looking to my right, I could just see the heads of about twelve or fifteen men firing upon me, from behind a breastwork; I moved on and got in; when Major Mitchell saw me, he asked me which way I came in. I told him over the bridge, he was astonished and said, "Sir, it is a thousand to one that you were not killed," and told me, "that we had a covered way to go in and out," which he conducted me through on my return. I stayed in this battery about a quarter of an hour, to give the necessary orders, in which time we were constantly skipping about to get out of the way of the shells thrown from their howitzers. They were not more than one hundred yards from our works, and throwing their shells in bushels on our front and left flanks.

"Damn me, the rebels are here!"

Heinrichs was surprised by an American sortie. One of his workmen suddenly cried, "Damn me, the rebels are here!"

> I jumped on the parapet and when I saw the enemy, who were already pressing upon our right wing from a barrier situated at their left wing front redoubt and were also rushing out of the gate-work, I had my workmen seize their muskets, withdrew the two jagers this side of the traverse, and opened a continuous fire along the unoccupied part of the parallel as far as the gate-work. The enemy, having penetrated our right wing, were already more than fifty paces behind us, partly between the third and second parallels. I ordered some jagers and Corporal Rubenkoenig behind the traverse and had them fire behind the trench across the plain.

His men in the trench behind began to fire, which caused the rebels to retire leaving twenty dead on the ground:

> But they covered their retreat with so excessive a shower of canisters which were loaded with old burst shells, broken shovels, pickaxes, hatchets, flatirons, pistol barrels, broken locks, etc., etc. (these pieces we found in our trench) and so enfiladed us at the same time from the front redoubt of their left wing (fifteen balls were embedded in the traverse I had thrown up) that one could hardly hear another close beside him. It was still

dark, and the smoke of the powder was so thick that one could not tell friend from enemy.

The parallels were completed by May 6. The British stood ready to storm the American lines. There was no hope of successful resistance. The guns were dismounted, the parapets lay in ruins. The British fleet dominated the harbor. Faced with no other course, Lincoln surrendered, handing over 300 cannon and 5,618 soldiers to the victor.

"Something happened which might have been foreseen."

A tragic incident marked the British take-over. The militiamen were ordered to unload and throw their muskets into a magazine half a dozen at a time. "Something happened which might have been foreseen," remarked Heinrichs. One militiaman omitted to unload his piece. "A musket went off; the bullet struck a barrel of powder and the magazine blew up." Two British officers, fifteen bombardiers, six guards, and a number of negroes were killed; wagons and powder-carts were destroyed. One man was dashed against the steeple of a church at great distance from the explosion and "left the marks of his body there for several days." Another magazine, 150 yards away and containing 180 barrels of powder, exploded, throwing muskets, ramrods, and bayonets onto the roofs of houses. Two thousand muskets were destroyed, those intended to arm the back-country people.

Tarleton's quarters

The fall of Charleston, the Americans' only southern seaport, and the surrender of its garrison, was a serious blow to the patriot cause—their worst disaster since the war began. Wasting no time, Clinton dispatched expeditions to subjugate the back-country and encourage the loyalists to kill and pillage their neighbors.

"The blood will be upon your head."

Tarleton caught up with 350 Virginians, commanded by Colonel Abraham Buford at Waxhaw's Creek, near Hillsborough. When Buford rejected the offered terms, Tarleton sent him a message, "If you are rash enough to reject the terms, the blood will be upon your head." Tarleton's legionaries charged in. Perceiving that their resistance was useless, Buford hoisted a white flag, and his men laid down their arms, expecting the usual treatment sanctioned by civilized warfare. Dr. Robert Brownfield, a Virginia surgeon, described the tragic aftermath:

> This, however, made no part of Tarleton's creed. His ostensible pretext for the relentless barbarity that ensued was that his horse was killed under him, just as the flag was raised. He affected to believe that this was done afterwards and imputed it to the treachery of Buford.

"Massacre by Tarleton"

The ensign who advanced with the flag was instantly cut down. Realizing their danger, the Virginians took up their arms; before they could fire Tarleton was in their midst.

> The demand for quarter, seldom refused to a vanquished foe, was at once found to be in vain. Not a man was spared, and it was the concurrent testimony of all the survivors that for fifteen minutes after every man was prostrate, they went over the ground plunging their bayonets into everyone that exhibited any signs of life, and in some instances, where several had fallen one over the other, these monsters were seen to throw off on the point of the bayonet the uppermost, to come to those beneath.

Tarleton's men massacred 113 Virginians, and severely wounded a further 150. His work that day, May 29, 1780, earned him the title of "Bloody" Tarleton, and it coined the term, "Tarleton's Quarter" for that type of atrocity. "This bloody day," wrote Harry Lee, "only wanted the war dance and the roasting fire to have placed it first in the records of torture and death in the west." Throughout the two states, Georgia and South Carolina, the loyalists flocked to join the Royal army. Many patriots took the oath of allegiance to King George. Throughout the colonies there was talk of surrender. Defeatism reached such proportions that Congress felt impelled to issue the statement:

> That this Confederacy is most sacredly pledged to support the liberty and independence of every one of its members; and . . . will unremittingly persevere in their exertions . . . for the recovery and preservation of any and every part of these United States that has been or may hereafter be invaded or possessed by the common enemy.

Believing that the South had been subdued, Clinton returned to New York, leaving Lord Cornwallis to command the mopping up operations against the guerrillas who continued to attack isolated British posts and supply columns.

For the Americans there was one bright spark. Admiral du Ternay reached Rhode Island, carrying six thousand French soldiers commanded by the Comte de Rochambeau. Washington rode to Connecticut to confer with his new allies.

–Sketch by Kay Smith

CAMDEN

Congress, ignoring Washington's disapproval, sent Horatio Gates to retrieve the situation in the south. "Take care lest your northern laurels turn to southern willows," warned Charles Lee. Gates reached the American base camp at Deep River on July 25. The soldiers had been many days without food, there were no wagons and, in his own words, the army suffered from "multiplied and increasing wants." He ordered an immediate march. His plan was sound and it might have proved effective had his army been capable of executing it. The British had spread their force of 3,500 soldiers over twelve exposed ports, strung out over South Carolina and Georgia.

Baron DeKalb

Gates planned to attack the chief depot at Camden before the enemy could concentrate their forces. His army was not inconsiderable, for it had been augmented to 1,400 men by the arrival of two regiments from Delaware and Maryland and a force of dragoons commanded by the French volunteer, the "Baron" (as he styled himself) de Kalb. Gates told his troops to hold themselves in readiness to march at a moment's notice, an order which caused great astonishment to his officers who knew the army's condition.

Ignoring the advice of the local officers, who urged the adoption of a circuitous route through unravaged, patriot-held country, Gates advanced through poor, hostile country where his army, which he described as being in "inconceivable distress," could find no food. Starting on July 27, Gates put off their fears with the promise that he would call a council of war when the troops halted at noon. His deputy adjutant general, Colonel Otto Williams, did not know if he did:

> After a short halt at noon, when the men were refreshed *upon the scraps in their knapsacks*, the march was resumed. The country exceeded the representation that had been made of it—scarcely had it emerged from a state of sterile nature—the few rude attempts at improvements that were to be found were most of them abandoned by the owners and plundered by the neighbors. Everyone, in this uncivilized part of the country, was flying from his home and joining in parties under adventurers who pretended to yield them protection until the British army should appear—which they seemed confidently to expect. The distresses of the soldiery daily increased—they were told that the banks of the Pee Dee River were extremely fertile—and so indeed they were; but the preceding crop of corn (the

General Francis Marion crossing the Pee Dee River

principal article of produce) was exhausted, and the new grain, although luxuriant and fine, was unfit for use. Many of the soldiery, urged by necessity, plucked the green ears and boiled them with the lean beef, which was collected in the woods, made for themselves a repast—not unpalatable to be sure, but which was attended with painful effects. Green peaches also were substituted for bread and had similar consequences. Some of the officers, aware of the risk of eating such vegetables, and in such a state, with poor fresh beef and without salt, restrained themselves from taking anything but the beef itself, boiled or roasted. It occurred to some that the hair powder which remained in their bags would thicken soup, and it was actually applied.

The officers appeased their men by showing their own empty canteens, and they persuaded them to continue the march towards Camden where, unknown to Gates, Lord Cornwallis had arrived on August 15. He set out that night intending to attack the rebel army at dawn. That same night Gates began a forced march, believing that he could surprise and capture Lord Rawdon's small garrison. According to Williams, Gates believed that he commanded some seven thousand soldiers. Williams showed him the roster which enumerated only 3,052 men. "These are enough for our purpose," Gates replied. The officers protested, pointing out that two-thirds of the army were untried militia. On Gates's reiteration that only a small force of the enemy lay ahead, the men "acquiesced with their usual cheerfulness and were ready to march at the hour appointed."

A surprise meeting

To buoy up the men's spirits, the hospital stores were broached and each man was given a gill of molasses and a full ration of oatmeal and meat. Their hasty meal operated so cathartically "as to disorder very many of the men, who were breaking the ranks at night and were certainly much debilitated." The French officer, Colonel Armand, led the advance with his cavalry, supported by Colonel Porterfield's light infantry. Between two and three in the morning, they ran into Cornwallis's horsemen. Both armies, stated Williams, were ignorant of each other's intentions:

> The first revelation of this new and unexpected scene was occasioned by a smart, mutual salutation of small arms between the advanced guards. Some of the cavalry of Armand's legion were wounded, retreated, and threw the whole corps into disorder; which, recoiling suddenly on the front of the column of infantry, disordered the First Maryland Brigade and occasioned a general consternation through the whole line of the army. The light infantry under Porterfield, however, executed their orders gallantly; and the enemy, no less astonished than ourselves, seemed to acquiesce in a sudden suspension of hostilities.
>
> Some prisoners were taken on both sides. From one of these, the deputy adjutant general of the American army extorted information respecting the situation and numbers of the enemy. He informed that Lord Cornwallis commanded in person about three thousand regular British troops, which were in line of march, about five or six hundred yards in front. Order was soon restored in the corps of infantry in the American army, and the officers were employed in forming a front line of battle when the deputy adjutant general communicated to General Gates the information which he had from the prisoner. The general's astonishment could not be concealed. He ordered the deputy adjutant general to call another council of war. All the general officers immediately assembled in the rear of the line. The unwelcome news was communicated to them.

Artillery used by colonial troops in the Southern campaigns
—Sketch by Kay Smith

General Horatio Gates

"It is too late now to do anything but fight."

"Gentlemen, what is best to be done?" Gates asked. The officers stood mute, until General Stevens exclaimed, "It is too late now to do anything but fight." Gates ordered his officers back to their commands. Williams hovered between the soldiers and their General:

> Lieutenant Colonel Porterfield, in whose bravery and judicious conduct great dependence was placed, received in the first *rencontre* a mortal wound (as it long afterwards proved) and was obliged to retire. His infantry bravely kept the ground in front; and the American army was formed in the following order: the Maryland division, including the Delawares, on the right—the North Carolina militia in the center—and the Virginia militia on the left. It happened that each flank was covered by a marsh, so near as to admit the removing of the First Maryland Brigade to form a second line, about two hundred yards in the rear of the first. The artillery was removed from the center of the brigades and placed in the center of the front line; and the North Carolina militia under Major Armstrong, which had retreated at the first *rencontre*, was ordered to cover a small interval between the left wing and the swampy grounds on that quarter.
>
> Frequent skirmishes happened during the night between the advanced parties—which served to discover the relative situations of the two armies—and as a prelude to what was to take place in the morning.
>
> At dawn of day (on the morning of the 16th of August) the enemy appeared in front, advancing in column. Captain Singleton, who commanded some pieces of artillery, observed to Colonel Williams that he plainly perceived the ground of the British uniform at about two hundred yards in front. The deputy adjutant general immediately ordered Captain Singleton to open his battery, and then rode to the general, who was in the rear of the second line, and informed him of the cause of the firing which he heard. He also observed to the general that the enemy seemed to be displaying their column by the right; the nature of the ground favored this conjecture, for yet nothing was clear.

Gates seemed disposed to await events. He gave no orders, and when Williams suggested an attack by Stevens's brigade, he answered, "That's right, let it be done." Williams carried the order to Stevens, who—

> . . . observing the enemy to rush on, put his men in mind of their bayonets; but the impetuosity with which they advanced, *firing* and *huzzaing*, threw the whole body of the militia into such a panic that they generally threw down their *loaded* arms and fled in the utmost consternation. The unworthy example of the Virginians was almost instantly followed by the North Carolinians; only a small part of the brigade commanded by Brigadier General Gregory made a short pause. A part of Dixon's regiment of that brigade, next in line to the Second Maryland Brigade, fired two or three rounds of cartridges. But a great majority of the militia (at least two-thirds of the army) fled without firing a shot. The writer avers it of his own knowledge, hav-

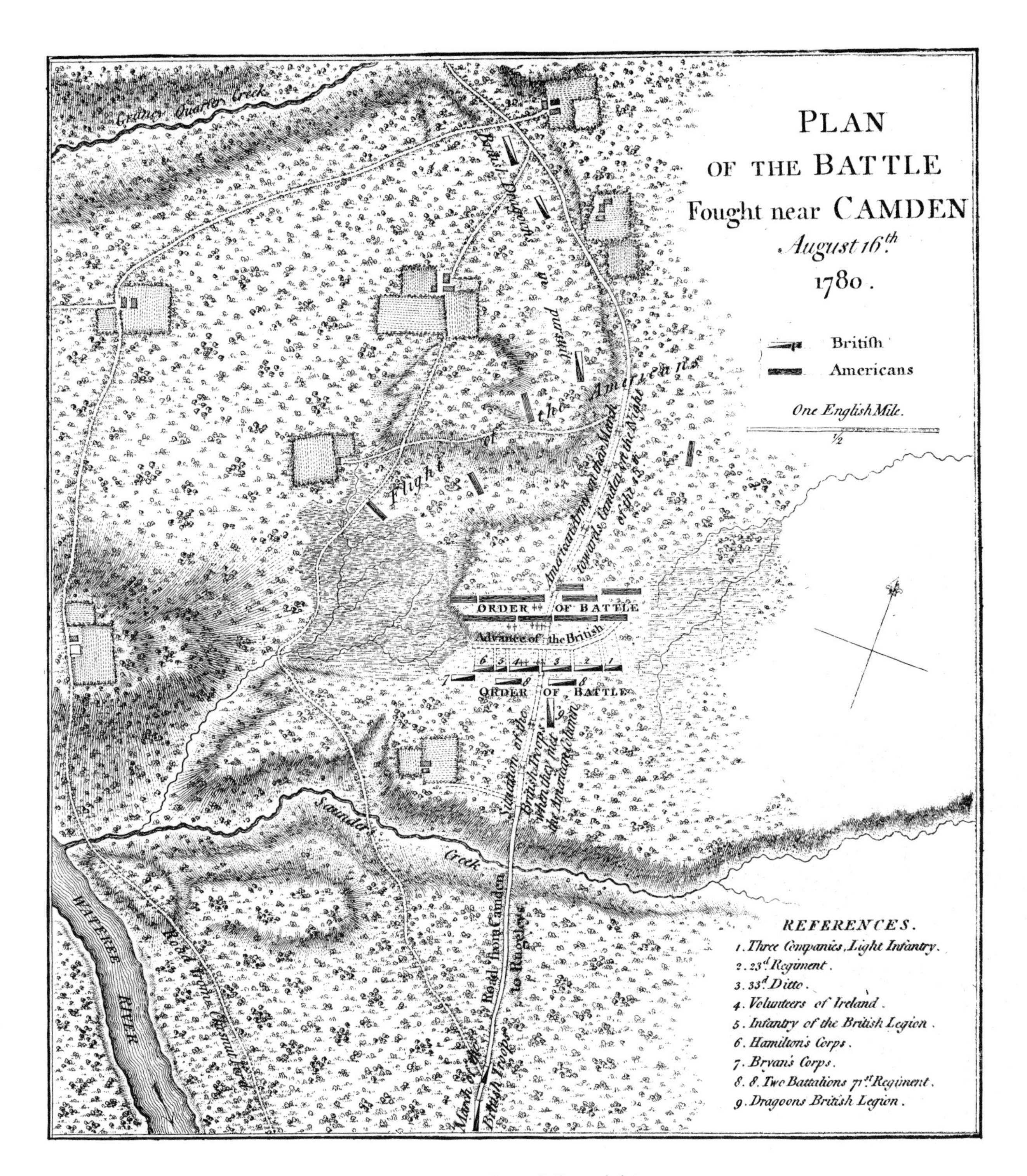

ing seen and observed every part of the army, from left to right, during the action.

Observing the movement on the left of the American lines, Cornwallis had directed Lieutenant Colonel Webster to begin the attack. His disciplined soldiers' steady front and stout advance dismayed the raw militiamen, as Williams saw:

> He who has never seen the effect of a panic upon a multitude can have but an imperfect idea of such a thing. The best disciplined troops have been enervated and made cowards by it.

Armies have been routed by it, even where no enemy appeared to furnish an excuse. Like electricity, it operates instantaneously—like sympathy, it is irresistible where it touches. But, in the present instance, its action was not universal. The regular troops, who had the keen edge of sensibility rubbed off by strict discipline and hard service, saw the confusion with but little emotion. They engaged seriously in the affair; and, notwithstanding some irregularity, which was created by the militia breaking pell-mell through the second line, order was restored there—time enough to give the enemy a severe check, which abated the fury of their assault and obliged them to assume a more deliberate manner of acting. The Second Maryland Brigade, including the battalion of Delawares, on the right, was engaged with the enemy's left, which they opposed with very great firmness. They even advanced upon them and had taken a number of prisoners, when their companions of the First Brigade (which formed the second line), being greatly outflanked and charged by superior numbers, were obliged to give ground.

The Marylanders stood fast, until the whole of Gates's army had become enveloped by Lord Rawdon, who came up in support of Webster. Williams, himself a Marylander, called upon them not to fly. Colonel Ford called back, "They have done all that can be expected of them. We are outnumbered and outflanked. See the enemy charge with bayonets." Lord Cornwallis, perceiving the Marylanders' perseverance and obstinacy, called up the dragoons and ordered the infantry to put an end to their resistance at bayonet point.

Death of Baron de Kalb

His victory was complete. All the artillery and a very great number of prisoners fell into his hands. Many fine fellows lay on the field, and the rout of the remainder was entire. Not even a company retired in any order. Everyone escaped as he could. If in this affair the militia fled too soon, the regulars may be thought almost as blamable for remaining too long on the field, especially after all hope of victory must have been despaired of.

Let the commandants of the brigades answer for themselves. Allow the same privilege to the officers of the corps comprising those brigades, and they will say that they never received orders to retreat, nor any order from any *general* officer, from the commencement of the action until it became desperate. The brave Major General, the Baron de Kalb, fought on foot with the Second Brigade and fell, mortally wounded, into the hands of the enemy, who stripped him even of his shirt—a fate which probably was avoided by other generals only by an opportune retreat.

The flight became a stampede.

The flight became a stampede. Gates was swept away in the torrent, unaware of the stout resistance put up by the Marylanders. All the heavy baggage fell into the enemy's hands. Two wagons, those furnished with the sturdiest horses, escaped:

Other wagons also had got out of danger from the enemy; but the cries of the women and the wounded in the rear and the consternation of the flying troops so alarmed some of the wagoners that they cut out their teams and, taking each a horse,

Alexander Hamilton

left the rest for the next that should come. Others were obliged to give up their horses to assist in carrying off the wounded, and the whole road, for many miles, was strewn with signals of distress, confusion, and dismay.

What added not a little to this calamitous scene was the conduct of Armand's Legion. They were principally foreigners, and some of them, probably, not accustomed to such scenes. Whether it was owing to the disgust of the colonel at general orders, or the cowardice of his men, is not with the writer to determine; but certain it is, the Legion did not take any part in the action of the 16th. They retired early and in disorder, and were seen plundering the baggage of the army on their retreat.

The North Carolina militia scattered through the wilderness, intent on making the shortest way home. The Virginians hurried to Hillsborough, where they discharged themselves, claiming that their term of service had expired.

A disgraced general

Gates, who was accompanied by General Richard Caswell, did not stop until he had put sixty miles between himself and the British. He rode a further sixty miles to Hillsborough. "Was there ever such an instance of a general running away from his whole army? Was there ever so precipitate a flight?" inquired Alexander Hamilton, who thought "it does admirable credit to the activity of a man at his time of life." But, it disgraced the general and the soldier.

Gates suffered from the unpopularity for which he was alone responsible. No one liked the vainglorious hero of Saratoga, and he was gleefully criticized by friend and foe. The Tory News Letter, Rivington's *Royal Gazette*, published in New York, advertised:

REWARD.

STRAYED, DESERTED, OR STOLEN, from the subscriber, on the 16th of August, last, near Camden, in the State of South Carolina, a whole ARMY, consisting of horse, foot, and dragoons, to the amount of near TEN THOUSAND (as has been said) with all their baggage, artillery, wagons, and camp equipage. The subscriber has very strong suspicions, from information received from his aide-de-camp, that a certain CHARLES, EARL CORNWALLIS, was principally concerned in carrying off the said ARMY with their baggage, etc. Any person or persons, civil or military, who will give information, whether to the subscriber, or to Charles Thompson, Esq., Secretary to the Continental Congress, where the said ARMY is, so that they may be recovered and rallied again, shall be entitled to demand from the Treasurer of the United States the sum of

THREE MILLION OF PAPER DOLLARS

as soon as they can be spared from the public funds, and

ANOTHER MILLION

for apprehending the person principally concerned in taking the said ARMY off. Proper passes will be granted by the President of the Congress to such persons as incline to go in search of the said ARMY. And as a further encouragement, no deduction will be made from the above reward on account of any of the Militia (who composed the said ARMY) not being found or heard of, as no dependence can be placed on their services, and nothing but the most speedy flight can ever save their Commander.

HORATIO GATES, M.G.
and late Commander in Chief
of the Southern Army,
August 30, 1780.

A most disastrous defeat

One of the early historians of the Revolution, John Fisk, who wrote in 1891, described the battle of Camden as "the most disastrous defeat ever inflicted on an American army." By it, Gates lost North Carolina and, possibly, Virginia. Foolish as Gates had been to strike blindly at Camden, his defeat may not have been so disastrous as his contemporaries believed. It gave the headstrong Cornwallis dangerous overconfidence. Clinton had warned his venturesome subordinate to be careful. Emboldened by his easy victory, and confident that he could crush all rebel resistance, Cornwallis hurried in pursuit of Gates, entangling his small army, weakened by the casualties of Camden, 68 killed and 256 wounded, in the North Carolina backwoods.

KING'S MOUNTAIN

Congress relieved Gates of his command, and invited Washington to name his successor. The General was in no doubt. Nathanael Greene traveled south, overtaking Gates's shattered army at Charlotte on the Virginian border:

> The appearance of the troops was wretched beyond description, and their distress, on account of provisions was little less than their suffering for want of clothing and other necessaries. General Gates had lost the confidence of the officers, and the troops all their discipline, and so addicted to plundering, that they were a terror to the inhabitants. The General and I met upon very good terms, and parted so. The old gentleman was in great distress, having but just heard of the death of his son before my arrival.

Unless his army was supported "the country is lost beyond redemption," Greene reported. It was impossible, he believed, for the people of the south to struggle much longer without aid. He underestimated the resource and courage of the backwoodsmen. While Greene debated his strategy, a force of volunteers assembled to rid the Carolinas of the Tory bands who were led by the British major, Patrick Ferguson. Too late, Cornwallis learned that Ferguson's 1,100 New York and Carolinian loyalists, marching parallel with his own army, were under attack. Pursued by the North Carolina and Virginian backwoodsmen – three thousand strong and skilled marksmen – Ferguson took refuge on King's Mountain, a spur of the Blue Ridge, in South Carolina, a few miles from the North Carolina border. The hill was about half a mile long and several hundred yards wide, its slopes thickly wooded.

Writing in 1823, Colonel Isaac Shelby recalled how the volunteer army was assembled. He led 240 North Carolinians, Colonel Charles McDowell commanded 160, Colonel John Sevier had 240, Colonel Benjamin Cleveland raised 350. Colonel William Campbell brought 400 Virginians, and Colonel James Williams of South Carolina, a similar force.

Shelby described Major Ferguson as "one of the best and most enterprising of the British officers in America." He had sent a message to Shelby warning him that if he did not surrender, he would cross the mountains, put him to death and ravage the country. This threat roused Shelby's patriotic indignation. He determined to raise a force, in connection with others,

A view of King's Mountain battlefield

strong enough to surprise and defeat the boaster. With this object in view, he went to a horse race to engage others in the enterprise:

> The force having been raised by officers of equal rank, and being without any higher officer entitled to command the whole corps, there was a general want of organization and arrangement. It was then determined that a board of officers should convene each night and decide on the plan of operations for the next day; and further, that one of the officers should see those orders executed as officer of the day, until they should otherwise conclude.

Following this friendly discussion, Colonel Campbell was appointed to command as officer of the day:

> Finding that Ferguson was retreating, and learning what was his real strength, it was determined on Thursday night, the 5th of October, to make a desperate effort to overtake him before he should reach any British post or receive any further reinforcements. Accordingly, they selected all who had good horses, who numbered about nine hundred and ten, and started the next morning in pursuit of Ferguson as soon as they could see.

"I will not stop till night"

The volunteers did not stop until late afternoon. They halted at Cowpens, shot some oxen, ate, and fed their horses:

> This done, the line of march was resumed, and continued through the whole night, amidst an excessively hard rain. In the morning Shelby ascertained that Campbell had taken a wrong road in the night and had separated from him. Men were posted off in all directions and Campbell's corps found and put in the right road. They then crossed Broad River, and continued their pursuit until twelve o'clock, the 7th of October. The rain con-

tinued to fall so heavily that Campbell, Sevier, and Cleveland concluded to halt, and rode up to Shelby to inform him of their determination. Shelby replied, "I will not stop till night, if I follow Ferguson into Cornwallis's lines!" Without replying, the other colonels turned off to their respective commands and continued the march. They had proceeded but a mile when they learned that Ferguson was only seven miles from them at King's Mountain.

The next day, Shelby reconnoitered the enemy position which he considered very strong and "so confident was Ferguson that he declared that the Almighty could not drive him from it." The patrols, coming near the mountain, tethered their horses and prepared for an immediate attack. The young North Carolinia officer, Robert Campbell, stated that they "were fortunate enough to come up on him (Ferguson) undiscovered and took his pickets, they not having it in their power to give the alarm." The South Carolina loyalist, Alexander Chesney, had returned to the mountaintop to report that "all was quiet and the pickets were on the alert," and was in the act of dismounting when "we heard a firing about half a mile off." It was about three o'clock in the afternoon.

The patriot force, stated Shelby, was led to the attack in four columns:

Col. Campbell commanded the right center column, Col. Shelby the left center, Col. Sevier the right flank column, and Col. Cleveland the left flank. As they came to the foot of the mountain, the right center and the right flank columns deployed to the right, and the left center and left flank columns to the left, and thus surrounding the mountain they marched up, commencing the action on all sides.

"Every man's fate is before him"

The plan, said young James Collins, who wrote his autobiography:

. . . was to surround the mountain and attack them on all sides, if possible. In order to do this, the left had to march under the fire of the enemy to gain the position assigned to them on the stream on the right of the enemy, while the right was to take possession of the other stream. In doing this they were not exposed, the cliff being so steep as to cover them completely.

Each leader made a short speech in his own way to his men, desiring every coward to be off immediately. Here I confess I would willingly have been excused, for my feelings were not the most pleasant. This may be attributed to my youth, not being quite seventeen years of age—but I could not well swallow the appellation of coward. I looked around. Every man's countenance seemed to change. Well, thought I, fate is fate; every man's fate is before him and he has to run it out.

"We were soon in motion," he recalled. Every man threw four or five balls into his mouth to prevent thirst, also to be in readiness to reload quickly. "The orders," said another boy, Thomas Young, "were at the firing of the first gun for every man to raise a whoop, rush forward and make his way as best he could."

The officer gave the word of command to raise the Indian war whoop, and "next moment King's Mountain resounded with their shouts," recalled Robert Campbell.

Assaulting the bare ridge

Ferguson's men were drawn up on the steep ridge. The wooded slopes provided excellent cover for the assailants, many of whom were armed with rifles. Ferguson, declared Shelby, did all that an officer could do under the circumstances:

> His men, too, fought bravely. But his position, which he thought impregnable against any force the Patriots could raise, was really a disadvantage to him. The summit was bare, whilst the sides of the mountain were covered with trees. Ferguson's men were drawn up in close column on the summit and thus presented fair marks for the mountaineers, who approached them under cover of the trees.

"The British," said Robert Campbell, "beat to arms, and immediately formed on top of the mountain behind a chain of rocks that appeared impregnable, and had their wagons drawn up on their flank across the end of the mountain, by which they made a strong breastwork."

Alexander Chesney perceived both the advantages and disadvantages of the position:

> King's Mountain from its height would have enabled us to oppose a superior force with advantage, had it not been covered with wood which sheltered the Americans and enabled them to fight in the favorite manner; in fact, after driving in our piquets, they were able to advance in three divisions under separate leaders to the crest of the hill in perfect safety until they took post and opened an irregular but destructive fire from behind trees and other cover.

On the first fire, stated Robert Campbell, the British guards retreated, leaving some of their men to fight a rear guard. The enemy's shot "soon began to pass over us like hail," recalled Collins. Concealed by the trees, the patriots advanced to the charge. In fifteen minutes the wings came round and the action became general. Shelby ordered Campbell and his men to post themselves behind rocks and get near the enemy. Collins was soon in a profuse sweat:

> My lot happened to be in the center, where the severest part of the battle was fought. We soon attempted to climb the hill, but were fiercely charged upon and forced to fall back to our first position. We tried a second time, but met the same fate; the fight then seemed to become more furious.

Shelby said that—

> . . . as either column would approach the summit, Ferguson would order out a charge with fixed bayonet, which was always successful, for the riflemen retreated before the charging column slowly, still firing as they retired. When Ferguson's men

FROM A WATER-COLOR PAINTING BY KAY SMITH

The House of Burgesses, Williamsburg, Virginia, where the Virginia assembly, which included many of the most famous figures in American history, met and enacted laws.

FROM A WATER-COLOR SKETCH BY KAY SMITH

FROM A WATER-COLOR SKETCH BY KAY SMITH

The Governor's Palace, Williamsburg, Virginia.

(left) Interior of the House of Burgesses where Patrick Henry delivered many of his most famous addresses.

FROM A WATER-COLOR SKETCH BY KAY SMITH

Bruton Parish Church, Williamsburg, Virginia, designed by Governor Spotswood, has been in continuous use since 1715.

> returned to regain their position on the mountain, the patriots would again rally and pursue them. In one of these charges Shelby's column was considerably broken; he rode back and rallied his men, and when the enemy retired to the summit he pressed on his men and reached the summit whilst Ferguson was directing a charge against Cleveland.

Thomas Young, who with Ben Hollingsworth climbed the side of the mountain, fighting "from tree to tree," recollected, "I stood behind one tree and fired until the bark was nearly all knocked off and my eyes pretty well filled with it. One fellow shaved me pretty close, for his bullet took a piece out of my own gun-stock. Before I was aware of it, I found myself apparently between my own regiment and the enemy." He judged that from spotting the white paper worn in their hats by the patriots, and the pine knots displayed by the Tories. Collins saw "their leader, Ferguson, come in full view, within rifle-shot as if to encourage his men, who by this time were falling fast." He soon disappeared.

The wings reached the summit at the same time as did the center, led by Shelby. Robert Campbell reported:

> This scene was not of long duration, for it was the brave Virginia volunteers and those under Col. Shelby on their attempting rapidly to ascend the mountain, that were charged with the bayonet. They obstinately stood until some of them were thrust through the body, and having nothing but their rifles by which to defend themselves, they were forced to retreat. They were soon rallied by their gallant commanders, Campbell, Shelby and other brave officers, and by a constant and well-directed fire of their rifles drove them back in their turn, strewing the face of the mountain with their assailants, and kept advancing until they drove them from some of their posts.

Alexander Chesney estimated that this stage of the action lasted nearly an hour, the "mountaineers flying whenever there was danger of being charged by the bayonet, and returning again as soon as the British detachment had faced about to repel another of their parties." Another Tory officer, Lieutenant Allaire, noted in his journal that "their numbers enabled them to surround us." His "poor little detachment," consisting of seventy, lost all but twenty killed or wounded.

The united patriots drove the enemy to one end of the ridge. They pressed forward, firing as they came up. The slaughter was very great. "The enemy was completely hemmed in on all sides, and had no chance of escape. Besides, their leader had fallen," remembered James Collins.

"He never would yield to such a d— —d banditti"

Robert Campbell declared that Major Ferguson was attempting to escape on horseback when he fell, and the two officers with him shared his fate. Neither Shelby nor Alexander Chesney made any such suggestion. Shelby stated, "He swore that he never would yield to such a d— —d banditti and rushed from his men, sword in hand, and cut away until his sword was broken and he was shot down."

Chesney saw his leader fall:

> Col. Ferguson was at last recognized by his gallantry, although wearing a hunting shirt, and fell pierced by seven balls at the moment he had killed the American Col. Williams with his left hand (the right being useless).

Ferguson's right arm had been shattered by a bullet at the battle of Brandywine.

Sixteen-year-old Thomas Young saw Williams fall, on the top of the mountain in the thickest of the fight:

> I had seen him but once before that day. It was in the beginning of the action, as he charged by me at full speed around the mountain. Toward the summit a ball struck his horse under the jaw, when he commenced stamping as if he were in a nest of yellow-jackets. The Colonel threw his reins over the animal's neck, sprang to the ground and dashed forward. The moment I heard the cry that Colonel Williams was shot, I ran to his assistance, for I loved him as a father. He had ever been so kind to me and almost always carried a cake in his pocket for me and his little son, Joseph.

"For God's sake, boys, don't give up the mountain"

His men sprinkled water in Williams's face. He revived and his first words were, "For God's sake, boys, don't give up the mountain." Young left him in the arms of his son Daniel, and returned to the field to avenge his fate.

Captain de Peyster succeeded to Ferguson's command. Robert Campbell watched him march a full company of British regulars to reinforce "the extreme post," possibly a reference to the end of the ridge. But when de Peyster reached his place of destination, he found, to his astonishment, that he had almost no men, "being exposed in that short distance to the constant fire of the patriots' rifles." He ordered his cavalry to mount, but to no purpose for "as quick as they mounted they were taken down by some bold marksman."

De Peyster, said Campbell, raised a flag and called for quarter. Chesney declared that the enemy ignored the flag and renewed their fire. "A dreadful havoc took place until the flag was sent out a second time. Then the work of destruction ceased."

Shelby said that Ferguson's men, "seeing their leader fall immediately surrendered." He meant probably at the first raising of the flag. It took some time and exertion by the officers to stop the men firing. Robert Campbell was more precise:

> As soon as Captain de Peyster observed that Col. Ferguson was killed, he raised a flag and called for quarters. It was soon taken out of his hand by one of the officers on horseback and raised so high that it could be seen by our line, and the firing immediately ceased. The Loyalists, at the time of their surrender, were driven into a crowd, and being closely surrounded, they could not have made any further resistance.

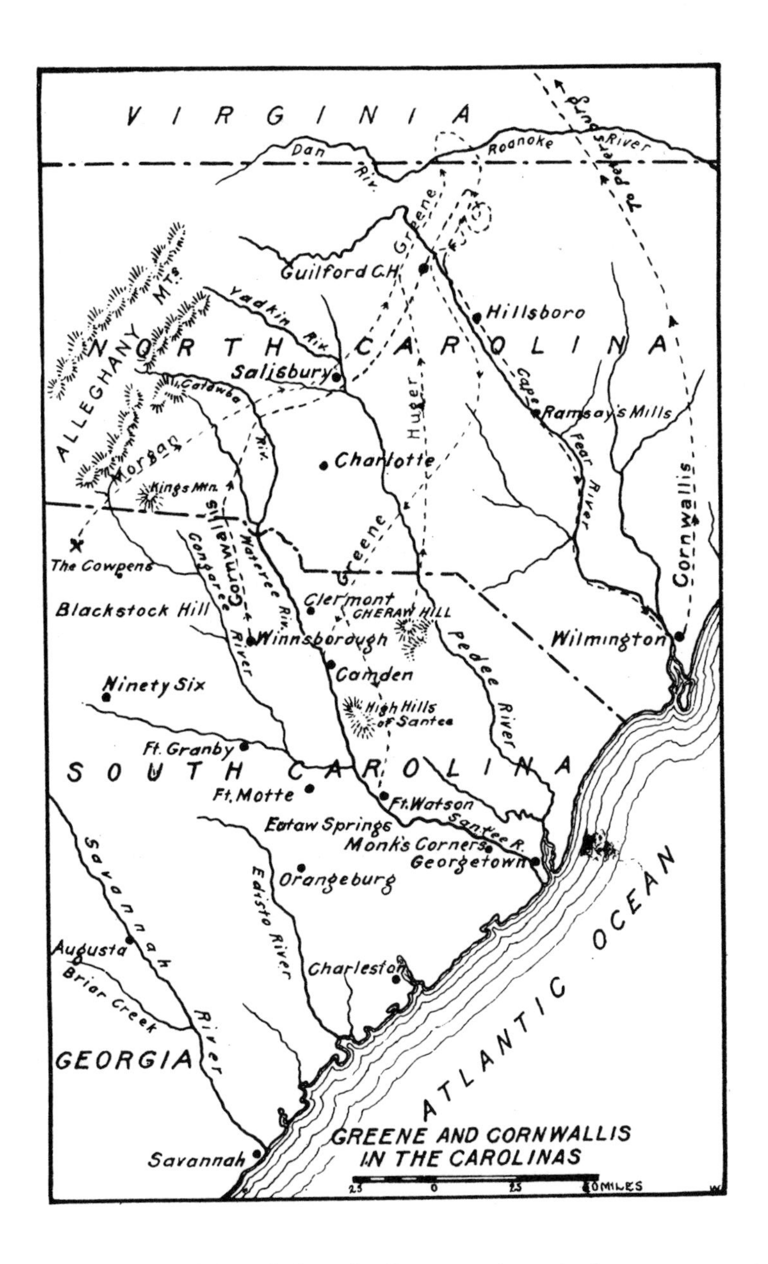

GREENE AND CORNWALLIS IN THE CAROLINAS

Chesney considered that de Peyster thought it necessary to surrender to save the lives of the brave men who were left.

"The dead lay in heaps on all sides"

After the fight was over, Collins thought the condition of "the poor Tories" was really pitiable; "the dead lay in heaps on all sides, while the groans of the wounded were heard in every direction. I could not help turning away from the scene before me with horror and, though exulting in victory, could not refrain from shedding tears."

He examined Ferguson's body. "It appeared that almost fifty rifles must have been leveled at him at the same time. Seven rifle balls had passed through his body, both of his arms were broken, and his hat and clothing were literally shot to pieces."

He explained the British defeat. "Their great elevation above us had proved their ruin. They overshot us altogether, scarce touching a man, except those on horseback, while every rifle from below seemed to have the desired effect."

As regards what happened next, the British and American accounts disagree. Chesney suggests that the wounded and the prisoners were ill treated.

> I had been wounded by the first fire but was so much occupied that I scarcely felt it until the action was over. We passed the night on the spot where we surrendered amidst the dead and groans of the dying who had not surgical aid, or water to quench their thirst.

James Collins took a more sympathetic view:

> Next morning, which was Sunday, the scene became really distressing. The wives and children of the poor Tories came in, in great numbers. Their husbands, fathers, and brothers lay dead in heaps, while others lay wounded or dying—a melancholy sight indeed—while numbers of the survivors were doomed to abide the sentence of a court martial, and several were actually hanged.

A mock trial was held and twenty-four Tories were sentenced to death, ten of whom were executed. The patriots took vengeance on their Tory neighbors who had chosen to fight for their King.

"I die contented, since we have gained the victory."

The British forces lost 150 killed and more than that wounded, plus 810 taken prisoner including 100 regular troops. The patriots lost 30 killed and about 50 wounded. Colonel Williams, remembered Robert Campbell, lived long enough to hear of the surrender. He then said, "I die contented, since we have gained the victory."

The loot included 1,500 muskets. In the evening, recalled James Collins, there was a distribution of the plunder. He and his father drew two fine horses, two guns, some articles of clothing, with a share of powder and lead. They returned home convinced that "for a short time every man could visit his home or neighbor without being afraid."

Alexander Chesney escaped from captivity and managed to reach Cornwallis's army, which, though warned of his predicament by Ferguson, failed to come up in time to rescue him. On hearing of the patriot victory, Cornwallis retraced his steps to Camden, where he remained for three months, his supply route plagued by the patriot guerrillas, who were led by Francis Marion, Thomas Sumter, and Andrew Pickens.

Only Tarleton could cope with them, Cornwallis told Clinton. He did so by barbarous methods, declared the patriots. William Moultrie quoted an example. Having dined at the house belonging to General Richardson, Tarleton burnt it on the pretext that its owner had gone to join the rebels, whereas "had he opened the grave before the door, he might have seen to the contrary."

COWPENS

The Tide Has Turned

Colonel William Washington

Nathanael Greene called the patriot victory at King's Mountain, "the first turn in the tide in favor of the Americans." For years the current had been strong against them, but now it began to change. Knowing that there was no prospect of contending with the British on equal terms, he determined to contain Cornwallis and render it difficult for his army to exist in the back country. To accomplish this, Greene, early in 1781, organized and equipped a "flying army." Following his gallant conduct at Freeman's Farm and Bemis Heights, where his genius had won the battles against Burgoyne, Daniel Morgan, resentful of lack of appreciation by Congress, had retired to his home. The news of the disaster at Camden brought him out, and he rejoined the army. Greene dispatched him to harass the British posts in the western part of South Carolina. Cornwallis sent Tarleton with 1,000 troops to intercept him, promising that he would himself move to bar Morgan's retreat.

Morgan led a mixed force, Colonel Washington's cavalry, two battalions of Maryland Continentals commanded by Colonel Eager Howard, and militia from the two Carolinas, Virginia, and Georgia. They were commanded by several colonels ("With the militia everyone is a colonel," observed Greene), Andrew Pickens, Thomas and Brannon from South Carolina, McDowell (who had fought at King's Mountain) from North Carolina, Trippett and Tate from Virginia, Beatie and Cunningham from Georgia.

"Colonel Tarleton is on his way."

Morgan crossed the Broad River, where he was joined by many local volunteers. There, on January 13, he received a letter from Greene warning him that "Colonel Tarleton is said to be on his way to pay you a visit." The General had no doubt that Morgan would give him a decent reception and a proper dismission. Morgan determined to stand and fight. He took position between the Broad River and its tributary, the Pacolet River, at Cowpens, the local farmers' winter pasture. Another tributary, Thickety Creek, intersected the pasture. These rivers, swamps, and streams made retreat impossible in case of defeat. Following the battle, Greene recounted that "a better place for the British regulars to attack, and a worse place for ordinary troops to defend, could not be imagined."

Scene at the Cowpens battlefield

Morgan placed Washington's cavalry in the rear, the Continentals in front, and beyond them the various militia who were commanded by Pickens. He afterwards justified the confidence in his command qualities that caused General Greene to appoint him. He did not want any protection on his flanks for he knew his adversary well and was satisfied that he would have nothing but hard fighting. As for resting his flanks on a swamp: "I would not have had a swamp in the view of my militia on any consideration. They would have made for it, and nothing could have detained them from it." And as for a river at his back, it was what he wanted to keep the militia from going away, and to make them fight. "Had I crossed the river," said Morgan, "one half of the militia would have abandoned me."

"Be firm and steady and fire with good aim."

By sunrise on the morning of January 17, Morgan's army stood ready. He walked through the ranks of the militia, urging them to fire two rounds carefully aimed and then to retire around the left flank of the Continentals, but not to run or take fright. He reminded the Continentals of the confidence he reposed in their skill and energy, and he exhorted them to be firm and steady and to fire with good aim. If they would pour in but two volleys at killing distance, he would guarantee victory. Walking to his own post, Morgan waited in determined silence for the enemy.

"We were very anxious for battle," wrote Thomas Young, who had come out to fight again. Now well mounted, he attached himself to Colonel Washington's cavalry. He was given a saber and told he had authority to seize any horse not belonging to a dragoon or required by an officer. He was convinced of Morgan's qualities to command. "He went among the volunteers, helped them fix their swords, joked with them about their sweethearts, told them to keep in good spirits and the day would be ours." He said, "Hold up your heads, three fires and you are free, and then, when you return to your homes, how the old folks will bless you, and the girls kiss you for your gallant conduct."

Tarleton learned from a prisoner that he was close to Morgan. He roused his soldiers at three o'clock in the morning, and marched rapidly towards the Broad River. Reaching it, he deployed his troops – the infantry in line, with two fieldpieces; the cavalry on either flank; and a battalion of regulars in the rear. He ordered his men to charge the militia, 200 yards ahead.

The other youthful veteran of King's Mountain, James Collins, watched, about sunrise, "the enemy come into full view." He thought the sight imposing. They halted for a short time

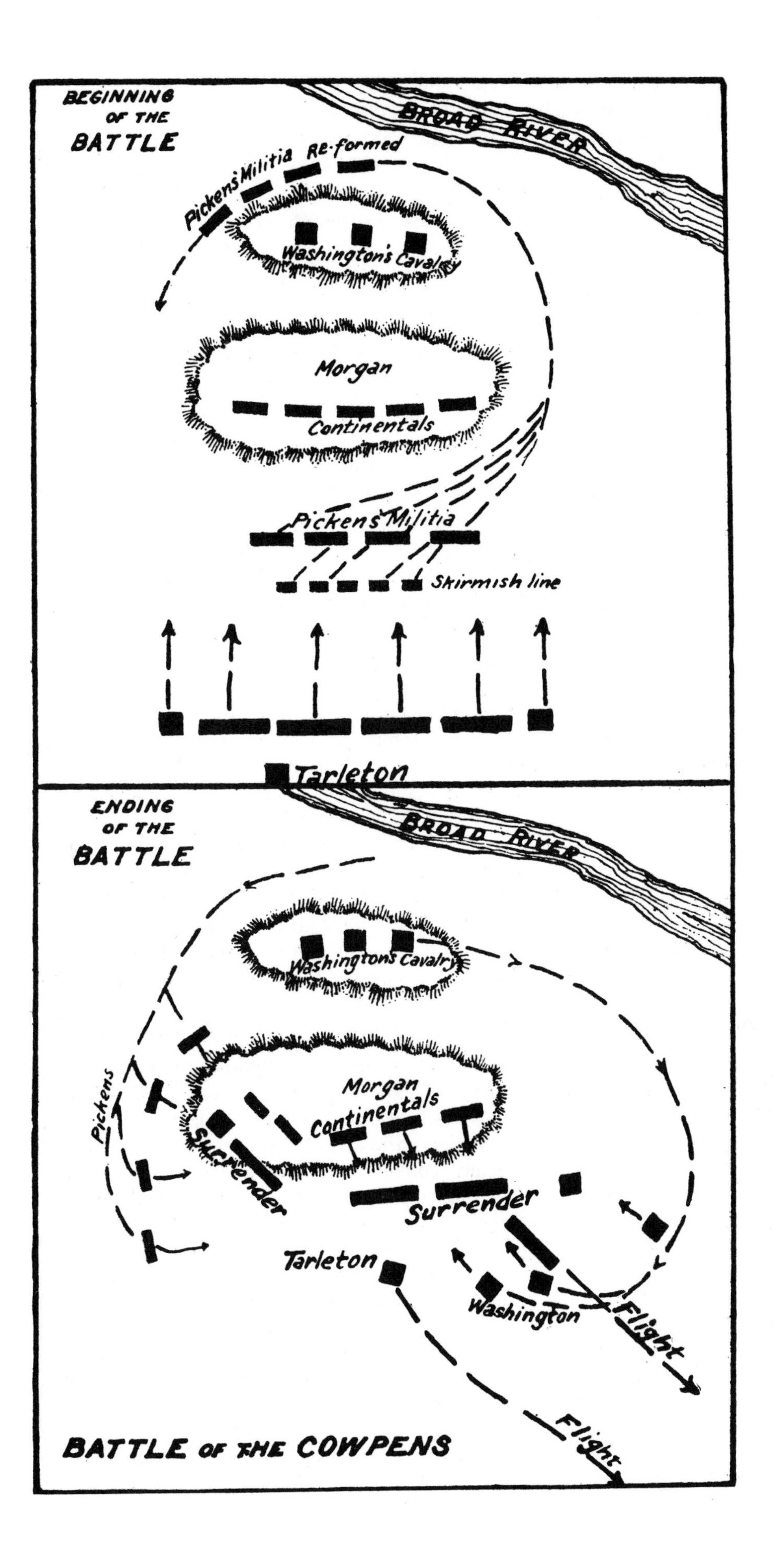

BEGINNING OF THE BATTLE
BROAD RIVER
Pickens' Militia Re-formed
Washington's Cavalry
Morgan
Continentals
Pickens' Militia
Skirmish line
Tarleton
ENDING OF THE BATTLE
BROAD RIVER
Washington's Cavalry
Pickens
Morgan
Continentals
Surrender
Surrender
Tarleton
Washington
Flight
Flight
BATTLE OF THE COWPENS

and then advanced rapidly, as if certain of victory. Collins stood in the front line of the militia.

The whole British line moved with the greatest impetuosity, shouting as they advanced. Thomas Young thought it "the most beautiful line I ever saw. When they shouted, I heard Morgan say, 'They give us the British halloo, boys. Give them the Indian halloo, by God.' "

"Don't fire until you can see the whites of their eyes."

Morgan galloped along the lines, cheering the men and telling them not to fire until "we could see the whites of their eyes." Every officer was crying, "Don't fire," and "it was a hard matter to keep us from it," Young found.

The British line advanced under cover of their artillery, which opened fiercely. The militia fired. To Young it sounded, "pop–pop–pop–and then a whole volley." The British fired too, "It seemed like one sheet of flame from right to left." He thought it "beautiful." James Collins was not so certain:

> We gave the enemy one fire; when they charged us with their bayonets, we gave way and retreated for our horses. Tarleton's cavalry pursued us. "Now," thought I, "my hide is in the loft."

In his more laconic report, Morgan said:

> McDowell and Cunningham gave them a heavy and galling fire and retreated to the regiments intended for their support. The whole of Col. Pickens's command then kept up a fire by regiments, retreating agreeably to their orders. When the enemy advanced to our line, they received a well-directed and incessant fire. But their numbers being superior to ours, they gained our flanks, which obliged us to change our position. We retired in good order about fifty paces, formed, advanced on the enemy and gave them a fortunate volley, throwing them into disorder.

The militia had retired, as they had been ordered. The British followed, overtaking James Collins, who had jumped on his horse. He made a few hacks at his pursuers, without doing much injury, and got clear.

Tarleton's regulars charged the Continentals. It was the crisis of the battle. Colonel Howard described the moment:

> Seeing my right flank was exposed to the enemy, I attempted to change the front of Wallace's company (Virginia regulars); in doing it, some confusion ensued, and first a part, and then the whole of the company, commenced a retreat. The officers along the line seeing this and supposing that orders had been given for a retreat, faced their men about and moved off. Morgan, who had mostly been with the militia, quickly rode up to me and expressed apprehensions of the event; but I soon removed his fears by pointing to the line and observing that men were not beaten who retreated in that order. He then ordered me to keep with the men until we came to the rising ground near Washington's horse; and he rode forward to fix on the most proper place for us to halt and face about.
>
> In a minute we had a perfect line. The enemy were now very near us. Our men commenced a very destructive fire, which they little expected, and a few rounds occasioned great disorder

in their ranks. While in this confusion, I ordered a charge with the bayonet, which order was obeyed with great alacrity. As the line advanced, I observed their artillery a short distance in front and called to Captain Ewing, who was near me, to take it.

"Form, form, my brave fellows."

Seeing the Continentals charge, the militia rallied, and prepared, in James Collins's words to "redeem their credit." Morgan rode up and waving his sword called "Form, form, my brave fellows; give them one more fire and the day is ours." Collins joined their advance:

> We then advanced briskly and gained the right flank of the enemy, and they, being hard pressed in front by Howard and falling very fast, could not stand it long. They began to throw down their arms and surrender themselves prisoners of war.

Collins saw the cavalry charge:

> In a few moments Col. Washington's cavalry was among them like a whirlwind, and the poor fellows began to keel from their horses without being able to remount. The shock was so sudden and violent, they could not stand it and immediately betook themselves to flight. There was no time to rally, and they appeared to be as hard to stop as a drove of wild Choctaw steers going to a Pennsylvania market. In a few moments, the clashing of swords was out of hearing and quickly out of sight.

The British broke and "fled with such precipitation," said Morgan, "that they left their fieldpieces behind. We pushed our advantage so effectually that they never had an opportunity of rallying."

Tarleton, in his account of the action, failed to explain his men's sudden collapse, other than to say "an unexpected fire at this instant from the Americans, who came about us as they were retreating, stopped the British, and threw them in confusion." It was impossible to make them advance. The cavalry fell into disorder and an unaccountable panic extended along the whole line. Taking advantage of the situation, the Americans advanced on the British troops and "augmented their astonishment." A general flight ensued. The cavalry, which had not been engaged, fled through the woods.

Colonel Howard encountered broken squads of the enemy. He called upon them to surrender, to lay down their arms, and for the officers to deliver up their swords. Captain Duncanson, a Grenadier officer, gave Howard his sword and stood by him:

> Upon getting on my horse, I found him pulling at my saddle, and he nearly unhorsed me. I expressed my displeasure and asked him what he was about. The explanation was that they had orders to give no quarter, and they did not expect any; and as my men were coming up, he was afraid they would use him ill. I admitted his excuse and put him into the care of a sergeant.

"I fear they are incorrigible."

In his report, Morgan thought it well to remark, "For the honor of the American arms, although the progress of this

Brigadier General Daniel Morgan

(Tarleton's) corps was marked with burning and devastation, and although they waged the most cruel warfare, not a man was killed, wounded, or even insulted after he surrendered. Had not Britons during this contest received so many lessons of humanity, I should flatter myself that this might teach them a little. But I fear they are incorrigible."

Morgan listed the British losses as 110 noncommissioned officers and privates killed, 10 commissioned officers killed, and 200 rank and file wounded. The prisoners numbered 502 soldiers and 29 officers. The booty amounted to 800 muskets, 100 horses, 2 guns, 35 wagons, a traveling forge, and band instruments. His own losses were 12 killed and 60 wounded. He ended his report with these words:

> Such was the inferiority of our numbers that our success must be attributed to the justice of our cause and the bravery of our troops. My wishes would induce me to mention the name of every sentinel in the corps I have the honor to command. In justice to the bravery and good conduct of the officers, I have taken the liberty to enclose a list of their names, from a conviction that you will be pleased to introduce such characters to the world.

Tarleton rode off, followed by forty horsemen. He was nearly caught by Colonel Washington, who succeeded in slashing Tarleton in the face with his saber, before he himself received a bullet wound in the knee. On his return to camp, Tarleton criticized Cornwallis for failing to support him. He declared with some bitterness that "as Ferguson's disaster made the first invasion of North Carolina, so the battle of Cowpens would probably make the second equally disastrous."

Fearing that Cornwallis would come in pursuit, Morgan marched northwards into North Carolina. His victory, commanding an inferior force over the redoubtable Tarleton, electrified the patriots. Congress awarded Morgan a gold medal, Brigadier Pickens a sword, and Colonels Howard and Washington silver medals.

GUILFORD COURT HOUSE

General Greene hurried to join Daniel Morgan, no easy task when half his army was "in a manner naked; so much so that we cannot put them on the least kind of duty. Indeed there is a great number that have not a rag of clothes on them, except a little piece of blanket, in the Indian form, around their waists." This was written during the freezing January weather. Greene rode ahead of his men 120 miles to meet Morgan on the banks of the Catawba River, where he arrived on January 31. The heavy rains and swollen river kept Cornwallis on the opposite bank, 12 miles behind Morgan. To speed his pursuit, Cornwallis had disposed of his heavy baggage.

During the next forty days, the two generals played cat-and-mouse. Cornwallis sought to catch Greene and force him to battle. Greene kept out of reach, seeking to draw Cornwallis deeper into the interior and lengthen his supply line. The two armies moved northward through North Carolina, seldom more than twelve miles apart. Cornwallis believed that Greene would be unable to cross the Dan, into Virginia and safety. Greene had prepared for that eventuality by assembling boats at Boyd's Ferry. On February 14, 1781, he crossed the river. Deprived of his prey, Cornwallis halted at Hillsborough.

Greene raged at the supineness of the militiamen who had failed to come to his aid in North Carolina. He told Joseph Reed:

> We were obliged to retire out of the State, upon which the spirits of the people sank, and almost all classes of the inhabitants gave themselves up for lost. They would not believe themselves in danger until they found ruin at their doors.

It was astonishing, he thought, "how these people could place such a confidence in a militia scattered over the face of the whole earth, and generally destitute of everything necessary to their own defense. The militia in the back country are formidable, the others are not, and all are very ungovernable and difficult to keep together. As they have generally come out, twenty thousand might be in motion, and not five hundred in the field."

Morgan's solution—"Shoot down the first man that runs."

Daniel Morgan, who had been forced to return home because he was crippled by arthritis, advised Greene on how to combine militia with Continentals:

General Greene crossing the Dan River

I expect Lord Cornwallis will push you until you are obliged to fight him, on which much will depend. You'll have, as what I see, a great number of militia. If they fight, you'll beat Cornwallis; if not, he will beat you, and perhaps cut your regulars to pieces. I am informed that among the militia will be a number of old soldiers. I think it would be advisable to select them from the militia, and put them in the midst of the regulars. *Select the riflemen also and fight them on the flanks, under enterprising officers who are acquainted with that kind of fighting, and put the remainder of the militia in the center with some picked troops in their rear with orders to shoot down the first man that runs.* If anything will succeed, a disposition of this kind will. I hope you will not look upon this as dictating, but as my opinion in a matter that I am much concerned in.

The battle shortly to be fought proved the wisdom of Morgan's advice.

Without waiting for the militia he expected to join him, Greene recrossed the Dan on February 23. Five days later he forded the Haw River and its two tributaries, Troublesome Creek and Reedy Forks. Cornwallis marched in pursuit. For ten days he and Greene sparred for position. Greene moved each night, keeping to the opposite bank of the Haw. Finally, joined by the Virginia militia, he halted at the village of Guilford Court House. He determined to stand and fight. Cornwallis was twelve miles behind.

Guilford Court House was situated on a hill from which the ground sloped gradually for half a mile to the southward, ending in a small rivulet. A road ran down the slope and it and the Court House were flanked by fields, intersected by fences and surrounded by woods. From the Court House another road branched to Reedy Forks.

Greene commanded 4,360 men – 1,600 of them Continentals, 2,600 militia, and 160 cavalry. He placed his army in three lines.

The first line was composed of two brigades of North Carolina militia – one brigade commanded by General John Butler, on the right of the road, and the other, General William Eaton's men, on the left of the road. On their flanks stood the cavalry – William Washington on the right and Harry Lee on the left.

In the second line, three hundred yards behind the first, Greene put the Virginia militia, commanded by Generals Stevens and Lawson, the former on the right and the latter on the left.

The action begins.

Four hundred yards in the Virginians' rear, on the clearing south of the Court House, were drawn up the Continentals – General Huger's Virginia brigade on the right, and Colonel Otto Williams's Maryland brigade on the left. In the space between the two brigades, Greene put two guns. Greene himself stood behind the Continentals, at the head of the slope from where he could view the action. It began about noon, when Lee, who had been sent forward to scout, encountered Tarleton's Dragoons. Lee fell back at once. It was about one o'clock. Cornwallis's advance guard came in sight thirty minutes later.

Spotting the waiting patriots, Cornwallis deployed his army. His 2,400 soldiers, British and Hessian, were regulars, disciplined and experienced. On the right, General Alexander Leslie led the Seventy-first Highlanders and the Hessian regiment of Bose. Colonel James Webster, commanded the Twenty-third regiment and the Jagers on the left. Two battalions of Guards brought up the rear.

"Charge!"

Both armies opened with salvos of artillery. The firing lasted about twenty minutes. As the cannon fell silent, the British moved forward, marching at the quickstep. Among Webster's men was Seargeant Roger Lamb, who, we recall, had surrendered with Burgoyne and shared his captivity. Seeing his opportunity, when the "Convention Army" was marched southward, Lamb escaped to the British lines. He saw Colonel Webster ride up to Cornwallis, who—

> . . . gave the word "*Charge!*" Instantly, the movement was made, in excellent order, in a smart run, with arms charged. When arrived within forty yards of the enemy's line, it was perceived that their whole force had their arms presented and resting on a rail fence, the common partition in America. They were taking aim with the nicest precision.
>
> At this awful period a general pause took place. Both parties surveyed each other for the moment with the most anxious suspense. Nothing speaks [characterizes] the general more than seizing on decisive moments. Colonel Webster rode forward in the front of the Twenty-third Regiment and said with more than even his usual commanding voice (which was well known to his brigade), "Come on, my brave Fusileers!" This operated like an inspiring voice; they rushed forward amidst the enemy's fire. Dreadful was the havoc on both sides.

"This unaccountable panic"

Undismayed by the patriots' fire, the British advanced and, having reached a proper distance, discharged their muskets and rent the air with shouts. "To our infinite distress and mortification," Lee recalled, the North Carolina militia took flight. Abandoning their good position behind fences, they threw away their guns and scattered headlong in every direction through the woods without firing a shot. The North Carolina Colonels, whom Lee joined, failed to stop what he called "this unaccountable panic." Had the North Carolina militia done their duty, Greene said afterwards, victory was certain:

> They had the most advantageous position I ever saw, and left it without making scarcely the shadow of opposition. Their general and field officers exerted themselves, but the men would

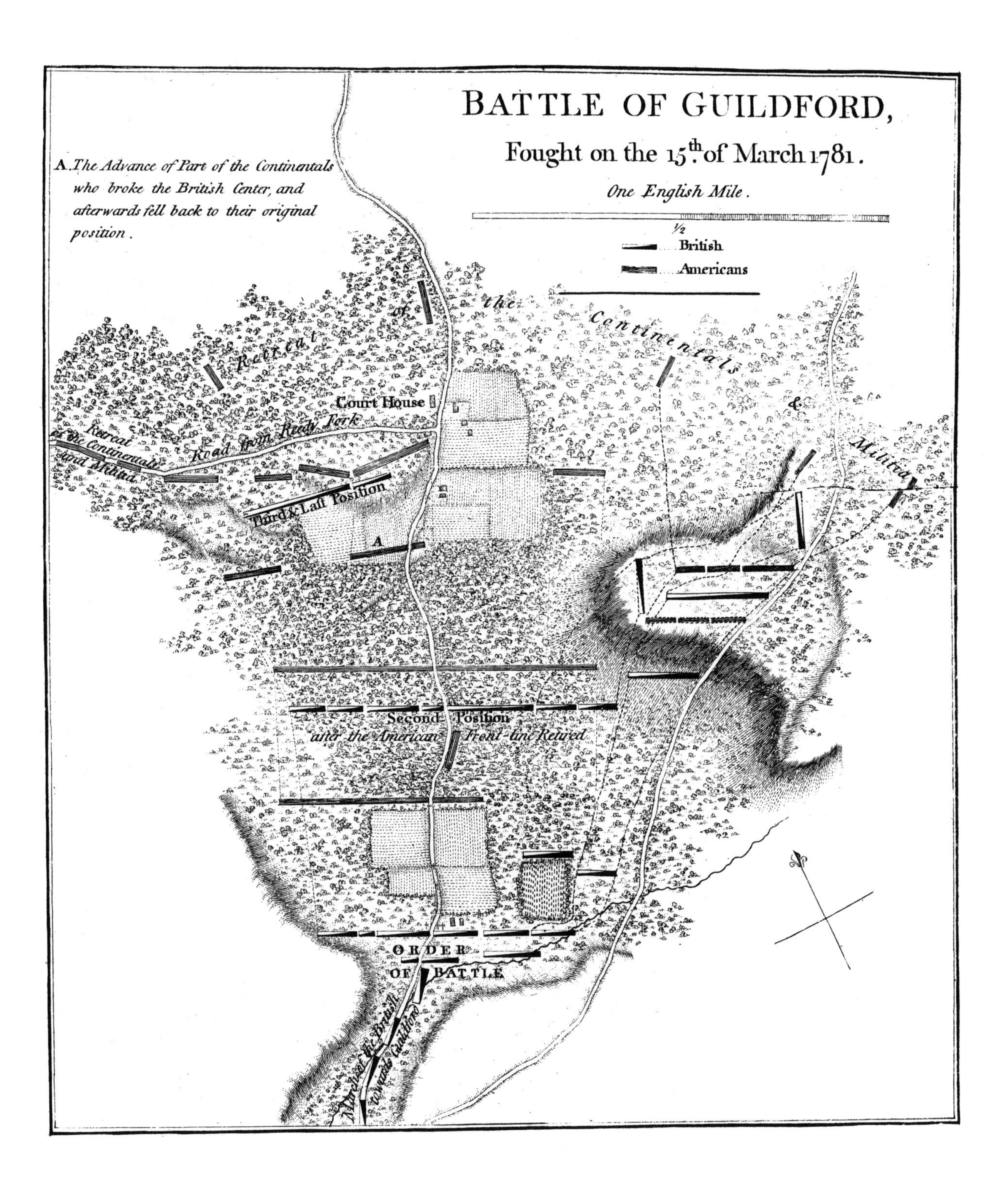
BATTLE OF GUILDFORD,
Fought on the 15th. of March 1781.
One English Mile.
½
British
Americans
A. The Advance of Part of the Continentals who broke the British Center, and afterwards fell back to their original position.
Retreat of the Continentals & Militia
Court House
Road from Reedy Fork
Retreat of the Continentals and Militia
Third & Last Position
A
Second Position after the American Front-line Retired
ORDER OF BATTLE
March of the British towards Guildford

not stand. Many threw away their arms and fled with the utmost precipitation even before a gun was fired at them.

"Not a man of this corps was even wounded," Lee remarked. Leslie and Webster advanced to attack the second line. "Here the conflict became still more fierce," noted Lamb:

> I saw Lord Cornwallis riding across the clear ground. His Lordship was mounted on a dragoon's horse, his own having been shot; the saddle-bags were under the creature's belly, which much retarded his progress, owing to the vast quantity of underwood which was spread over the ground. His Lordship was evidently unconscious of his danger. I immediately laid hold of the bridle of his horse and turned his head. I then mentioned to him that if his Lordship had pursued the same direction, he would have been surrounded by the enemy, and, perhaps, cut to pieces or captured. I continued to run along the side of his horse, keeping the bridle in my hand, until his Lordship gained the Twenty-third Regiment, which was at that time drawn up in the skirt of the wood.

The Virginians in the second line poured in a galling fire upon the advancing redcoats. It did great execution. "At this period," said Tarleton, "the event of the action was doubtful, and victory alternatively presided over each army." On the left, the Virginians held firm, but their right gave way. "We discovered them (the British) in our rear," Major St. George Tucker wrote to his wife next day.

> This threw the militia into such confusion that, without attending in the least to their officers who endeavored to halt them and make them face about and engage the enemy, Holcombe's regiment and ours instantly broke off without firing a gun and dispersed like a flock of sheep frightened by dogs.

Tucker, with another officer, rallied about sixty or seventy men and brought them to the charge:

> Holcombe was not so successful. He could not rally a man though assisted by John Woodson, who acted very gallantly. With the few men which we had collected, we at several times sustained an irregular kind of skirmishing with the British, and were once successful enough to drive a party for a very small distance. On the ground we passed over I think I saw about eight or ten men killed and wounded.

Tucker was forced to ride over one British officer. He saw one of his men give the wounded officer a dram and heard him bid the officer to die like a brave man—a sight which brought from Tucker the comment, "How different this conduct from that of the barbarians he had commanded." About his own men he said:

> The Virginia militia had the honor to receive General Greene's thanks for their conduct. Some were undoubtedly entitled to them, while others ought to blush that they were undeservedly included in the number of those who were supposed to have behaved well. I believe the rest of the Virginia militia behaved better than Holcombe's regiment and ours. The surprise at finding the enemy in their rear I believe contributed to the disgrace-

FROM A WATER-COLOR SKETCH BY KAY SMITH

Raleigh Tavern, Williamsburg, Virginia, reconstructed after the original, where political leaders of the day, including Patrick Henry and Richard Henry Lee, met in 1769 and formed a nonimportation association against England to protest the import duties set up by the Townshend Acts.

FROM A WATER-COLOR SKETCH BY KAY SMITH

The Courthouse of 1770, Williamsburg, Virginia.

FROM A WATER-COLOR SKETCH BY KAY SMITH

Raleigh Tavern, Williamsburg, Virginia, reconstructed after the original, where political leaders of the day, including Patrick Henry and Richard Henry Lee, met in 1769 and formed a nonimportation association against England to protest the import duties set up by the Townshend Acts.

FROM A WATER-COLOR SKETCH BY KAY SMITH

The Courthouse of 1770, Williamsburg, Virginia.

FROM A WATER-COLOR SKETCH BY KAY SMITH

The King's Arms, a tavern in Williamsburg, Virginia.

FROM A WATER-COLOR SKETCH BY KAY SMITH

This Tower, the only 17th century ruin left standing above ground at Jamestown, Virginia, was built after the completion of the first church 1639-1647. At this location, on July 30, 1619, Governor George Yeardley convened the first legislative assembly to be elected by the people in the new world.

ful manner in which they fled at first. But it is not a little to the honor of those who rallied that they fired away fifteen or eighteen rounds—and some, twenty rounds—a man, after being put into such disorder. Such instances of the militia rallying and fighting well are not very common, I am told. Perhaps it is more honorable than making a good stand at first, and then quitting the field in disorder.

Lee praised the Virginia militia.

Lee thought the stand of the Virginia militia was noble. "They contended for victory against the best officer (Webster) in the British army, at the head of two regiments distinguished for intrepidity and discipline." He attributed the Virginians' stand partly to the resolution with which "the corps under Lee" sustained their left. "So bravely did the Virginia militia support the action on the right, that, notwithstanding the injurious desertion of the first line without exchanging a shot, every corps of the British army, except the cavalry, had been necessarily brought into battle, and many of them had suffered badly."

Lee thought, "Had the North Carolina militia rivaled that of Virginia upon this occasion, Lord Cornwallis must have been defeated." Still, with the Continental troops in full vigor, and the cavalry unhurt, there was chance of victory. Lee watched the assault on the third line:

Persevering in his determination to die or conquer, the British general did not stop to concentrate his force, but pressed forward to break our third line. The action, never intermitting on his right, was still sternly maintained by Colonel Norton's battalion of guards and the regiment of Bose, with the rifle militia and the Legion infantry; so that this portion of the British force could not be brought to bear upon the third line, supported by Colonel Washington at the head of the horse, and Kirkwood's Delaware company.

General Greene was well pleased with the present prospect, and flattering himself with a happy conclusion, passed along the line, exhorting his troops to give the finishing blow. Webster, hastening over the ground occupied by the Virginia militia, sought with zeal the Continental line, and presently approached its right wing. Here was posted the first regiment of Maryland, commanded by Colonel Gunby, having under him Lieutenant Colonel Howard. The enemy rushed into close fire; but so firmly was he received by this body of veterans, supported by Hawes's regiment of Virginia and Kirkwood's company of Delawares (being weakened in his contest with Stevens' brigade, and, as yet unsupported, the troops to his right not having advanced, from the inequality of ground or other impediments), that with equal rapidity he was compelled to recoil from the shock.

Recrossing a ravine in his rear, Webster occupied an advantageous height, waiting for the approach of the rest of the line. Very soon Lieutenant Colonel Stuart, with the first battalion of guards, appeared in the open field, followed successively by the remaining corps, all anxious to unite in the last effort. Stuart,

An American private in the colonial army

discovering Ford's regiment of Maryland on the left of the first regiment, and a small copse of wood concealing Gunby, pushed forward upon Ford who was strengthened by Captain Finley with two six-pounders. Colonel Williams, commanding the Maryland line, charmed with the late demeanor of the first regiment, hastened forward the second, expecting a similar display, and prepared to combine his whole force with all practicable celerity; when, unaccountably, the second regiment gave way, abandoning to the enemy the two fieldpieces.

"Each corps manfully struggling for victory."

Colonel Gunby wheeled his Maryland regiment left and fell upon Stuart who was pursuing the second regiment:

Here the action was well fought—each corps manfully struggling for victory—when Lieutenant Colonel Washington, who had, upon the discomfiture of the Virginia militia, placed himself upon the flank of the Continentals, agreeably to the order of battle, pressed forward with his cavalry.

Stuart beginning to give ground, Washington fell upon him sword in hand, followed by Howard with fixed bayonets, now commanding the regiment in consequence of Gunby being dismounted. This combined operation was irresistible. Stuart fell by the sword of Captain Smith of the first regiment: the two fieldpieces were recovered: his battalion was driven back with slaughter, its remains being saved by the British artillery, which, to stop the ardent pursuit of Washington and Howard, opened upon friends as well as foes; for Cornwallis, seeing the vigorous advance of these two officers, determined to arrest their progress, though every ball leveled at them must pass through the flying guards. Checked by this cannonade and discovering one regiment passing from the woods on the enemy's right, across the road, and another advancing in front, Howard believing himself to be out of support, retired, followed by Washington.

The guards, Lee explained, filled the intervals between the British wings. Webster renewed the action with vigor.

Meanwhile, the long impending contest upon the enemy's right continued without intermission, each of the combatants getting gradually nearer to the flanks of their respective armies, to close with which was the desired object of both. At length, Lieutenant Colonel Norton, with his battalion of guards, believing the regiment of Bose adequate to the contest, and close to the great road to which he had been constantly inclining, pressed forward to join the Seventy-first. Relieved from this portion of the enemy, Lieutenant Colonel Lee dispensed with his cavalry, heretofore held in the rear to cover retreat in case of disaster, ordering it to close with the left of the Continental line, and there to act until it should receive further orders.

Upon Bose, the rifle and the Legion infantry now turned with increased animation, and with confidence of success. Major De Buy, of the regiment of Bose, continued to defend himself with obstinacy; but pressed as he was by superior force, he at length gave ground, and fell back into the rear of Norton. Still annoying him with the rifle corps under Campbell, Lee hastened with his infantry to rejoin his cavalry upon the flank of the Continentals, the point so long and vainly contended for. In his route, he found the battalion of guards under Norton in possession of the height first occupied by Lawson's brigade of Virginia militia. With this corps, again the Legion infantry renewed action; and supported by the van company of the riflemen, its rear, still waiting upon Major De Buy, drove it back upon the regiment of Bose. Every obstacle now removed, Lee pressed forward, followed by Campbell, and joined his horse close by Guilford Court House.

General Greene ordered a retreat.

General Greene, believing that his army was in danger of being destroyed, and not wishing to risk its annihilation, decided to retreat—mistakenly, Lee thought:

> Had General Greene known how severely his enemy was crippled, and that the corps under Lee had fought their way to his Continental line, he would certainly have continued the conflict; and in all probability would have made it a drawn day, if not having secured to himself the victory. Ignorant of these facts, and finding Webster returned to battle—O'Hara, with his rallied guards in line—and General Leslie, with the seventy-first connected with them on the right, and followed, as he well knew, by the remnant of his wing—he persevered in his resolution, and directed a retreat, which was performed deliberately under cover of Colonel Green.

"One of the bravest of the brave"

Colonel Green, whom Lee described as "one of the bravest of the brave," commanded one of the Virginia regiments which had not "tasted battle."

Abandoning his artillery, Nathanael Greene withdrew his army, halting three miles away to collect stragglers. "Thus the battle terminated," Lee observed:

> It was fought on the 15th of March, a day never to be forgotten by the southern section of the United States. The atmosphere calm, and illumined with a cloudless sun; the season rather cold than cool; the body braced and the mind high toned by the state of the weather. Great was the stake, willing were the generals, to put it to hazard, and their armies seemed to support with ardor the decision of their respective leaders.

A costly victory for the British army

The British were outnumbered two to one, but, in Lee's opinion, because of the much greater experience of the British, they had the advantage in the quality of their soldiers. To Cornwallis, the battle of Guilford Court House proved a costly victory. "Another such victory would destroy the British army," remarked the British Opposition Leader, Charles James Fox. Cornwallis had lost one-fourth of his total strength, 93 killed, 413 wounded, and 26 missing. Webster, Stuart and 9 other officers had been killed. O'Hara, Tarleton and 17 more wounded. On the American side the losses, though serious, were less crucial, for they could be replaced. They had lost 78 men killed, 83 wounded, and 1,043 missing, for the North Carolina militia had fled.

"The militia are leaving us in great numbers to return home to kiss their wives and sweethearts."

The advantage remained with Greene. He had previously expressed his firm determination never to put his army in a position where its total destruction was possible. Though the temptation was great, he rigidly adhered to this position. He had achieved his purpose. He had weakened Cornwallis. Writing to Joseph Reed, the President of Pennsylvania, immediately after the battle, Greene said:

> The Virginia militia behaved nobly and annoyed the enemy greatly. The horse, at different times in the course of the day, performed wonders. Indeed, the horse is our great safeguard, and without them the militia could not keep the field in this country. Never did an army labor under so many disadvantages as this; but the fortitude and patience of the officers and soldiery rise superior to all difficulties. We have little to eat, less to drink, and lodge in the woods in the midst of smoke. Indeed, our fatigue is excessive. I was so much overcome night before last that I fainted.
>
> Our army is in good spirits, but the militia are leaving us in great numbers to return home to kiss their wives and sweethearts.
>
> I have never felt an easy moment since the enemy crossed the Catawba until since the defeat of the 15th, but now I am perfectly easy, being persuaded it is out of the enemy's power to do us any great injury. Indeed, I think they will retire as soon as they can get off their wounded.

Cornwallis's next move proved Greene right. Encumbered with wounded men, the strength of his army severely diminished, his food supply in danger, Cornwallis abandoned his attempt to subjugate the interior of the Carolinas, and he retreated to Wilmington, on the coast of North Carolina.

Greene was too worn out to realize at first how well he had done. He had not taken off his clothes for six weeks, and he had hardly slept for ten days. While making his rounds one night at Troublesome Creek, where his army had halted, he found a colonel in command of a large outpost asleep. Greene asked him how he could sleep when he was in contact with the enemy and might be attacked at any time. The colonel answered, "Why, General, we all knew *you* would be awake."

HOBKIRK'S HILL

I am determined to carry the war into South Carolina," Greene wrote to General Washington on March 29. The enemy, he believed, would "be obliged to follow us or give up their posts in that State:"

> If the former takes place it will draw the war out of this State and give it an opportunity to raise its proportion of men. If they leave their posts to fall, they must lose more than they can gain here. If we continue in this State (North Carolina) the enemy will hold their possessions in both. All things considered I think the movement is warranted by the soundest reasons both political and military. The maneuver will be critical and dangerous, and the troops exposed to every hardship. But as I share it with them, I hope they will bear up under it with that magnanimity which has already supported them, and for which they deserve everything of their country.

View at the spring— Hobkirk's Hill

Greene planned to oust the British from both South Carolina and Georgia where they held six strong posts, Georgetown, Camden, Ninety-Six (so called because it stood that number of miles from the chief town of the Cherokee Indians) Watson, Motte, Granby (all on the Santee River and its tributaries) and Augusta in Georgia. The British garrisons numbered 7,254 soldiers. Greene sent Lee to join the partisan leaders, Marion, Pickens, and Sumter. While they besieged the lesser posts, he would assault Camden in the center of the chain.

Greene marched from Deep River on April sixth, hoping to surprise Lord Rawdon, the British Commander in South Carolina, at Camden, where he commanded fifteen hundred troops. Greene had about the same number of Continentals. The North Carolina militia had deserted and the Virginians had returned home on the expiration of their term of service. Following a march of 140 miles in fourteen days, Greene reached Camden on April nineteenth. Learning that Rawdon had been reinforced and knew of his approach, Greene took position on the narrow ridge called Hobkirk's Hill, which straddled the road north from Camden to Charlotte, where his flanks were protected by dense woods. The Virginia Continentals, under Brigadier General Isaac Huger, occupied the ground on the right of the road, and the Marylanders, led by Colonel Otto Williams, stood on its left. Greene kept the small force of South Carolina militia under his own eye in the rear with

Colonel Washington's cavalry. The American officers were confident of victory, should Rawdon attack.

Rawdon marched from Camden, one and a half miles away, at nine o'clock the morning of April 25. Within an hour his advance guard had made contact with Greene's pickets. The crack of muskets warned the troops, who were at breakfast, that the British were approaching from the southeast.

Following the battle, the local farmer, Samuel Mathis, gathered the stories of several participants in the action, the start of which he himself heard.

Rawdon, who had made a wide detour in the hope of surprising Greene, came up on a narrow front. The Sixty-third British Regiment advanced on the right, the New York loyalists in the center, and the King's Royal Americans (another Tory contingent) on the left. Rawdon's own regiment, the Volunteers of Ireland, followed, as did contingents of South Carolina loyalists and Dragoons.

Advance with fixed bayonets

Greene, as Mathis learned, directed Colonel Campbell, with his Virginia Continental regiment, and Colonel Ford, with his Maryland regiment, to turn the enemy's flanks. He instructed the two center regiments, those led by Colonels Hawes and Gunby, to advance with fixed bayonets "withholding their fire until the British line was broken." He sent Colonel Washington with his cavalry to attack the British rear. Washington was almost too successful. He took too many prisoners, which impeded him from acting when it was necessary.

Francis Rawdon Hastings better known as Lord Rawdon

The British pressed up the slope and succeeded, Mathis was told, in "turning our left." The British right, the Royal Americans, crept up on the patriots' right, "under cover of thick woods and could scarecely be seen," until they rose over the hill. The Dragoons rode up the "great Road," as Mathis called the highway. Greene had prepared for such an eventuality by placing his cannon to command the road; "It opened upon them, the canister and grape doing great execution, and soon cleared the road."

The battle stood equal, or "rather in our favor," Mathis was told. The British were stalled on the slope to the crest; "Their left, at least their cavalry, was routed, many killed and many prisoners." Lord Rawdon, stunned at hearing the cannon which he did not know Greene possessed, and seeing his horse dispersed, galloped to the scene of the disaster; "He was quickly surrounded by Washington's horse and his sword demanded. One of his aides received a severe wound from the sword of a dragoon." It was a critical moment.

"A single word turned the fate of the day."

"Only *one* word, a single *word*, and that only because it was spoken out of season, turned the fate of the day."

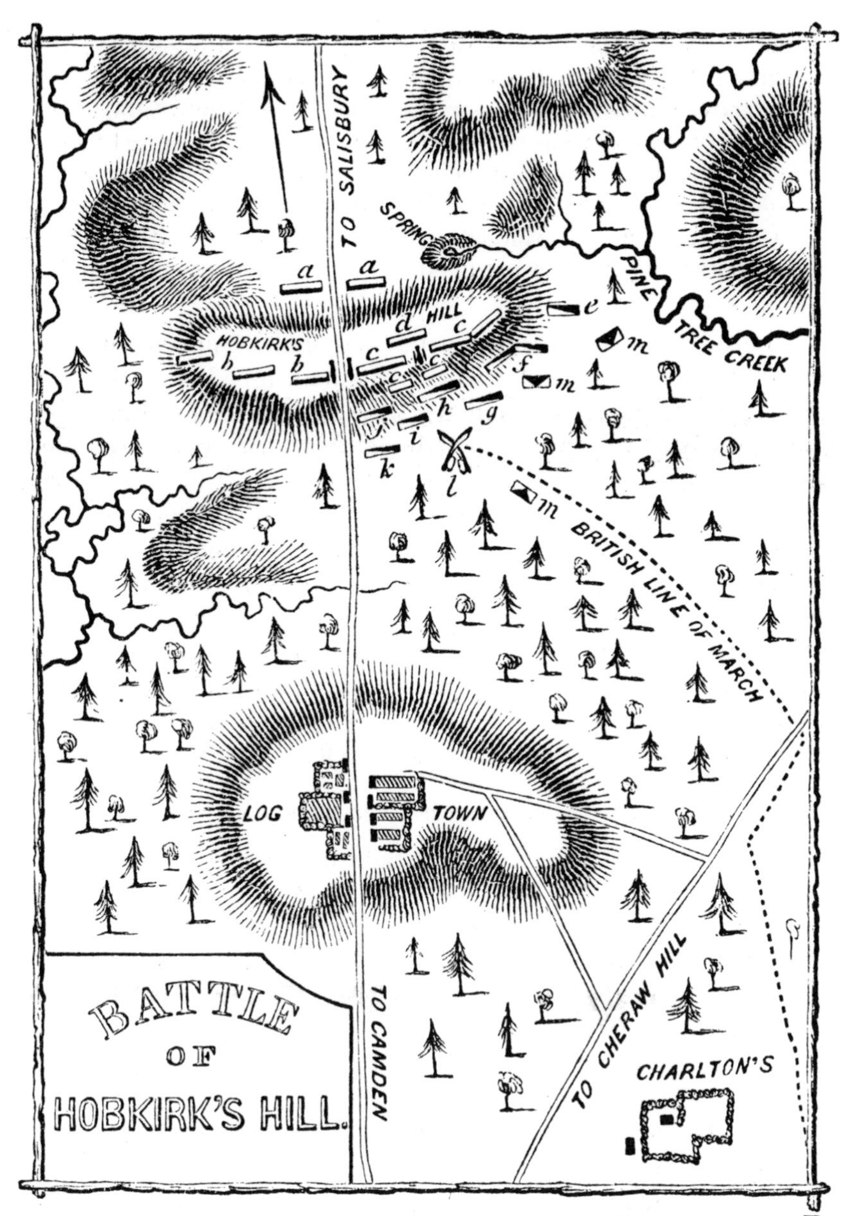

Explanation of the Plan—This plan of the battle on Hobkirk's Hill is copied from Stedman. *a a*, are the American militia, on the Waxhaw road, leading from Camden to Salisbury; *b b*, the Virginia line; *c c*, the Maryland line; *d*, the reserve, with General Greene; *e*, British light infantry, approaching the American camp from Pine Tree Creek; *f*, volunteers from Ireland; *g*, South Carolina Loyalists; *h*, 63d regiment; *i*, New York Loyalists; *j*, King's American regiment; *k*, convalescents; *l*, with swords crossed, the place where the first attack was made; *m m*, British dragoons. The spring was known as Martin's.

Colonel Ford, who commanded one Maryland regiment, fell mortally wounded. Though his men "were neither killed nor prisoners," they began to yield:

> Altho' our left was giving way, yet Gen. Huger on our right was gaining ground and was beginning to advance upon the enemy and Col. Gunby's regiment of brave soldiers, veterans of the Maryland line, had all got to their arms, were well formed and in good order, but too impatient waiting the word of command. Some of them had begun to fire in violation of orders and, seeing the British infantry coming up the hill in front of them, Col. Gunby suffered them to come up within a few paces and

then ordered his men to charge without firing. Those near him, hearing the word, first rushed forward, whereby the regiment was moving forward in the form of a bow. Col. Gunby ordered a "halt" until the wings should become straight. This turned the fate of the day. Previously being ordered not to fire, and now ordered to *halt*, while the British were coming up with charged bayonets, before the colonel could be understood and repeat the charge, the enemy were in among them and made them give way.

Gunby's mistake in retiring some companies to re-form, declared Greene, "gave the whole regiment an idea of retreat, which soon spread through the second regiment, which fell back accordingly. They both rallied afterwards, but it was too late."

Lord Rawdon, heard Mathis, "was surrounded near the head of this regiment and saw the scene and also that some of his cavalry had rallied and with infantry were coming to his relief, while he very politely bowed and seemed to acquiesce with the demand of the dragoons around him, pretended that his sword was hard to get out of the scabbard, feigned to endeavor to draw or unhook it for the surrender required, until the party that took him were attacked and had to fly."

The prisoners attacked their captors.

The scene was quickly changed. Washington's horsemen were in turn attacked by both horse and foot, and "the very prisoners that they had mounted behind them seized the arms of their captors and overcame them."

Greene struggled personally, pulling at the drag ropes, to bring the cannon to bear on the British regiments that were pursuing his Continentals. Observing that the enemy had gained the crest of the hill, he ordered the guns to be hauled into the bushes at the rear of the hill. He told his buglers to sound the retreat.

The Americans halted four miles in the rear at Saunders Creek. Colonel Washington succeeded in carrying off "all the British surgeons and several officers" he had made prisoner. The Americans were less fortunate in the matter of their artillery, as Mathis learned. The artillerymen got entangled among the trees and could not get along, but cut their horses and fled, leaving the limbers of both pieces of cannon in the woods where they were found by the British and taken:

Under these circumstances General Greene galloped up to Capt. John Smith and ordered him to fall into the rear and save the cannon. Smith instantly came and found the artillery men hauling off the pieces with the drag ropes; he and his men laid hold, and off they went in a trot, but had not gone far until he discovered that the British cavalry were in pursuit. He formed his men across the road, gave them a full fire at a short distance and fled with the guns as before. This volley checked the horses and threw many of the riders; but they after some time remounted and pushed on again. Smith formed his men, gave

Lieutenant Colonel Henry Lee

> them another fire with the same effect, and proceeded as before. This he repeated several times until they had got two or three miles from the field of action. Here one of Smith's men fired or his gun went off by accident, before the word was given, which produced a scattering fire, on which the cavalry rushed in among them and cut them all to pieces. They fought like bull-dogs and were all killed or taken. This took up some time, during which the artillery escaped.

Rawdon did not pursue. The losses on the American side were 19 killed, 115 wounded, and 136 missing—total, 270; on the British side, 258, of whom 38 were killed.

"We fight, get beat, rise and fight again."

Greene was frantically disappointed. He seemed fated never to win a battle. He did not lose heart. To the Frenchman, Luzerne, he wrote, "We fight, get beat, rise and fight again."

Elsewhere the partisans were successful. Francis Marion and Henry Lee besieged Fort Watson on the Santee River, surrounding the stockade. Having no artillery, they were unable to make any impression on the garrison, commanded by Lieutenant McKay, whereupon, in Lee's words:

> One of Marion's officers, Colonel Maham, suggested a device similar to those employed by the Romans. The surrounding

General Francis Marion

country was heavily wooded and Marion's men were good backwoodsmen. They promptly set to work with the axes which were gathered from neighboring farms, and after they had cut a sufficient amount of timber, a large force of the besiegers were employed one night in bringing it up on their shoulders to the immediate vicinity of the stockade; and there a high wooden tower was erected during the night, completely dominating the interior of the stockade. When day broke on the morning of April 23rd, the garrison was treated to a fusillade fired from the top of this tower by a picked detachment of skilled marksmen selected from Harry Lee's Legion. Under cover of this fire a breach was made in the stockade. McKay saw that resistance was useless, and at once surrendered his entire garrison. Marion lost only two killed and six wounded.

Marion captured two more forts and Pickens secured Augusta. Marion and Lee besieged Fort Motte. "This post," Lee stated in his *Memoirs*, "was the principal depot of the convoys from Charleston to Camden, and sometimes of those destined for Forts Granby and Ninety-Six."

The British occupied the large, new house belonging to Mrs. Motte, a lady of impeccable patriotism whose daughter was the wife of Major Pickney of the South Carolina Continental Line. Driven from her house, she resided in an old farmhouse where she entertained the American officers.

Captain McPherson, who commanded the British garrison, refused to surrender. Only by burning it, believed Lee, could he be forced to vacate the mansion.

An order to burn the house down

Orders were instantly issued to prepare bows and arrows with missile-combustible matter. This measure was reluctantly adopted, because the destruction of private property was repugnant to the principles which swayed the two commandants, and upon this occasion was peculiarly distressing.

Lee ("the famous father of a more famous son, Robert E. Lee") was as much the southern gentleman as Mrs. Motte was the southern lady:

> While her richly spread table presented with taste and fashion all the luxuries of her opulent country, and her sideboard offered without reserve the best wines of Europe—antiquated relics of happier days—her active benevolence found its way to the sick and to the wounded; cherishing with softest kindness infirmity and misfortune, converting despair into hope, and nursing debility into strength.

Nevertheless, the obligations of duty were imperative. To Mrs. Motte, Lee imparted the impending measure, lamenting the sad necessity, and assuring her of the deep regret which the unavoidable act excited in his and every breast.

> With a smile of complacency this exemplary lady listened to the embarrassed officer, and gave instant relief to his agitated feelings, by declaring that she was gratified with the opportunity of contributing to the good of her country, and that she should view the approaching scene with delight. Shortly after, seeing accidentally the bow and arrows which had been prepared, she sent for the lieutenant colonel, and presenting him with a bow and its apparatus imported from India, she requested his substitution of these, as probably better adapted for the object than those we had provided.
>
> Receiving with silent delight this opportune present, the lieutenant colonel rejoined his troops, now making ready for the concluding scene. The lines were manned, and an additional force stationed at the battery, lest the enemy, perceiving his fate, might determine to risk a desperate assault, as offering the only chance of relief. As soon as the troops reached their several points, a flag was again sent to McPherson, for the purpose of inducing him to prevent the conflagration and the slaughter which might ensue, by a second representation of his actual condition.

McPherson remained immovable.

> It was now about noon, and the rays of the scorching sun had prepared the shingle roof for the projected conflagration. The return of Irvine (the officer carrying the flag) was immediately followed by the application of the bows and arrows. The first arrow struck, and communicated its fire; a second was shot at another quarter of the roof, and a third at a third quarter; this last also took effect, and, like the first, soon kindled a blaze.

Unable to contain the fire, McPherson surrendered. Not a drop of blood was shed, declared Lee. McPherson and his officers accompanied their captors to enjoy a sumptuous dinner at Mrs. Motte's.

General Marion inviting the British officers to dine

Rawdon evacuated the chief post at Camden and retreated to Charleston, and he withdrew the garrison from Ninety-Six. He handed over his command to Colonel Alexander Stuart and returned to England, suffering capture by an American privateer on the voyage. He became, in turn, the Earl of Moira and Marquess of Hastings, and a famous Governor-General of India.

EUTAW SPRINGS

During the hot, sticky season Greene rested his army on the Santee hills, an elevated and comparatively healthy region, ninety miles from Charleston. He was desperately short of soldiers, money and food. He punished plunderers and deserters with death. It sickened his kindly nature for, as he wrote to his wife, he could not repress his longing "for a peaceful retirement, where love and softer pleasures are to be found. Here, turn what way you will, you have nothing but the mournful widow and the plaints of the fatherless child, and behold nothing but houses desolated and plantations laid waste. Ruin is in every form and misery in every shape." It was more than six years since he had left his home, and nearly two years since the last glimpse of his wife at the winter camp at Morristown.

In August, he sallied forth from his camp to fight the British army once more, hoping to inflict a disastrous defeat upon it and drive the remnants into Charleston, where the French fleet would bottle them up. Greene learned that Colonel Stuart had moved to Eutaw Springs, a hundred miles west of Charleston. Greene went in pursuit, reaching within seven miles on the evening of September 7, 1781.

Uprooting the "rooting parties"

The two armies were about equal in strength, each numbering approximately twenty-three hundred men. The British were camped in a clearing about two hundred yards west of the Springs, at the head of the creek which ran into the Santee River. The surrounding country was heavily wooded. Unaware that Greene was so close, on the morning of the eighth, the usual detachment of "rooting parties" sallied out to dig for sweet potatoes. A detachment of cavalry commanded by Captain Coffin went to reconnoiter. They rode headlong into Greene's advance guard, leaving forty prisoners behind in their escape. All the men of the rooting parties were captured. Alerted to his danger, Stuart formed his line of battle. A battalion of light infantry under Major Marjoribanks guarded the right flank, which was protected by the steep bank of the Eutaw Creek. Marjoribanks concealed his three hundred men in a close thicket. Next in line stood the Irish Buffs, a regiment fresh to America. The American Royalists, under Lieutenant Colonel Cruger, took position in the center, with the Sixty-third and Sixty-fourth Regiments on their left.

Colonel Stuart made one astute move. He placed a small force of New York loyalists under Captain Sheridan in the three-storied brick house which stood by the Springs. This dwelling house, with its palisaded garden, was to prove as efficient a point of resistance as had Chew's house at the battle of Germantown. He told Sheridan, at the first symptoms of misfortune, to throw his men into the house and cover the retreat of the army from its upper windows.

Greene began his advance at four o'clock in the morning. Andrew Pickens on the left, Francis Marion on the right, and Malmédy in the center led the North and South Carolina militias. Behind came three small Continental brigades, from North Carolina, Virginia, and Maryland, respectively commanded by Jethro Sumner, William Campbell and Otto Williams. Robert Kirkwood's Delaware troops and William Washington's cavalry formed the reserve. Lee, with his Legion, composed of both infantry and cavalry, covered the right flank, and Lieutenant Colonel Henderson with State troops, the left flank. Greene placed his four guns on the road. The battle began around nine o'clock.

Following its termination, Colonel Otto Williams collected the stories told by other officers to augment his own account. Greene and Stuart both composed reports.

"The militia fought with spirit and firmness."

"By an unknown mistake", said Stuart, "the British left wing advanced and drove the North Carolinians before them, but,

General Otto Williams

unexpectedly finding the Virginia and Maryland line formed, and receiving a heavy fire, occasioned some confusion." Sumner quickly restored the line, closing the gap that had been formed. "This was done with the utmost promptness, and the battle again raged with redoubled fury," learned Williams, who was stationed on the left. Greene said, "The militia fought with a degree of spirit and firmness that reflects the highest honor upon that class of soldier." He was at a loss which most to admire, "the gallantry of the officers or the good conduct of the men." The bayonet was freely used.

> They kept up a heavy and well-directed fire, and the enemy returned it with equal spirit for they really fought worthy of a better cause and great execution was done on both sides. In this stage of the action, the Virginians under Lieutenant Colonel Campbell and the Marylanders under Colonel Williams were led on to a brisk charge, with trailed arms, through a heavy cannonade and a shower of musket balls. Nothing could exceed the gallantry and firmness of both officers and soldiers upon this occasion. They preserved their order, and pressed on with such unshaken resolution that they bore down all before them. The enemy were routed in all quarters.

Stuart brought up the reserves and the struggle was obstinately fought by both sides.

The brunt of the action took place on the American left, under the eye of Williams. As to what happened on the right, he relied on others;

> From the first commencement of the action, the infantry of the American covering parties, on the right and left, had been steadily engaged. The cavalry of the Legion, by being on the American right, had been enabled to withdraw into the woods and attend on its infantry, without being at all exposed to the enemy's fire. But the State troops under Henderson had been in the most exposed situation on the field. The American right, with the addition of the Legion infantry, had extended beyond the British left. But the American left fell far short of the British right; and the consequence was that the State troops were exposed to the oblique fire of a large proportion of the British right, particularly of the battalion commanded by Marjoribanks.

Lee, stated Greene, "with great address, gallantry and good conduct" turned the British right, as the Virginia and Maryland troops charged them in front. "The enemy instantly gave way," said Lee.

On the left, Henderson, who was followed by Colonel Washington, charged against Marjoribanks. Henderson was wounded and the command was taken by Lieutenant Colonel Wade Hampton. Washington plunged into the thicket, where he was unhorsed and taken prisoner. "Never was the constancy of a party of men more severely tried," Williams observed.

"Let Williams advance and sweep the field with his bayonets."

Elsewhere "the British line became deranged." This was exactly the moment for which Greene had been anxiously

American cannon on the fringe of the woods
—Sketch by Kay Smith

waiting. "Let Williams advance and sweep the field with his bayonets," he ordered. Williams, who commanded the Maryland Continentals, obeyed the order with alacrity, as did Campbell's Virginians:

> The two brigades received it with a shout. Eager to wipe away the recollections of Hobkirk's Hill, they advanced with a spirit

FROM A WATER-COLOR SKETCH BY KAY SMITH

Castillo de San Marcos in Saint Augustine, Florida, is the oldest masonry fort in the United States, dating back to beginning construction by the Spaniards in 1672. The British controlled the fort during the Revolutionary War, using it as a base of supplies.

FROM A WATER-COLOR SKETCH BY KAY SMITH

This house, the oldest in Saint Augustine, the oldest city in the United States, was built about 1703 and is now open to the public as a museum.

expressive of the impatience with which they had hitherto been passive spectators of the action. When approached within forty yards of the enemy, the Virginians delivered a destructive fire, and the whole second line, with trailed arms and an animated pace, advanced to the charge. Until this period their progress had been in the midst of showers of grape, and under a stream of fire from the line opposed to them. But eyewitnesses have asserted that the roll of the drum and the shouts which followed it drew every eye upon them alone; and a momentary pause in the action, a suspension by mutual consent, appeared to withdraw both armies from a sense of personal danger to fix their attention upon this impending conflict. It may well be supposed with what breathless expectation the Southern commander hung upon a movement on which all his hopes depended. Had it failed, he must have retired under cover of his cavalry.

The British left had swung back, but their right still held. Their left had made a retrograde movement in some disorder, Williams learned:

This was confirmed by the good conduct of Col. Lee. The Legion infantry had steadily maintained its order in its position on the extreme right, and the advance of the British left having exposed its flank, the Legion infantry were promptly wheeled and poured in upon them a destructive enfilading fire; then joining in the charge, the British left wing was thrown into irretrievable disorder. But their center and right still remained, greatly outnumbering the assailing party and awaiting the impending charge with unshaken constancy.

Major Marjoribanks' men, reported Stuart, "having repulsed and driven off everything that attacked them," made a rapid move to the left, driving off the enemy, killing upwards of two hundred, taking many prisoners and capturing two guns. Otto Williams saw for himself:

If the two lines on this occasion did not actually come to the mutual thrust of the bayonet, it must be acknowledged that no troops ever came nearer. They are said to have been so near that their bayonets clashed and the officers sprang at each other with their swords, before the enemy actually broke away.

"Shouts of victory resounded through the American line."

The retreat on the left, and now Marjoribanks' withdrawal, exposed the British center to the onslaught of Greene's Continentals:

But the scales of victory, fortunately for man, are never long in equipoise on these occasions. In this instance, the left of the British center appear to have been pressed upon and forced back by their own fugitives, and began to give way from left to right. At that moment, the Marylanders delivered their fire, and along their whole front the enemy yielded. The shouts of victory resounded through the American line, affording a gleam of consolation to many a brave man bleeding and expiring on the field. Among these was the gallant Campbell, who received a ball in the breast during this onset.

To Williams, victory seemed certain:

> The carnage among the Americans had but commenced; it was in the effort to prevent the enemy from rallying and to cut him off from the brick house, which was all that remained to compel the army to surrender, that their great loss was sustained.

"A road strewn with bodies of men and horses"

From his vantage point on the left, where the ground was obscured by trees, Williams contemplated the scene:

> The field of battle was, at this instant, rich in the dreadful scenery which disfigures such a picture. On the left, Washington's cavalry routed and flying, horses plunging as they died or coursing the field without their riders, while the enemy with poised bayonet issued from the thicket upon the wounded or unhorsed rider. In the foreground, Hampton covering and collecting the scattered cavalry, while Kirkwood, with his bayonets, rushed furiously to revenge their fall, and a road strewn with the bodies of men and horses, and the fragments of dismounted artillery. Beyond these, a scene of indescribable confusion, viewed over the whole American line advancing rapidly and in order. And on the right, Henderson borne off in the arms of his soldiers, and Campbell (the Virginia Colonel) sustained in his saddle by a brave son, who had sought glory at his father's side.

In the British camp everything was given up for lost:

> The commissaries destroyed their stores; the numerous retainers of the army, mostly loyalists and deserters, who dreaded falling into the hands of the Americans, leaping on the first horse they could command, crowded the roads and spread alarm to the very gates of Charleston. The stores on the road were set fire to, and the road itself obstructed by the felling of trees, for miles, across it.

"The whole British line was now flying before the American bayonet."

The survivors of Washington's and Hampton's commands were led by Kirkwood in a final charge against Marjoribanks, whose men were the only obstacle to the American advance. Marjoribanks retreated successfully to the palisaded garden of the house by the Springs. Otherwise, recalled Williams, "the whole British line was now flying before the American bayonet. The latter pressed closely upon their heels, took many prisoners, and might have cut off the retreat of the rest, or entered pell-mell with them into the house, but for one of these occurrences which have often snatched victory from the grasp of a pursuing enemy."

Colonel Williams told the sad story:

> The retreat of the British army lay directly through their encampments, where the tents were all standing and presented many objects to tempt a thirsty, naked and fatigued soldiery to acts of insubordination. Nor was the concealment afforded by the tents at this time a trivial consideration, for the fire from the windows of the house was galling and destructive, and no cover from it was anywhere to be found except among the tents or behind the building to the left of the front of the house. Here it

> was that the American line got into irretrievable confusion. When their officers had proceeded beyond the encampment, they found themselves nearly abandoned by their soldiers, and the sole marks for the party who now poured their fire from the windows of the house.
>
> Everything now combined to blast the prospects of the American commander. The fire from the house showered down destruction upon the American officers, and the men, unconscious or unmindful of consequences, perhaps thinking the victory secure and bent on the immediate fruition of its advantages, dispersing among the tents, fastened upon the liquors and refreshments they afforded, and became utterly unmanageable.

Unaware of the disorderly conduct of his infantry, Greene ordered Lee on the right to charge the retreating enemy, and the artillery to lay its guns on the house and batter its garrison into submission. Before its door could be barred, one of Lee's soldiers got halfway in, "Lieutenant Manning pressing him in, and Sheridan forcing him out. The latter prevailed and the door was closed." Williams watched the assault on the house:

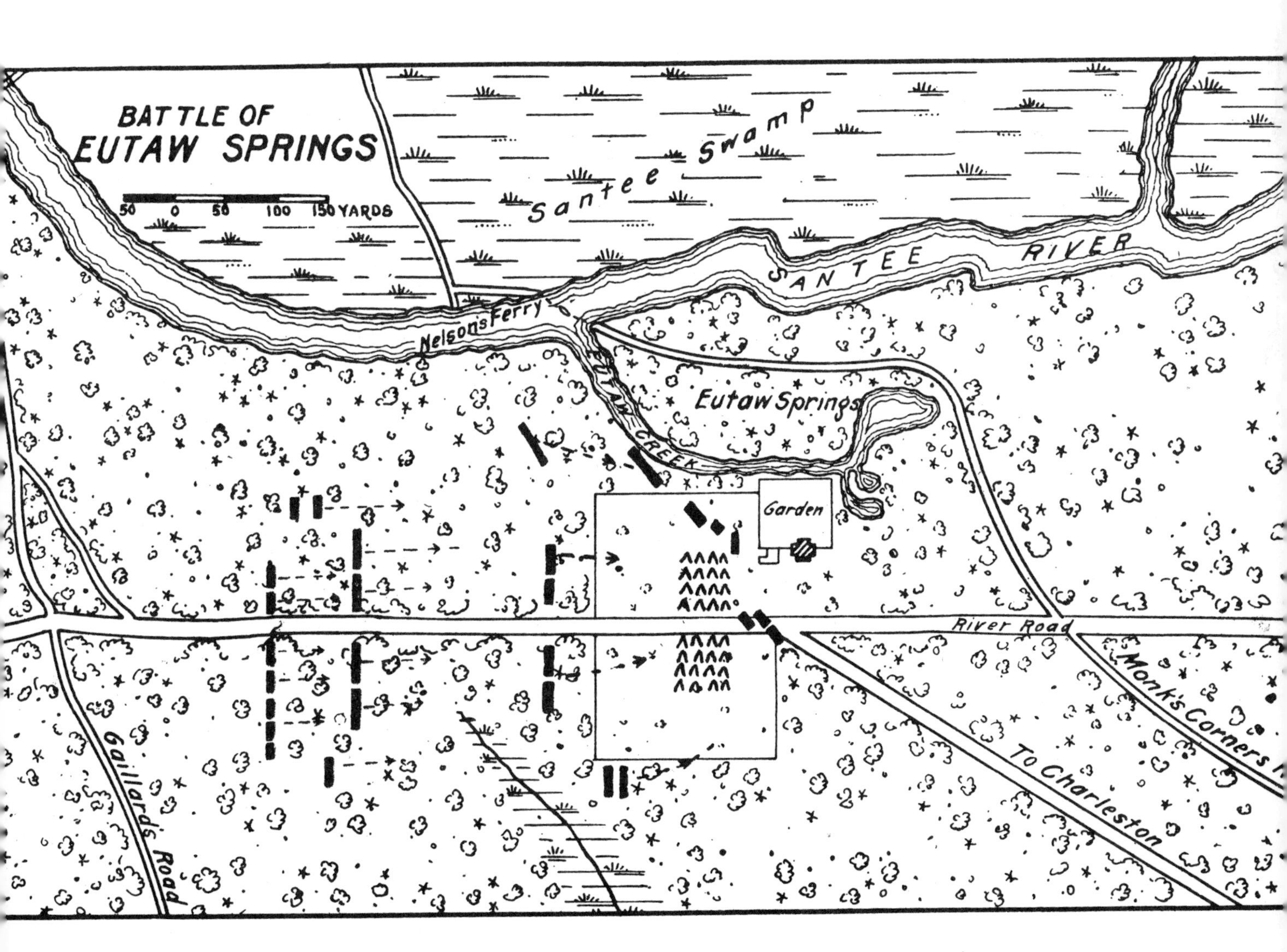

> The artillery of the second line had followed on, as rapidly as it could, upon the track of the pursuit, and, together with two six-pounders abandoned by the enemy in their flight, had been brought up to batter the houses. Unfortunately, in the ardor to discharge a pressing duty, the pieces had been run into the open field, so near as to be commanded by the fire from the house. The pieces had scarcely opened their fire when the pressing danger which threatened the party in the house and, consequently, the whole army, drew all the fire from the windows upon the artillerists, and it very soon killed or disabled nearly the whole of them.

Marjoribanks seized the abandoned cannons and dragged them under cover of the house. Reinforced by its defenders, he charged the Americans dispersed among the tents, driving them before him. Simultaneously, Captain Coffin, who had fallen to the rear, repulsed Lee's Legion. Rallying his cavalry, Hampton galloped to the rescue, receiving a fatally destructive fire from the soldiers posted in the palisaded garden. Colonel Polk described this part of the action to Otto Williams by saying that he thought every man killed but himself.

When he was acquainted with this misfortune, Greene ordered a retreat. Sheridan, by his defense of the house, and Marjoribanks, by his quick response, had saved the British army from total defeat.

Both commanders claimed victory. The British army having been chased from the field, took refuge in a fortress. The Americans were repulsed from that fortress. Williams believed that had not the Continentals stopped to pillage the tents, there would have been certainty in "reducing the whole to submission."

"A most bloody battle"

In his dispatch to General Washington, Greene called it, "a most bloody battle—by far the most obstinate I ever saw."

The Americans suffered 408 casualties, the British 693. Collecting his wounded, Greene fell back seven miles. The next day, Stuart abandoned his British wounded and, leaving behind a thousand muskets, beat a hasty retreat to Charleston.

Lee called the result "mortifying." Washington perceived the truth. He congratulated Greene on his "splendid victory." Between them, Greene and the partisan leaders had driven the British from the interior of South Carolina and Georgia, where they retained only the two ports, Charleston and Savannah.

Lord Cornwallis, we recall, following his hollow victory at Guilford Court House, had retreated to Wilmington in North Carolina.

CHESAPEAKE CAPES

Admiral De Grasse

Cornwallis and Clinton, the one overbold, the other too cautious, disagreed. Clinton wanted his subordinate to remain in the Carolinas, or perhaps return to New York. He instructed him not to risk his army in Virginia, where Cornwallis wished to campaign in order to cut the rebels' communications between north and south. The controversy about which British general was right still arouses lively debates in military circles. In any case, by their vacillation they played into the rebels' hands.

In May, 1781, Cornwallis, "tired out marching about the country in quest of adventures," led his 1,435 troops to Portsmouth, Virginia, where he superseded Arnold, who had been sent there earlier. He combined those 7,200 troops with his own, and Arnold returned to New York. Cornwallis had taken the first fateful step which would lead to eventual disaster.

The second step was taken hundreds of miles to the north at Wethersfield, Connecticut, on May 21. Washington conferred with the French general, the Comte de Rochambeau. He informed the Commander-in-Chief that Admiral de Grasse had sailed from France for the West Indies with a powerful fleet. "If," he asked Washington, "the fleet from the West Indies

General Comte de Rochambeau

should arrive in these (American) waters," what operations had he in mind?

Washington did not yet know that Cornwallis was in Virginia, where Lafayette commanded a small army. His own army was shrinking. The winter of 1780–1781 marked the nadir of the American cause. The people were apathetic, some believing the war already won, others convinced it was lost. The French alliance had proved a bitter disappointment. Rochambeau's army was stuck in Rhode Island, unable to move while the Royal Navy held the seas. Washington faced the prospect of another "gloomy, defensive" campaign.

To Rochambeau's question, Washington replied that the French and American armies should unite on the Hudson and either attack New York or move against the enemy in some other quarter "as circumstances shall dictate."

Far away in Virginia, Lafayette saw the situation clearly. The issue of American independence rested upon naval superiority. He reported Cornwallis's arrival to Washington.

Momentous news

De Grasse took the third step. From Brest he wrote to Rochambeau stating that his stay in West Indian and American waters would be short, from mid-July to mid-October. On his arrival in the West Indies, he wrote that he would sail on August 5 for Chesapeake Bay, "the point which appears to me as the one from which the advantage may be most certainly gained." He was embarking three thousand troops, field artillery and siege guns. His momentous news reached Washington on August 14.

The uncertainty was over. From Lafayette, Washington learned that Cornwallis had established a base at Yorktown on Chesapeake Bay. He told the young French general to prevent Cornwallis's escape—that he would "shortly have occasion to communicate matters of great importance."

It was the crisis of the war. Washington expressed his thoughts in his *Journal:*

> I was obliged from the shortness of Count de Grasse's promised stay on this coast, the apparent disinclination of their naval officers to force the harbor of New York, and the feeble compliance of the States with my requisitions for men hitherto, and the little prospect of greater exertion in future—to give up all ideas of attacking New York, and instead thereof to remove the French troops and a detachment from the American army to the head of Elk (Chesapeake Bay), to be transported to Virginia, for the purpose of cooperating with the force from the West Indies against the troops in that State.

The end of hesitancy and doubt

The years of hesitancy and doubt, of sparring and retreating, were over. The French alliance was about to bear fruit. Moving by sea and land, the Americans and their allies would combine to crush Cornwallis and destroy his army, a blow from which the British cause would not recover.

Would de Grasse be able to establish naval superiority on the American coast? The Royal Navy was strong in West Indian and American waters. Admiral Sir George Rodney commanded twenty-three ships of the line in the Caribbean. Vice-Admiral Graves held five at New York. Together they would outnumber and outgun de Grasse's twenty-four vessels.

Rodney failed in his duty. In February he had captured the Dutch island of St. Eustatius (the Dutch, like the Spaniards, had declared war on Britain). The rich port yielded £3 million in booty. Depriving his fleet of four ships to carry it home, Rodney sailed for England, sending Sir Samuel Hood to follow de Grasse.

Leaving General Heath with two thousand soldiers to deceive Clinton into thinking that New York was threatened, Washington collected his fifteen hundred ragged veterans and Rochambeau's fresh and smart Frenchmen on the Hudson. He marched southward on August 19. Dr. James Thacher, whose journal has already contributed to this story, set out thinking:

> Our situation reminds me of some theatrical exhibition, where the interest and expectations of the spectators are continually increasing, and where curiosity is wrought to the highest point. Our destination has been for some time a matter of perplexing doubt and uncertainty; bets have run high on one side that we

were to occupy the ground marked out on the Jersey shore, to aid in the siege of New York, and on the other, that we are stealing a march on the enemy and are actually destined for Virginia in pursuit of the army under Lord Cornwallis.

Passing over the old battlefield at Princeton, the army pursued its route towards Philadelphia with increasing rapidity:

> Our destination can no longer be a secret. The British army under Lord Cornwallis is unquestionably the object of our present expedition. It is now rumored that a French fleet may soon be expected to arrive in Chesapeake Bay, to cooperate with the allied army in that quarter. The great secret respecting our late preparations and movements can now be explained. It was a judiciously concerted strategem, calculated to menace and alarm Sir Henry Clinton for the safety of the garrison of New York and induce him to recall a part of his troops from Virginia for his own defense, or, perhaps, keeping an eye on the city, to attempt its capture, provided that by the arrival of a French fleet favorable circumstances should present. The deception has proved completely successful; a part of Cornwallis' troops are reported to have returned to New York. His Excellency General Washington, having succeeded in a masterly piece of *generalship*, has now the satisfaction of leaving his adversary to ruminate on his own mortifying situation, and to anticipate the perilous fate which awaits his friend Lord Cornwallis in a different quarter.

Thacher chuckled to think that Clinton's eyes remained veiled, and he would wake up too late to help Cornwallis.

Dust like a smothering snowstorm

Washington and Rochambeau reached Philadelphia on August 30, in advance of their soldiers. At the City Tavern they were received by "the universal acclamations of the citizens." Robert Morris, the Superintendent of Finance, took them to his house, where the party drank toasts to the United States, the Kings of France and Spain, and to the speedy arrival of de Grasse. Three days later the army—the ill-kempt Continentals and the spick and span Frenchmen—marched through the American capital, raising a dust "like a smothering snowstorm," to the head of Elk. It had made the two hundred miles from the Hudson in fifteen days. The lack of news of de Grasse distressed Washington "beyond expression." He feared that the French fleet had been intercepted by the Royal Navy.

On September 5, he learned that de Grasse was off the Chesapeake. "I never saw a man so thoroughly and openly delighted," wrote the Duc de Lauzun that day. To his army Washington expressed his anticipation of "the glorious events which may be expected from the combined operations now in contemplation." No prospect ever promised more opportunity of success. "Nothing but want of exertion" could blast the pleasing prospect.

A month's pay to all loyal troops

Washington ordered that all troops should at once be given a month's pay, excepting those who had been "so lost to all sense of honor, the pride of their profession, and the love of their country, as to desert the Standard of Freedom at this critical moment." One soldier, Major William Popham, thought September 8 "famous in the annals of history for being the first in which the troops of the United States received one month's pay in specie," in hard cash. Robert Morris raised the money by borrowing it from the French.

Unknown to Washington, the successful issue of the campaign hung in the balance.

On the morning of September 5, the British fleet hove over the horizon. Admiral Samuel Hood, coming from the West Indies, and Admiral Thomas Graves, from New York, had linked up, giving Graves, the senior officer, nineteen ships to oppose de Grasse's twenty-four. The arrival of Graves caught de Grasse unawares. His transports were close in shore, unloading troops, his fleet cooperating. He beat out against wind and tide, his ships straggling. Graves missed the opportunity. He bore down too slowly. The fleets clashed at 4:15 in the afternoon. Hood in the rear failed to understand his admiral's signals and sheered off. De Grasse brought sixteen ships to bear upon eleven British. The engagement lasted until dark. Badly mauled, Graves limped to New York. De Grasse sailed triumphantly into Chesapeake Bay. Five days later his fleet was increased to thirty-six ships by the arrival of Admiral de Barras from Rhode Island. Cornwallis's chance of escape, or rescue, by sea was blocked. He was trapped at Yorktown.

The adjoining residences of General Washington and Robert Morris in Philadelphia
—Drawn from memory by C. A. Poulson

YORKTOWN

Lafayette in 1777

De Grasse's 3,000 soldiers joined Lafayette, who placed them across the peninsula on which Yorktown stands. To complete the military strategy, it remained only for Washington and Rochambeau to spread their men between the James and York rivers, and to assault Cornwallis's stronghold. While his army advanced, Washington took Rochambeau to Mount Vernon, revisiting his home for the first time in six years. He reached Lafayette's headquarters at Williamsburg on September 14, 1781. De Grasse told him that he could not remain in American waters later than the end of October. "If he does not leave us . . . our work is sure," wrote Adjutant General Hand. The Virginia Colonel, St. George Tucker, gave his wife the "torrent of good news," to which he hoped soon to add that Lord Cornwallis and his army were "in our possession." Another Virginian, General George Weedon, was even more elated. He told Nathanael Greene, "I am all on fire. By the Great God of War, I think we may all hang up our swords by the last of the year."

Writing in cypher, Cornwallis informed Clinton of his condition. His 7,000 soldiers were in good spirits, he had provisions for six weeks, he hoped for relief. He occupied both banks of the York River, the single street of seventy houses at York, and the village of Gloucester a mile distant on the opposite shore. At Yorktown, two creeks "nearly embraced the port." He had constructed ten redoubts, housing sixty-five guns. The frigates *Guadaloupe* and *Charon* lay moored between York and Gloucester, which was defended by nineteen guns. Nonetheless, Yorktown was not particularly favorable for defense. Cornwallis had not anticipated the contingency of a siege. "Nothing but the hope of relief would have induced me to attempt its defense," he said afterwards.

It took the allies fourteen days to get their 16,000 soldiers into position. Major Generals Lafayette, Lincoln (who had been exchanged) and Von Steuben commanded the Continentals, General Knox the artillery. The 3,000 militia were all Virginians. The Americans occupied the right, the Frenchmen under Rochambeau the center and left.

"We prepared to pay the British a visit."

Diarist Martin, now a member of the corps of Sappers and Miners, was an early arrival:

British fortification at Yorktown overlooking Chesapeake Bay

—Sketch by Kay Smith

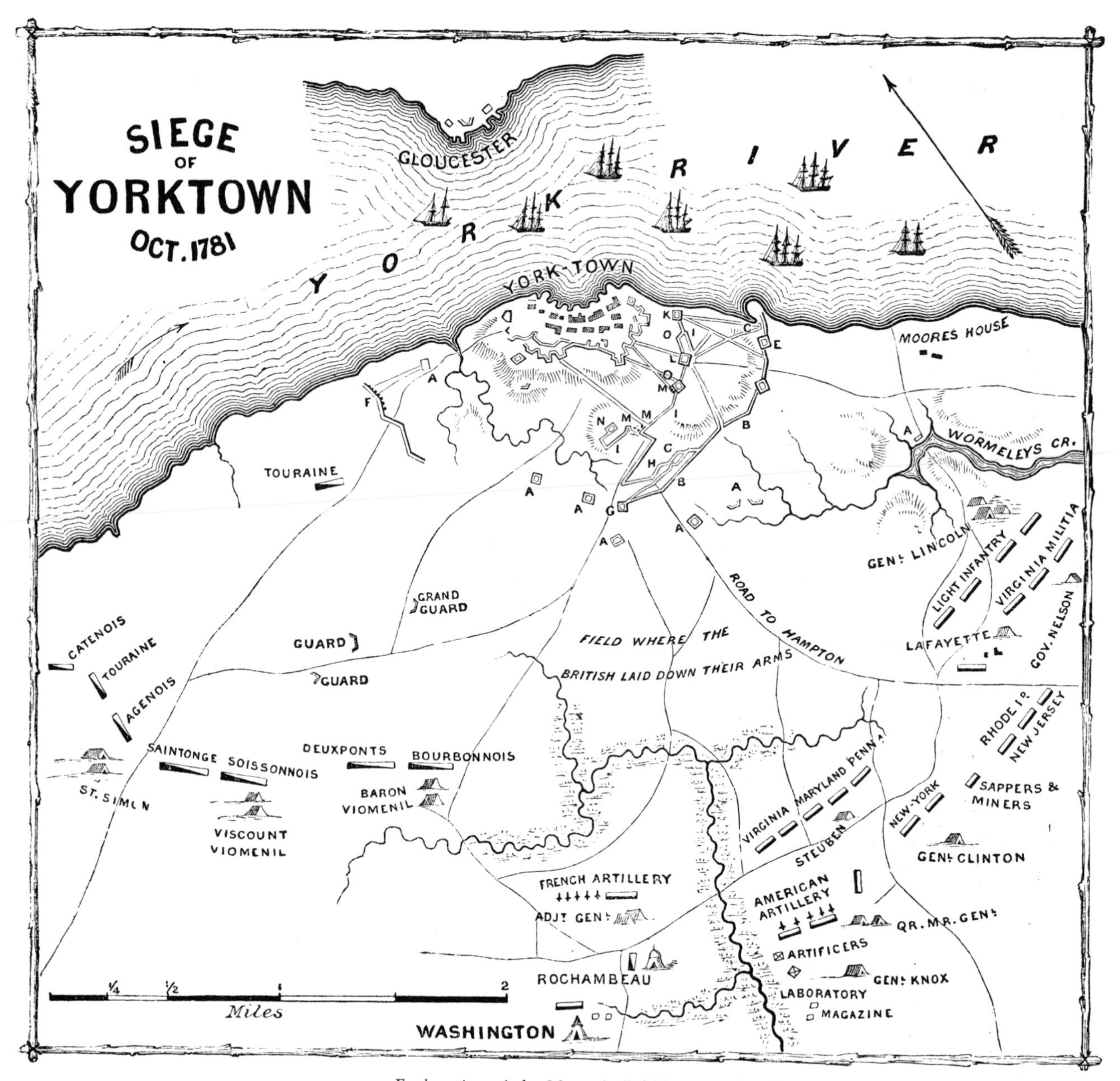

Explanation of the Map.—A, British outworks taken possession of by the Americans on their arrival. B, first parallel. C, D, American batteries. E. a bomb battery. G, French battery. H, French bomb battery. I, second parallel. K, redoubt stormed by the Americans. L, redoubt stormed by the French. M M M, French batteries. N, French bomb battery. O, American batteries.

Soon after landing we marched to Williamsburg, where we joined General Lafayette, and very soon after, our whole army arriving, we prepared to move down and pay our old acquaintance, the British, at Yorktown, a visit. I doubt not but their wish was not to have so many of us come at once as their accommodations were rather scanty. They thought, "The fewer the better cheer." We thought, "The more the merrier." We had come a long way to see them and were unwilling to be put off with excuses.

"We commenced our march for the Investiture of the enemy at York," Washington wrote in his journal on September 28. He spent the day "reconnoitering the enemy's position and determining upon a plan of attack." During the night, the British abandoned their outer defenses. Cornwallis had received a letter from Clinton. He promised to sail from New York with 5,000 soldiers and twenty-three ships of the line on the fifth of October. Cornwallis replied that he had no doubt that "if relief arrives in reasonable time, York and Gloucester will both be in possession of His Majesty's troops."

"Scarce a gun fired this day"

The besiegers occupied the abandoned outer works on September 30. "Scarce a gun fired this day," noted Washington's secretary, Jonathan Trumbull. Like many other diarists, he noted the death of the popular Colonel Alexander Scammell, a veteran of Saratoga. Scammell was wounded and taken prisoner by members of Tarleton's Legion while reconnoitering the abandoned works. He was returned to the American lines where he died on the sixth of October, "much lamented by all ranks," stated his friend Henry Dearborn.

"We now began to make preparations for laying close siege to the enemy," wrote Martin. "We had holed him and nothing remained but to drag him out." The work went slowly, the heavy artillery being hard to move, recorded Colonel Butler of the Pennsylvania line; "Indeed, I discover very plainly we are young soldiers in a siege." What they lacked in experience, they made up in perseverance. One militia man became impatient. Another Pennsylvania colonel, James Duncan, told the story. Possessed of more bravery than prudence, the man "stood constantly on the parapet and d–d his soul if he would dodge for the buggers. He had escaped longer than could have been expected, and, growing foolhardy, brandished his spade at every ball that was fired, till, unfortunately, a ball came and put an end to his capers."

A minor skirmish occurred on the Gloucester front. A foraging party commanded by Colonel Tarleton encountered a squadron of French Hussars led by the Duc de Lauzun, who told the story in his *Memoirs*. From a contingent of Virginia troops, he learned that the English Dragoons were in the neighborhood:

> I went forward to learn what I could. I saw a very pretty woman at the door of a little farmhouse on the high road; I went up to her and questioned her; she told me that Colonel Tarleton had left her house a moment before; that he was very eager to shake hands with the French Duke. I assured her that I had come on purpose to gratify him. She seemed very sorry for me; judging from experience, I suppose that Tarleton was irresistible; the American troops seemed to be of the same opinion.
>
> I was not a hundred steps from the house when I heard pistol shots from my advance guard. I hurried forward at full speed to find a piece of ground where I could form a line of battle. As I arrived I saw the English cavalry in force three times my own; I charged it without halting; we met hand to hand. Tarleton saw me and rode towards me with pistol raised. We were about to

fight single-handed between the two troops when his horse was thrown by one of his own dragoons pursued by one of my lancers. I rode up to him to capture him; a troop of English dragoons rode in between us and covered his retreat; he left his horse with me. He charged me twice without breaking my line; I charged the third time, overthrew a part of his cavalry and drove him within the entrenchment of Gloucester. He lost an officer, some fifty men, and I took quite a number of prisoners.

Tarleton ordered a retreat.

Tarleton, in his *Memoirs*, explained the incident. A Dragoon's horse plunged, on being struck with a spear, and overthrew Lieutenant Colonel Tarleton and his horse. He obtained another, and "perceiving the broken state of his cavalry, occasioned by their anxiety for his safety," ordered a retreat.

The heavy siege guns were in position by October sixth, and the trenches or "parallels," as they were called, were progressing, zigzagging towards the enemy's position. Martin continued his story:

One-third part of all the troops were put in requisition to be employed in opening the trenches. A third part of our Sappers and Miners were ordered out this night to assist the engineers in laying out the works. It was a very dark and rainy night. However, we repaired to the place and began by following the engineers and laying laths of pine wood end-to-end upon the line marked out by the officers for the trenches. We had not proceeded far in the business before the engineers ordered us to desist and remain where we were and be sure not to straggle a foot from the spot while they were absent from us. In a few minutes after their departure, there came a man alone to us, having on a surtout, as we conjectured, it being exceeding dark, and inquired for the engineers. We now began to be a little jealous for our safety, being alone and without arms, and within forty rods of the British trenches. The stranger inquired what troops we were, talked familiarly with us a few minutes, when, being informed which way the officers had gone, he went off in the same direction, after strictly charging us, in case we should be taken prisoners, not to discover to the enemy what troops we were. We were obliged to him for his kind advice, but we considered ourselves as standing in no great need of it, for we knew as well as he did that Sappers and Miners were allowed no quarters, at least, are entitled to none, by the laws of warfare, and of course should take care, if taken, and the enemy did not find us out, not to betray our own secret.

The stranger proved to be General Washington.

The engineers returned, bringing the stranger with them:

They discoursed together some time, when, by the officers often calling him "Your Excellency," we discovered that it was General Washington. Had we dared, we might have cautioned him for exposing himself too carelessly to danger at such a time, and doubtless he would have taken it in good part if we had. But nothing ill happened to either him or ourselves.

Washington came and struck a few blows with a pickaxe, so that it might be said, "General Washington with his own hands first broke ground at the siege of Yorktown." He also fired the first shot. It was singularly fatal, recorded the British captain, Samuel Graham. It crashed into the house where a party of officers were dining, killing Commissary General Perkins and wounding others.

Thomas Nelson directed fire at his own residence.

This house, which Cornwallis had made his headquarters, belonged to the one-time governor of Virginia, Thomas Nelson. Old and decrepit, he had been allowed to pass the American lines, where his accurate knowledge of Yorktown was put to use.

"To what particular spot," he was asked, "would your Excellency direct that we should point the cannon?"

"To that house," he replied, pointing to his own magnificent mansion. "There you will be almost certain to find Lord Cornwallis and the British headquarters."

Another discharge, this time loaded with red-hot shot set on fire the *Charon* and several smaller vessels. Dr. Thacher watched her burn:

The Thomas Nelson house showing the cannon shot still imbedded in the walls
—Photo by Kay Smith

From the bank of the river I had a fine view of this splendid conflagration. The ships were enwrapped in a torrent of fire, which, spreading with vivid brightness among the combustible rigging, and running with amazing rapidity to the tops of the several masts, while all around was thunder and lightning from our numerous cannon and mortars, in the darkness of night, presented one of the most sublime and magnificent spectacles which can be imagined. Some of our shells, over-reaching the town, are seen to fall into the river and, bursting, throw up columns of water like the spouting of the monsters of the deep.

Rear Admiral Bartholomew James thought the loss of the *Charon* trivial in comparison to the distressing scenes he witnessed within the town:

I now want words to express the dreadful situation of the garrison, for it is scarcely possible to describe the calamitous condition we were in during the remainder of the siege. The enemy on this evening began their second parallel, having advanced three hundred yards nearer to us; their fire continued then incessant from heavy artillery and mortars, and we opened fresh embrasures to flank the enemy's works, keeping up a constant fire with all the howitzers and small mortars then in the garrison. Upwards of a thousand shells were thrown into the works on this night, and every spot became alike dangerous. The noise and thundering of the cannon, the distressing cries of the wounded, and the lamentable sufferings of the inhabitants, whose dwellings were chiefly in flames, added to the restless fatigues of the duty, must inevitably fill with pity and compassion every mind possessed of any feelings for his fellow creatures.

Yet amidst all this dire destruction no murmuring was heard, no wish to give up the town while the most distant hope was in view of being relieved. On the contrary, this very distinguished little army, taking example from their chief, went through the business of the siege with a perfect undaunted resolution, and hourly discovered proofs of their attachment to the general, who had so often led them to the field with success.

"I felt a secret pride swell my heart when I saw the 'star-spangled banner' waving majestically."

The siege progressed slowly. Martin lost count of the days:

The French, who were upon our left, had completed their batteries a few hours before us, but were not allowed to discharge their pieces till the American batteries were ready. Our commanding battery was on the near bank of the river and contained ten heavy guns; the next was a bomb battery of three large mortars; and so on through the whole line. The whole number, American and French, was ninety-two cannons, mortars and howitzers. Our flagstaff was in the ten-gun battery, upon the right of the whole.

I was in the trenches the day that the batteries were to be opened. All were upon the tiptoe of expectation and impatience to see the signal given to open the whole line of batteries, which was to be the hoisting of the American flag in the ten-gun battery. About noon, the much-wished-for signal went up. I con-

FROM A WATER-COLOR SKETCH BY KAY SMITH

Carter's Grove plantation was built between 1750 and 1755 by Carter Burwell on the 1400-acre estate purchased by his grandfather, Robert King Carter. For three generations that followed, this mansion was the home of the Burwell family. There are many legends about this great property, which has been restored and is now open to the public. In a room on the ground floor, a youthful George Washington is said to have proposed marriage and been refused. Some time later in this same house, Thomas Jefferson proposed to Rebecca Burwell and was refused. In 1781, General Banastre Tarleton, the British dragoon, used Carter's Grove as his headquarters. The story goes that on one occasion he was so angered by failure of subordinates to respond promptly to his summons from outside the house that he rode his horse up the magnificent staircase hacking at the banister rail with his cavalry sword—a story borne out by the marks still visible in the rail.

FROM A WATER-COLOR PAINTING BY KAY SMITH

The Yorktown battlefield. On this Virginia field the final major battle of the war with England ended on October 19, 1781, with the surrender of Lord Cornwallis. The redoubt in the foreground with its abatis pickets made of trees embedded in the bank of the fort illustrates the strong positions that had to be captured by the American and French troops.

FROM A WATER-COLOR SKETCH BY KAY SMITH

The residence of Thomas Nelson, a Virginia signer of the Declaration of Independence who, during the siege of Yorktown, observing that his own home, this mansion, was the only one that had not been struck by the American artillery, even though it was being used as General Cornwallis' headquarters, urged that it be fired upon at once and had the pleasure of seeing the British officers flee as the house was struck by cannon balls.

fess I felt a secret pride swell my heart when I saw the "star-spangled banner" waving majestically in the very faces of our implacable adversaries. It appeared like an omen of success to our enterprise, and so it proved in reality. A simultaneous discharge of all the guns in the line followed, the French troops accompanying it with "Huzza for the Americans!"

Dr. Thacher, who acted as surgeon to the light infantry, watched the work:

The siege is daily becoming more and more formidable and alarming, and his lordship must view his situation as extremely critical, if not desperate. Being in the trenches every other night and day, I have a fine opportunity of witnessing the sublime and stupendous scene which is continually exhibiting. The bomb-shells from the besiegers and the besieged are incessantly crossing each other's path in the air. They are clearly visible in the form of a black ball in the day, but in the night they appear like a fiery meteor with a blazing tail, most beautifully brilliant, ascending majestically from the mortar to a certain altitude and gradually descending to the spot where they are destined to execute their work of destruction.

It is astonishing with what accuracy an experienced gunner will make his calculations, that a shell shall fall within a few feet of a given point, and burst at the precise time, though at a great distance. When a shell falls, it whirls round, burrows, and excavates the earth to a considerable extent, and bursting, makes dreadful havoc around. I have more than once witnessed fragments of the mangled bodies and limbs of the British soldiers thrown into the air by the bursting of our shells, and by one from the enemy, Captain White, of the Seventh Massachusetts Regiment, and one soldier were killed and another wounded near where I was standing. About twelve or fourteen men have been killed or wounded within twenty-four hours. I attended at the hospital, amputated a man's arm and assisted in dressing a number of wounds.

"The enemy seems embarrassed, confused and indeterminate."

"The enemy," thought Colonel Butler, "seems embarrassed, confused and indeterminate; their fire seems feeble to what might be expected; their works, too, are not formed on any regular plan, but thrown up in a hurry occasionally." Most of the enemy's guns were silenced, noted Martin:

We now began our second parallel, about halfway between our works and theirs. There were two strong redoubts held by the British, on their left. It was necessary for us to possess those redoubts before we could complete our trenches. One afternoon, I, with the rest of our corps that had been on duty in the trenches the night but one before, were ordered to the lines. I mistrusted something extraordinary, serious or comical, was going forward, but what I could not easily conjecture.

We arrived at the trenches a little before sunset. I saw several officers fixing bayonets on long staves. I then concluded we were about to make a general assault upon the enemy's works, but before dark I was informed of the plan, which was to storm the redoubts, one by the Americans and the other by the French.

Alexander Hamilton
from the painting by John Trumbull, 1792

The siege could not be allowed to drag on indefinitely.

The investment was complete. The siege could not be allowed to drag on indefinitely. The allies determined to precipitate its end. By the eleventh of October, the "shovel and spade" parties had dug their second parallel up to the two redoubts alongside the river, on the southeast of the town, the easiest line of approach. Dr. Thacher learned the plan:

> The enemy having two redoubts, about three hundred yards in front of their principal works, which enfiladed into our entrenchment and impeded our approaches, it was resolved to take possession of them both by assault. The one on the left of the British garrison, bordering on the banks of the river, was assigned to our brigade of light infantry, under the command of the Marquis de Lafayette. The advanced corps was led on by the intrepid Colonel Alexander Hamilton, who had commanded a regiment of light infantry during the campaign, assisted by Colonel Gimat [a French volunteer officer with the American army].

The night of October 14 was selected for the attack. Four hundred French soldiers assembled on the left, commanded by Colonel William Deux-Ponts, the younger brother of the general of that name. His comrades came to wish him success and glory, expressing regret that they could not go with him. "That moment," he wrote in his journal "seemed to me very sweet, and was very elevating to the soul and animating to the courage. My brother, especially my brother—and I shall never forget it. It gave me marks of tenderness which penetrated to the bottom of my heart."

"Who goes there?"

At the given signal, the firing of six shells in rapid succession, as dusk fell, the two parties advanced. The Frenchmen reached within a hundred yards of redoubt No.9 before they were challenged. "Who goes there?" shouted the Hessian sentry. Deux-Ponts led the charge over the parapet. The Hessians threw down their arms. "*Vive le roi*," cried the French. They had carried the redoubt in less than half an hour, with the loss of fifteen killed and seventy-seven wounded. Deux-Ponts was ecstatic in praise of his soldiers:

> With troops so good, so brave, and so disciplined as those I have the honor to lead against the enemy, one can undertake anything, and be sure of succeeding, if the impossibility of it has not been proved. I owe them the happiest day of my life, and certainly the recollection of it will never be effaced from my mind.

The sappers led the advance.

The Americans were no less successful against the redoubt by the river. It was somewhat smaller than No.9 and was defended by Major Campbell with seventy men. While Hamilton and his column attacked from the front, Colonel Laurens

The Yorktown monument commemorating the men who won the last major battle of the Revolutionary War
—Photo by Kay Smith

marched to take the garrison in the rear. The sappers led the advance, in order to break down the obstructions short of the parapet. Martin went with them:

> The word *up, up*, was then reiterated through the detachment. We immediately moved silently on toward the redoubt we were to attack, with unloaded muskets. Just as we arrived at the abatis, the enemy discovered us and directly opened a sharp fire upon us. We were now at a place where many of our large shells had burst in the ground, making holes sufficient to bury an ox in. The men, having their eyes fixed upon what was transacting before them, were every now and then falling into these holes. I thought the British were killing us off at a great rate. At length, one of the holes happening to pick me up, I found out the mystery of the huge slaughter.
>
> As soon as the firing began, our people began to cry, "The fort's our own!" and it was "Rush on boys." The Sappers and Miners soon cleared a passage for the infantry, who entered it rapidly. Our Miners were ordered not to enter the fort, but there was no stopping them. "We will go," said they. "Then go to the d–l", said the commanding officer of our corps, "if you will." I could not pass at the entrance we had made, it was so crowded. I therefore forced a passage at a place where I saw our shot had cut away some of the abatis; several others entered at the same place. While passing, a man at my side received a ball in his head and fell under my feet, crying out bitterly. While crossing the trench, the enemy threw hand grenades (small shells) into it. They were so thick that I at first thought them cartridge papers on fire, but was soon undeceived by their cracking. As I mounted the breastwork, I met an old associate hitching himself down into the trench. I knew him by the light of the enemy's musketry, it was so vivid. The fort was taken and all quiet in a very short time.

Dr. Thacher followed the assault party:

> I was desired [requested] to visit the wounded in the fort even before the balls had ceased whistling about my ears, and saw a sergeant and eight men dead in the ditch. A captain of our infantry, belonging to New Hampshire, threatened to take the life of Major Campbell to avenge the death of his favorite, Colonel Shammel; but Colonel Hamilton interposed, and not a man was killed after he ceased to resist.
>
> During the assault, the British kept up an incessant firing of cannon and musketry from their whole line. His Excellency General Washington, Generals Lincoln and Knox, with their aides, having dismounted, were standing in an exposed situation awaiting the result.
>
> Colonel Cobb, one of General Washington's aides, solicitous for his safety, said to His Excellency, "Sir, you are too much exposed here. Had you not better step a little back?"
>
> "Colonel Cobb," replied His Excellency, "if you are afraid, you have liberty to step back."

The Americans suffered the loss of eight men killed and thirty wounded. Rear Admiral James watched from the British side:

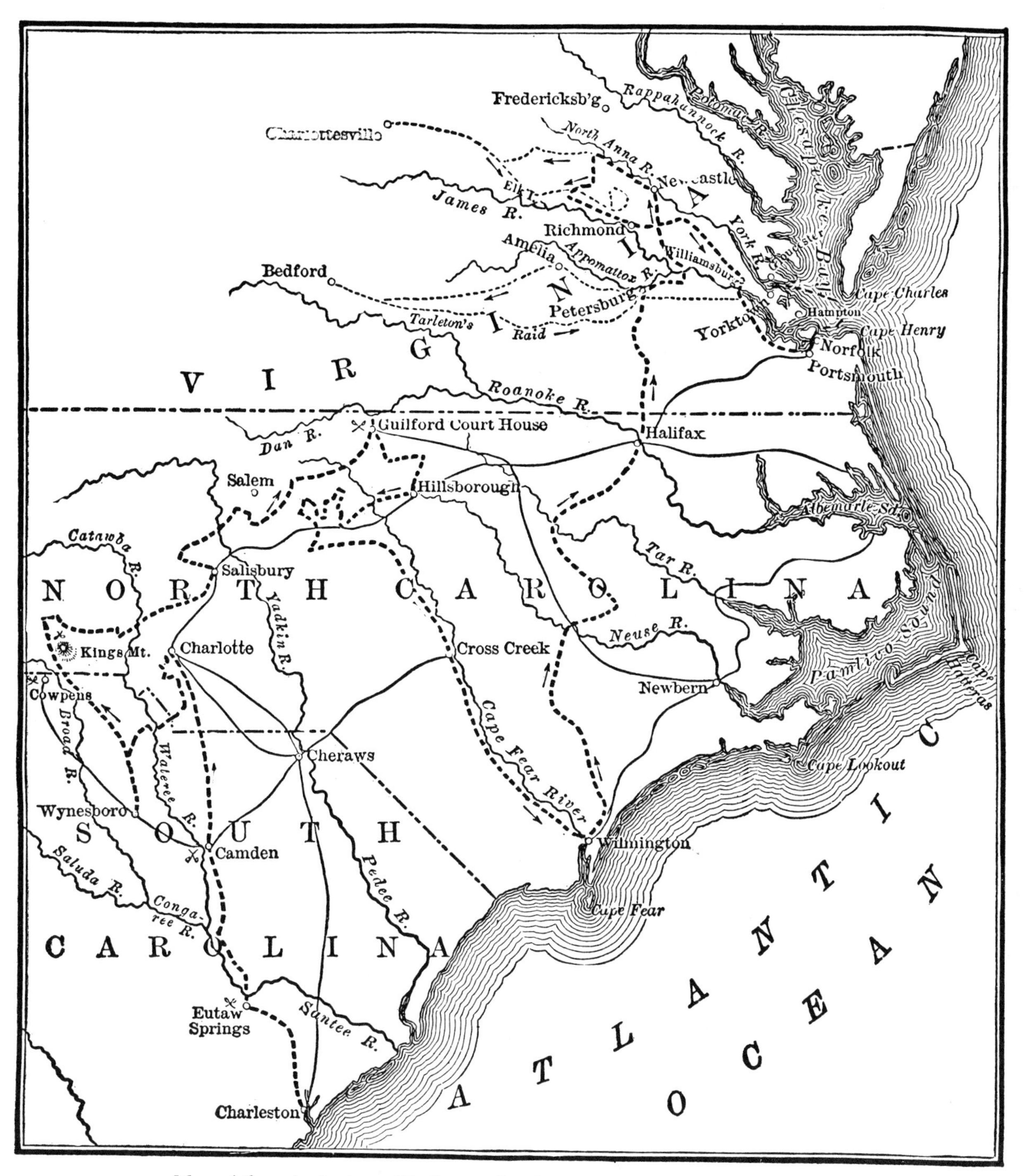

Map of the colonies from Charleston, South Carolina to Fredericksburg, Virginia

At nine o'clock they stormed from right to left with seventeen thousand men, advancing with drums beating and loud huzzas, when the whole garrison was a scene of fire throughout the lines, which, added to the thunder of the heavy artillery and the blaze of musketry from so prodigious an army within a few yards of each other, opened to view a scene which will ever make an impression on my mind and which I cannot attempt to describe. In this storm the enemy carried two of our flanking re-

> doubts to the left which had hitherto retarded their approaches, and most of the unhappy fellows were put to the bayonets, as usual in cases of storms.

James was incorrect. Lafayette affirmed that no retaliation or brutality was encouraged or indulged in.

Washington praised his troops unstintingly. "There was no difficulty which they would not bravely overcome."

Cornwallis realized the effect of the loss of the key redoubts. The next day he wrote to Clinton, "My situation now becomes very critical. We dare not show a gun to their old batteries, and I expect that their new ones will open tomorrow morning. Experience has shown that our fresh earthen works do not resist their powerful artillery, so that we shall soon be exposed to an assault in ruining works, in a bad position with weakened numbers." He warned his Commander-in-Chief that the safety of Yorktown was so precarious "that I cannot recommend that the fleet and army should run any great risk in endeavoring to save us."

"Push on, my brave boys, and skin the hounds."

The British made a sortie, an attempt to recapture the redoubts, and upon the American second parallel. In his journal Washington dismissed the incident in a few words: "(They) spiked four French pieces of Artillery and two of ours, but the guards in the Trenches advancing rapidly upon them, they retreated precipitately." Fortunately, Colonel Butler's report was more elucidating:

Front and back of medal awarded to General Washington to commemorate the recovery of Boston from the British

About twelve o'clock at night, Major Abercrombie of the British with a party of light infantry and guards made a sally and, passing between two small redoubts that were unfinished where the line was weak, got possession of the trench. Thence they pushed rapidly to a French battery and spiked the guns and drove off the people, having killed four or five. Thence to the covert way or communication leading from the first to the second parallel, where they halted. They there discovered a battery commanded by Captain Savage of the Americans and challenged "What troops?" The answer was "French," on which the order of the British commander was, "Push on, my brave boys, and skin the hounds."

The shout was heard by Count de Noailles, who led the advance of the covering party crying "*Vive le roi!*" They routed the assailants who, according to Butler, "executed the sortie with secrecy and spirit."

The next night, October 16, Cornwallis attempted to transfer his army across the river to Gloucester, with the idea of breaking through the besiegers and marching rapidly to New York. The desperate effort was prevented by a storm which arose at midnight. Further resistance was useless. "We at that time could not fire a single gun," reported Cornwallis. "I therefore proposed to capitulate."

He had never listened to music "so delightful as the sound of that drum."

At ten o'clock on October 17, a date vividly remembered by the Americans as the fourth anniversary of Burgoyne's surrender at Saratoga, a British drummer mounted the parapet and beat a "parley." Lieutenant Denny of the Pennsylvania line thought he had never listened to music "so delightful as the sound of that drum."

Washington hurried the negotiations. The British fleet might come or de Grasse might leave. The situation could change in an hour. He demanded and obtained the terms he wanted. "The troops shall march out with colors cased and drums beating a British or German march."

The British and German troops marched out on October 19, their bands playing the old British march with the appropriate title, *The World Turned Upside Down.*

Several of our diarists watched the surrender. Dr. Thacher thought it a "most glorious day, but to the English one of chagrin and disappointment."

At about twelve o'clock, the combined army was arranged and drawn up in two lines extending more than a mile in length. The Americans were drawn up in a line on the right side of the road, and the French occupied the left. At the head of the former, the great American commander, mounted on his noble courser, took his station, attended by his aides. At the head of the latter was posted the excellent Count Rochambeau and his suite. The French troops, in complete uniform, displayed a martial and noble appearance; the music of their bands, of which the tim-

An artist's conception of the surrender at Yorktown which appears to be historically inaccurate inasmuch as the officer on the right presenting the sword to General Washington is Lord Cornwallis, whereas in fact General O'Hara represented the British and Major General Lincoln accepted the surrender, representing General Washington, who refused to meet with anyone inferior in rank.

brel formed a part, is a delightful novelty and produced, while marching to the ground, a most enchanting effect. The Americans, though not all in uniform, nor their dress so neat, yet exhibited an erect soldierly air, and every countenance beamed with satisfaction and joy. The concourse of spectators from the country was prodigious, and in point of numbers was probably equal to the military, but universal silence and order prevailed.

It was about two o'clock when the captive army advanced through the line formed for their reception. Every eye was prepared to gaze on Lord Cornwallis, the object of peculiar interest and solicitude, but he disappointed our anxious expectations. Pretending indisposition, he made General O'Hara his substitute as the leader of his army. This officer was followed by the conquered troops in a slow and solemn step, with shouldered arms, colors cased and drums beating a British march. Having arrived at the head of the line, General O'Hara, elegantly mounted, advanced to his excellency the commander-in-chief, taking off his hat, and apologized for the non-appearance of Lord Cornwallis. With his usual dignity and politeness, his excellency pointed to Major General Lincoln for directions, by whom the British army was conducted into a spacious field, where it was intended they should ground their arms.

The royal troops, while marching through the line formed by the allied army, exhibited a decent and neat appearance, as respects arms and clothing, for their commander opened his store and directed every soldier to be furnished with a new suit complete, prior to the capitulation. But in their line of march we remarked a disorderly and unsoldierly conduct; their step was irregular, and their ranks frequently broken.

But it was in the field, when they came to the last act of the drama, that the spirit and pride of the British soldier was put to the severest test; here their mortification could not be concealed. Some of the platoon officers appeared to be exceedingly chagrined when giving the word *ground arms*, and I am a witness that they performed this duty in a very unofficer-like manner; and that many of the soldiers manifested a *sullen temper*, throwing their arms on the pile with violence, as if determined to render them useless. This irregularity, however, was checked by the authority of General Lincoln. After having grounded their arms and divested themselves of their accoutrements, the captive troops were conducted back to Yorktown and guarded by our troops till they could be removed to the place of their destination.

"No spectacle could be more impressive."

Harry Lee thought, "No spectacle could be more impressive than the one now exhibited."

The road through which they marched was lined with spectators, French and American. On one side the commander-in-chief, surrounded by his suite and the American staff, took his station; on the other side, opposite to him, was the Count de Rochambeau, in like manner attended. The captive army approached, moving slowly in column with grace and precision. Universal silence was observed amid the vast concourse, and the utmost decency prevailed; exhibiting in demeanor an awful

The British fleet, always a dominent force in helping England control its colonies, failed to arrive at Yorktown in time to influence the outcome of the battle

FACSIMILE OF THE SURRENDER OF LORD CORNWALLIS AT YORKTOWN

Articles of Capitulation settled between his
Excellency General Washington Comander in
Chief of the combined Forces of America & France
— His Excellency The Count de Rochambeau
Lieutenant General of the Armies of the King
of France — Great Cross of the Royal & Military
Order of St Louis — Commanding the Auxiliary

Troops of his most Christian Majesty in Ame-rica — And His Excellency the Count de Grasse Lieutenant General of the Naval Armies of his Most Christian Majesty, Commander of the Order of St Louis, comand[g] in Chief the Na-val Army of France in the Chesapeak — on the One Part — And His ~~Excellency~~ The Right Hon[ble] Earl Cornwallis Lieut General of His Britannick Majesty's Forces, Commanding the Garrisons of York & Gloucester and Thomas Symonds Esq[r] Commanding His Britannick Majestys Naval forces in York river in Virginia on the other part.

Article 1st	Article — 1st
The Garrisons of York & Gloucester including the Officers & Seamen of his Britannic Majestys Ships as well as other Mariners, to sur-render themselves Prisoners of War to the Combined Forces of America & France. — The Land Troops to	Granted —

sense of the vicissitudes of human life, mingled with commiseration for the unhappy.

The head of the column approached the commander-in-chief. O'Hara, mistaking the circle, turned to that on his left, for the purpose of paying his respects to the commander-in-chief and requesting further orders, when, quickly discovering his error, with much embarrassment in his countenance he flew across the road, and, advancing up to Washington, asked pardon for his mistake, apologized for the absence of Lord Cornwallis, and begged to know his further pleasure. The General, feeling his embarrassment, relieved it by referring him with much politeness to General Lincoln for his government. Returning to the head of the column, it again moved under the guidance of Lincoln to the field selected for the conclusion of the ceremony.

"You could not have heard a whisper or seen the least of a motion throughout our whole line," the Virginia colonel, Fontaine, told his friend Major Penn. Private Martin was his usual matter-of-fact self:

It was a noble sight to us, and the more so, as it seemed to promise a speedy conclusion to the contest. The British did not make so good an appearance as the German forces, but there was certainly some allowance to be made in their favor. The English felt their honor wounded. The Germans did not greatly care whose hands they were in. The British seemingly paid the Americans but little attention as they passed them, but they eyed the French with considerable malice depicted in their countenances.

Lord Cornwallis found the treatment received from the conquerors perfectly good and proper, "but the kindness that has been shown to us by the French officers in particular—their delicate sensibility of our situation—their generous and pressing offer of money, both public and private, to any amount—has really gone beyond what I can possibly describe, and will, I hope, make an impression on the breast of every British officer, whenever the fortune of war should put any of them into our power."

"The American, French, and English generals visited each other."

Lord Cornwallis and his officers were hospitably entertained by the victors. They were guests at the tables of Washington and Rochambeau. "The American, French, and English generals," said Lafayette, "visited each other, and everything passed with every possible mark of attention." Cornwallis and his officers were allowed to go to New York on parole. The soldiers marched to captivity in Virginia. En route, Roger Lamb made another escape; he returned home to Ireland where his family had given him up for lost.

On October 19, 1781, the day of surrender, Clinton reached the Capes of Chesapeake Bay. His attempt to relieve Cornwallis came too late. He returned to New York.

"Oh God! It is all over," exclaimed Prime Minister Lord North, when he heard the news of the surrender at Yorktown. He expressed the realistic and popular view.

The triumphant return of General Washington to New York in 1783

FAREWELL

Following Cornwallis's surrender, hostilities virtually ceased. De Grasse returned to the West Indies, where, on April 19, 1782, he was heavily defeated and captured by Sir George Rodney at the Saintes. Against their traditional enemy the British had won the last battle. It took a year of hard pleading by Lord North to persuade King George to recognize the United States of America.

The peace was signed in Paris on February 3, 1783. The news of the cessation of hostilities was announced in America on April 19, eight years to the day since the first shots had been fired at Lexington and Concord.

Liberty had triumphed.

The final victory vindicated Washington's fundamental strategy—to harass the enemy at every point, but never to allow them the opportunity of crushing his army. It justified the American cause. The men of liberal minds had prevented the

The desk on which the Treaty of 1783 was signed
—Sketch by Kay Smith

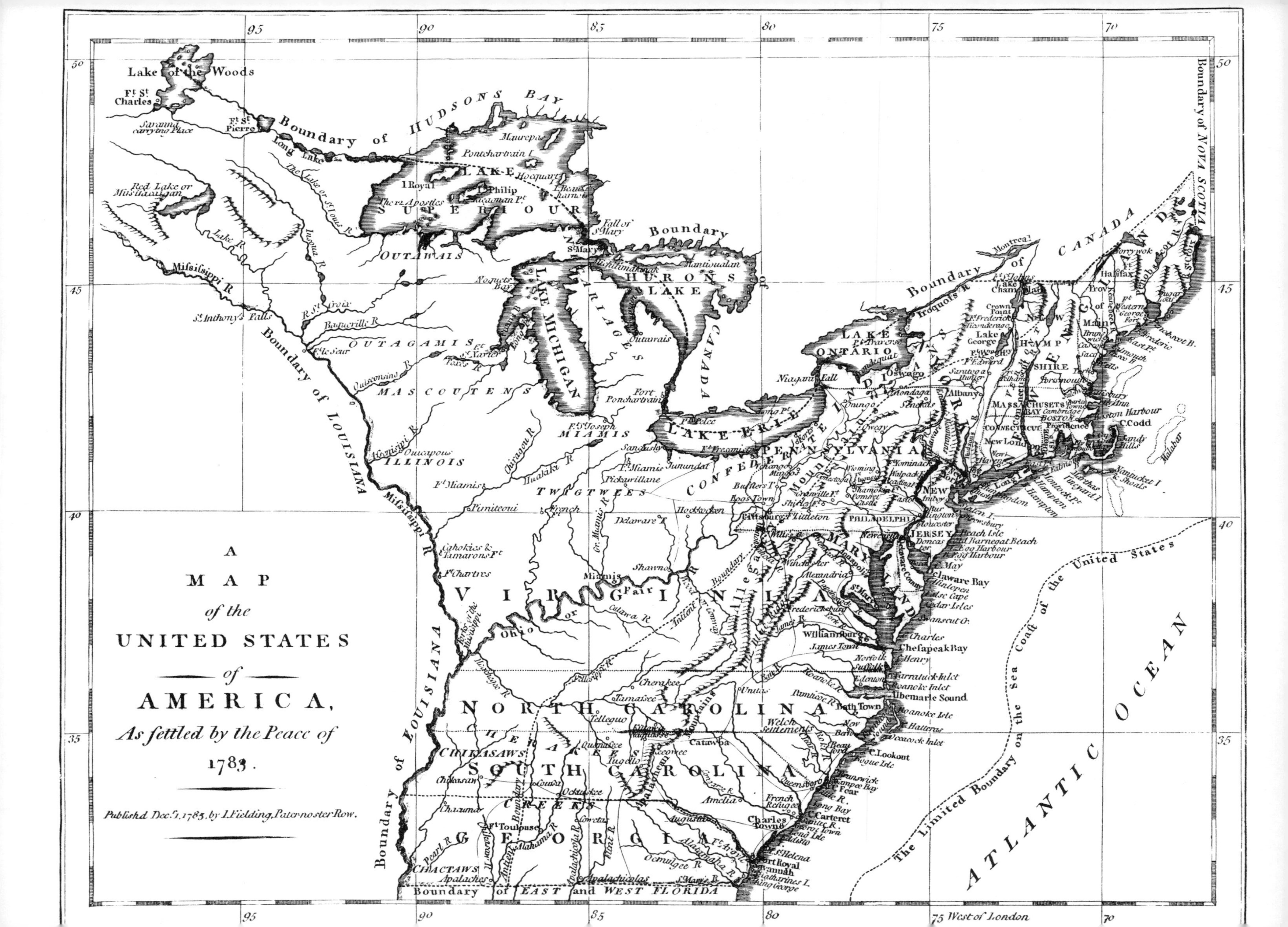
A MAP
of the
UNITED STATES
of
AMERICA,
As settled by the Peace of
1783.
Publish'd Dec. 1, 1783, by J. Fielding, Paternoster Row.
ATLANTIC OCEAN
The Limited Boundary on the Sea Coast of the United States
Boundary of HUDSONS BAY
Boundary of LOUISIANA
Boundary of EAST and WEST FLORIDA
Boundary of NOVA SCOTIA
Boundary of CANADA
CANADA
Lake of the Woods
LAKE SUPERIOUR
LAKE MICHIGAN
HURONS LAKE
LAKE ERIE
LAKE ONTARIO
NORTH CAROLINA
SOUTH CAROLINA
GEORGIA
VIRGINIA
PENNSYLVANIA
MARYLAND
JERSEY
CONNECTICUT
MASSACHUSETS BAY
BOSTON
PHILADELPHIA
ILLINOIS
MIAMIS
TWIGTWEES
MASCOUTENS
OUTAGAMIS
OUTAWAIS
CHICKASAWS
CREEKS
CHACTAWS
Misisipi R
Ohio
Chesapeak Bay
Delaware Bay
Albemarle Sound
75 West of London

Revolution from degenerating into a terror, and from becoming a military dictatorship. The victors were exalted but did not exult. Liberty had triumphed.

The British evacuated New York on November 23, 1783. Washington marched in, leading his ill-clad, ragged army. "They were *our* troops," thought one spectator, "and I admired and gloried in them the more, because they were weather-beaten and forlorn." Major Benjamin Tallmadge saw Washington bid farewell to his officers and soldiers;

> At twelve o'clock the officers repaired to Fraunces Tavern in Pearl Street, where General Washington had appointed to meet them and to take his final leave of them. We had been assembled but a few moments when His Excellency entered the room. His emotion, too strong to be concealed, seemed to be reciprocated by every officer present.
>
> After partaking of a slight refreshment, in almost breathless silence, the General filled his glass with wine, and turning to his officers he said, "With a heart full of love and gratitude, I now take leave of you. I most devoutly wish that your latter days may be as prosperous and happy as your former ones have been glorious and honorable."
>
> After the officers had taken a glass of wine, General Washington said, "I cannot come to each of you, but shall feel obliged if each of you will come and take me by the hand."
>
> General Knox, being nearest to him, turned to the Commander-in-Chief, who, suffused in tears, was incapable of utterance, but grasped his hand, when they embraced each other in silence. In the same affectionate manner, every officer in the room marched up to, kissed, and parted with his General-in-Chief.

Not a word broke the solemn silence.

Tallmadge had never witnessed such a scene of sorrowful weeping, and he hoped he never would again. Not a word broke the solemn silence.

> The simple thought that we were then about to part from the man who had conducted us through a long and bloody war, and under whose conduct the glory and independence of our country had been achieved, and that we should see his face no more in this world, seemed to me utterly insupportable.
>
> But the time of separation had come, and waving his hand to his grieving children around him, he left the room, and passing through a corps of light infantry who were paraded to receive him, he walked silently on to Whitehall, where a barge was waiting. We all followed in mournful silence to the wharf, where a prodigious crowd had assembled to witness the departure of the man who, under God, had been the great agent in establishing the glory and independence of these United States. As soon as he was seated, the barge put off into the river, and when out in the stream, our great and beloved General waved his hat and bid us a silent adieu.

On his way home, Washington called upon Congress to whom he resigned "with satisfaction" the command which he had taken "with diffidence."

Three months' pay and their muskets.

The soldiers of the Continental Army were dismissed with a note for three months' arrears of pay and their muskets as a gift. Joseph Plumb Martin, the typical Revolutionary soldier, may be allowed to say the last word. Few soldiers, he wrote in 1830, received the land they had been promised:

> The truth was, none cared for them. The country was served, and faithfully served, and that was all that was deemed necessary. It was, soldiers, look to yourselves; we want no more of you. I hope I shall one day find land enough to lay my bones in. If I chance to die in a civilized country, none will deny me that. A dead body never begs a grave—thanks for that.

"The thousandth part of their sufferings has not, nor ever will be told."

Reminiscing, he recalled the miserable clothes and blankets the soldiers had been forced to wear:

> How often have I had to lie whole stormy, cold nights in a wood, on a field, or a bleak hill, with such blankets and other clothing like them, with nothing but the canopy of the heavens to cover me. All this too in the heart of winter, when a New England farmer, if his cattle had been in my situation, would not have slept a wink from sheer anxiety for them. And if I stepped into a house to warm me, when passing, wet to the skin and almost dead with cold, hunger, and fatigue, what scornful looks and hard words have I experienced.
>
> Almost everyone has heard of the soldiers of the Revolution being tracked by the blood of their feet on the frozen ground. This is literally true, and the thousandth part of their sufferings has not, nor ever will be told.

Martin was granted in 1818 a pension of ninety-six dollars a year. He died at the age of ninety on May 2, 1850, and was buried in Sandy Point Cemetery at Prospect, Maine. His fellow townsmen placed at his grave a monument bearing the simple inscription—

A Soldier of the Revolution

It would have made a fitting epitaph for thousands of others.

Whether or not the Americans owed their success to French help—whether or not the British bungled the war, or could never have won it—it was the soldiers, by their steadfastness in adversity, who had gained the victory.

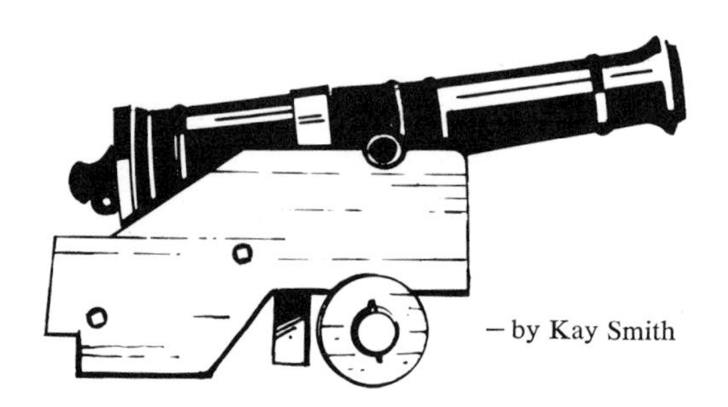

—by Kay Smith

FROM A WATER-COLOR SKETCH BY KAY SMITH

Fraunces Tavern, still standing on the corner of Broad and Pearl Streets in New York City, where George Washington said farewell to his troops on December 4, 1783.

FROM A WATER-COLOR SKETCH BY KAY SMITH

Federal Building, New York City, where George Washington took his oath of office as the first President of the United States of America.

BIBLIOGRAPHY

CONTEMPORARY SOURCES: CONSULTED AND QUOTED

Adams, John	*Works* 10 Vols. *Familiar Letters*	Boston, 1856 New York, 1876
Adams, Samuel	*Warren-Adams Letters* 2 Vols.	Mass. Hist. Soc. Coll. LXXII, LXXIII
Allaire, Anthony	*Diary*	New York, 1881
Allen, Ethan	*Narrative of Captivity*	Burlington, 1838
Anbury, Thomas	*Travels Through the Interior Parts of America.* 2 Vols.	London, 1789
André, John	*Journal*	New York, 1866
Armstrong, John	*Letter*	Gates Papers, New York Public Library
Arnold, Benedict	*Letters* *Memorandum Book,*	Maine Hist. Soc. Coll. I Penn. Mag. Hist. & Biog. VIII
Atlee, Samuel	*Journal*	Penn Archives 2nd Series I
Baldwin, Jeduthan	*Revolutionary Journal*	Bangor, Maine, 1906
Bangs, Isaac	*Journal*	Cambridge, 1890
Barker, John	*Military Journal*	Cambridge, 1924
Barrett, Amos	*The Concord Fight*	Boston, 1924
Barton, William	*Journals of Sullivan's Expedition* Cook, F.	New York, 1887
Beatty, William	*Journal*	Maryland Hist. Mag. III
Beebe, Lewis	*Military Surgeon's Journal*	Penn. Mag. Hist. & Biog. LIX
Belknap, Jeremy	*Journal*	Mass. Hist. Soc. Proc. 1st Series IV
Bixby, Samuel	*Journal*	Mass. Hist. Soc. Proc. 1st Series XIV
Boardman, Oliver	*Journal*	Conn. Hist. Soc. Coll. 1899
Boudinot, Elias	*Journal*	Philadelphia, 1894
Bowdoin, James	*Papers*	Mass. Hist. Soc. Coll. 6th Series VI
Bradford, William	*Letter*	Penn. Archives, 1st Series V
Brooks, John	*Letter*	Mass. Hist. Soc. Proc. XIII
Brown, Peter	*Literary Diary of Ezra Stiles* Vol. I	New York, 1901
Burgoyne, Sir John	*State of the Expedition* *Letter to Lord Stanley*	London, 1780 Force, Am. Archives 4th Series, II
Burnett, E. C.	*Letters of Members of Continental Congress* 8 Vols.	Washington, 1921-26
Butler, Richard	*Journal*	Hist. Mag. VIII
Cadwalader, John	*Military Papers*	Penn. Mag. Hist. & Biog. XXXII
Caldwell, Henry	*Letter. MSS Relating to Early History of Canada*	Lit. Hist. Soc. of Quebec 2nd Series V
Campbell, Robert	*Autobiography*	North Carolina State Records XV
Chastellux, Marquis de	*Travels in North America* 2 Vols.	New York, 1827
Chesney, Alexander	*Journal*	Columbus, Ohio, 1921

Chester, John	*Letter*. Frothingham, R. *Siege of Boston*	Boston, 1849
Clark, George Rogers	*Campaign in Illinois*	Columbus, Ohio, 1869
Clark, Joseph	*Diary*	New Jersey Hist. Soc. Proc. VII
Clark, Jonas	*Journal* Hudson C. *History of Concord and Lexington*	Boston, 1913
Clinton, Sir Henry	*The American Rebellion*	New Haven, Conn. 1954
Clinton, George	*Public Papers*	Albany, 1904
Collier, Sir George	*Journal.*	Long Isl. Hist. Soc. Memoirs II
Collins, James	*Autobiography*	Clinton, La., 1859
Cooke, Nicholas	*Revolutionary Correspondence*	Am. Antiq. Soc. Proc. XXXVI
Cornwallis, Charles, Marquis of	*Correspondence,* 3 Vols.	London, 1859
Cresswell, Nicholas	*Journal*	New York, 1924
Cross, Ralph	*Journal*	Hist. Mag. XVII
Cruger, John	*Letters.*	Mag. American Hist. II
Dale, Richard	*Account of Action with Serapis*	Sherburne, H. *Life of J. P. Jones* Washington, 1825
Darlington, William	*Letter*	Hist. Soc. of Penn. Bulletin I
Davis, Nathan	*Expedition Against Five Nations*	Hist. Mag. 2nd Series III
Dearborn, Henry	*Journal*	Mass. Hist. Soc. Proc. 2nd Series III
	Ed. Peckham, H. H. & Brown, L. A.	Chicago, 1939
De Peyster, J.	*The Affair at Kings Mountain*	Mag. Am. Hist. V
Deux Ponts, Comte William	*My Campaigns in America*	Boston, 1868
Digby, William	*The British Invasion from the North.*	Albany, 1887
Drinker, Mrs. Henry	*Journal*	Mag. Am. Hist. XIII
Duncan, James	*Journal.*	Penn. Archives. 2nd Series XV Mag. Am. Hist. XXV
Du Ponceau, Pierre	*Autobiography*	Penn. Mag. Hist. & Biog. LXIII
Elliott, Barnard	*Charleston, 1775*	Gibbes, R.W. *Doc. Hist. of Am. Revolution* New York, 1853-57
Elliott, Andrew	*Letter*	Stevens, B.F. Facsimiles London, 1889-95
Elking, Peter	*Life During American Revolution.*	New York, 1861
Elmer, Ebenezer	*Journal*	Penn. Mag. Hist. & Biog. XXXV
Emerson, William	*Diary*	Emerson, R. W. Miscellanies. Boston, 1863
Ewing, Thomas	*Soldier of Valley Forge*	Yonkers, N.Y. 1928
Fanning, Nathaniel	*Memoirs*	New York, 1808
Farnsworth, Amos	*Journal*	Mass. Hist. Soc. Proc. 2nd Series IX
Fitch, Jabez	*Journal*	Mass. Hit. Soc. Proc. 2nd Series IX
Fithian, P. V.	*Journal*	Princeton, N.J. 1934
Fleury, Vicomte de	*Journal*	Ford, W.C. Defenses of Philadelphia. Philadelphia, 1897
Force, Peter	*American Archives.* 9 Vols.	Washington, 1837-53
Franks, Rebecca	*Letter*	Penn. Mag. Hist. & Biog. I
Franklin, Benjamin	*Writings,* 10 Vols.	New York, 1905-7
Gage, Thomas	*Correspondence,* 2 Vols.	New Haven, Conn. 1931
Gates, Horatio	*Papers* *Camden Letters*	New York Public Library Mag. Am. Hist. V

Gibbes, R. W.	*Documentary History of the American Revoution* 2 Vols.	New York, 1853-57
Glover, John	*Letter*	Force, P. *Am. Arch.* 5th Series II *Memoir,* Upham W.W. Marblehead, Mass., 1853
Graves, Admiral Thomas	*Papers*	New York, 1916
Graydon, Alexander	*Memoirs*	Harrisburg, Pa., 1811
Greene, Nathanael	*Life and Correspondence*	Johnson W. Charleston, 1822
	Life	Greene, G. W. New York, 1867
Hadden, James	*Journal*	Albany, 1884
Hamilton, Alexander	*Writings,* 9 Vols. *Works.* 12 Vols.	New York, 1850 New York, 1903
Hand, Edward	*Papers*	Penn. Archives 2nd Series X
Hart, A.B.	*American History Told By Contemporaries*	New York, 1898
Harrison, Richard	*Evidence*	Lee Court Martial, Philadelphia, 1778
Hay, Samuel	*Letter*	Penn. Archives. 2nd Series I
Heth, William	*Memoirs*	New York, 1904
Heinrichs, Johann	*Journal of Siege of Charleston*	Ann Arbor, Michigan, 1938
	Letter	Penn. Mag. Hist. & Biog. XXII
Henry, John Joseph	*Account of Arnold's Expedition Against Quebec,*	Albany, 1877
Heth, William	*Letter*	New York. Hist. Soc. I. No. 217
Hewes, George	*Retrospect of Boston Tea Party*	New York, 1834
Hodgkins, Joseph	*Letters.* Wade, H.T. & Lively, R.A. *This Glorious Cause*	Princeton, N.J. 1958
Howard, Eager	*Account of Cowpens* Lee, H. *Campaign of 1781.*	Philadelphia, 1824
Howe, Sir William	*Narrative*	London, 1781
Hull, William	*Memoirs,* Campbell, M.H. *Gen. William Hull*	New York, 1848
Hulton, Ann	*Letters of a Loyalist Lady*	Cambridge, 1927
Hunter, Sir Martin	*Journal*	Edinburgh, 1894
James, Rear Admiral Bartholomeux	*Journal*	London, 1896
Jarvis, Stephen	*An American's Experience in the British Army*	Journal of Am. Hist. I
Jefferson, Thomas	*Papers.* Ed Boyd, J.P. 10 Vols.	Princeton, 1954
Jones, Thomas	*History of New York During Revolutionary War*	New York, 1879
Jones, John Paul	*Life and Character,* Sherburne, J.H.	Washington, 1825
	Life and Correspondence, Taylor, J.	New York, 1830
	A Sailor's Biography, Morison, S.E.	Boston, 1959
Kalb, Baron Johann de	*Life of,* Kapp, F.	New York, 1884
Knox, Henry	*Life and Correspondence* Drake, F.S.	Boston, 1973
	A Soldier of the Revolution Brooks, N.	New York, 1900
	Diary	New Eng. Hist. & Genealogical Reg. XXX
Krafft, J.C.	*Journal*	New York, Hist. Soc. Coll., 1882
Lacey, John	*Memoirs*	Penn. Mag. & Biog. XXV
Lafayette, Marquis de	*Memoirs, Correspondence*	New York, 1837

Lamb, Roger	*An Authentic Account of Occurrences During the Late American War*	Dublin, 1809
Laurens, John	*Army Correspondence*	New York, 1867
Lauzun, Duc de	*Narrative*	Mag. Am. Hist. VI
Leach, John	*Journal*	New Eng. Hist. & Genealogical Soc. XIX
Lee, Ezra	*Letter*	Mag. Am. Hist. XXIX
Lee, Henry	*Campaign of 1781 in the Carolinas*	Philadelphia, 1824
	Memoirs of the War in the Southern Department	New York, 1827
Lukens, Jesse	*Letter*	Am. Hist. Record I
Lyman, Simeon	*Journal*	Conn. Hist. Soc. Coll. II
Marion, Francis	*Life.* James W.D.	Charleston, S.C., 1821
Martin, Rev.	*Literary Diary of Ezra Stiles*	New York, 1901
Martin, Joseph Plumb	*Narrative*	Hallowell, La. 1830
Mathis, Samuel	*Letter*	Am. Hist. Record II
Melvin, James	*Journal*	Portland, Maine, 1902
Miles, Samuel	*Journal*	Penn. Archives 2nd Series I, Long Is. Hist. Soc. III
Moore, Frank	*Diary of the Revolution*	New York 1861
Morgan, Daniel	*Life and Correspondence.* Graham, J.	New York, 1859
Morison, George	*Journal*	Penn. Mag. Hist. & Biog. XIV
Morton, Robert	*Diary*	Penn. Mag. Hist. & Biog. I
Moultrie, William	*Memoirs.* 2 Vols.	New York, 1802
Munchausen, Frederick von	*Journal*	Penn. Mag. Hist. & Biog. XVI
Mutiny of Pennsylvania Line	*Materials of*	Penn. Archives. 2nd Series XI
Mackenzie, Frederick	*Diary* 2 Vols.	Cambridge, 1930
McMichael, James	*Diary*	Penn. Mag. Hist. & Biog. XVI
Newel, Timothy	*Journal*	Mass. Hist. Soc. Coll. 4th Series I
Niles, H.	*Principles & Acts of the Revolution in America*	New York, 1876
Onderdonk, Henry	*Revolutionary Incidents*	New York, 1849
Paine, Thomas	*Writings.* Conway, M.D. 4 Vols.	New York, 1894-96
Paoli Massacre	*British Officer*	Penn. Mag. Hist. & Biog. XXIX
Parker, Robert	*Journal*	Penn. Mag. Hist. & Biog. XXVII
Pausch, Georg	*Journal*	Albany, 1886
Percy, Hugh. (2nd Duke of Northumberland)	*Letters and Papers*	Boston, 1902
Pickering, Timothy	*Letter*	North Am. Rev. XXIII
	Life. Pickering O.	Boston, 1867
Pinckney, Charles	*Letter*	Hist. Mag. X
Prescott, William	*Letters.* Frothingham, R. *Siege of Boston*	Boston, 1849
R. Sergeant	*Battle of Princeton*	Penn. Mag. Hist. & Biog. XX
Rawdon, Lord	*Letters. Rawdon MSS*	Great Britain Hist. MSS Commission, 1930-47
Reed, Joseph	*Narrative*	Penn. Mag. Hist. & Biog. VIII
Reed, William	*Life & Correspondence.* Reed, W.B.	Philadelphia, 1847
Reeves, Enos	*Letters*	Penn. Mag. Hist. & Biog. XX, XXI
Revere, Paul	*Letter*	Mass. Hist. Soc. Coll. V
Riedesel, Frederica von	*Letters and Journals*	Albany, 1867
Rochambeau, Comte de	*Operations of French Army*	Philadelphia, 1817
Rodney, Thomas	*Diary*	Hist. Soc. of Delaware. VIII.

Rogowski Major	*Pulaski's Charge.* Jones C.C. *Siege of Savannah*	Albany, 1874
Rowe, John	*Journal*	Mass. Hist. Soc. Coll. 2nd Series X
Senter, Isaac.	*Journal*	Philadelphia, 1846
Serle, Ambrose	*American Journal*	San Marino, Calif. 1940
Scott, Morin	*Letter*	Long Is. Hist. Soc. III
Shaw, Janet	*Journal of Lady of Quality*	New York, 1921
Shelby, Isaac	*Battle of Kings Mountain*	Journal of Southern History IV
Shewkirk, Rev.	*Memoirs*	Long Is. Hist. Soc. III
Simcoe, John	*Military Journal*	New York, 1844
Sparks, Jared	*Correspondence of American Revolution* 4 Vols.	Boston, 1853
Stark, John	*Memoirs*	Concord, N.H. 1860
Steele, Robert	*Letter.* French *A Siege of Boston*	Boston, 1911
Steuben, William von	*Life of;* Kapp, F.	New York, 1859
Stevens, Elisha	*Memoranda*	Meriden Conn. 1922
Stevens, B.F.	*Facsimiles of Mss in European Archives*	London, 1889-95
Stocking, Abner	*Journal*	Mag. of Hist. No. 75
Sullivan, John	*Papers.* Hammond O. *Journals Expedition Ag. Six Nations*	Concord, N.H., 1930 Auburn, N.Y., 1887
Sutherland, William	*Relation. Gage Correspondence*	New Haven, Conn., 1931-33
Tallmadge, Benjamin	*Memoirs*	New York, 1851
Tarleton, Banastre	*History of Campaigns of 1780, 1781*	Dublin, 1787
Thacher, James	*Military Journal*	Boston, 1827
Thacher, Peter	*Narrative*	Hist. Mag. 2nd Series III
Thayer, Simeon	*Journal*	Rhode Is. Hist. Soc. Coll. VI
Tilghman, Tench	*Memoir* *Letter*	Albany, 1876 Penn. Mag. Hist. & Biog. XXXII
Trumbull, Benjamin	*Journal*	Connecticut Hist. Soc. Coll. VII
Trumbull, John	*Reminiscences*	New York, 1841
Trumbull, Jonathan	*Journal*	Mass. Hist. Soc. Proc. IV, XIV
Tucker, St. George	*Journal*	Mag. Am. Hist. VII William & Mary Quart 3rd Series V
Waldo, Albigence	*Diary*	Hist. Mag. V Penn. Mag. Hist. & Biog. XXI
Washington, George	*Writings.* Sparks, J. 12 Vols. Fitzpatrick, C. 39 Vols.	Boston, 1834-37 Washington, 1931-44
Wayne, Anthony	*Life.* Stille, C.	Philadelphia 1893
Webb, Samuel	*Correspondence & Journal* 3 Vols.	New York, 1894
Wild, Ebenezer	*Journal*	Mass. Hist. Soc. Proc. 2nd Series VI
Wilkinson, James	*Memoirs of My Own Times,* 3 Vols.	Philadelphia, 1816
Willard, M.W.	*Letters On The American Revolution*	Boston, 1925
Williams, Otto	*Narrative.* Appendix to Johnson W. *Life & Correspondence of Nathanael Greene* *Battle of Eutaw.* Gibbes R.W. *Doc. Hist. Am. Rev.*	Charleston, 1822 New York, 1853-57
Wood, Sylvanus	*True Account,* Dawson W.B. *Battles of U.S.*	New York, 1858

Winthrop, Hannah	*Letter.* Warren-Adams *Letters. II*	Boston, 1925
Wright, Aaron	*Journal*	Hist. Mag. VI
Young, Thomas	*Memoir*	Orion III

SUPPLEMENTARY SOURCES

Alden, J.R.	*The American Revolution*	New York, 1953
Barker, J.	*The British in Boston*	Cambridge, 1924
Becker, C.	*Declaration of Independence*	New York, 1937
Bill, A.H.	*Valley Forge*	New York, 1952
Bolton, A.H.	*The Private Soldier Under Washington*	New York, 1902
Canby, H.S.	*The Brandywine*	New York, 1941
Carrington, H.B.	*Battles of American Revolution*	New York, 1876
Chidsey, D.B.	*Valley Forge*	New York, 1959
Codman, J.	*Arnold's Expedition to Quebec*	New York, 1902
Dawson, H.B.	*Battles of the U.S.* 2 Vols.	New York, 1858
Draper, L.C.	*Kings Mountain & Its Heroes*	Cincinnati, 1881
Eelking, Max von	*German Allied Troops in North American War of Independence*	Albany, 1893-
Fiske, J.	*The American Revolution* 2 Vols.	Boston, 1893
French, A.	*Siege of Boston*	Boston, 1911
	Day of Concord & Lexington	Boston, 1923
	First Year of American Revolution	Boston, 1934
	The Taking of Ticonderoga in 1775	Cambridge, 1928
Frothingham, R.	*The Siege of Boston*	Boston, 1849
Frothingham, T.G.	*Sequence That Led to Yorktown*	New York, 1930
Furneaux, R.	*Saratoga; the Decisive Battle*	New York, 1971
Garden, A.	*Anecdotes of American Revolution.* 3 Vols.	Brooklyn, 1885
Heathcote, C.W.	*Battle of Germantown*	Valley Forge, Pa., 1955
Heyl, R.F.	*Battle of Germantown*	Philadelphia, 1908
Hough, F.B.	*Siege of Savannah*	Albany, 1866
	Siege of Charleston	Albany, 1867
Hudson, C.	*History of Lexington, Mass.*	Boston, 1913
James, W.M.	*British Navy in Adversity*	New York, 1926
Johnston, W.M.	*Campaign of 1776 Around New York, and Battle of Long Island*	Brooklyn, 1878
	The Yorktown Campaign	New York, 1881
Lister, J.	*The Concord Fight*	Cambridge, 1931
Lossing, B.	*The Two Spies. Nathan Hale and John André*	New York, 1886
Lowell, E.	*The Hessians and Other German Auxiliaries of Gt. Britain*	New York, 1884
Lundin, C.H.	*The Cockpit of the American Revolution. The War in New Jersey*	Princeton, 1940
Matthews, W.	*American Diaries to the Year 1861*	Berkeley, Calif., 1945

Montross, L.	*Rag, Tag and Bobtail. The Story of the Continental Army*	New York, 1951
Morison, S.E.	*Sources & Documents Illustrating the American Revolution*	New York, 1923
Smith, J.H.	*Arnold's March 1775-76*	New York, 1903
Stoudt, J.	*Ordeal at Valley Forge*	New York, 1962
Stone, F.D.	*Battle of Brandywine*	Philadelphia, 1895
Stryker, W.S.	*Battles of Trenton & Princeton*	Boston, 1898
	Battle of Monmouth	Princeton, 1927
Van Doren, C.	*Secret History of the American Revolution*	New York, 1945

BIBLIOGRAPHY

CONTEMPORARY SOURCES: CONSULTED AND QUOTED

Adams, John	*Works* 10 Vols. *Familiar Letters*	Boston, 1856 New York, 1876
Adams, Samuel	*Warren-Adams Letters* 2 Vols.	Mass. Hist. Soc. Coll. LXXII, LXXIII
Allaire, Anthony	*Diary*	New York, 1881
Allen, Ethan	*Narrative of Captivity*	Burlington, 1838
Anbury, Thomas	*Travels Through the Interior Parts of America.* 2 Vols.	London, 1789
André, John	*Journal*	New York, 1866
Armstrong, John	*Letter*	Gates Papers, New York Public Library
Arnold, Benedict	*Letters* *Memorandum Book,*	Maine Hist. Soc. Coll. I Penn. Mag. Hist. & Biog. VIII
Atlee, Samuel	*Journal*	Penn Archives 2nd Series I
Baldwin, Jeduthan	*Revolutionary Journal*	Bangor, Maine, 1906
Bangs, Isaac	*Journal*	Cambridge, 1890
Barker, John	*Military Journal*	Cambridge, 1924
Barrett, Amos	*The Concord Fight*	Boston, 1924
Barton, William	*Journals of Sullivan's Expedition* Cook, F.	New York, 1887
Beatty, William	*Journal*	Maryland Hist. Mag. III
Beebe, Lewis	*Military Surgeon's Journal*	Penn. Mag. Hist. & Biog. LIX
Belknap, Jeremy	*Journal*	Mass. Hist. Soc. Proc. 1st Series IV
Bixby, Samuel	*Journal*	Mass. Hist. Soc. Proc. 1st Series XIV
Boardman, Oliver	*Journal*	Conn. Hist. Soc. Coll. 1899
Boudinot, Elias	*Journal*	Philadelphia, 1894
Bowdoin, James	*Papers*	Mass. Hist. Soc. Coll. 6th Series VI
Bradford, William	*Letter*	Penn. Archives, 1st Series V
Brooks, John	*Letter*	Mass. Hist. Soc. Proc. XIII
Brown, Peter	*Literary Diary of Ezra Stiles* Vol. I	New York, 1901
Burgoyne, Sir John	*State of the Expedition* *Letter to Lord Stanley*	London, 1780 Force, Am. Archives 4th Series, II
Burnett, E. C.	*Letters of Members of Continental Congress* 8 Vols.	Washington, 1921-26
Butler, Richard	*Journal*	Hist. Mag. VIII
Cadwalader, John	*Military Papers*	Penn. Mag. Hist. & Biog. XXXII
Caldwell, Henry	*Letter. MSS Relating to Early History of Canada*	Lit. Hist. Soc. of Quebec 2nd Series V
Campbell, Robert	*Autobiography*	North Carolina State Records XV
Chastellux, Marquis de	*Travels in North America* 2 Vols.	New York, 1827
Chesney, Alexander	*Journal*	Columbus, Ohio, 1921

Chester, John	*Letter.* Frothingham, R. *Siege of Boston*	Boston, 1849
Clark, George Rogers	*Campaign in Illinois*	Columbus, Ohio, 1869
Clark, Joseph	*Diary*	New Jersey Hist. Soc. Proc. VII
Clark, Jonas	*Journal* Hudson C. *History of Concord and Lexington*	Boston, 1913
Clinton, Sir Henry	*The American Rebellion*	New Haven, Conn. 1954
Clinton, George	*Public Papers*	Albany, 1904
Collier, Sir George	*Journal.*	Long Isl. Hist. Soc. Memoirs II
Collins, James	*Autobiography*	Clinton, La., 1859
Cooke, Nicholas	*Revolutionary Correspondence*	Am. Antiq. Soc. Proc. XXXVI
Cornwallis, Charles, Marquis of	*Correspondence,* 3 Vols.	London, 1859
Cresswell, Nicholas	*Journal*	New York, 1924
Cross, Ralph	*Journal*	Hist. Mag. XVII
Cruger, John	*Letters.*	Mag. American Hist. II
Dale, Richard	*Account of Action with Serapis*	Sherburne, H. *Life of J. P. Jones* Washington, 1825
Darlington, William	*Letter*	Hist. Soc. of Penn. Bulletin I
Davis, Nathan	*Expedition Against Five Nations*	Hist. Mag. 2nd Series III
Dearborn, Henry	*Journal*	Mass. Hist. Soc. Proc. 2nd Series III
	Ed. Peckham, H. H. & Brown, L. A.	Chicago, 1939
De Peyster, J.	*The Affair at Kings Mountain*	Mag. Am. Hist. V
Deux Ponts, Comte William	*My Campaigns in America*	Boston, 1868
Digby, William	*The British Invasion from the North.*	Albany, 1887
Drinker, Mrs. Henry	*Journal*	Mag. Am. Hist. XIII
Duncan, James	*Journal.*	Penn. Archives. 2nd Series XV Mag. Am. Hist. XXV
Du Ponceau, Pierre	*Autobiography*	Penn. Mag. Hist. & Biog. LXIII
Elliott, Barnard	*Charleston, 1775*	Gibbes, R.W. *Doc. Hist. of Am. Revolution* New York, 1853-57
Elliott, Andrew	*Letter*	Stevens, B.F. Facsimiles London, 1889-95
Elking, Peter	*Life During American Revolution.*	New York, 1861
Elmer, Ebenezer	*Journal*	Penn. Mag. Hist. & Biog. XXXV
Emerson, William	*Diary*	Emerson, R. W. Miscellanies. Boston, 1863
Ewing, Thomas	*Soldier of Valley Forge*	Yonkers, N.Y. 1928
Fanning, Nathaniel	*Memoirs*	New York, 1808
Farnsworth, Amos	*Journal*	Mass. Hist. Soc. Proc. 2nd Series IX
Fitch, Jabez	*Journal*	Mass. Hit. Soc. Proc. 2nd Series IX
Fithian, P. V.	*Journal*	Princeton, N.J. 1934
Fleury, Vicomte de	*Journal*	Ford, W.C. Defenses of Philadelphia. Philadelphia, 1897
Force, Peter	*American Archives.* 9 Vols.	Washington, 1837-53
Franks, Rebecca	*Letter*	Penn. Mag. Hist. & Biog. I
Franklin, Benjamin	*Writings,* 10 Vols.	New York, 1905-7
Gage, Thomas	*Correspondence,* 2 Vols.	New Haven, Conn. 1931
Gates, Horatio	*Papers* *Camden Letters*	New York Public Library Mag. Am. Hist. V

Montross, L.	*Rag, Tag and Bobtail. The Story of the Continental Army*	New York, 1951
Morison, S.E.	*Sources & Documents Illustrating the American Revolution*	New York, 1923
Smith, J.H.	*Arnold's March 1775-76*	New York, 1903
Stoudt, J.	*Ordeal at Valley Forge*	New York, 1962
Stone, F.D.	*Battle of Brandywine*	Philadelphia, 1895
Stryker, W.S.	*Battles of Trenton & Princeton*	Boston, 1898
	Battle of Monmouth	Princeton, 1927
Van Doren, C.	*Secret History of the American Revolution*	New York, 1945

INDEX

Italic page numbers refer to illustrations.

F

G

H

I

J

K

L

M

N

O

P

Q

R

S

Y

F
D
E

OU are fortunate to receive this rare volume on what is, perhaps, a period of our country's history that we blushingly know very little about . . . but should. It is rare in that it combines the chronological narrative of an objective historian with the bonus of a valuable look at the very documentation that only the most industrious researcher is privileged to see. In so doing it also discloses the bravery and stupidity, folly and frustration, and spirit and determination displayed on both sides of this "insurgency." It applies to war then, and to all wars. One side chooses to define the war their way, the other side, theirs. It is a military book; it is a civilian book. It's a political barometer, it's a cultural footnote. It is fortunately, to restate, now your book. Read it for added insight and knowledge, not solely because the United States approaches her 200th birthday but because she has indeed earned her birthright. We all would be the wiser to feel and share in how it came to be.